HONDA 1971-1978
WORKSHOP MANUAL
500cc & 550cc SINGLE O.H.C. FOUR CYLINDER

A Floyd Clymer Publication
This edition published in 2023 by
www.VelocePress.com

All rights reserved. this work may not be reproduced or transmitted in any form without the express written consent of the publisher.

INTRODUCTION

Welcome to the world of digital publishing ~ the book you now hold in your hand was printed using the latest state of the art digital technology. The advent of print-on-demand has forever changed the publishing process, never has information been so accessible and it is our hope that this book serves your informational needs for years to come. If this is your first exposure to digital publishing, we hope that you are pleased with the results. Many more titles of interest to the classic automobile and motorcycle enthusiast, collector and restorer are available via our website at www.VelocePress.com. We hope that you find this title as interesting as we do.

NOTE FROM THE PUBLISHER

The information presented is true and complete to the best of our knowledge. All recommendations are made without any guarantees on the part of the author or the publisher, who also disclaim all liability incurred with the use of this information.

TRADEMARKS

We recognize that some words, model names and designations, for example, mentioned herein are the property of the trademark holder. We use them for identification purposes only. This is not an official publication.

INFORMATION ON THE USE OF THIS PUBLICATION

This manual is an invaluable resource for those interested in performing their own maintenance. However, in today's information age we are constantly subject to changes in common practice, new technology, availability of improved materials and increased awareness of chemical toxicity. As such, it is advised that the user consult with an experienced professional prior to undertaking any procedure described herein. While every care has been taken to ensure correctness of information, it is obviously not possible to guarantee complete freedom from errors or omissions or to accept liability arising from such errors or omissions. Therefore, any individual that uses the information contained within, or elects to perform or participate in do-it-yourself repairs or modifications acknowledges that there is a risk factor involved and that the publisher or its associates cannot be held responsible for personal injury or property damage resulting from the use of the information or the outcome of such procedures.

WARNING!

One final word of advice, this publication is intended to be used as a reference guide, and when in doubt the reader should consult with a qualified technician.

CONTENTS

1. REPAIR PROCEDURE.......... 1
2. SPECIAL TOOLS 3
3. MAINTENANCE OPERATIONS . 7
4. ENGINE 19
   1. Servicing with engine mounted in frame 20
   2. Engine removal and installation.... 20
   3. Cylinder head, cylinder and piston 24
   4. Valves and valve springs 33
   5. Oil pump and oil filter........... 36
   6. Clutch 40
   7. Gear shift mechanism........... 43
   8. Cam chain tensioner 46
   9. Crankshaft and connecting rod 47
   10. Transmission, kick starter and primary shaft 53
   11. Carburetor 57
5. CHASSIS 65
   1. Front wheel and front brake 65
   2. Rear wheel and rear brake 73
   3. Steering........................ 77
   4. Front suspension................. 79
   5. Rear suspension 82
   6. Frame body..................... 84
6. ELECTRICAL.................. 87
   1. General description 87
   2. Ignition system................... 88
   3. Charging system................. 93
   4. Starting system.................. 98
   5. Electrical equipment 103
7. INSPECTION AND ADJUSTMENT OF CB550...... 107
   1. Clutch 107
8. NEW FEATURES OF CB550.................. 108
   1. Blow-by Gas Scavenging Device........................ 108
   2. Starting Motor Safety........... 109
   3. Front Suspension 110
   4. Brake Lining Wear Indicator.... 112
9. COMPARISON OF CB550 TO CB500 113
10. ENGINE 121
    1. Clutch 121
    2. Gearshift 124
11. TROUBLE SHOOTING........ 128
12. MAINTENANCE SCHEDULE.................... 134
13. TECHNICAL DATA............ 135
14. WIRING DIAGRAM 143
15. SUPPLEMENT TO CB550 K1... 149
16. SUPPLEMENT TO CB550F 153
17. SUPPLEMENT TO CB550 K2 ('76) 170
18. INDEX (Up to page 163) 173
19. SUPPLEMENT TO CB500 K3/CB550 K3 ('77)........ 175
20. SUPPLEMENT TO CB 550 F2 ('77) 185

1. SERVICE PRECAUTIONS

1. Always replace gaskets, O-rings, cotter pins, etc. with new ones when reassembling.
2. When tightening bolts, nuts or screws, begin with the larger-diameter or inner ones first and tighten them to the specified torque in a criss-cross pattern.
3. Use genuine Honda-recommended parts and lubricants when servicing.
4. Be sure to use special tools where specified.
5. When working with another person take safety precautions.
6. Clean engine parts when disassembling. Coat their sliding surfaces with a high-quality lubricant when reassembling.
7. Coat or pack grease where specified.
8. After reassembling, check that each part is tightened properly and operating properly.

ENGINE

	Item	Q'ty	Torque values	
			Kg-m	lbs-ft
1.	Tappet adjusting nut	8	1.1-1.5	8.0-10.8
2.	Cam sprocket knock bolt, 7×12	2	1.4-1.8	10.1-10.8
3.	Cylinder head nut, 8mm	12	2.0-2.3	14.5-16.6
4.	A. C. generator rotor set bolt	1	5.0-6.0	28.9-30.3
5.	Starting clutch screw, 6×18 cross flat head screw	3	0.8-1.2	14.5-17.3
6.	Upper crankcase bolt, 8×100 Flange hex bolt	3	2.0-2.5	14.5-18.1
7.	Upper crankcase bolt, 8×145 hex bolt	1	2.3-2.5	16.6-18.0
8.	Lower crankcase bolt, 8×100 hex bolt	10	2.0-2.5	14.5-18.1
9.	Connecting rod nut	8	2.0-2.2	14.5-15.9
10.	Oil pump screw, 6×35 cross flat head screw	3	0.8-1.2	5.7-8.6
11.	Clutch filter fixing bolt, 6×45 hex bolt	1	0.8-1.2	5.7-8.6
12.	Spark advancer bolt, 6×55 Flange hex bolt	1	1.1-2.5	8.0-10.8
13.	Tachometer gear holder screw, 6×16 cross flat head screw	1	1.0-1.4	7.2-10.0
14.	Exhaust pipe flange nut, 6mm	8	0.8-1.2	5.7-8.6
15.	Oil pressure switch	1	1.5-2.0	10.8-14.5
16.	Gear shift lever bolt, 6×20 hex bolt	1	0.8-1.0	5.7-7.2
17.	Oil filter center bolt	1	2.7-3.3	19.5-23.8
18.	Spark plug	4	1.2-1.6	8.6-11.6
19.	Oil drain bolt	1	3.5-4.0	25.3-28.9
20.	Clutch spring, 6×20 hex bolt	4	1.0-1.4	7.2-10.1
21.	Tappet hole cap	8	1.0-1.4	7.2-10.1
22.	Oil path cap	1	1.0-1.4	7.2-10.1
23.	Gear shift return spring, 8mm bolt	1	2.0-3.0	14.5-21.7
24.	Drive sprocket	1	1.1-1.5	
Standard parts			Kg-m	lbs-ft
	SCREW pan 6 mm		0.7-1.1	5.1-8.0
	SCREW flat 6 mm		0.8-1.2	5.8-8.7
	BOLT hex 6 mm		0.8-1.2	5.8-8.7
	BOLT flange 6 mm		1.0-1.4	7.2-10.1
	NUT hex 6 mm		0.8-1.2	5.8-8.7

I. SERVICE PRECAUTION

FRAME

	Item	Q'ty	Torque values	
			kg-m	lbs-ft
1.	Rear brake pedal bolt, 8×32 hex holt	1	1.8-2.5	13.0-18.1
2.	Foot peg nut, 12mm	2	5.0-6.0	36.2-43.4
3.	Engine hanger bolt A	5	3.0-4.0	21.7-28.9
4.	Engine hanger plate	6	1.8-2.5	13.0-18.1
5.	Rear fork pivot nut, 14mm	1	5.5-7.0	39.8-50.6
6.	Rear suspension upper nut, 10mm cap nut	2	3.0-4.0	21.7-28.9
7.	Rear suspension lower bolt, 10×32 hex bolt	2	3.0-4.0	21.7-28.9
8.	Oil bolt	3	3.4-4.0	24.6-28.9
9.	Brake stop switch	1	3.0-4.0	24.6-28.9
10.	Front brake disc nut, 8mm	6	1.8-2.5	13.0-18.1
11.	Brake oil joint, 6×28 hex bolt	1	0.8-1.0	5.8-87.2
12.	Brake hose joint	1	0.6-1.0	4.3-7.2
13.	Master cylinder bolt, 6×28 hex bolt	2	0.8-1.0	5.7-7.2
14.	Caliper set bolt	2	3.4-4.0	24.6-28.9
15.	Holder joint bolt, 8×40, 8×50 hex bolt	3	1.8-2.3	13.0-16.6
16.	Front fork bolt	2	5.5-6.5	39.8-47.0
17.	Steering stem nut	1	8.0-12.0	57.9-86.7
18.	Steering stem bolt, 10×40 hex bolt	2	3.0-4.0	21.7-28.9
19.	Rear wheel axle nut	1	8.0-10.0	57.8-72.3
20.	Front axle holder nut, 8mm	4	1.8-2.3	13.0-16.6
21.	Handlebar holder bolt, 8×40 hex bolt	4	1.8-2.3	13.0-16.6
22.	Front wheel axle nut	1	5.5-6.5	39.8-47.0
23.	Rear brake stopper arm bolt and nut, 8mm	1	1.8-2.3	13.0-16.6
24.	Fork top bridge bolt, 8×56 hex bolt	2	1.8-2.3	13.0-16.6
25.	Drive chain adjuster bolt and nut, 8mm hex bolt	2	1.5-2.0	10.8-14.5
26.	Drive chain adjuster stopper bolt	2	1.8-2.3	13.0-16.6
27.	Main stand pivot bolt, 8×40 hex bolt	2	1.5-2.0	10.8-14.5
28.	Rear foot peg nut, 12mm	2	4.5-6.0	32.5-43.4
29.	Caliper joint pin	1	1.8-2.5	13.0-18.1
30.	Bottom bridge	2	3.0-4.0	21.7-28.9
31.	Final driven sprocket	4	3.0-4.0	21.7-28.9
Standard parts				
	Bolt hex. 6mm		0.8-1.2	5.8-8.7
	Bolt hex. 8mm		1.5-2.3	10.8-16.6

2. SPECIAL TOOLS

* Except U.S.A. model, ○=USED, ×=NOT USED, (op)=optional tool

Ref. No.	Tool No.	Tool Name	CB 500	CB 550	Q'ty	Remarks
①	07902-2000000	Spanner, pin 48mm	○	○	1	
*②	07906-3230000	Wrench, box 12mm	○	○	1	Cylinder head locking nut
③	07908-3230000	Wrench, tappet adjusting	○	○	1	
*④	07909-3000000	Wrench, spark plug	○	○	1	
⑤	07910-3230101	Wrench, F retainer	○	○	1	Front hub dis/assembling
⑥	07910-3230201	Wrench, R retainer	○	○	1	Rear hub dis/assembling
⑦	07914-3230000	Pliers, Snap ring	○	○	1	Master cylinder piston dis/assembling
*⑧	07917-3230000	Wrench, hollow set 6mm	○	○	1	Front fork bottom case dis/assembling
⑨	07933-2160000	Puller, rotor	○	○	1	
⑩	07936-3230100	Shaft, hammer	○	×	1	Primary shaft removing (Use with item No. 11)
⑪	07936-3230200	Weight, hammer	○	×	1	
*⑫	07936-3740100	Shoft, sliding hammer	×	○	1	Primary shaft removing (Use with item No. 17)
⑬	07942-3290100	Driver, valve guide	○	○	1	
⑭	07942-3290200	Remover, valve guide	○	○	1	
*⑮	07945-3230100	Driver A, bearing	○	×	1	
⑯	07945-3230200	Driver B, bearing	○	×	1	
*⑰	07945-3000500	Weight, sliding hammer	×	○	1	
⑱	07945-3330300	Bearing driver attachment	×	○	1	
⑲	07945-3330200	Driver, attachment	×	○	1	Transmission bearing inner driver 6205 (Use with item No. 23)
⑳	07946-3600000	Driver, attachment	×	○	1	Rear hub bearing driver ATT 6305 (Use with item No. 23)
㉑	07946-9350200	Driver, attachment	×	○	1	Front hub bearing driver ATT 6302 Use with item No. 23)
㉒	07947-3290000	Guide, fork seal	○	○	1	
㉓	07949-6110000	Driver, handle	×	○	1	Use with item Nos. 18, 19, 20, and 21
㉔	07953-3330000	Remover, ball race	×	○	1	
㉕	07954-3230000	Compressor, piston ring	○	○	2	
㉖	07957-3290000	Compressor, valve spring	○	○	1	
㉗	07958-2500000	Base, Piston	○	○	2	
㉘	07959-3290000	Compressor, shock absorber	○	○	1	
㉙	07967-3230100	Attachment A, driver	○	×	1	
㉚	07967-3230200	Attachment B, driver	○	×	1	
㉛	07967-3230000	Attachment remover	○	×	1	
㉜	07974-3230100	Piston cup guide	○	○	1	
㉝	07974-3230200	Cup guide	○	×	1	
㉞	07984-0980000	Reamer, valve guide	×	○	1	
㉟	07908-3230200	Wrench, carburetor adjusting	○	○	1	(op)
㊱	07504-3000100	Gauge set, vacuum	○	○	1	Carburetor adjusting (op)
㊲	07975-3000001	Tool set, chain joint	○	○	1	(op)
	07401-0010000	Gauge, flot level	○	○	1	

2. SPECIAL TOOLS

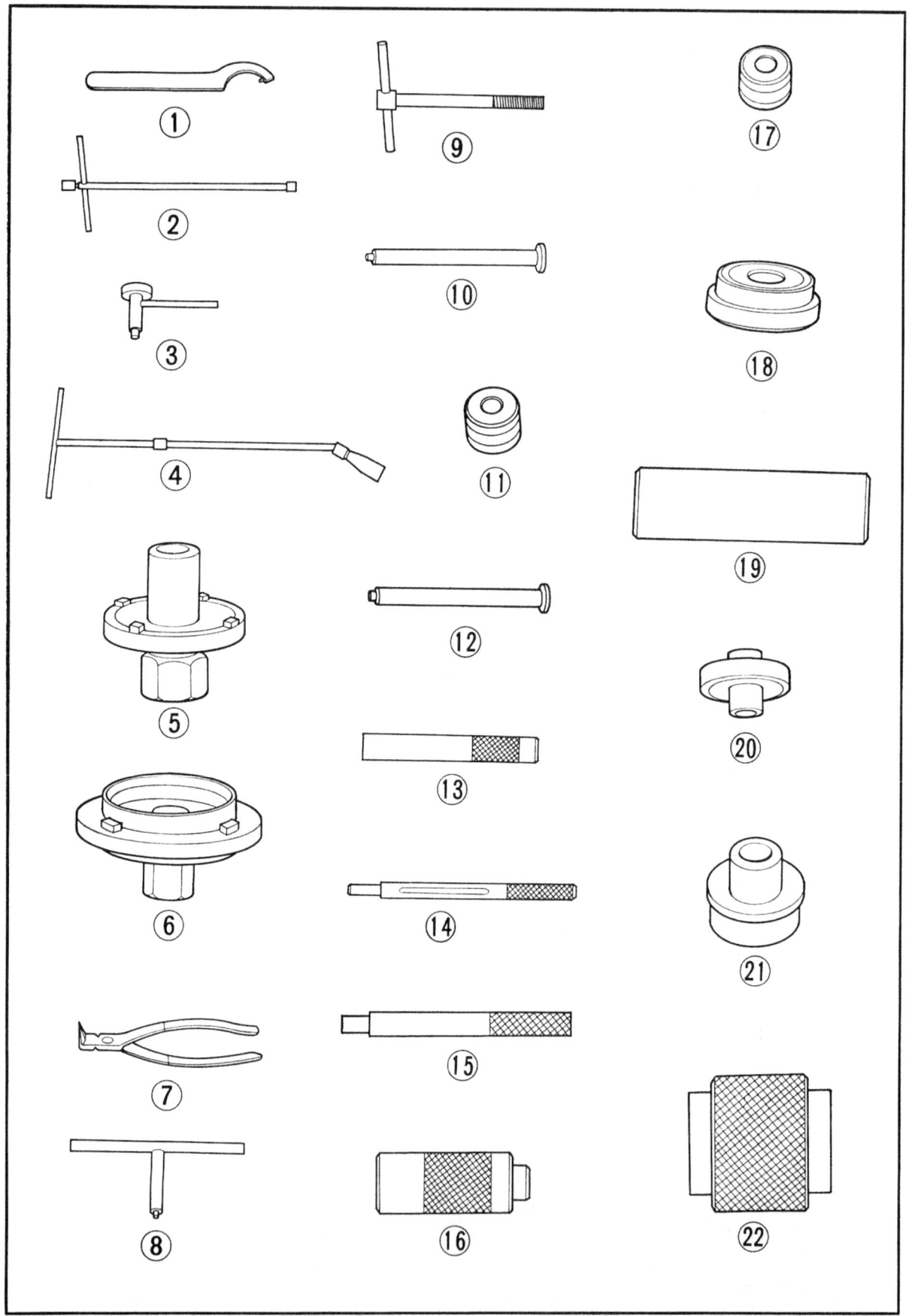

2. SPECIAL TOOLS

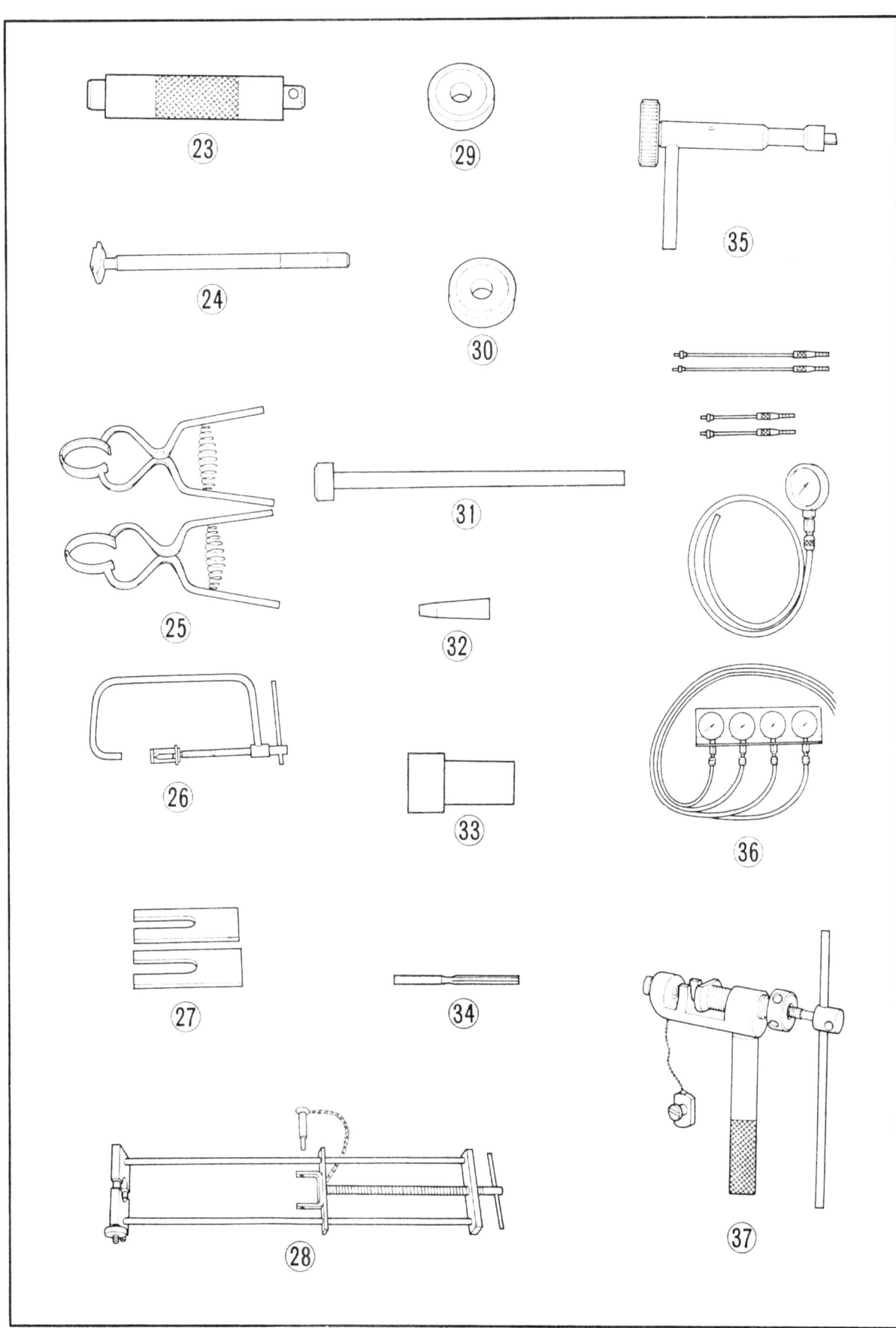

MEMO

3. MAINTENANCE OPERATIONS

1. TAPPET ADJUSTMENT

Adjust tappet clearance when the engine is cold.

Note:
Pistons are numbered left to right from the rider's position.

1. Remove the tank.
2. Loosen the tappet hole caps.
3. Remove the point cover and align the "T" (1·4) mark on the spark advancer to the timing mark when the No. 1 piston is at top-dead-center of the compression stroke.
4. Check and adjust valve tappet clearances indicated by "O" in the chart below.
5. Measure the clearances using a feeler gauge. Adjust by loosening the lock nut and turning the adjusting screw. Tighten the lock nut.
   Valve tappet clearances:
   INTAKE——0.05 mm (0.002 in.)
   EXHAUST —0.08 mm (0.003 in.)
6. Rotate the crankshaft one revolution and realign the "T" (1·4) mark on the spark advancer to the timing mark. In this position, the No. 4 piston is at top-dead-center of the compression stroke. Check and adjust the valve tappet clearances indicated by "X" in the chart below. See step 5 above for proper valve tappet clearances.

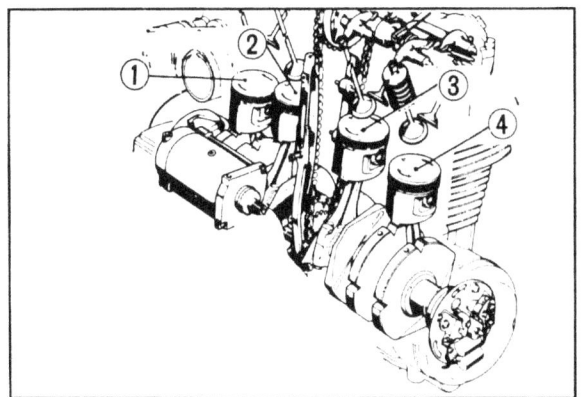

Fig. 1 ① No. 1 piston ③ No. 3 piston
        ② No. 2 piston ④ No. 4 piston

Fig. 2 ① T mark   ③ 1·4 mark
        ② Timing mark

Fig. 3 ① Lock nut   ③ Feeler gauge
        ② Adjusting screw

	No. 1 cylinder	No. 2 cylinder	No. 3 cylinder	No. 4 cylinder
Intake valve	O	X	O	X
Exhaust valve	O	O	X	X

Note:
- Hold the adjusting screw so that it does not turn when tightening the lock nut.
- Make sure the clearance is not disturbed when the lock nut is tightened.

2. CARBURETOR ADJUSTMENT

Adjust the carburetor after warming up the engine (60–70°C/140–158°F).

Idle adjustment

Adjust the engine idle speed to **950-1050** rpm with the throttle stop screw. Turn the screw clockwise to increase the idle speed and counterclockwise to decrease the idle speed.

Synchronization adjustment

1. Remove the fuel tank.
   Note:
   Position the tank about 50 cm (20 in.) higher than the mounting position and reconnect with a longer fuel line.
2. Adjust the throttle stop screw so that the throttle lever is **49±1.5 mm** ($1^{15}/_{16} \pm {}^1/_{16}$ **in.**) from the stay.
3. Install the vacuum gauge in the intake manifolds. Remove the plugs from the intake manifolds. Install the long A adaptors of the vacuum gauge to the two inside manifolds and the short B adaptors to the outside manifolds.
4. Start the engine, loosen the adjusting lock nuts and turn the adjusting screws so that all four carburetors are uniform **(16-24 cm Hg)** on the vacuum gauge (H/C 39340).

   Turn the screws clockwise to increase vacuum. Turn the screws counterclockwise to decrease vacuum. All the carburetors should be adjusted to within **3.0 cm Hg** of each other.

Note:
If the gauge needle is oscillating over a wide range, dampen the movement with the vacuum adjuster on the gauge.

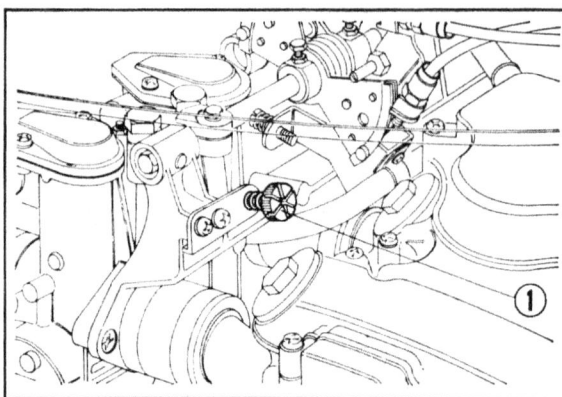

Fig. 4 ① Throttle stop screw

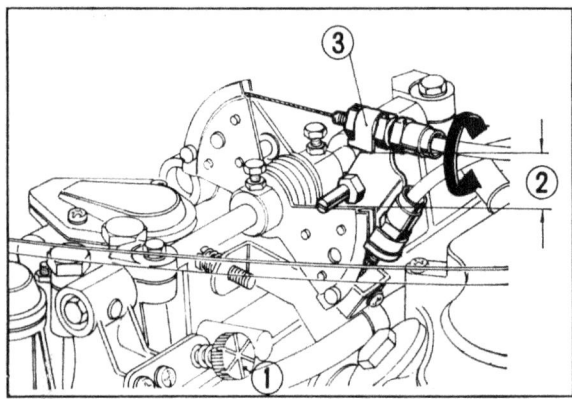

Fig. 5 ① Throttle stop screw
② 49±1.5 mm (1.929±0.059 in.)
③ Stay

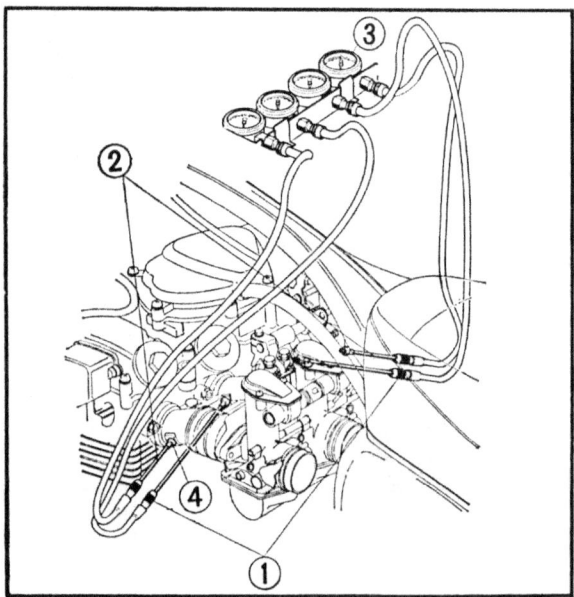

Fig. 6 ① A adaptor
② B adaptor
③ Vacuum gauge
④ Plug hole

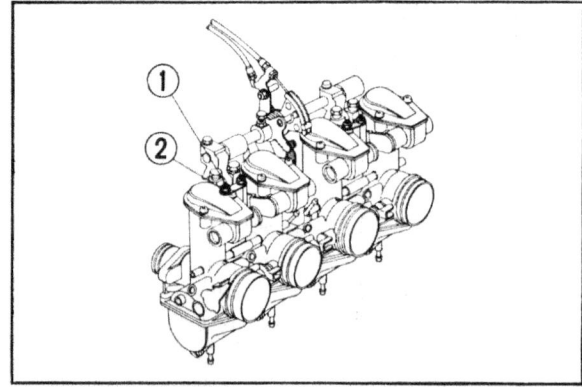

Fig. 7 ① Screw
② Lock nut

3. MAINTENANCE OPERATIONS

5. Snap the throttle back several times and recheck the vacuum pressures after the four carburetors indicate the same vacuum pressure.

   Repeat the adjustment in step 4 if the vacuum pressures lack uniformity.

   Check the following items if the vacuum pressure is less than **15 cm Hg** for any of the carburetors:
   1. Be sure the ignition timing is
      −5°/1,150 − 30°/2,500 rpm BTDC.
   2. Check the tappet clearances.
      Intake: **0.05mm (0.002in.)**
      Exhaust: **0.08mm (0.003in.)**
   3. Check the spark plug gap.
      Gap: **0.6-0.7 mm (0.024-0.028 in.)**
   4. Check the compression pressure.
      Pressure: **11-12 kg/cm²**
      (156.45-170.67 psi.)

6. After all four carburetors have been adjusted to the same vacuum pressure, adjust the throttle stop screw to an idle speed of **950~1,050 rpm**.

7. Adjust the air screw on each carburetor. (The standard adjustment for the air screws is **1±3/8** turns open from the fully closed position.)

8. Readjust the engine idle speed to **950 −1,050** rpm with the throttle stop screw.

Note:
Tighten the intake manifold plugs after synchronizing the carburetors.

Throttle Cable Adjustment

1. Turn the adjuster counterclockwise at the handlebar end to increase free play in the throttle cable. Turn it clockwise to decrease the free play.

   Note:
   Leave about 3 mm (0.12 in) range of adjustment at the cable adjuster for final microadjustment.

2. Loosen the cable lock nut and turn the adjuster at the carburetor end to provide **3~4 mm** (1/8~5/32 in.) free play at the throttle grip flange.

   Note:
   The throttle lever should hit the eccentric pin when the grip is forced to the fully closed position. If it doesn't, replace the return cable with a new one.

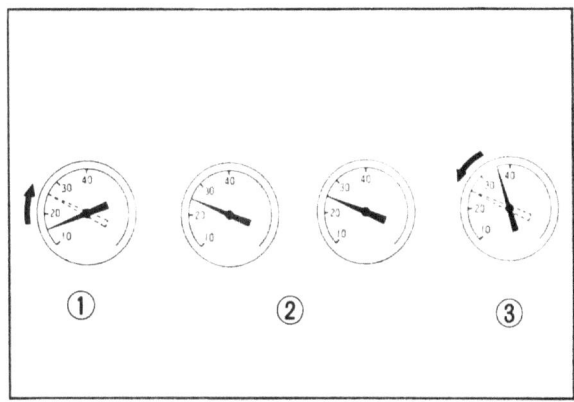

Fig. 8 ① Low vacuum   ③ High vacuum
        ② Normal

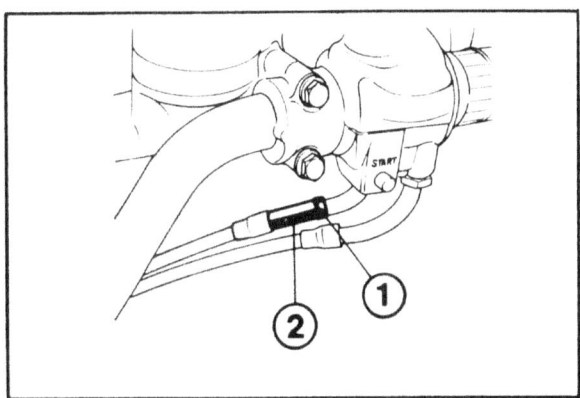

Fig. 9 ① Lock nut   ② Adjuster

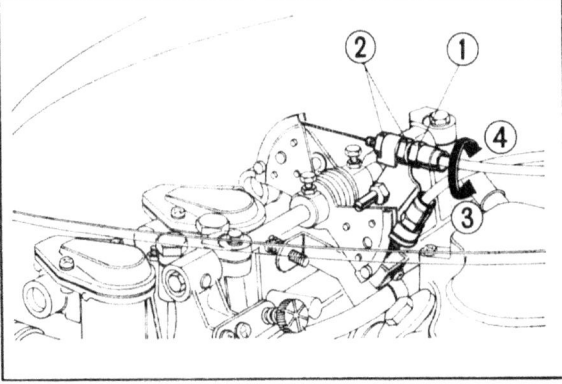

Fig. 10 ① Adjuster   ③ Decrease
         ② Lock nut   ④ Increase

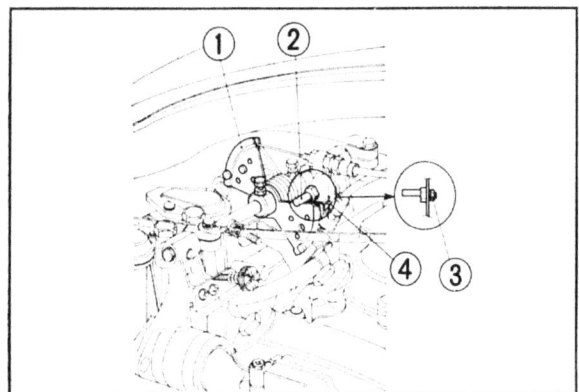

Fig. 11 ① Throttle lever   ③ Lock nut
② Eccentric pin
④ 2~3 mm (0.08~0.12 in.)

Overtravel stopper adjustment
Loosen the lock nut and turn the eccentric pin. Clearance between the throttle lever and the eccentric pin should be **2~3 mm (0.08~0.12 in)**.

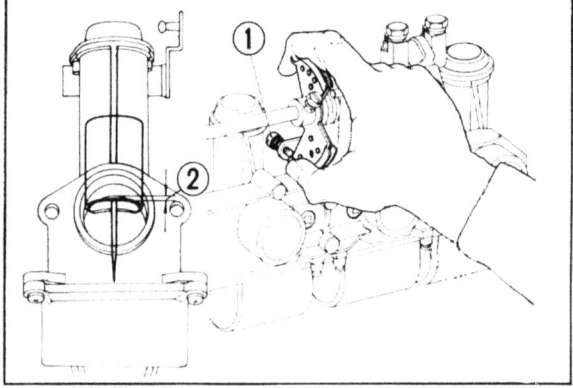

Fig. 12 ① Stop screw ② 0~1.0 mm (0~0.04 in.)

Full throttle opening stopper adjustment
Adjust the stop screw so that the throttle valve extends **0~1.0 mm (0~0.04 in.)** above the throttle bore in the fully open position.

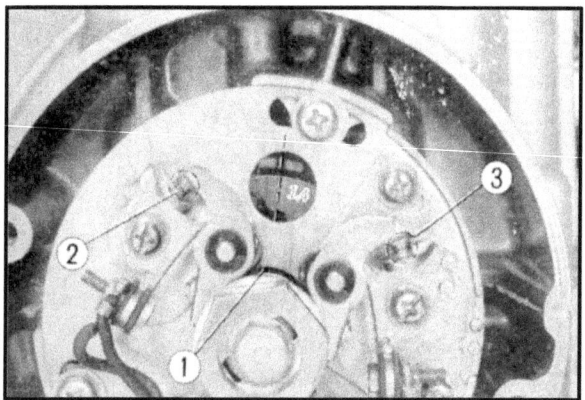

Fig. 13 ① Slipper   ③ 2·3 points
② 1·4 points

3. BREAKER POINT GAP AND IGNITION TIMING ADJUSTMENT

Check the condition of the contact points, point gap and ignition timing. Adjust the ignition timing of the 1·4 points first.

Breaker point gap adjustment, 1·4 points
1. Rotate the crankshaft until the contact breaker slipper comes up on the highest position of the cam lobe. Measure the point gap with a feeler gauge.
   Standard point gap: **0.3~0.4 mm (0.012~0.016 in.)**
2. Loosen the screw ⓐ and move the breaker point assembly if it needs to be adjusted.

Breaker point gap adjustment, 2·3 points
Adjust the 2·3 point gap in the same manner as the 1·4 points by loosening the screw ⓑ.

Note:
Clean the point surfaces with a point file or an oil stone if they are pitted or rough.

Fig. 14 ① Screw ⓐ   ③ Breaker   ⑤ 2·3 points
② Screw ⓑ   ④ 1·4 points

3. MAINTENANCE OPERATIONS

Ignition timing adjustment, 1·4 points

1. Connect a 12V test lamp to 1·4 points primary wire (blue) and to ground. (See Fig. 15)
2. Turn the main switch to the "ON" position.
3. Rotate the crankshaft clockwise slowly. If the test lamp comes on when the "F" (1·4) mark on the spark advancer is aligned to the timing mark, the timing is correct.
4. If the adjustment is necessary, align the "F" (1·4) mark to the timing mark and loosen the screws ⓑ, and then move the base ⓑ until the lamp goes on. Tighten the screws.

Ignition timing adjustment, 2·3 points

1. Connect the 12V test lamp to the primary cord (yellow) of the opposite contact breaker and align the "F" (2·3) mark to the timing mark.
2. Loosen the screw ⓒ and move the base ⓒ as shown above.

Ignition timing adjustment with a stroboscopic timing light

The use of the stroboscopic timing light is recommended to obtain the most accurate timing.

1. Plug the timing light cord into the timing light receptacle.
2. Remove the spark plug cap from the No. 4 cylinder and install the timing attachment between the spark plug and the cap.
3. Connect the high tension cord of the timing light to the timing attachment, position the switch knob to TIMING, and start the engine.
   The timing light will flash.
4. Aim the timing light toward the timing mark and make sure the "F" (1·4) mark and the timing mark are aligned.
   Increase the engine rpm to approximately 2500 rpm. At this speed, if the timing mark is between the two index lines located 23.5~26.5° before the "F" mark, the ignition timing at full advance condition is satisfactory.

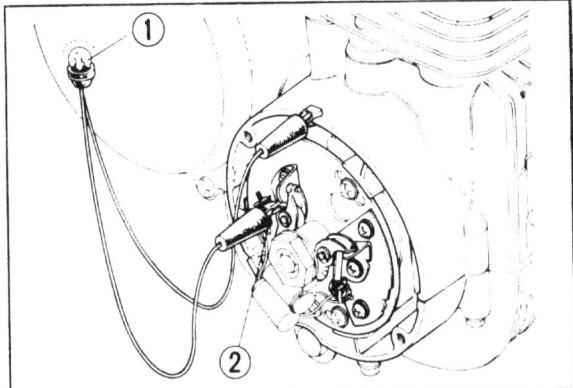

Fig. 15 ① 12V Lamp ② Blue cord

Fig. 16 ① "F" (1·4) Mark ② Timing mark

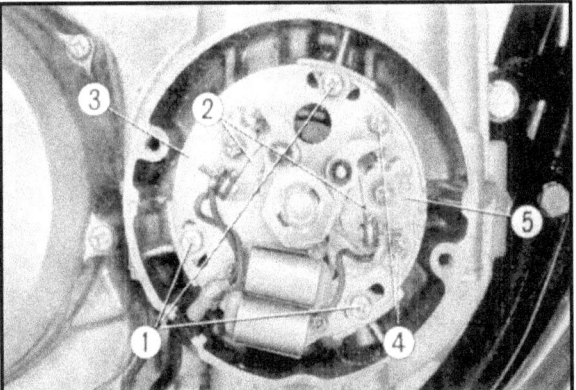

Fig. 17 ① Screw ⓑ ③ Base ⓑ ⑤ Base ⓒ
② Breaker ④ Screw ⓒ

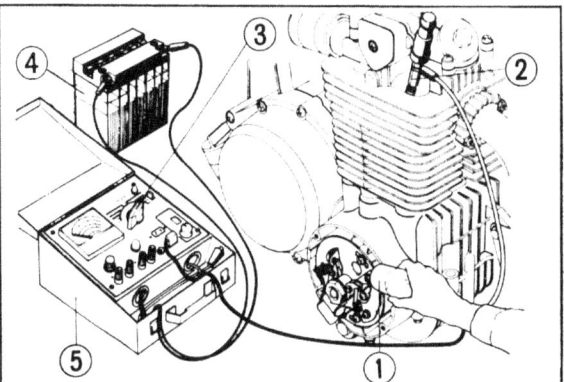

Fig. 18 ① Timing light ④ Battery
② Timing attachment ⑤ Service tester
③ Switch knob

3. MAINTENANCE OPERATIONS

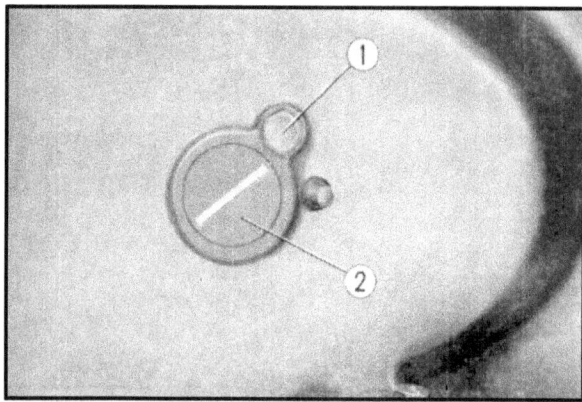

Fig. 19 ① Lock bolt ② Adjuster

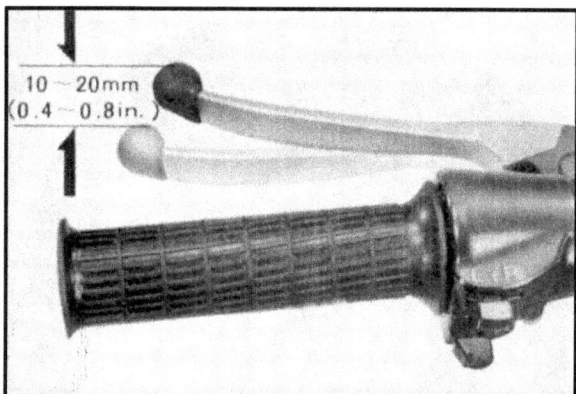

Fig. 20

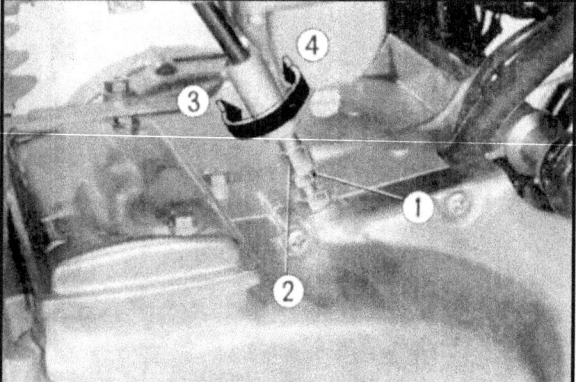

Fig. 21 ① Lock nut ③ Increase free play
② Adjuster ④ Decrease free play

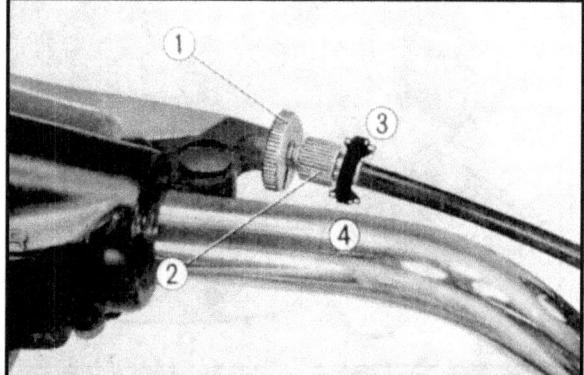

Fig. 22 ① Lock nut ③ Increase free play
② Adjuster ④ Decrease free play

5. Remove the spark plug cap from the No. 3 cylinder and install the timing attachment between the spark plug and the cap. Check the ignition timing ("F" 2·3) as described in steps 1~4.
6. Adjust if the timing is incorrect.

4. CLUTCH ADJUSTMENT

1. To provide free play in the clutch cable, loosen the clutch adjuster lock bolt.
2. Turn the adjuster clockwise until a slight resistance is felt, and then turn counter-clockwise about **3 mm** (¹/₈ **in.**). At that point, tighten the lock bolt.
3. Adjust free play in the clutch cable at the lock nut and adjuster on the engine. The play should be **10~20 mm** (**0.4~0.8 in.**). Perform micro adjustment with the adjuster at the clutch lever.

5. CAM CHAIN ADJUSTMENTS

Perform cam chain tension adjustment in the following manner.

1. Remove the tappet hole caps from the No. 1 cylinder.
2. Remove the point cover, and align the "T" (1·4) mark to the timing mark.
3. Check both valves of the No. 1 cylinder. If both valves are free, proceed to the **next** step. If either or both of the valves are

tight, rotate the crankshaft 360°, and proceed with the next step.

4. Rotate the crankshaft clockwise until the spring peg on the advancer assembly at the 1·4 position is at the right of a line from the timing mark. This position is 15° ATDC.
5. At this point, loosen the lock nut so that proper chain tension can be obtained automatically.
6. Retighten the lock nut, and reinstall the point cover and tappet covers.

6. SPARK PLUG INSPECTION

Remove the spark plug with a spark plug wrench and check the gap and the insulator for damage or fouling.

1. Clean the plug with a spark plug cleaner or a wire brush.
2. Check the gap with a feeler gauge and adjust the opening to the standard **0.6~0.7 mm (0.02~0.03 in)**.
3. Replace the plug or plug gasket if the insulator or gasket is damaged.
   Standard spark plugs: **D-7ES (NGK)**
   X 22 ES (DENSO)

7. ENGINE OIL INSPECTION AND CHANGE

Oil Level Inspection

Check the oil level with the dipstick gauge without screwing it into the case. If the level is below the lower mark on the gauge, add oil to the upper mark.
Recommended oil classification:
Honda 4-stroke oil or equivalent
SAE 10W-40 or SAE 20W-50

Oil change

Perform the oil change while the engine is warm so that the oil will drain properly.

1. Loosen the drain bolt and remove the filler cap to assist draining.
2. Remove the oil filter to drain the oil completely.
3. Tighten the drain bolt and fill with **2.5 l (2.6 U.S. qt., 2.2 Imp. qt.)** of clean oil through the filler opening. Add oil as necessary to bring the oil level to the upper mark on the gauge.
   Oil capacity: **3.0 liters (3.2 U.S. qt., 2.6 Imp. qt.)**

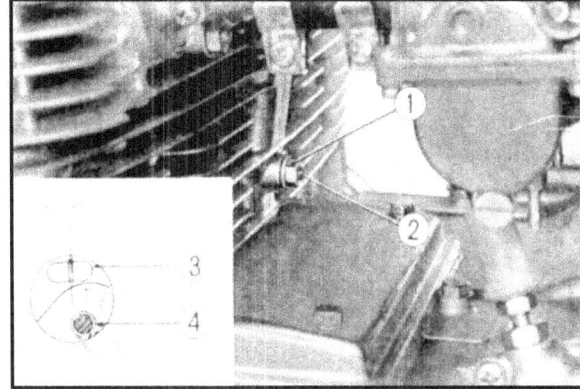

Fig. 23 ① Nut   ③ Timing mark
        ② Adjusting screw ④ Spring peg

Fig. 24 ① Gap

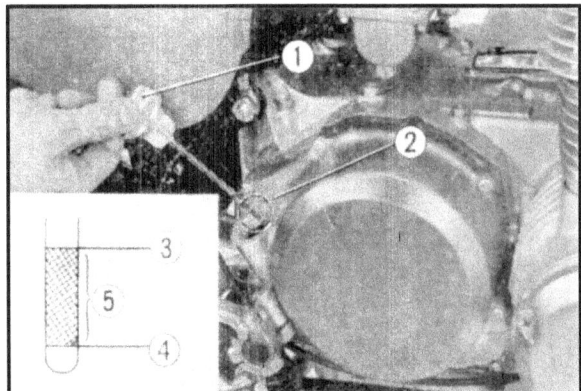

Fig. 25 ① Filler cap   ④ Lower level
        ② Oil level gauge   ⑤ Serviceable range
        ③ Upper level

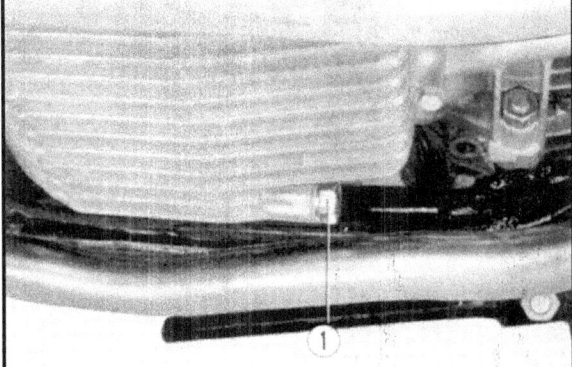

Fig. 26 ① Drain bolt

3. MAINTENANCE OPERATIONS

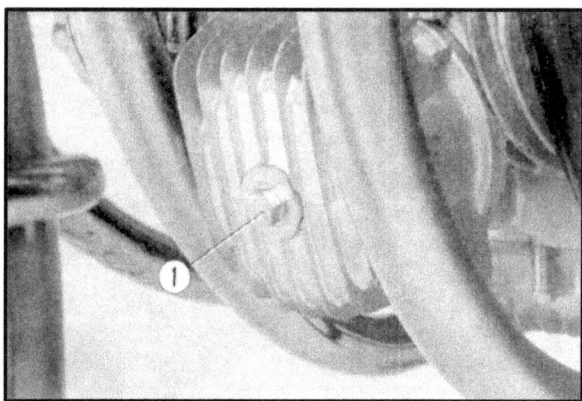

Fig. 27 ① Oil filter center bolt

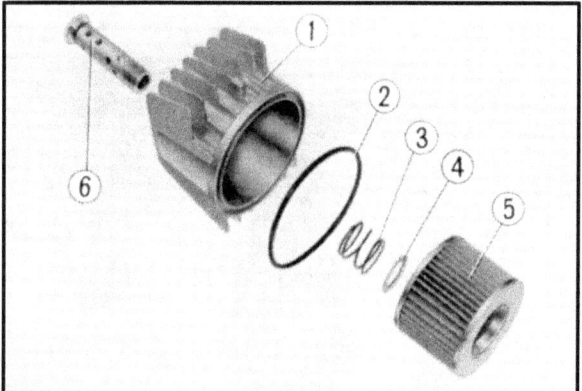

Fig. 28 ① Oil filter cover ④ Washer
② O ring ⑤ Oil filter element
③ Spring ⑥ Oil filter center bolt

8. OIL FILTER SERVICING

Service the oil filter when changing the engine oil.

1. Loosen the oil filter center bolt and remove the filter element.

Note:
- A small amount of oil will drip from the filter when it is removed.
- When reinstalling the element, replace all parts. Any pieces of rubber left on the seat will cause poor sealing.
- Replace the oil filter element every 6,000 km (4,000 miles).

9. BRAKE INSPECTION AND ADJUSTMENT

Adjusting Brake Caliper

Whenever the brake pads are replaced, the brake caliper must be adjusted. The adjustment is made in the following manner, so that there is a small clearance between the fixed friction pad and the brake disc.

1. Raise the front wheel off the ground using a block or jack.
2. Loosen the caliper stopper bolt lock nut.
3. Turn the stopper bolt in direction Ⓐ until the friction pad contacts the brake disc. When the wheel is rotated, a slight drag should be noticed.
4. While rotating the front wheel, turn the stopper bolt in direction Ⓑ until the front wheel rotates freely.
5. Turn the stopper bolt 1/2 turn in direction Ⓑ further and tighten the lock nut.

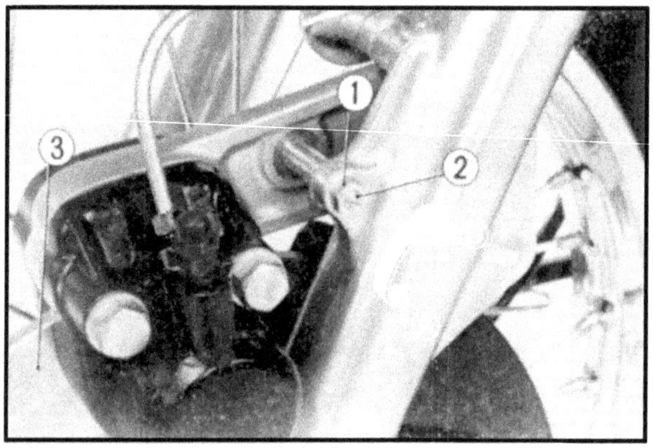

Replenishing Brake Fluid

Remove the reservoir cap, washer and diaphragm, and if the level is lower than the level mark engraved inside the reservoir, fill the reservoir with **DOT 3 BRAKE FLUID** to the level mark. Reinstall the diaphragm and washer, and tighten the reservoir cap securely.

Note:
- Do not mix brands of brake fluid. A chemical reaction may occur or brake problems could result.
- Do not use any other fluid in the brake system.

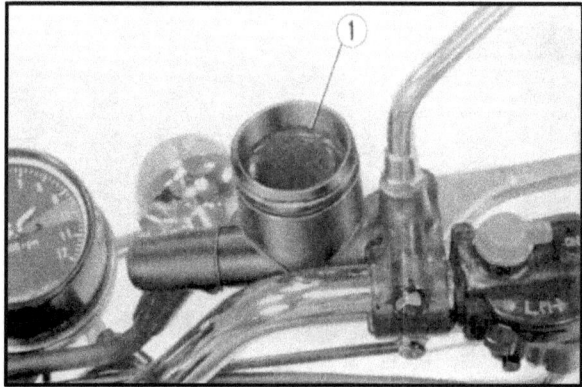

Fig. 29 ① Stopper bolt lock nut ③ Disc
② Stopper bolt

Fig. 30 ① Level mark

- Remove any brake fluid which may have spilled on a painted surface, rubber parts, and meter components. It may produce a chemical reaction and damage those parts.

Brake Pad Inspection
Replace pads A and B with new ones when either of the pads is worn to the red serviceable limit mark around the pad.

Brake Bleeding
The brakes must be bled subsequent to work performed on the brake system, when the lever becomes soft or spongy, or when lever travel is excessive. The procedure is best performed by two mechanics.

1. Remove the dust cap from the bleeder valve and attach the bleeder hose.
2. Place the free end of the bleeder hose in a glass container which has some hydraulic brake fluid in it so that the end of the hose can be submerged.
3. Fill the reservoir using only the recommended brake fluid. Screw the cap partially on the reservoir to prevent entry of dust.
4. As shown in Fig. 33 attach a piece of rubber about 15 mm thick to the end of the handle grip to decrease the stroke as measured at the tip of the handle lever. Pump the brake lever several times until pressure can be felt. Holding the lever tight, open the bleeder valve about $1/2$ turn and squeeze the lever all the way down.
   Do not release the lever until the bleeder valve has closed again. Repeat this procedure until bubbles cease to appear in the fluid at the end of the hose.
5. Remove the bleeder hose, tighten the bleeder valve and install the bleeder valve dust cap.
6. Do not allow the fluid reservoir to become empty during the bleeding operation or air will enter the system again. Replenish the fluid as often as necessary while bleeding.

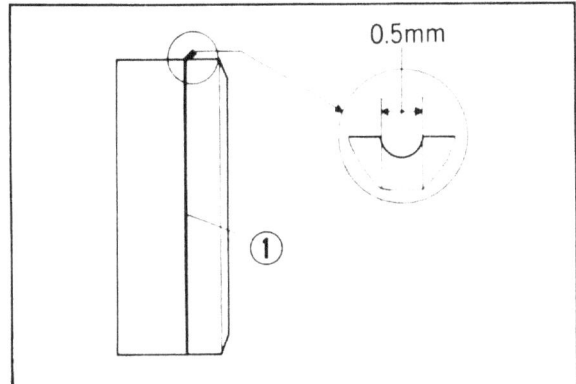

Fig. 31　① Red line

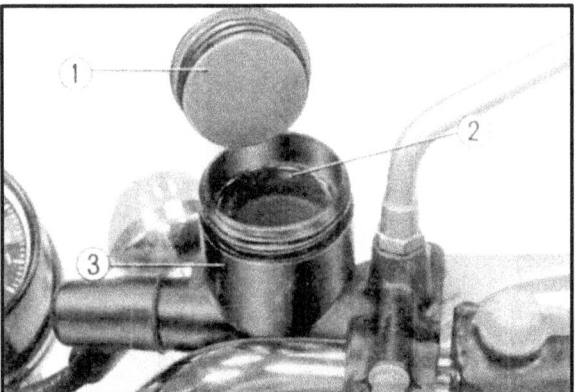

Fig. 32　① Diaphragm　③ Master cylinder
　　　　② Brake fluid

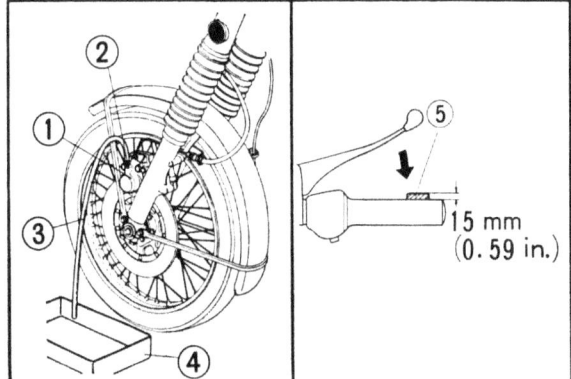

Fig. 33　① Caliper　③ Bleeder hose　⑤ Rubber
　　　　② Bleeder　④ Drip pan

7. Check for proper effect of bleeding and absence of leaks in the front brake lines while holding pressure against the brake lever. Replenish the fluid in the reservoir when bleeding is completed. Reinstall the diaphragm, washer and reservoir cap and tighten.

After the hydraulic brake system has been drained, it should be filled as outlined below.
1. Fill the fluid reservoir.
2. Open the bleeder valve by $1/2$ turn, squeeze the brake lever, close the valve and release the brake lever. This procedure must be repeated in this sequence until hydraulic fluid begins to flow through the bleeder hose. After filling the hydraulic system with fluid, proceed with the actual bleeding operation.

Note:
- Brake fluid which has been pumped out of the system must not be used again.
- Brake fluid will damage the paint finish and instrument lenses.

3. MAINTENANCE OPERATIONS

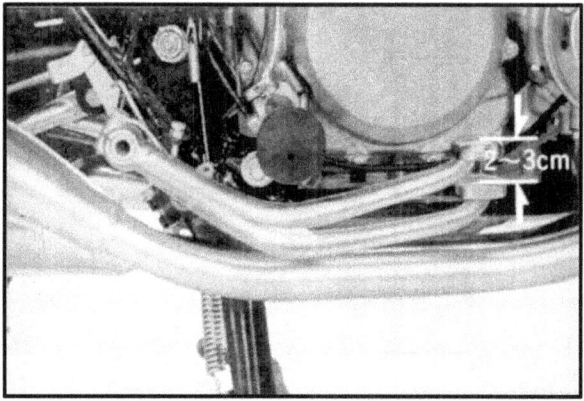

Fig. 34

Rear Brake Adjustment
1. Normal free play at the end of the brake pedal is **2–3 cm** ($^3/_4 \sim 1^3/_{16}$ **in.**).

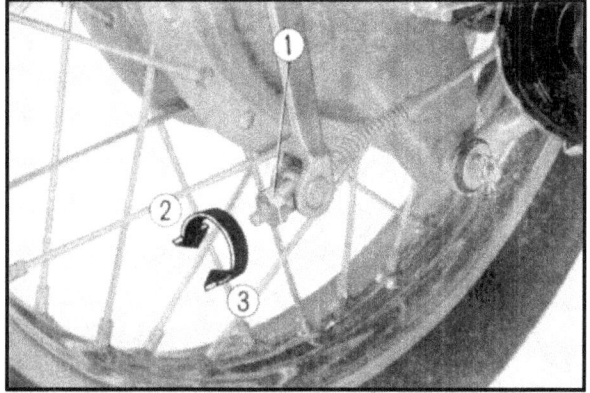

Fig. 35 ① Adjuster nut ③ Decrease free play
② Increase free play

2. Perform the adjustment with the adjuster nut.

10. AIR CLEANER ELEMENT SERVICING

1. Open the seat and remove the tool tray.
2. Pull the spring clip out and remove the cleaner element.
3. Clean the element by tapping it lightly and blowing compressed air from inside.

Fig. 36 ① Seat lever ② Seat lock

Fig. 37 ① Air cleaner element ② Spring clip

11. DRIVE CHAIN INSPECTION AND ADJUSTMENT

1. Check the drive chain slack by raising and lowering the chain at the midpoint between the sprockets. The normal slack is **1~2cm** ($^3/_8$~$^3/_4$ **in**).
2. Adjust by loosening the rear axle nut and turning the adjusting bolts on both sides.

Note:
The marks on both adjusters should be at the same location when the chain is properly adjusted.

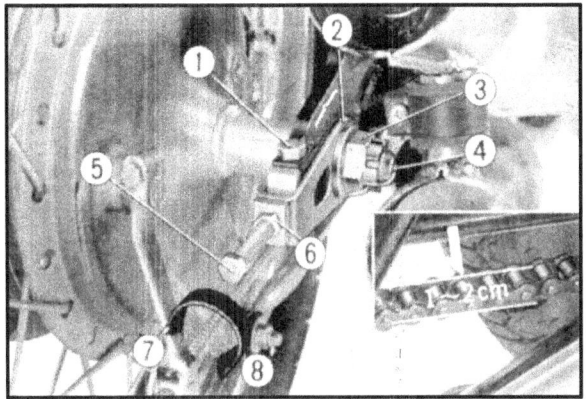

Fig. 38
1. Fork cap bolt
2. Mark
3. Axle nut
4. Cotter pin
5. Adjusting bolt
6. Lock nut
7. Loosen
8. Tighten

12. BATTERY ELECTROLYTE INSPECTION

Remove the right side cover and check the electrolyte level. The level should be at the upper limit.

1. If the level is low, open the seat and remove the tool tray to add distilled water to the battery.
2. Remove the six battery filler caps and fill each cell with water to the upper limit.

Fig. 39 ① Upper limit ② Lower limit

13. FRONT FORK OIL REPLACEMENT

1. Remove the fork bolt and drain bolt, and drain the oil.
   Actuate the forks up and down to drain the oil completely.
2. Flush the interior with solvent.
   Note:
   Do not use gasoline for flushing.
3. Tighten the drain bolt securely and add clean oil to the fork through the top of the fork pipe.
   Recommended oil: **AFT**
   Capacity: 160 cc (5.4 ozs)

Fig. 40 ① Fork bolts

Fig. 41 ① Drain bolt

Fig. 42 ① Compression gauge

14. COMPRESSION PRESSURE CHECK

1. Remove the spark plugs.
2. Insert the end of the compression gauge into the spark plug hole.
3. Set both the throttle and choke to the fully open position and kick the kick starter.
   Standard compression pressure:

$$12 \text{ kg/cm}^2 \text{ (170. 67 psi)}$$

Note:
- Open the throttle and choke fully so that the correct compression pressure will be indicated on the gauge.
- Continue the kicking until the compression reading is at the maximum. The reading will increase with each kick.
- To obtain the correct pressure reading, perform the measurement after warming the engine up.

(**Low compression pressure**)

When the compression pressure is below 10 kg/cm² (142. 23 psi), the probable causes are leaks around the valves and piston rings, or from the head and cylinder gaskets.

Adjust the valve tappet clearances, or disassemble the engine and inspect the piston rings and gaskets.

(**High compression pressure**)

When the pressure is greater than 12 kg/cm² (170. 67 psi), the probable cause is excessive carbon deposits on the combustion chamber, piston head and the valves. Disassemble the head and cylinder to remove the carbon.

4. ENGINE

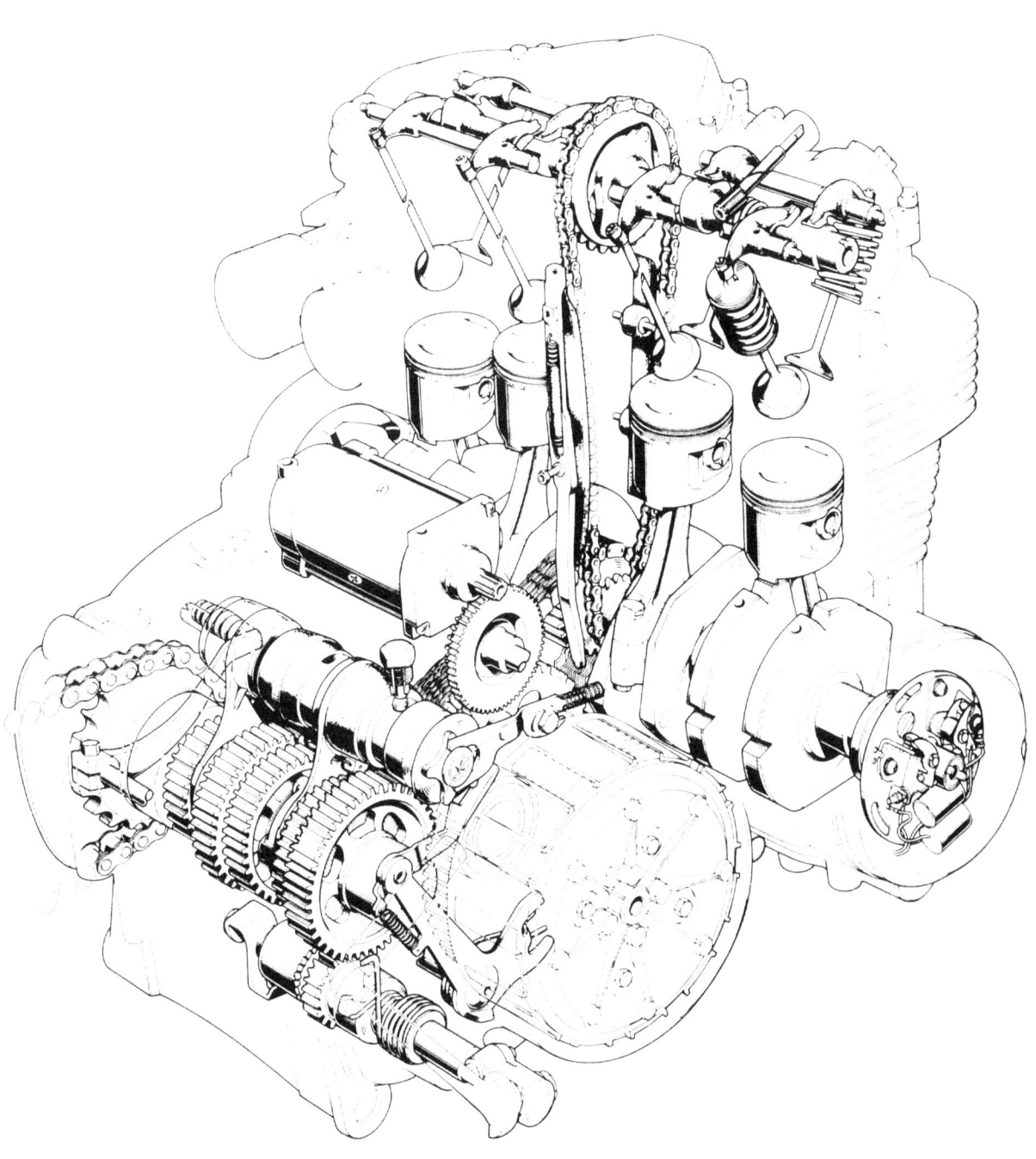

4. ENGINE

1. SERVICING WITH ENGINE MOUNTED IN FRAME

Items	Pages
1. Cylinder Head Cover and Camshaft	24
2. Cylinder Head	24
3. Cylinder and Piston	24
4. Cam Chain Tensioner	25
5. Oil Filter and Oil Pump	36
6. Clutch	40
7. Gear Shift Mechanism	43
8. Electrical System (i. e., Generator and Starting motor)	95

2. ENGINE REMOVAL AND INSTALLATION

A. Removal

1. Turn the fuel valve to the "STOP" position. Disconnect the fuel pipe at the tank and remove the fuel tank.
2. Loosen the oil drain bolt and the oil filter center bolt, and drain the engine oil.
3. Remove the exhaust pipe and the muffler.
4. Disconnect the high tension wires at the spark plugs.
5. Disconnect the ground cable at the battery terminal.
6. Loosen the 5 mm screw and disconnect the tachometer cable at the cylinder head cover.
7. Take the air cleaner element out, loosen the three 6 mm bolts and remove the air cleaner case.

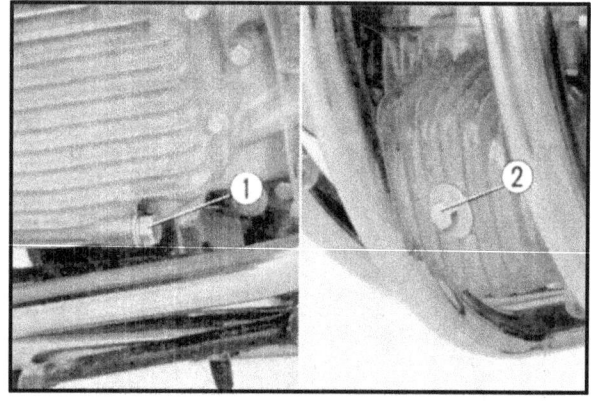

Fig. 43 ① Drain bolt   ② Oil filter center bolt

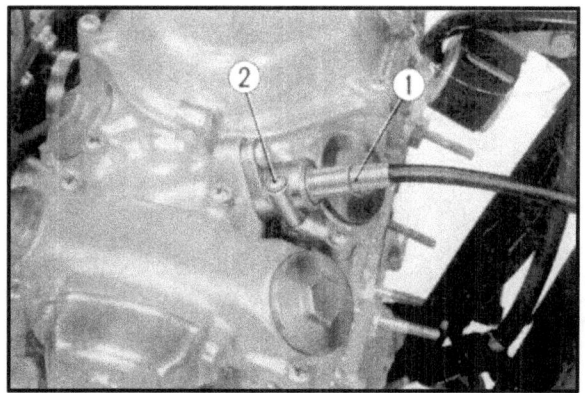

Fig. 44 ① Tachometer cable   ② 5 mm screw

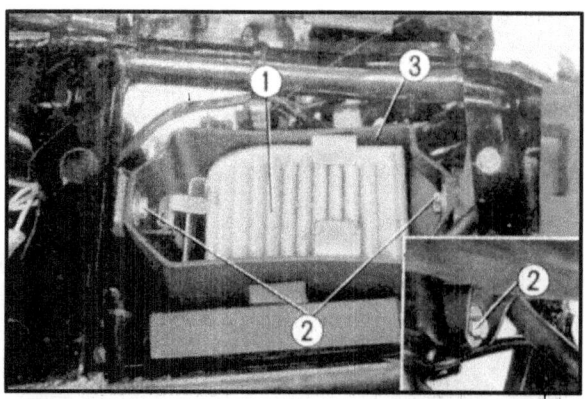

Fig. 45 ① Air cleaner element   ③ Air cleaner case
② 6 mm bolts

4. ENGINE   21

8. Disconnect the throttle cables at the carburetors.

Fig. 46 ① Throttle cable

9. Loosen the two 5 mm screws at the carburetor insulator and the 4 mm screws at the air cleaner chamber. Remove the carburetors.

Fig. 47 ① 5 mm screw   ② 4 mm screw

10. Disconnect the starting motor cable from the magnetic switch, and then the generator wiring at the coupler.

Fig. 48 ① Starting motor cable   ③ Wiring coupler
② Magnetic switch

11. Remove the gear change pedal, and loosen the starting motor cover bolts. Remove the starting motor cover and the left crankcase cover. Disconnect the clutch cable at the clutch lifter.

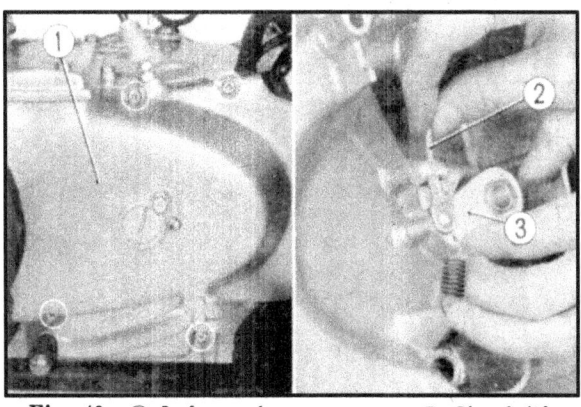

Fig. 49 ① Left crankcase cover   ③ Clutch lifter
② Clutch cable

4. ENGINE

Fig. 50 ① Contact breaker point leads

12. Remove the final driven sprocket and the drive chain.

13. Disconnect the contact breaker point leads (yellow and blue) at the connectors.

14. Loosen the nuts from the engine hanger bolts, and dismount the engine from the right side by raising the rear slightly.

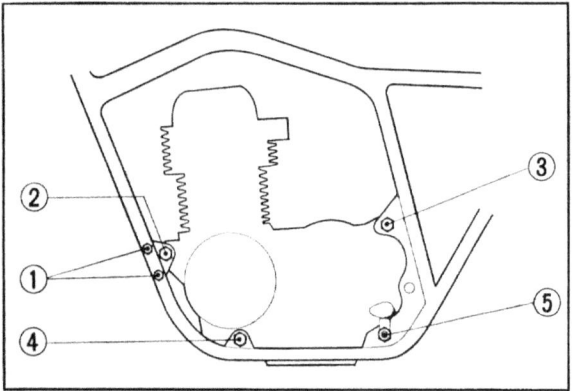

Fig. 51 Left side engine hanger bolts
① 8×50 hex bolt
② 10×50 hex bolt
③ Rear upper hanger bolt
④ 10×80 hex bolt
⑤ Rear lower hanger bolt

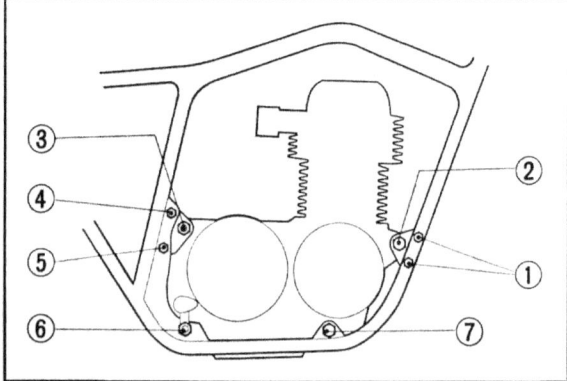

Fig. 52 Right side engine hanger bolts
① 8×50 hex bolt
② 10×50 hex bolt
③ Rear upper hanger bolt
④ 8×100 hex bolt
⑤ 8×40 hex bolt
⑥ Rear lower hanger bolt
⑦ 10×80 hex bolt

B. Engine Installation

1. Reinstall the engine in the reverse order of removal noting the following points:
   - Install the engine from the right side and tighten the hanger bolts. The battery ground cable terminal is installed with the rear hanger bolt.
   - Make sure that the generator cord and the starting motor cord are not pinched when the left crankcase cover is installed.
   - Make sure that the two mufflers on each side are properly connected with the muffler connecting band.
   - Perform the following adjustments after the engine is installed:
     Clutch adjustment
     Drive chain slack adjustment
     Carburetor adjustment

Fig. 53 ① Battery ground cable

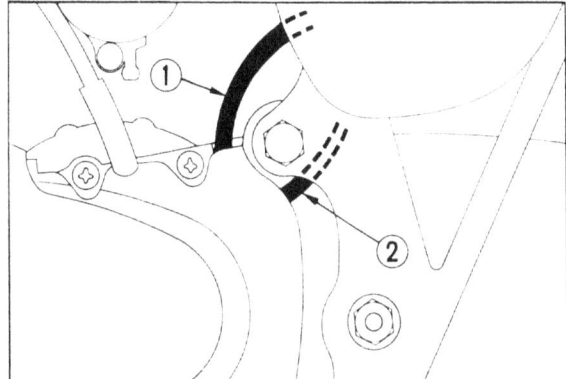

Fig. 54 ① Generator cord
         ② Starting motor cord

Fig. 55 ① Muffler connecting band

4. ENGINE

Fig. 56 ① Breather cover

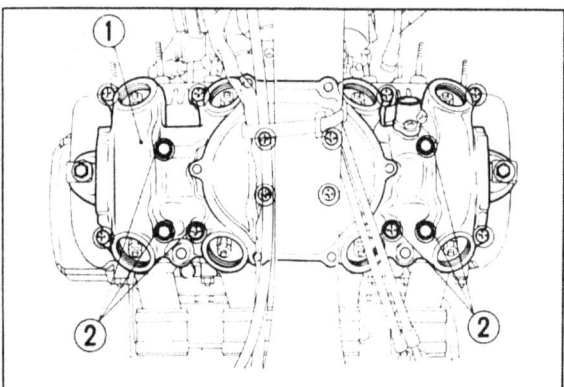

Fig. 57 ① Cylinder head cover
② 6 mm copper washers

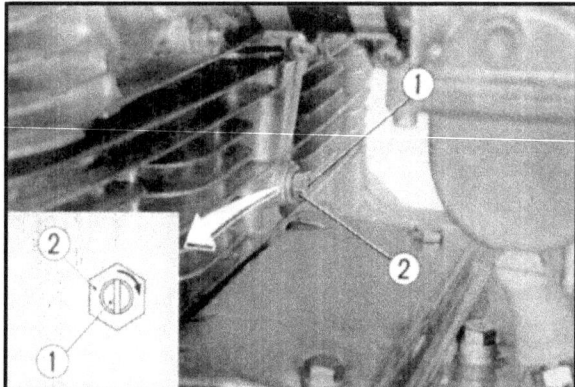

Fig. 58 ① Cam chain tension adjuster
② Lock nut

Fig. 59 ① Cam sprocket ③ Camshaft
② Cam chain ④ 7 mm bolt

3. CYLINDER HEAD, CYLINDER AND PISTON

A. Disassembly

1. Turn the fuel valve to the "STOP" position. Disconnect the fuel lines at the tank and remove the fuel tank.
2. Remove the exhaust pipe and muffler.
3. Disconnect the tachometer cable.
4. Disconnect the high tension cords at the spark plugs, loosen the six 6 mm screws and remove the breather cover.
5. Remove the tappet hole caps and the left and right side covers. Loosen the twelve 6 mm screws and six bolts, and remove the cylinder head cover.

Note:
· **Loosen the screws and bolts uniformly to relieve pressure gradually.**

6. Loosen the lock nut of the cam chain tension adjuster (leave the wrench on the nut). Turn the screw fully (approximately 90°) clockwise, and tighten the lock nut.
   In this condition the cam chain tensioner is not applying tension to the cam chain.

7. Loosen the two cam sprocket mounting bolts and remove the camshaft from the sprocket.
8. Remove the cam chain from the sprocket.

4. ENGINE

9. Separate the carburetor assembly from the cylinder head.
10. Loosen the cam chain tensioner mounting bolt.

Fig. 60 1 Cam chain tensioner
2 Cam chain tensioner mounting bolt

11. Loosen the twelve cylinder head mounting nuts and two 6 mm flange bolts, and remove the head. Loosen the nuts in the reverse order of tightening shown in Fig. 83.

Fig. 61 1 Cylinder head

12. Remove the cam chain guide from the cylinder by raising the cam chain guide slightly. Rotate the guide 90° and removing the chain guide.
    During this operation, do not drop the cam chain.

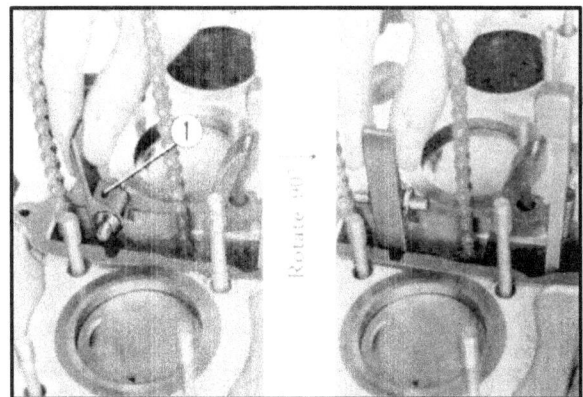

Fig. 62 ① Cam chain guide

13. Loosen the cam chain adjuster lock nut (Fig. 58) and remove the chain tensioner from the cylinder.
    To facilitate removal, raise the cylinder about 20 mm (1 in.), and remove the cam chain tensioner.

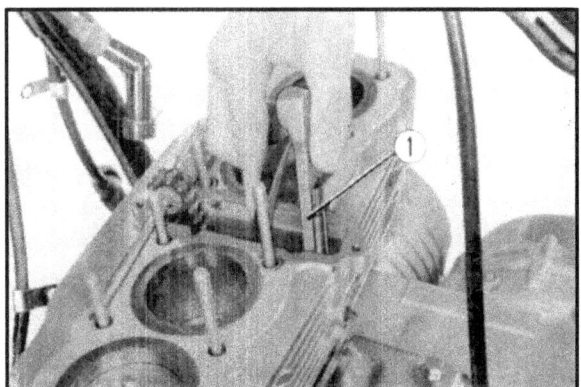

Fig. 63 ① Cam chain tensioner

Fig. 64 ① Cylinder　② Cylinder groove

14. Remove the cylinder.
    If the cylinder is stuck, pry if loose with a screwdriver placed in the groove at the base of the cylinder.

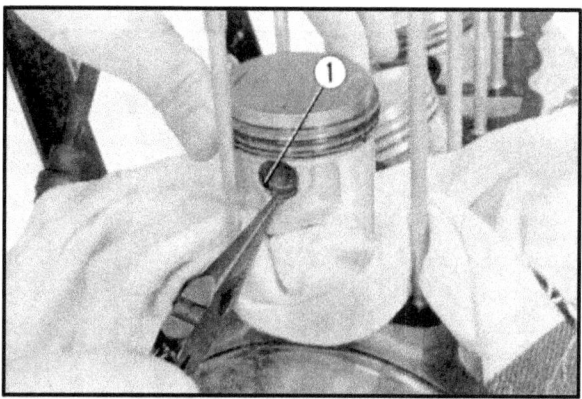

Fig. 65 ① Piston pin clip

15. Remove the piston pin clip, piston pin, and the piston.
    Note:
    When removing the pin clip, be careful not to drop the clip into the crankcase.

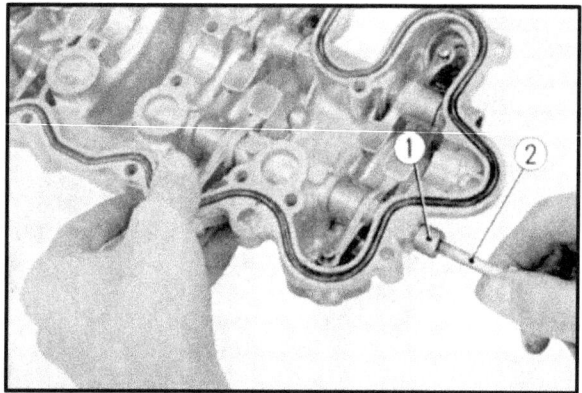

Fig. 66 ① Rocker arm shaft　② 6 mm bolt

16. Remove the piston rings.
17. Screw a 6 mm bolt into the rocker arm shaft and remove the rocker arm shaft from the cylinder head cover.

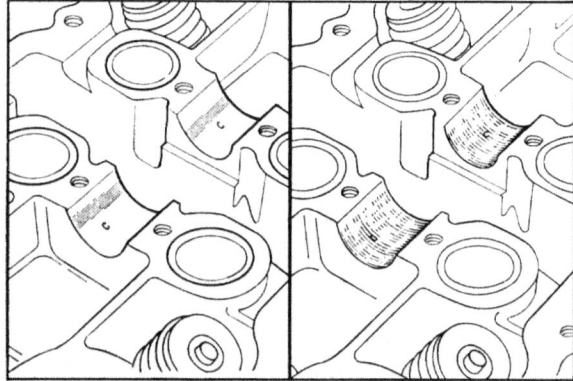

Fig. 67　Good　　No good

B. Inspection
1. Inspect the camshaft bearing surfaces. Camshaft bearing surfaces should be smooth and shiny. If it is scratched or excessively worn, it should be replaced.

2. Measure the can height with a micrometer.
   Replace the camshaft if it is beyond the serviceable limit.

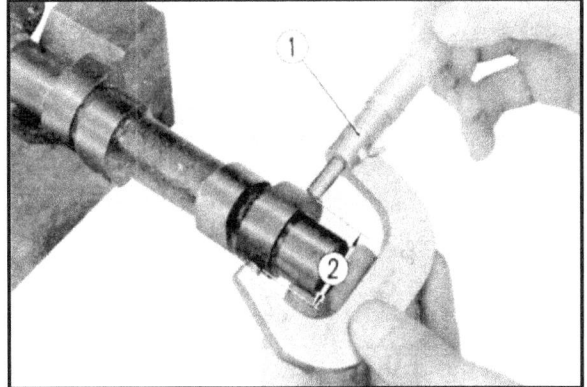

Fig. 68 1: Micrometer 2: Cam height

3. Measure camshaft runout.
   Support both ends of the camshaft on V-blocks. With a dial gauge, measure the radial runout by rotating the shaft. Replace the camshaft if it is beyond the serviceable limit.

4. Check the camshaft for scratches and wear and replace it if necessary.

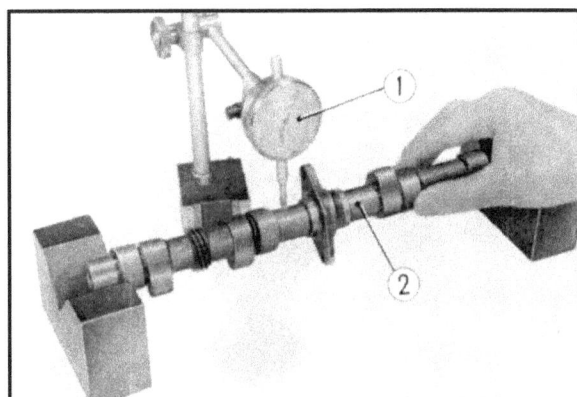

Fig. 69 1: Dial gauge 2: Camshaft

5. Measure the cylinder diameter at the top, center and bottom in both the X and Y axes. Rebore the cylinder if it is beyond the serviceable limit at any point. When reboring the cylinder, rebore it to fit one of the four standard oversize pistons available.
   Standard oversizes are **0.25, 0.50, 0.75 and 1.00 mm (0.009, 0.019, 0.029 and 0.039 in.)**.

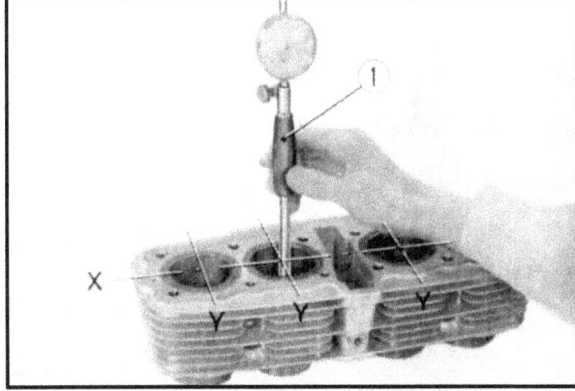

Fig. 70 1: Cylinder gauge

6. Measure piston diameter.
   Measure the diameter at the piston skirt, 90° to the piston pin with a micrometer. Replace the piston if the diameter is beyond the serviceable limit.

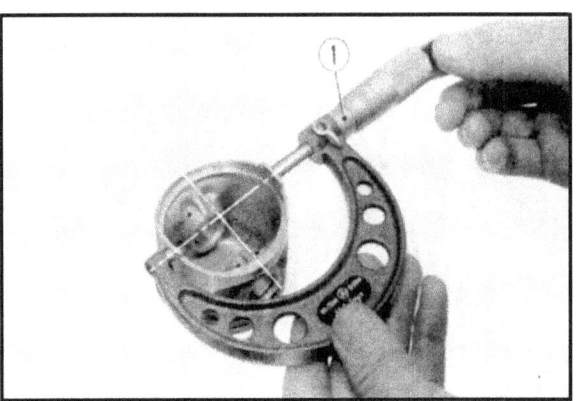

Fig. 71 1: Micrometer

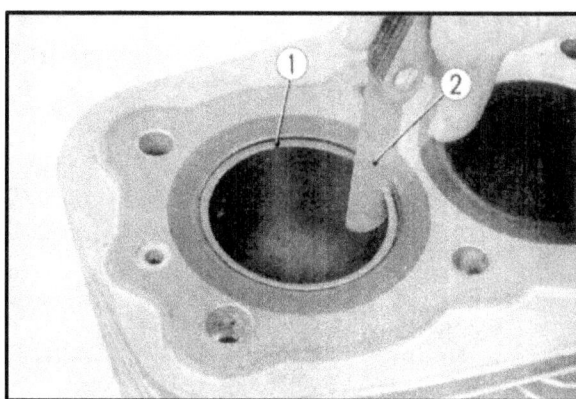

Fig. 72 ① Piston ring   ② Feeler gauge

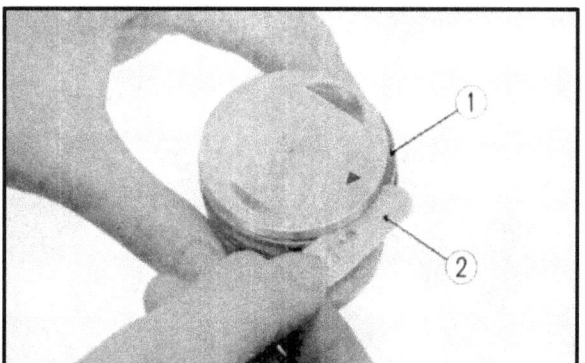

Fig. 73 ① Piston ring   ② Feeler gauge

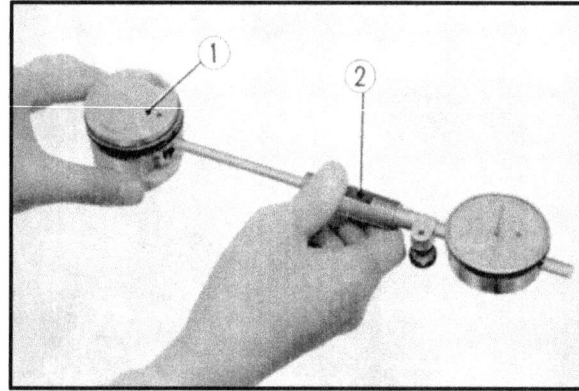

Fig. 74 ① Piston   ② Cylinder gauge

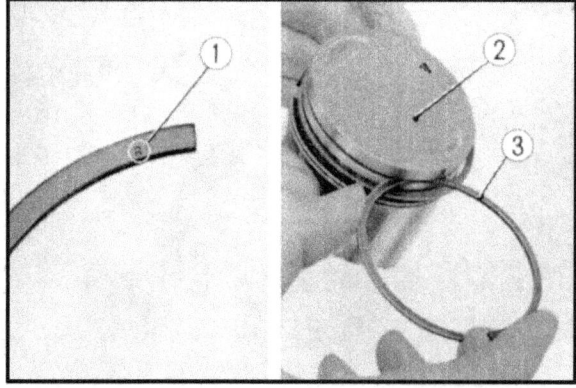

Fig. 75 ① Marks   ② Piston   ③ Piston ring

7. Measure piston ring end gap.
   Insert the piston ring into the skirt of the cylinder so that it is squarely positioned, and measure the gap with a feeler gauge.

8. Measure piston ring side clearance.
   Install the piston rings and measure the side clearance of the piston ring in the ring groove with a feeler gauge.

9. Measure the piston pin hole using an inside micrometer or a cylinder gauge.
10. Inspect the piston for damage, distortion and excessive wear.

C. Reassembly

1. Install the rocker arm and the rocker arm shaft in the cylinder head cover.
   Install the rocker arm shafts with the side having a hole facing outward.
2. Install the piston rings on the piston with the marking on the rings facing the top.

Note:
When installing new piston rings, roll the rings in the ring grooves to assure proper clearance. If the rings roll smoothly, the clearance is satisfactory.

Use piston rings of the same manufacturer as a set.

3. Install the piston on the connecting rod with the piston pin and clips so that the ▲ mark on the piston head points toward the front (exhaust side) as shown in the Fig. 74.
   Note:
   Always use new pin clips.

Fig. 76 ① ▲ marks

4. Stagger the end gaps of the top, 2nd and oil rings 120° apart.
   Install so that none of the gaps are on the piston boss axis or 90° away from it.

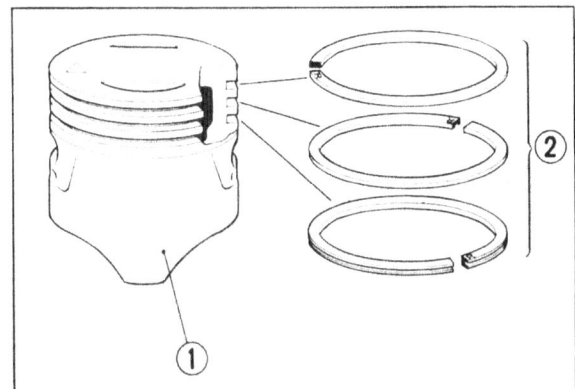

Fig. 77 ① Piston ② Rings

(Three-piece type oil ring)
a. When installing the oil ring, place the spacer and then the rails in position.
b. The spacer and rail gaps must be staggered **2~3cm (0.783~1.181 in.)**.
   Note:
   The gap of the oil ring is also that of the spacer.

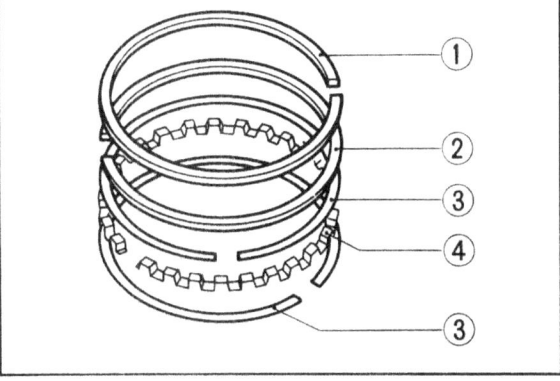

Fig. 77-1 ① Top ring   ③ Rails
              ② Second ring ④ Spacer

5. Install the cylinder gasket, two dowel pins (orifice valve) and two O-rings on the upper crankcase.
   Note:
   Before installing the dowel pin, blow compressed air through the hole to make sure it is not clogged.

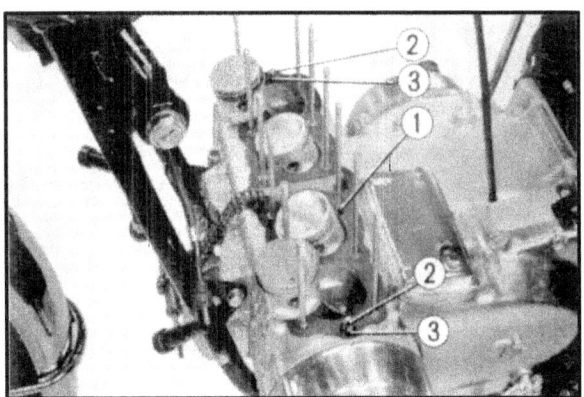

Fig. 78 ① Cylinder gasket ③ O-rings
            ② Dowel pins

Fig. 79 ① Piston bases ② Piston ring compressors

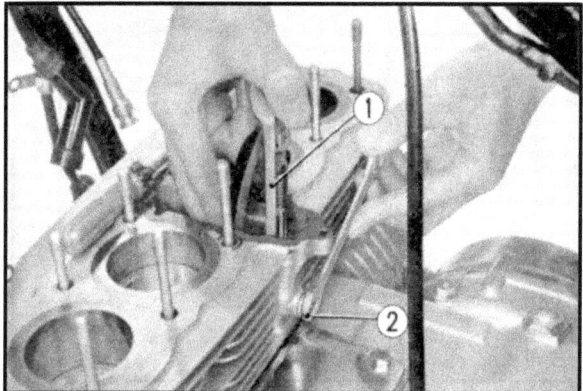

Fig. 80 ① Cam chain tensioner ② Lock nut

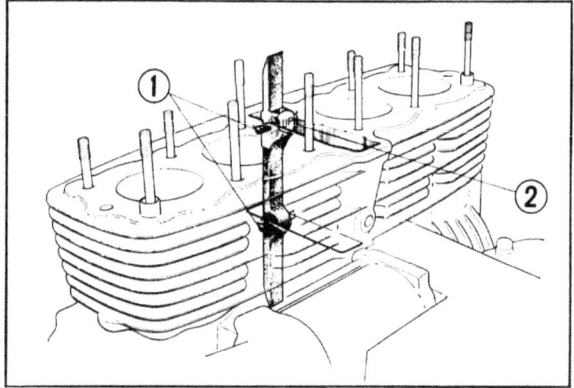

Fig. 81 ① Pins ② "UP" mark

Fig. 82 ① Cylinder head gasket ③ O-rings
② Dowel pins

6. Turn the crankshaft and place the piston base (Tool No. 07958-2500000) under the No. 2 and 3 pistons. Install the piston ring compressors (Tool No. 07957-3230000) on the piston rings, and insert the pistons into the cylinder. When the No. 2 and 3 pistons have entered the cylinder, remove the bases and piston ring compressors. Turn the crankshaft slightly and install the No. 1 and 4 pistons being careful not to expose the rings of the No. 2 and 3 pistons. Raise the cam chain at the same time.

7. With the cylinder held approximately 20 mm from the crankcase, install the cam chain tensioner in the cylinder, hold the tensioner down by hand and install the O ring, steel washer, and tighten the lock nut.

8. Insert the cam chain guide into the cylinder as shown in Fig. 81.

9. Install the cylinder head gasket, two dowel pins and two O-rings on the cylinder.

4. ENGINE

10. Place the cylinder head and hold the cam chain with a screwdriver to prevent the cam chain from dropping.
11. Tighten the twelve 8 mm nuts with the special tool to a torque of **2.0~2.2 kg-m. (14.46~16.63 ft-lbs)** in the sequence shown in Fig. 83.
    Install and torque two 6 mm flange bolts. Mount the cam chain tensioner on the cylinder head with the aluminum washer and 6 mm bolt.
    Note:
    Be careful not to drop nuts or washers into the cylinder head or will be difficult to remove them.

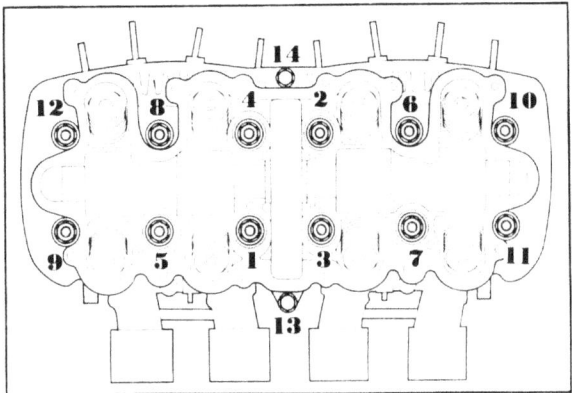

Fig. 83

12. Hold the cam chain sprocket and cam chain together and slide the camshaft through them from the right side, and set it on the cylinder head bearings. Install the cam chain on the cam sprocket.

Fig. 84　① Cam sprocket　③ Camshaft
　　　　② Cam chain

13. Valve timing adjustment
    Remove the point cover, rotate the crankshaft in the clockwise direction and align the "T" (1.4) mark of the spark advancer to the timing mark. Position the camshaft so that the center of the cutout notch on the right end of the camshaft is aligned to the cylinder head flange surface.

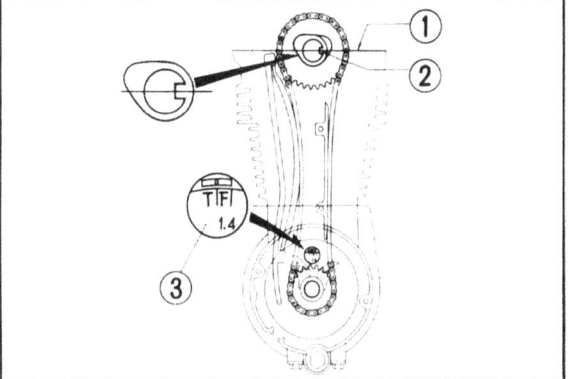

Fig. 85　① Cylinder head flange surface
　　　　② Cutout notch　③ Spark advancer

14. Mount the cam sprocket on the camshaft with two 7 mm bolts.
15. Mount the carburetor assembly on the cylinder head.
16. Install the two dowel pins and six sealing rubbers on the cylinder head.

Fig. 86　① Dowel pins　② Sealing rubbers

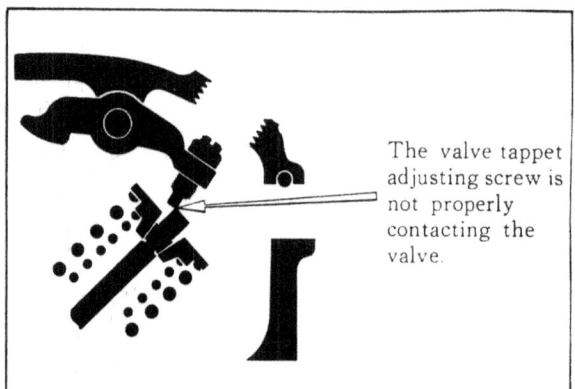

Fig. 87

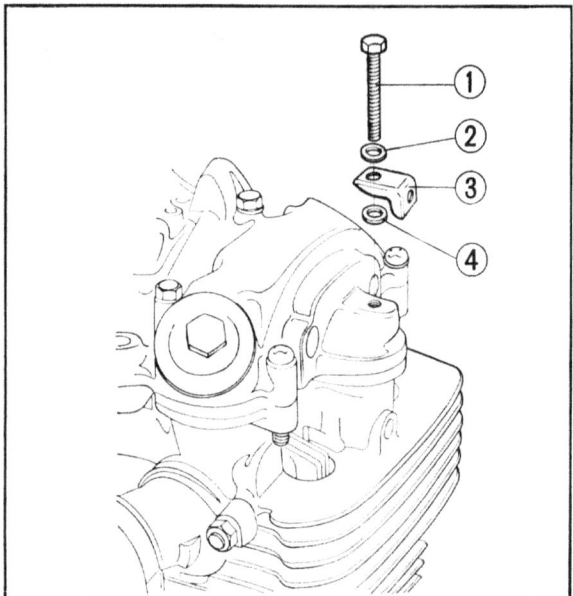

Fig. 88
① 6 mm screw
② Chromium-plated copper washer
③ Head side cover set plate
④ Alminum washer

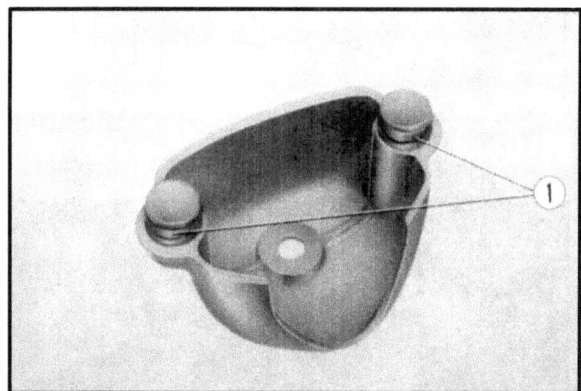

Fig. 89 ① O-ring

17. Install the cylinder head cover with the twelve 6 mm screws and six 6 mm bolts, and torque to **0.8~1.2 kg-m (5.78~8.67 lbs-ft)** so that the torque difference is not over **0.2 kg-m (1.44 lbs-ft)**.

Note:
- Insert fingers into the tappet hole cap opening and lift the valve tappet adjusting screw to check that they are properly meeting the valves.
- Use the six 6 mm copper washers as shown in Fig. 88.
- Install the head side cover set plate with washers mounted on both sides of the 6 mm screws (Chromium-plated copper washer on top and aluminum washer on bottom).

18. Install O-rings on the dowel pins of the left and right side covers, and install the side covers on the cylinder head.
19. Install the breather cover with six 6 mm screws.

Note:
High tension cord clips are mounted on both sides with the clips facing forward.

20. Adjust the cam chain by referring to page 12.
21. Adjust the tappets by referring to page 7.

4. VALVES AND VALVE SPRINGS

A. Disassembly

1. Remove the cylinder head by referring to section 3. A.
2. Compress the valve springs with a valve spring compressor (Tool No. 07957-3290000). Remove the valve cotters and the valves.

Note:
Do not compress the springs more than necessary. Compressing them excessively may damage the valve stem seals.

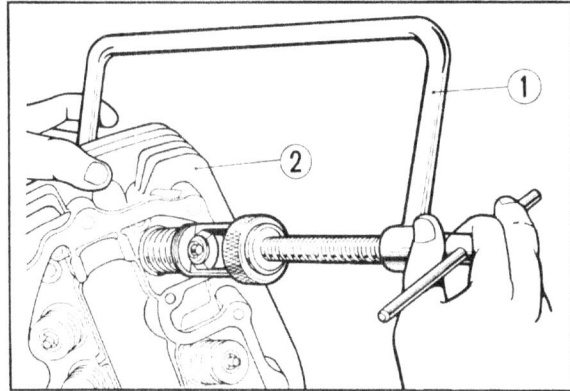

Fig. 90　① Valve spring compressor
　　　　② Cylinder head

3. Drive the valve guide out of the cylinder head using the valve guide remover (Tool No. 07046-32301).

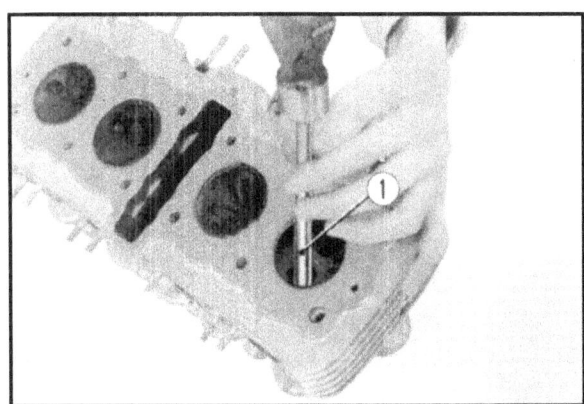

Fig. 91　① Valve guide remover

B. Inspection

1. Measure valve stem clearance.
   Insert the valve into the guide and measure the clearance in both the X and Y directions using a dial gauge. Replace both the valve and guide as a set if the clearance is beyond the serviceable limit. Drive the guide into the cylinder head using a valve guide driver (Tool No. 07942-3290100) and finish ream the guide to the proper size with the reamer (Tool No. 07984-0980000). Standard valve guide inside diameter for both the intake and exhaust is **5.475~5.485 mm (0.2153 in.~0.2157 in.)**

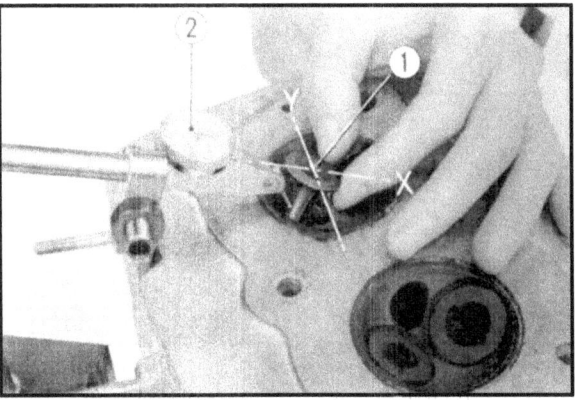

Fig. 92　① Valve　② Dial gauge

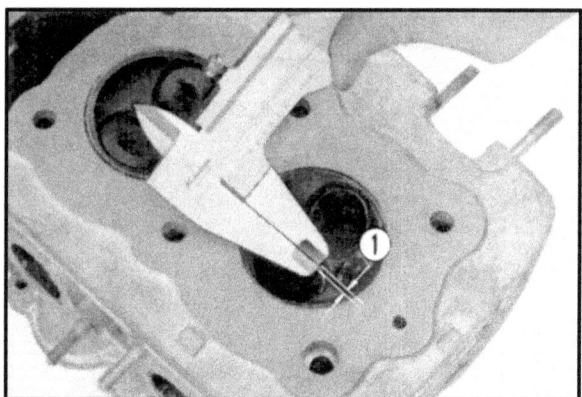

Fig. 93 ① Valve seat width

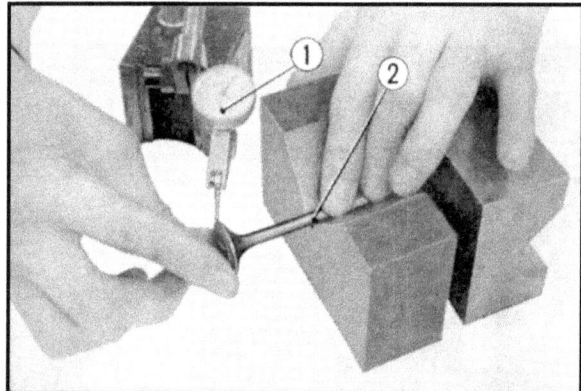

Fig. 94 ① Dial gauge ② Valve

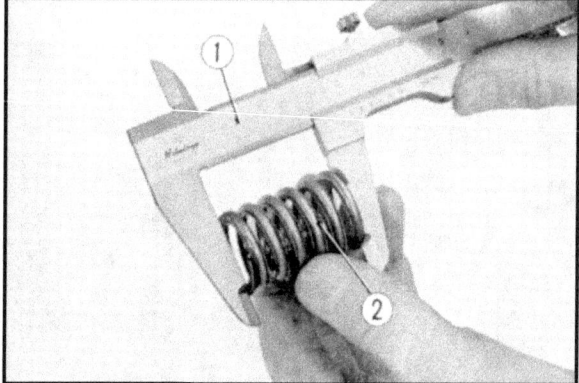

Fig. 95 ① Vernier caliper ② Valve spring

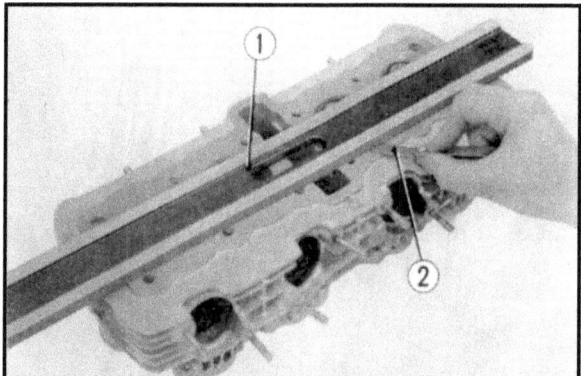

Fig. 96 ① Straight edge ② Feeler gauge

2. Check the valve seat contact width and recondition if necessary.
   Apply a thin coat of red lead to the valve seat surface. Press the valve against the seat and rotate it to check if the contact width is uniform. If not, lap the valve seat and again check the contact width. If necessary, recondition the valve seat using a valve seat grinder. Seat width **1.0~1.5 mm (0.039~0.059 in.)**.

3. Measure valve runout.
   Place the valve on a V-block and measure the runout of the valve with a dial gauge applied to the face of the valve while turning it. Replace the valve if the runout exceeds the serviceable limit.

4. Measure the valve springs.
   Measure the free length of the valve spring with a vernier caliper.

5. Measure the flatness of the cylinder head. Place a straight edge on the cylinder head surface and measure the clearance at several points with a feeler gauge. If the clearance exceeds the serviceable limit, lap the cylinder head surface on the surface plate using lapping compound or replace the head if it cannot be repaired.

C. Reassembly

1. Wash all component parts in solvent and reassemble the parts in the reverse order of disassembly.

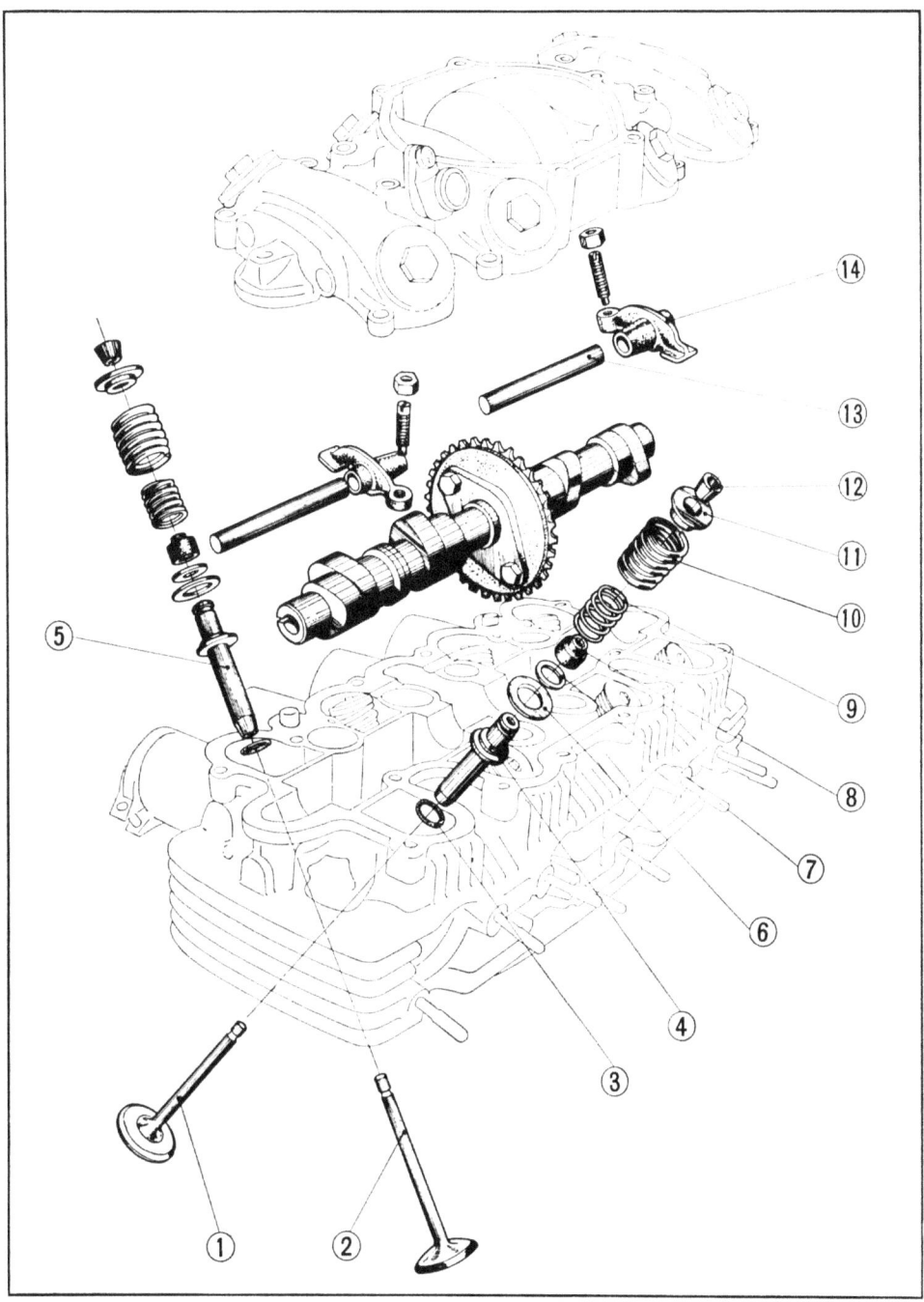

Fig. 97 Component parts of the cylinder head

① Exhaust valve
② Intake valve
③ 10×1.6 O ring
④ Exhaust valve guide
⑤ Intake valve guide
⑥ Valve spring outer seat
⑦ Valve spring inner seat
⑧ Valve stem seal
⑨ Inner valve spring
⑩ Outer valve spring
⑪ Retainer
⑫ Cotter
⑬ Valve rocker arm shaft
⑭ Valve rocker arm

Note:
When installing the valves, apply a liberal amount of oil on the valve stem.

2. Install the cylinder head in accordance with section 3. C, page 28.

5. Oil Pump and Oil Filter

The oil pump is a trochoid type driven by the primary shaft. The screen and paper element filters are used to provide clean oil to the engine.

Lubricating System Block Diagram

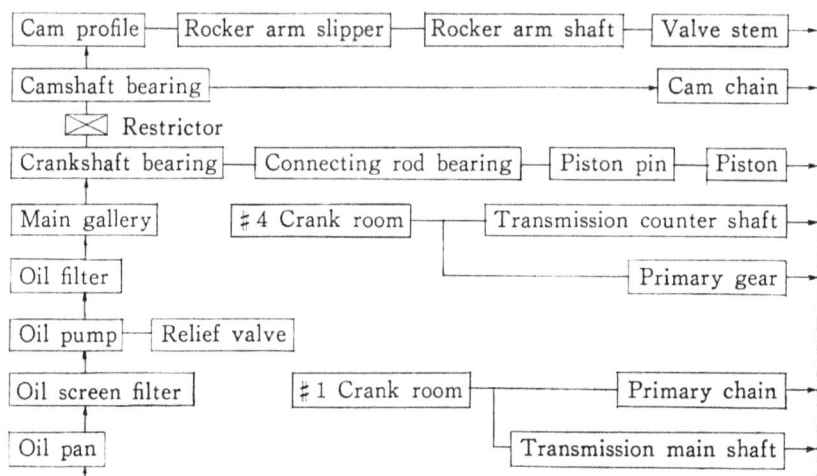

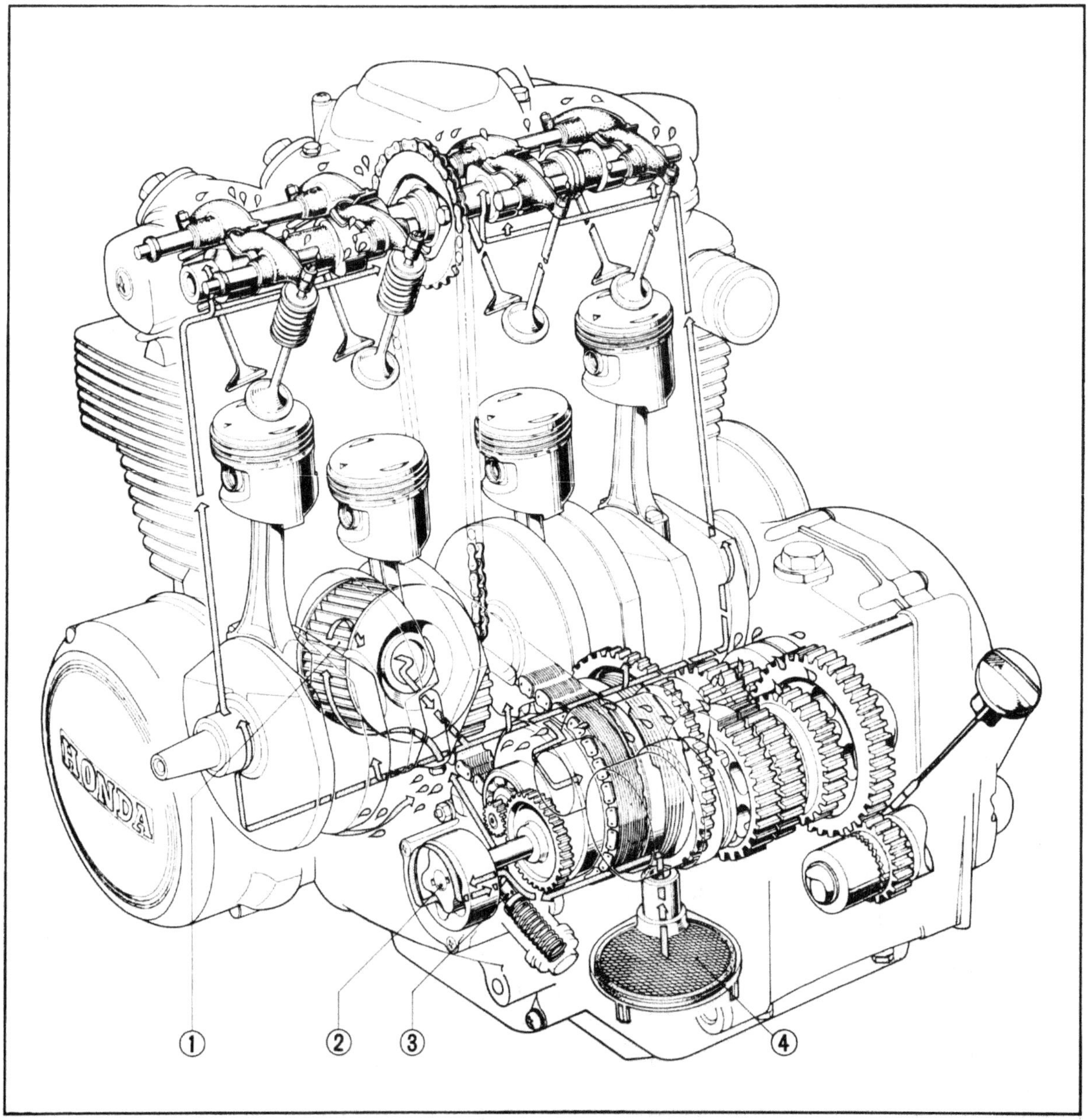

Fig. 98 Oil Lubricating Diagram
① Oil cleaner element ② Oil pump ③ Relief valve ④ Oil screen filter

A. Disassembly

Oil Pump

1. Drain the engine oil in accordance with section 7, page 13.
2. Remove the starting motor cover, shift lever and the left crankcase cover.
3. Loosen the 4 mm bolt and remove the pressure switch wiring. Remove the three 6 mm screws and the oil pump.

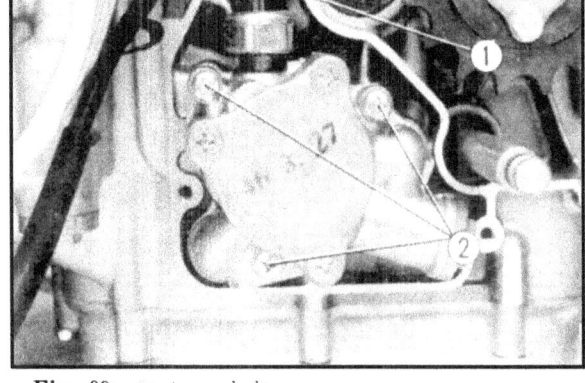

Fig. 99 1) 4 mm bolt
2) 6 mm screws

4. Remove the cap and disassemble the relief valve and spring.

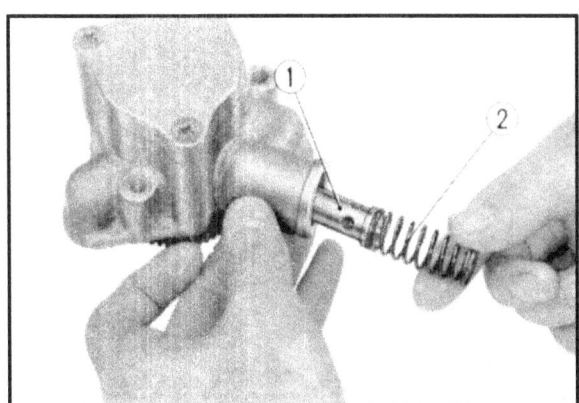

Fig. 100 1) Relief valve   2) Spring

Oil Screen Filter

1. Drain the engine oil in accordance with section 7, page 13.
2. Loosen the ten 6 mm bolts from the oil pan. Remove the oil pan, and the oil screen filter can be removed.

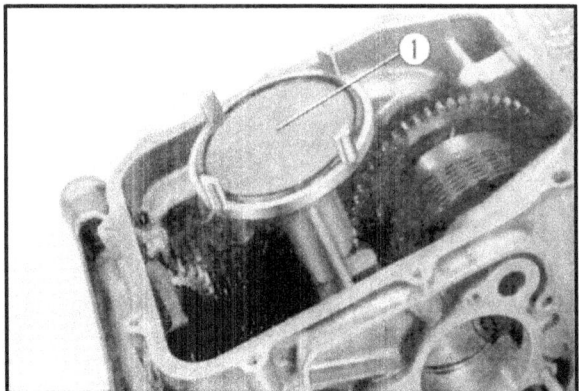

Fig. 101 1) Oil screen filter

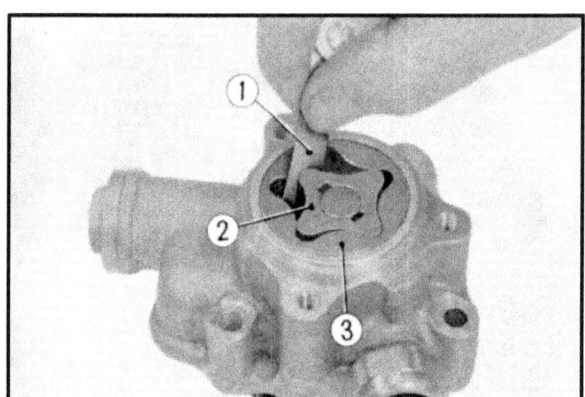

Fig. 102 ① Feeler gauge   ③ Outer rotor
② Inner rotor

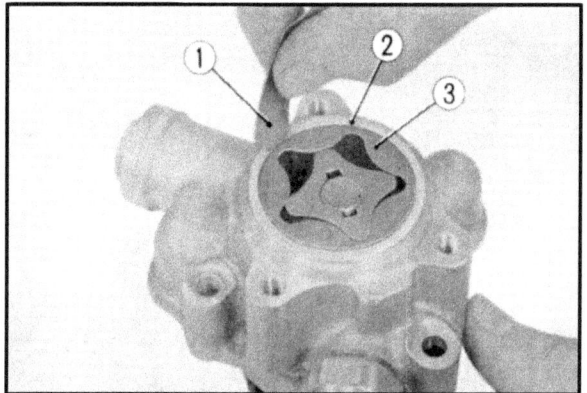

Fig. 103 ① Feeler gauge   ③ Outer rotor
② Pump body

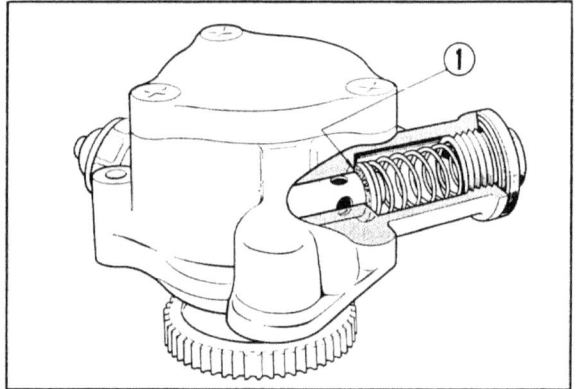

Fig. 104 ① Relief valve seat

Oil Filter

1. Drain the engine oil in accordance with section 7, page 13.
2. Loosen the center bolt to remove the oil filter.

B. Oil Pump Inspection

1. Measure the clearance between the inner and outer rotors.

   Use a feeler gauge to measure the clearance between the rotors. If the clearance exceeds the serviceable limit, replace the pump.

2. Measure the clearance between the outer rotor and the pump body.

   Use a feeler gauge to measure the clearance between the outer rotor and the pump body. If the clearance exceeds the serviceable limit, replace the pump.

3. Inspect the operation of the relief valve. Make sure that the relief valve is not stuck in the pump body. Also check for any foreign objects which may be lodged between the valve and seat.

4. Inspect the screen filter.

   Wash and inspect the screen filter. Replace the filter if it is damaged.

4. ENGINE

C. Reassembly

Oil Filter

1. Insert the oil filter center bolt through the oil filter case and assemble the spring, spring seat and element. Screw the center bolt into the engine.

Oil Screen Filter

1. Mount the screen filter on the lower crankcase.
2. Mount the oil pan on the engine with the ten 6 mm bolts.

Oil Pump

1. Insert the drive pump shaft into the oil pump body and install the drive pin into the shaft.
2. Align the outer and inner rotor punch marks and install into the pump body. The surfaces with the punch marks may be set to the pump body side or the pump cover side.
3. Install the 47 mm O-ring on the oil pump body and install the oil pump cover with the three 6 mm screws.
4. Install the relief valve and spring into the oil pump body, and install the cap.
5. Install the two O-ring collars, two 14 mm O-rings, and a 47 mm O-ring into the oil pump body and then install the oil pump on the crankcase with the three 6 mm screws.
6. Connect the pressure switch wires.
7. Install the left crankcase with the four 6 mm screws and the gear change pedal.
8. Install the starting motor cover.

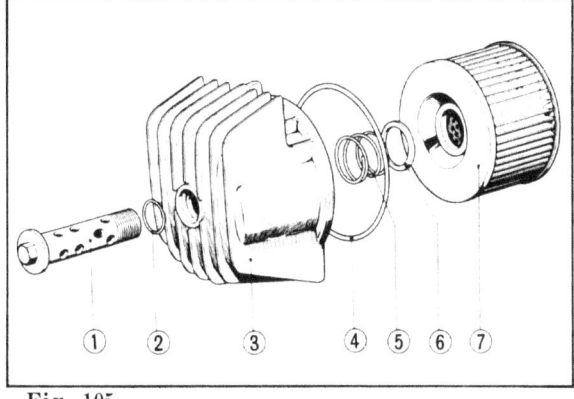

Fig. 105
1) Oil filter center bolt
2) 15 × 2.5 O-ring
3) Oil filter case
4) 89 × 4.5 mm O-ring
5) Filter element set spring
6) Oil filter spring seat
7) Oil filter element

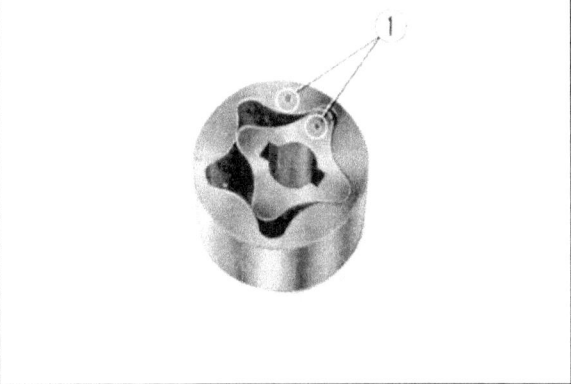

Fig. 106 1) Punch marks

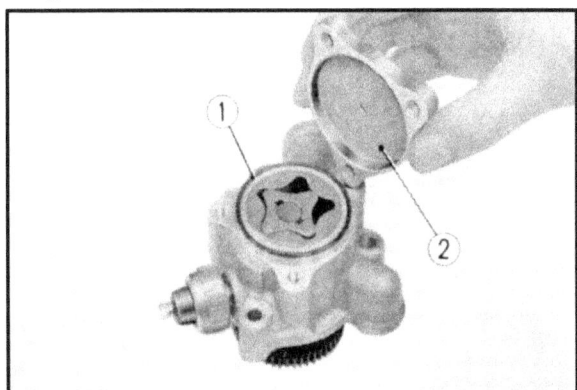

Fig. 107 1) 47 mm O-ring   2) Oil pump cover

Fig. 108 1) O-ring collar   3) 47 mm O-ring
2) 14 mm O-ring

6. CLUTCH

A. Disassembly

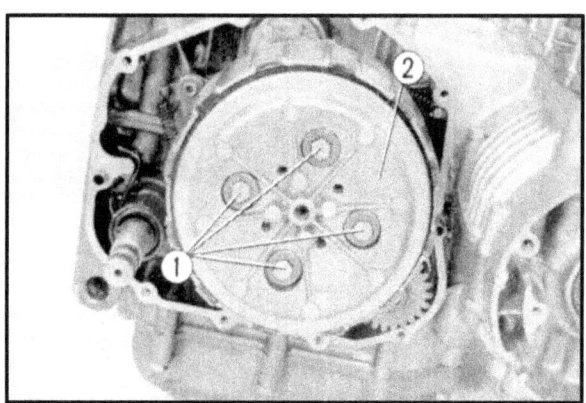

Fig. 109 ① Bolts ② Clutch pressure plate

1. Drain the engine oil in accordance with section 7, page 13.
2. Remove the kick starter pedal.
3. Loosen the ten 6 mm screws and remove the right crank case cover.
4. Loosen the four clutch pressure plate mounting bolts, and remove the clutch pressure plate and four clutch springs.

Fig. 110 ① 25 mm snap ring
② Clutch assembly

5. Remove the clutch lifter joint piece.
6. Remove the 25 mm snap ring, shims (some engines may not have shims installed), and the clutch assembly from the main shaft.

Fig. 111 ① Clutch adjuster

7. Disassemble the clutch disc, clutch plate and clutch center from the clutch outer.
8. Remove the left crankcase cover.
9. Disconnect the clutch cable from the clutch lifter.
10. Loosen the clutch adjuster lock bolt and remove the clutch adjuster from the left crankcase cover.

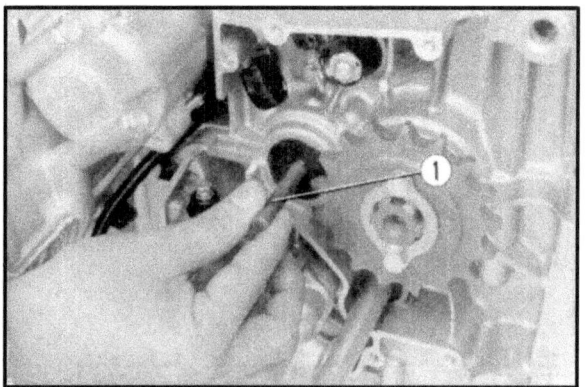

Fig. 112 ① Clutch lifter rod

11. Pull the clutch lifter rod out.

4. ENGINE

B. Inspection

1. Measure the friction disc thickness with a vernier caliper. Replace it if it exceeds the serviceable limit.

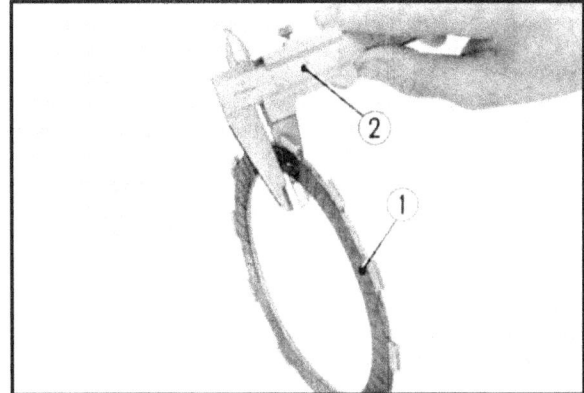

Fig. 113 (1) Friction disc   (2) Vernier caliper

2. Check the clutch plate for warp age. Place the clutch plate on the surface plate and measure the amount of warp age with a feeler gauge. If the warp exceeds the serviceable limit, replace the clutch plate.
3. Measure the clutch spring. Measure the free length of the clutch spring with a vernier caliper and replace it if it exceeds the serviceable limit.

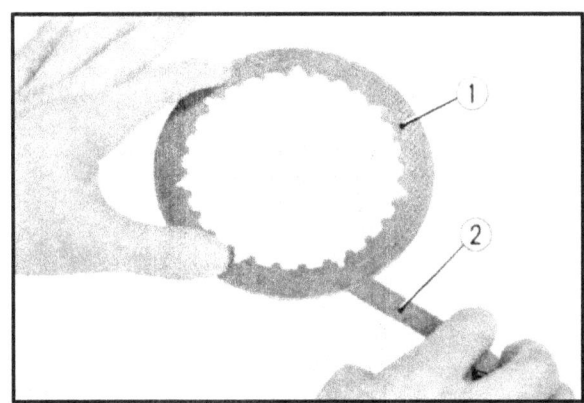

Fig. 114 (1) Clutch plate   (2) Feeler gauge

4. Inspect the rivets mounting the clutch outer to the driven gear for looseness, and replace the clutch outer if any of rivets are loose.

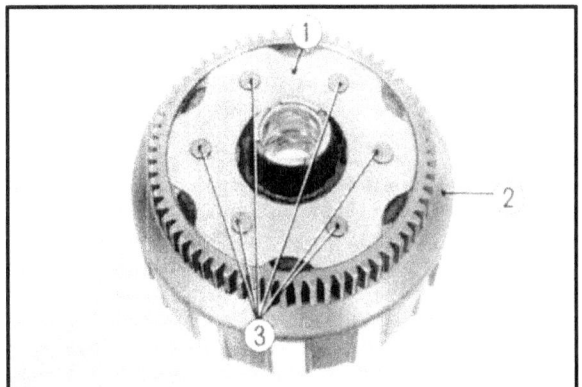

Fig. 115 (1) Driven gear   (3) Rivets
    (2) Clutch outer

C. Reassembly

1. Assemble the clutch lifter rod into the main shaft so that the spherical end is facing the right side.
2. Apply grease to the clutch lifter and assemble it to the left crankcase cover with the adjuster. Tighten the lock bolt and reconnect the clutch cable to the clutch lifter.
3. Install the clutch lifter rod, set the steel ball into the clutch lifter, and mount the left crankcase cover with four 6mm screws.

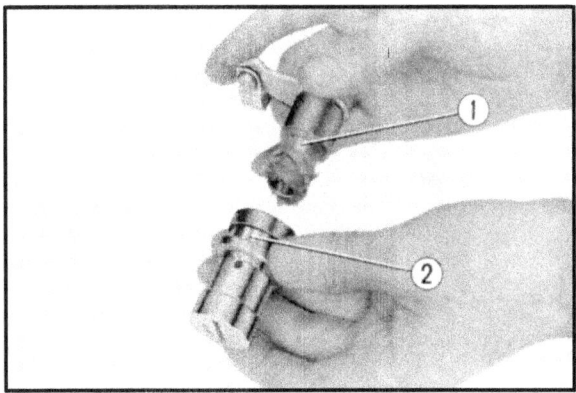

Fig. 116 (1) Clutch lifter   (2) Adjuster

Fig. 117 ① Clutch center ② Clutch outer

4. Install the clutch outer to the mainshaft and install the clutch center.

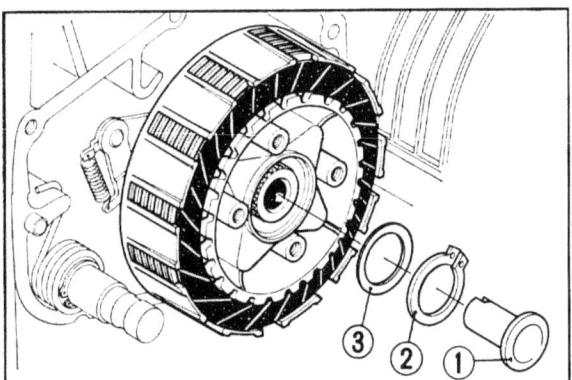

Fig. 118 ① Oil grooves

5. Apply engine oil on the friction discs (7 pieces) and assemble them on the clutch center alternately with the clutch plates (6 pieces). Assemble them into the clutch outer.

   Note:
   When assembling the friction discs, assemble them on the clutch center so that the oil grooves are facing as in Fig. 118.

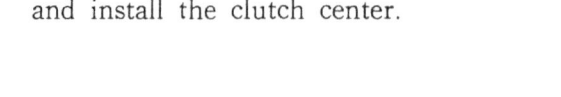

Fig. 119 ① Joint piece ③ 25 mm snap ring
         ② Spacer

6. After assembling the friction discs and clutch plates, set them with the 25 mm snap ring. Place a dial gauge against the end of the clutch assembly to check for looseness. If the measured value of looseness is greater than **0.1 mm (0.004 in.)**, install a spacer on the inside of the snap ring. Spacers are available in thicknesses of 0.1, 0.3 and 0.5 mm.

Fig. 120 ① Bolts ② Clutch pressure plate

7. Insert the clutch lifter joint piece into the mainshaft and fix the clutch plates with four pieces of the clutch spring, washer and 6 mm screw.
8. Install a new gasket and the right crank case cover.
9. Adjust the clutch.

7. GEAR SHIFT MECHANISM

A. Disassembly

1. Disassemble the clutch in accordance with section 6. A., page 40.
2. Remove the gear change pedal.
3. Remove the gear shift arm while holding the gear shift arm down.

Fig. 121　① Gear shift arm

4. Remove the shift drum stopper bolt and the shift drum neutral stopper bolt. Remove the shift drum stopper and shift drum neutral stopper.
5. Loosen the 6 mm screw and remove the oil guide plate and bearing set plate.
6. Loosen the 6 mm screw and cam plate.
7. Disassemble the upper and lower crankcase and disassemble the transmission gears in accordance with section 9. A., page 47.
8. Remove the neutral stopper switch from the gear shift drum.
9. Remove the shift drum guide screw from the upper crankcase and then remove the guide screw collar.
10. Remove the guide pin clip and guide pin and pull the gear shift drum out of the crankcase.

Fig. 122
① Shift drum stopper
② Shift drum stopper bolt
③ Shift drum neutral stopper
④ Shift drum neutral stopper bolt
⑤ Bearing set plate
⑥ 6 mm screw
⑦ Oil guide plate
⑧ Cam plate

Fig. 124　① Guide pin clip　③ Gear shift drum
　　　　　② Guide pin

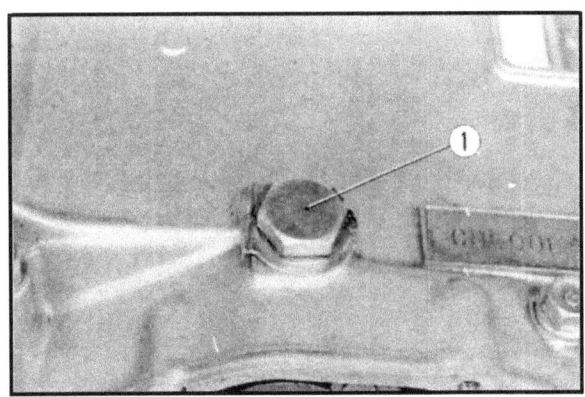

Fig. 123　① Shift drum guide screw

4. ENGINE

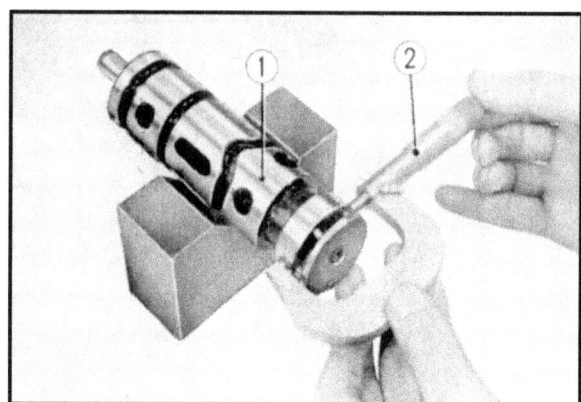

Fig. 125 ① Gear shift drum   ② Micrometer

B. Inspection

1. Measure the gear shift drum diameter with a micrometer and the shift fork with an inside micrometer. Replace any part that exceeds the serviceable limit.

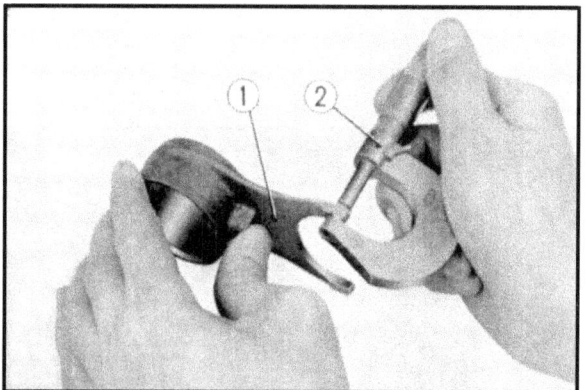

Fig. 126 ① Gear shift fork   ② Micrometer

2. Measure the width of the gear shift fork fingers with a micrometer.
   Replace if it exceeds the serviceable limit.

C. Reassembly

1. Set the left, right and center gear shift forks into the upper crankcase as shown in Fig. 127. Install the gear shift drum.

Fig. 127 ① Gear shift forks   ② Gear shift drum

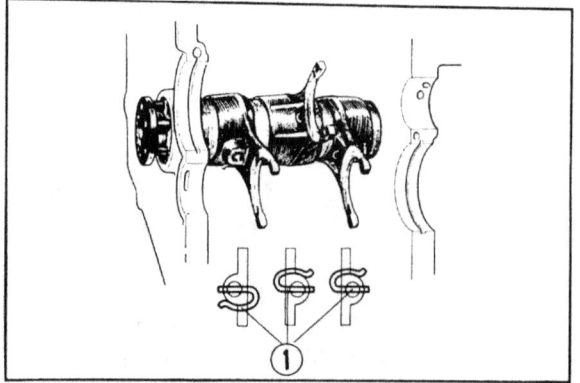

Fig. 128 ① Guide pin clips

2. Insert the guide pin into the shift fork and secure it with the guide pin clip.
   Note:
   Make sure that the guide pin clip is installed in the proper direction.

3. Place the counterbored section of the shift drum as shown in Fig. 128. Install the steel ball, the spring cap, and the spring. Lock with the shift drum screw. Bend the tab up on the guide screw lock washer to lock the guide screw.

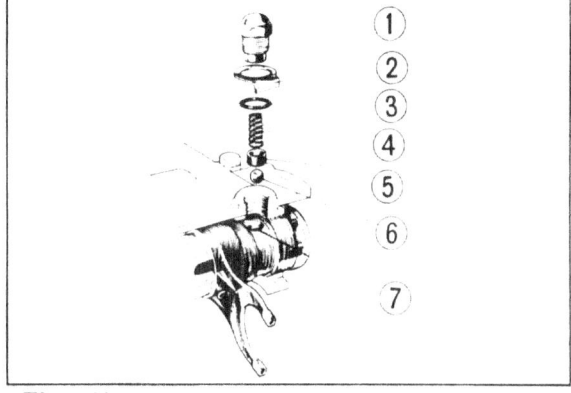

Fig. 129 ① Guide screw ④ Spring
② Guide screw lock washer ⑤ Spring cap
③ O-ring ⑥ Steel ball
⑦ Counterbored section

4. Align the neutral switch to the groove in the gear shift drum and lock in place with the 6 mm screw.

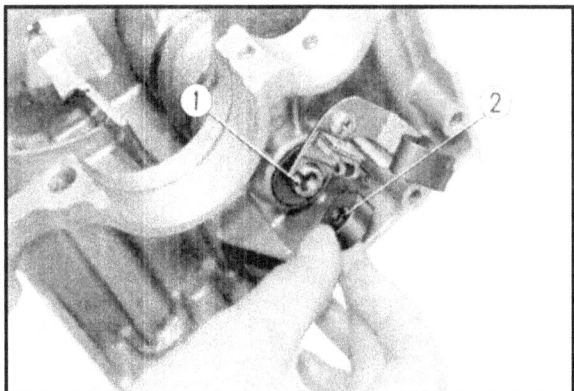

Fig. 130 ① Gear shift drum ② Neutral switch

5. Assemble the transmission into the upper crankcase in accordance with section 10. C, page 55 and assemble the upper and lower crankcases.
6. Install the cam plate on the pin of the gear shift drum with the 6 mm flat head screw which has been coated with thread lock cement.

Note:
The pin and the pin hole in the cam plate must be aligned.

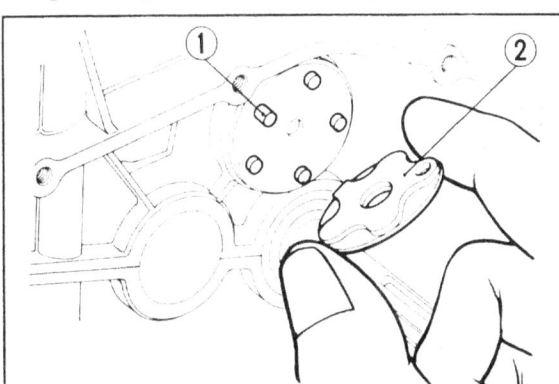

Fig. 131 ① Pin ② Cam plate

7. Attach the shift drum stopper spring to the drum stopper and the drum neutral stopper as shown in Fig. 132. Tighten the drum stop bolt and neutral stop bolt. Tighten the bearing set plate together.
8. Tighten the oil guide plate. After tightening, rotate the shift drum and check to be sure that each component part operates smoothly.

Note:
Make sure that the guide plate comes in contact with the primary drive gear.

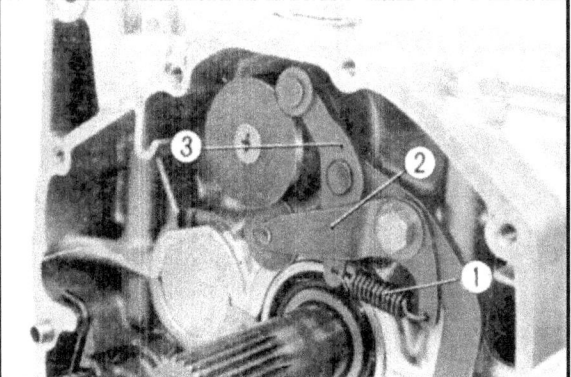

Fig. 132 ① Shift drum stopper spring
② Shift drum stopper
③ Shift drum neutral stopper

9. Install the gear shift arm and make sure that it operates smoothly in both directions.
10. Install the clutch in accordance with section 6. C., page 41.

8. CAM CHAIN TENSIONER

The cam chain tensioner is constructed of spring steel on which a layer of heat resistant rubber is vulcanized and a sheet of teflon cemented. It applies pressure against the cam chain and absorbs the shocks produced by the chain. The cam chain guide on the tension side of the cam chain also controls chain vibration.

An adjustment screw is located at the rear of the cylinder block.

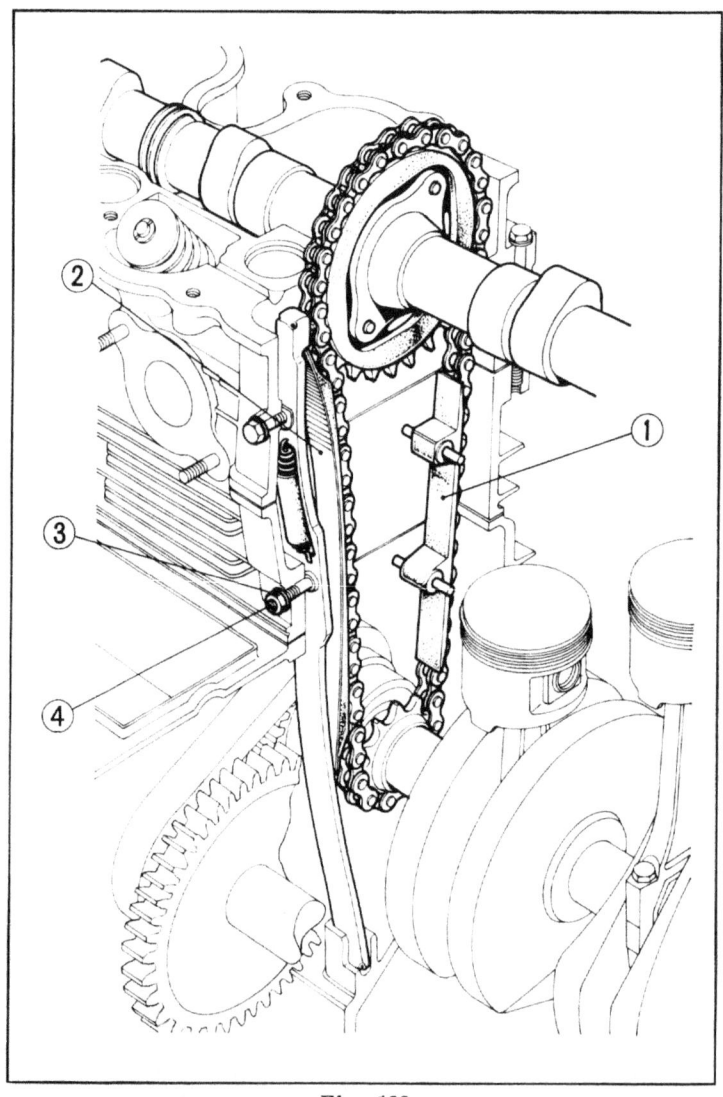

Fig. 133

① Cam chain guide   ③ Lock nut
② Cam chain tensioner   ④ Screw

4. ENGINE

A. Disassembly
1. Remove the cam chain tensioner and the chain guide in accordance with section 3. A., page 24.

B. Inspection
1. Make sure that the cam chain tensioner adjuster gear is properly meshed with the rack. Inspect for smooth operation. To adjust the cam chain, see page 14.

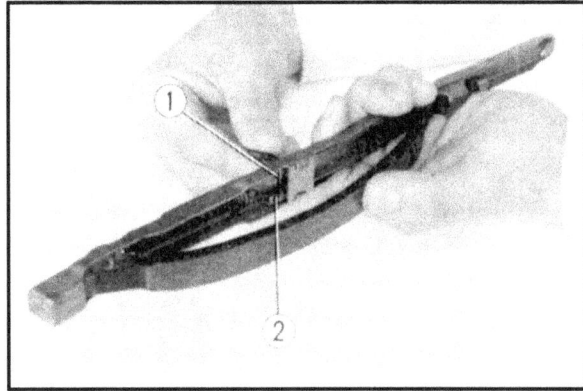

Fig. 134 ① Gear ② Rack

C. Reassembly
1. Perform reassembly in accordance with section 3. C., page 28.

9. CRANKSHAFT AND CONNECTING ROD

A. Disassembly
1. Dismount the engine in accordance with section 2. A., page 20.
2. Disassemble the cylinder head, cylinder, and piston in accordance with section 3. A., page 24.
3. Remove the generator cover and remove the rotor using a generator rotor puller. (Tool No. 07933-2160000)
4. Remove the point cover and the special washer by removing the 6 mm bolt. Loosen the three 5 mm screws and remove the contact breaker assembly and the spark advancer.

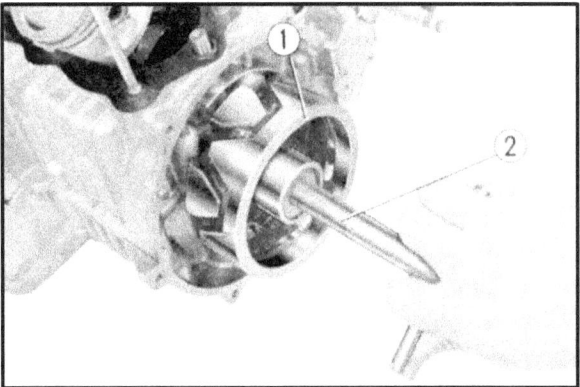

Fig. 135 ① Generator rotor
② Generator rotor puller

Fig. 136 ① 6 mm bolt
② Special washer
③ 5 mm screws
④ Contact breaker assembly

5. Remove the clutch and the gear shift arm in accordance with section 6. A., page 40.
6. Remove the starting motor cover and dismount the starting motor.

Fig. 137 ① Starting motor

48 4. ENGINE

Fig. 138 ① Bearing set plate

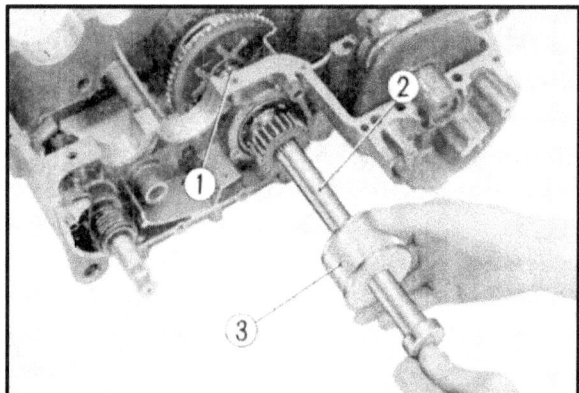

Fig. 139 ① Primary shaft ② Primary shaft puller
③ Weight hammer

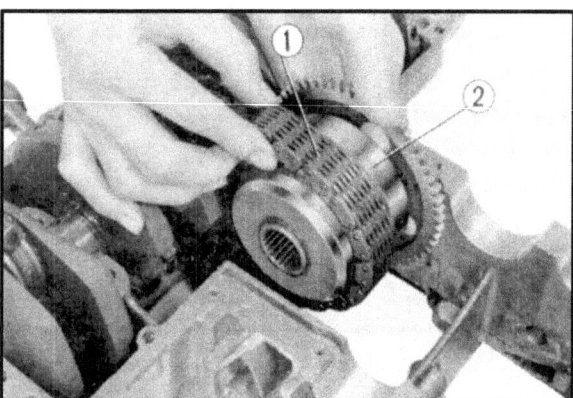

Fig. 140 ① Primary chain ② Starting clutch

Fig. 141 ① Dial gauge ② Crankshaft

7. Place the engine upside down and loosen the ten 6 mm bolts to remove the oil pan.
8. Loosen the ten 8 mm bolts and the twelve 6 mm bolts from the lower crankcase. Loosen the 8 mm bolts in the reverse order shown in Fig. 152.
9. Place the engine in an upright position and loosen the three 8 mm and 6 mm bolts. Tap the upper crankcase lightly with a wooden hammer and separate the upper and lower crankcases.
10. Loosen the two 6 mm bolts and remove the bearing set plate.
11. Pull the primary shaft out using a primary shaft hammer (Tool No. 07936-3230100) and a weight hammer (Tool. No. 07936-3230200). On the model CB550, use a primary shaft hammer (Tool No. 07936-3740100) and weight hammer (Tool No. 07945-3000500).

Note:

Disassembly of the primary shaft, transmission, and kick starter can be performed without removing the cylinder head, cylinder or piston. When removing the lower crankcase, follow the sequence 10, 11, 9 and 8 above.

12. Remove the starting clutch from the primary chain.
13. Remove the primary chain and the cam chain from the crankshaft.

B. Inspection

1. Measure crankshaft runout
   Support both ends of the crankshaft on a V-block and measure the amount of bend in the crankshaft by applying a dial gauge to the center journal and rotating the crankshaft. If the runout exceeds the serviceable limit on the dial gauge, replace the crankshaft.

2. Inspect the crankshaft journals with a micrometer for scoring and uneven wear. If any journal is out-of-round or tapered more than the serviceable limit, replace the crankshaft.

3. Measure the crankshaft journal wear.
   Cut a length of plasti-gauge to the width of the bearing cap. Place the gauge on the bearing parallel to the crankshaft. Assemble the crankshaft and torque the crankcase down in accordance with Fig. 152.
   Disassemble the crankcase and measure the plasti gauge using the scale provided. If there is a clearance in excess of **0.08 mm (0.0031 in.)**, replace the bearing.

Note:
When measuring with the plasti-gauge, do not turn the crankshaft.

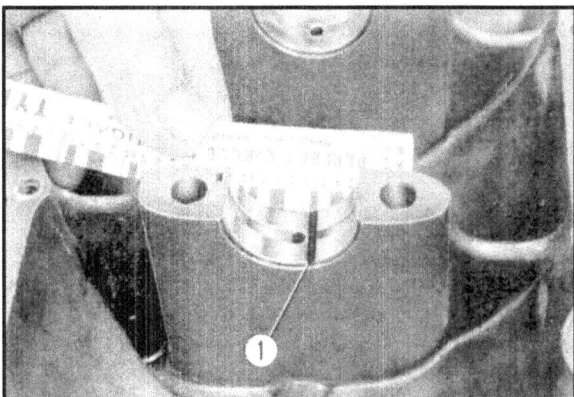

Fig. 142 1. Plasti-gauge

Bearing Selection

1. Remove the bearing. Assemble and tighten the upper and lower crankcases. Refer to Fig. 152.
2. Measure the inside diameter of all the bearing seats in the vertical direction with a cylinder gauge and select the corresponding letter from the table below.

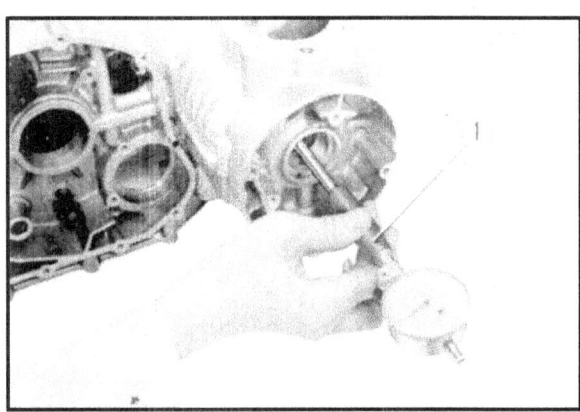

Fig. 143 1. Cylinder gauge

mm (in.)

C	36.016~36.024 (1.4179~1.4182)
B	36.008~36.016 (1.4176~1.4179)
A	36.000~36.008 (1.4173~1.4176)

3. Measure the diameter of the crankshaft journal with a micrometer and select the corresponding figure 1 or 2 from the table below.

1	2
32.99~33.00 (1.2987~1.2992)	32.98~32.99 (1.2983~1.2987)

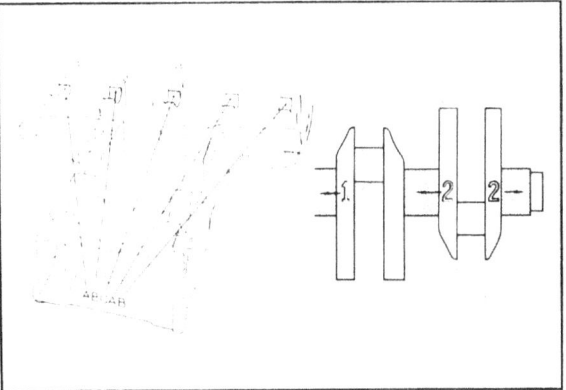

Fig. 144

Note:
The lower crankcase and crankshaft are marked with letters or numbers at the factory. These are production codes and should not be used or referred to during servicing or repairing.

4. According to the letter and the figure from items 2 and 3, select the proper bearing from A, B, C and D in the table below.

Crankshaft classification No. Crankcase classification mark	1	2
C	B (Brown)	A (Black)
B	C (Green)	B (Brown)
A	D (Yellow)	C (Green)

Fig. 145 ① Connecting rod cap

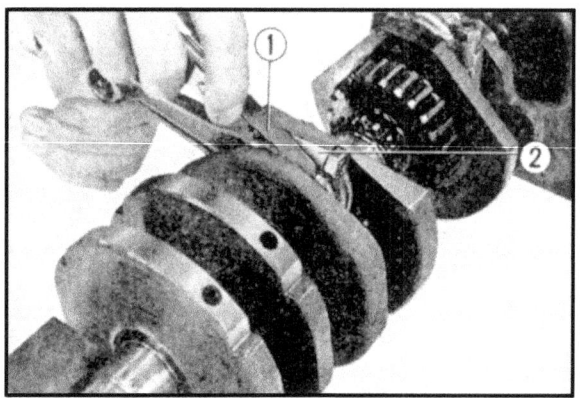

Code	Weight (gr.)
A	281~285
B	286~290
C	291~295
D	296~300
E	301~305
F	306~310
G	311~315

Fig. 146 ① Weight code number

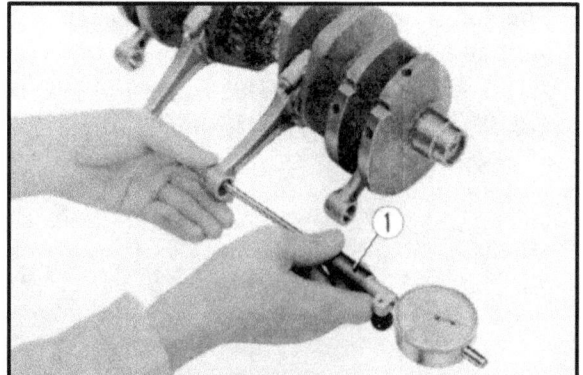

Fig. 147 ① Feeler gauge
② Connecting rod

5. Measure connecting rod large end wear. Separate the cap from the connecting rod. After setting the plasti-gauge in place, torque the two rod nuts to **2.0-2.2 kg-m (14.46-15.91 lbs-ft)**.
Disassemble the cap and measure the plasti-gauge. Replace the bearing with a new one if it exceeds the serviceable limit.
Note:
Do not turn the crankshaft while the plasti-gauge is installed.

6. Method of designating connecting rod weight.
When replacing the connecting rod, replace with one having the same weight code. The weight code is stamped at the large end of the connecting rod. When replacing all of the connecting rods, the tolerance of the respective rods should be within 5 grams.
Note:
The connecting rod weight includes the weight of the cap and two bolts, but not the bearings.

7. Measure axial clearance using a feeler gauge.
Replace if it exceeds the serviceable limit.

8. Measure the connecting rod small end. Measure the diameter of the connecting rod small end with an inside dial gauge. Replace if it exceeds the serviceable limit.

Fig. 148 ① Inside dial gauge

4. ENGINE

Selection of The Bearing

1. Measure crankshaft pin diameter with a micrometer and select the corresponding letter from the table below.

A	B
34.99~35.00 (1.3775~1.3780)	34.98~34.99 (1.3771~1.3775)

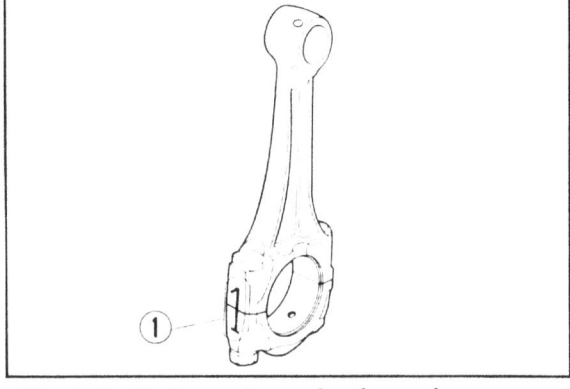

Fig. 149 ① Connecting rod code number

2. Select the bearing from the table below which coincides with the number (1, 2, 3) stamped on the large end of the connecting rod.

Crank pin classification mark / Connecting rod code No.	A	B
3	B (Brown)	A (Black)
2	C (Green)	B (Brown)
1	D (Yellow)	C (Green)

Note:
- The numbers marked on the crankshaft are production codes and should not be referred to during servicing.
- The bearings must be installed on the connecting rod with the key toward the front.

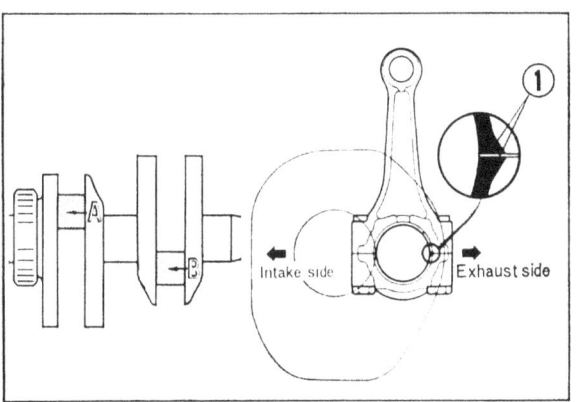

Fig. 150 ① Key (projection)

C. Reassembly

1. Install the primary chain and the cam chain on the crankshaft.
2. Install the crankshaft into the lower crankcase.
3. Position the starting clutch and starter gear as in Fig. 151, then drive the primary shaft in from the right to left. Use care in the needle bearing assembly sequence shown in Fig. 166.

Fig. 151 ① Starting clutch
② Starter gear ③ Primary shaft

Fig. 152 8 mm mounting bolts

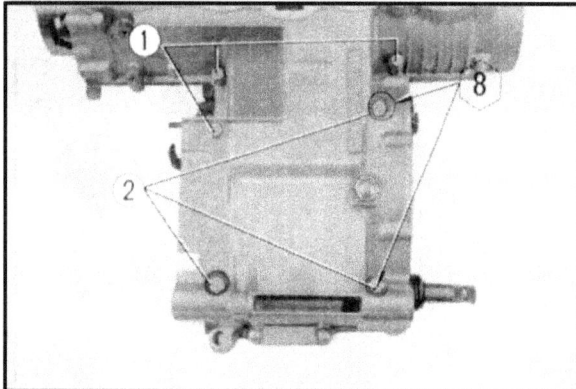

Fig. 154 ① 6 mm bolts
② 8 mm bolts

Fig. 155 ① Oil pan

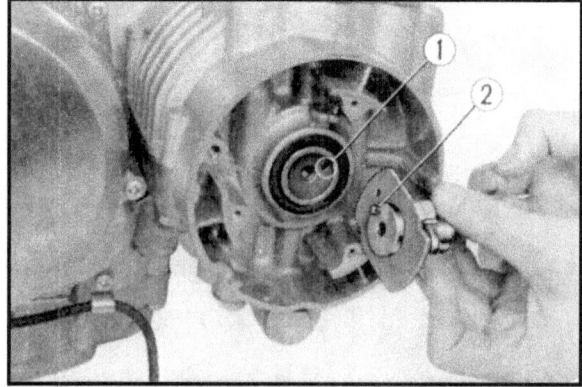

Fig. 156 ① Dowel pin hole ② Dowel pin

4. Install the bearing set plate with two 6 mm bolts.
5. Apply a thin coat of gasket paste on the mounting flange of the lower crankcase (a heavy coat will cause the paste to fall inside the crankcase).
   Install two dowel pins. Mount the upper crankcase on the lower crankcase.

Fig. 153 6 mm mounting bolts

6. Place the engine upside down so that the parting surfaces will not be separated. Install the ten 8 mm bolts. Torque the 8 mm bolts in the sequence shown in Fig. 152 to a torque of **2.3–2.5 kg-m. (16.63–18.08 lbs-ft)**.
   Tighten the thirteen 6 mm bolts. (Fig. 153)

Note:
Note the position of the two 8 mm bolts which are stamped on the bolt head with the number "9".

7. Position the upper crankcase on top and install with the three 6 mm and 8 mm bolts. (Fig. 154)

Note:
Note position of the two 8 mm bolts which are stamped on the bolt head with the number "8".

8. Install the oil screen filter and mount the oil pan with the ten 6 mm bolts.
9. Mount the starting motor with the two 6 mm bolts.
10. Install the gear shift arm in accordance with section 7. C., page 44.
11. Install the clutch in accordance with section 6. C., page 41.
12. Insert the spark advancer dowel pin into the pin hole in the crankshaft and mount the contact breaker with the three 5 mm screws.

4. ENGINE

13. Install the special advancer washer with the 6 mm bolt and install the point cover.
14. Adjust timing and point gap.
15. Mount the generator rotor with the 10 mm bolt.
16. Install the generator cover.
17. Assemble the piston, cylinder, cylinder head, and head cover in accordance with section 3. C., page 28.

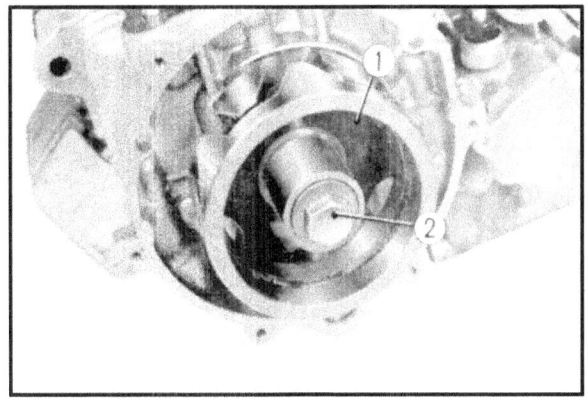

Fig. 157 ① Generator rotor
② 10 mm bolt

10. TRANSMISSION, KICK STARTER AND PRIMARY SHAFT

A. Disassembly

1. Dismount the engine from the frame in accordance with section 2. A., page 20.
2. Remove the clutch in accordance with section 6. A., page 40.
3. Separate the upper and lower crankcase in accordance with section 9. A., page 47.
4. Remove the transmission and disassemble the gears from the respective shafts.

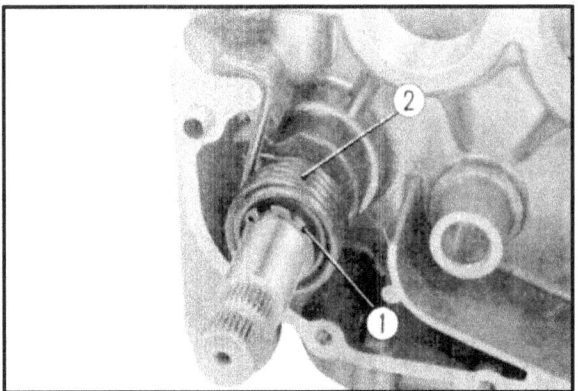

Fig. 158 ① 18 mm snap ring
② Return spring

Kick Starter

5. Remove the 18 mm snap ring and the return spring.
6. Remove the 12 mm snap ring and disassemble the kick starter shaft from the lower crankcase.

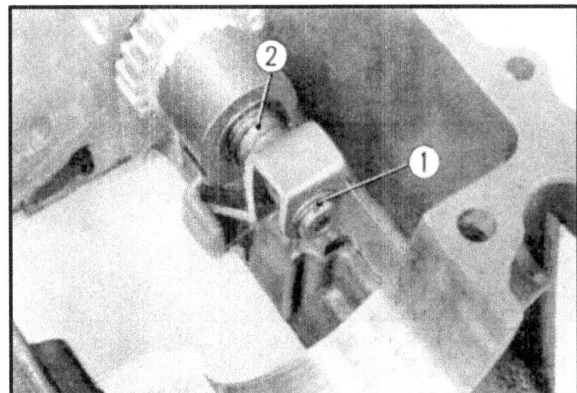

Fig. 159 ① 12 mm snap ring   ② Kick starter shaft

Fig. 160 ① Primary drive gear ② 20 mm snap ring

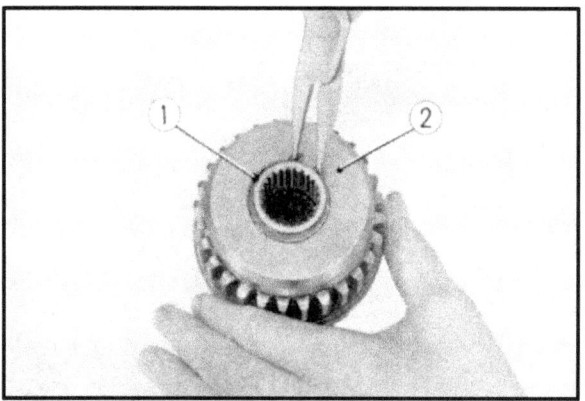

Fig. 161 ① 30 mm snap ring
② Primary driven sprocket

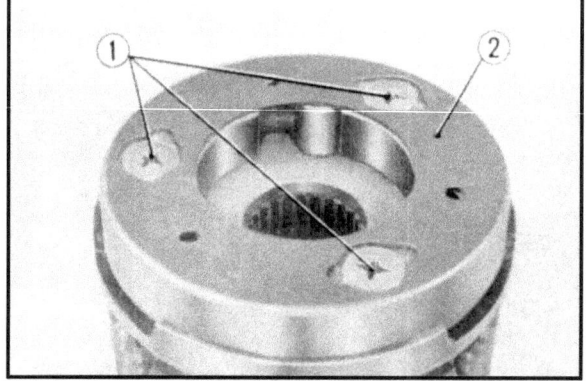

Fig. 162 ① 6 mm flat head screws
② Starting clutch outer

Fig. 163 ① Dial gauge

Primary Shaft

7. Remove the primary shaft in accordance with section 9. A, page 47 and remove the 20 mm snap ring and primary drive gear.

8. Remove the side collar and pull the #6205 ball bearing out.
9. Remove the 30 mm snap ring, primary driven sprocket, starting clutch, and pull the damper rubbers out.

10. Loosen the three 6 mm flat head screws and remove the starting clutch outer.

B. Inspection

1. Measure gear backlash.
   Set the pointer of a dial gauge against the tooth of the gear and measure the backlash.

4. ENGINE

2. Inspect the dogs and replace any gears with excessively worn dogs. Make sure that the gears slide smoothly over the splined shaft.

C. Reassembly

Primary Shaft

1. Install the starting clutch outer and primary driven sprocket hub with the three 6 mm flat head screws coated with thread lock cement. Then stake the screw heads with a punch to prevent looseness.

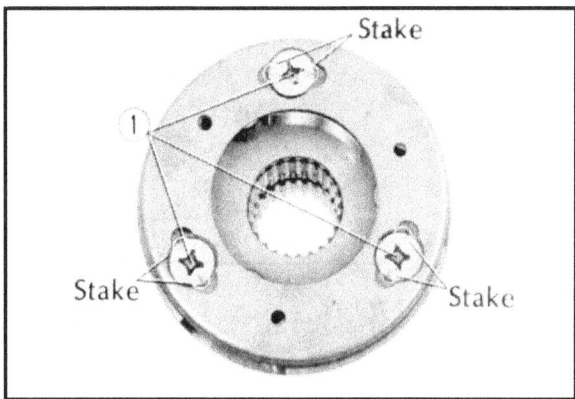

Fig. 164 ① 6 mm flat head screw

2. Assemble the damper rubbers on the primary driven sprocket, and install on the starting clutch with a 30 mm set ring.
3. Drive the #6205 ball bearing into the primary shaft.

Fig. 165 ① Primary driven sprocket
② Damper rubbers

4. Mount the starting clutch gear on the starting clutch, and insert the needle bearing and 25 mm spacer into the starting clutch gear. Fit the 25 mm thrust washer and the snap ring on the primary shaft, and install the primary shaft in the crankcase.

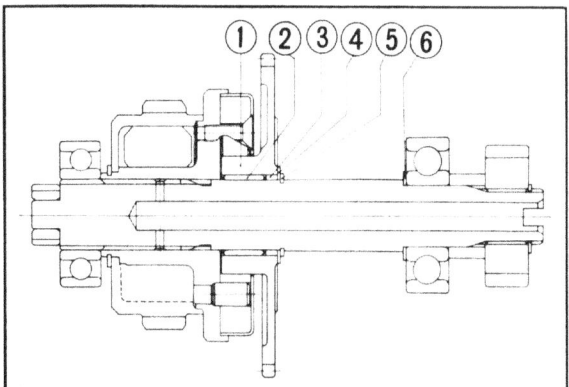

Fig. 166 ① Starting clutch gear
② Needle bearing (25 × 29 × 17)
③ 25 mm spacer
④ 25 mm thrust washer
⑤ 25 mm snap ring
⑥ 22 mm thrust washer

4. ENGINE

Kick Starter

5. Reassemble the kick starter components in accordance with Fig. 167.

Note:
Be sure to install the 18 mm washer.

Transmission

6. Assemble the transmission gears on the respective main and counter shafts.

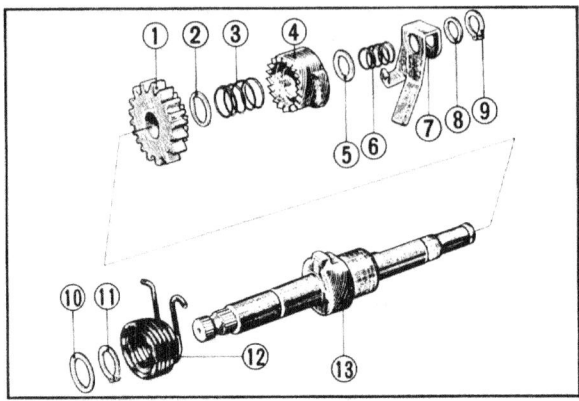

Fig. 167
① Kick starter pinion
② 20 mm thrust washer
③ Starter pinion set spring
④ Kick starter rachet
⑤ 15 mm thrust washer
⑥ Kick starter rachet spring
⑦ Rachet guide plate
⑧ Chain guide thrust
⑨ 12 mm snap ring
⑩ 18 mm washer
⑪ 18 mm snap ring
⑫ Kick starter spring
⑬ Kick starter spindle

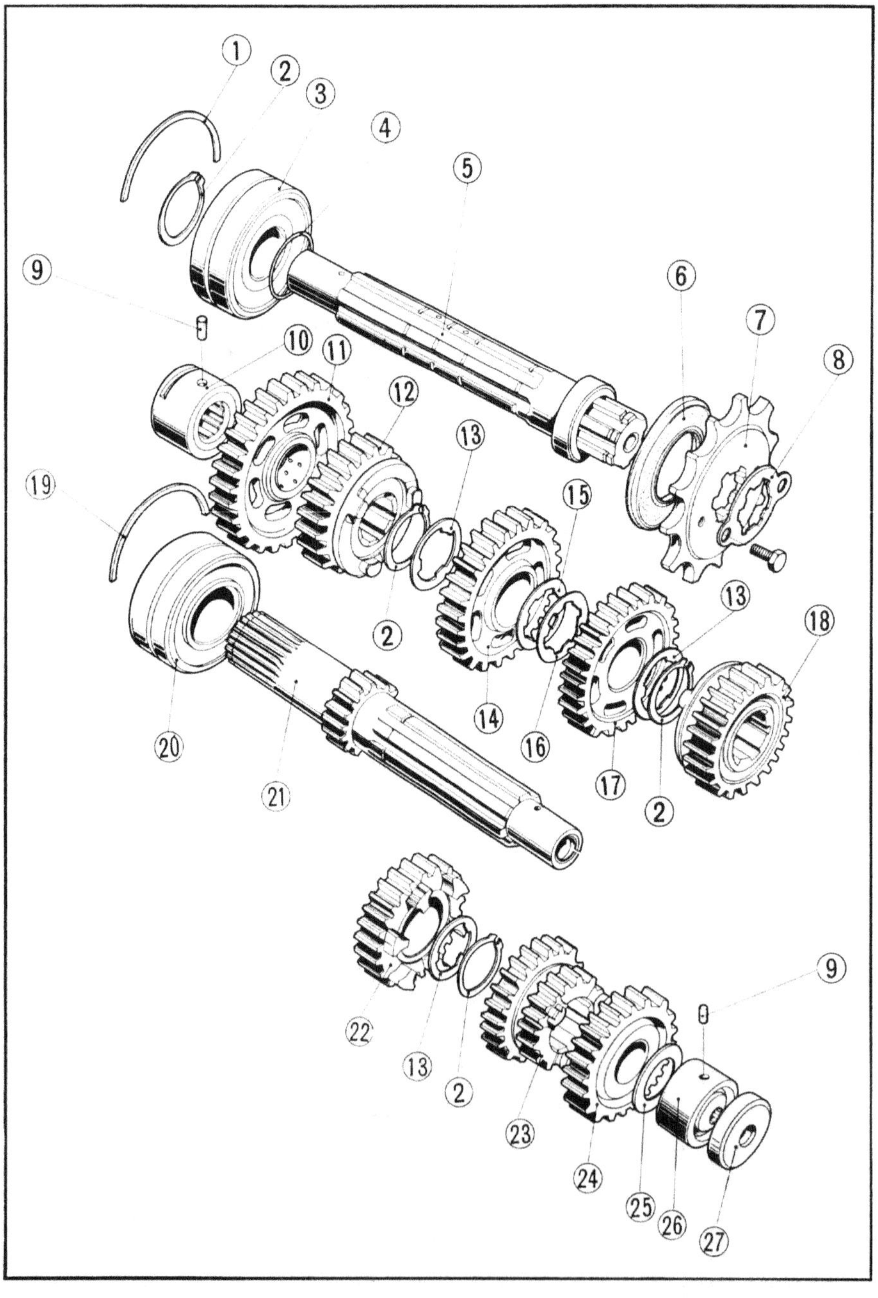

① 57 mm bearing set ring
② 25 mm snap ring
③ 5205 special ball bearing
④ 24.5 mm O-ring
⑤ Transmission counter shaft
⑥ 33×57×7 oil seal
⑦ Drive sprocket (17T)
⑧ Drive sprocket fixing plate
⑨ Gear shift fork pin
⑩ 20 mm needle bearing
⑪ Counter shaft low gear (40 T)
⑫ Counter shaft fourth gear (29 T)
⑬ 25 mm thrust washer
⑭ Counter shaft third gear (33T)
⑮ 25 mm lock washer
⑯ 25 mm thrust washer
⑰ Counter shaft second gear (36 T)
⑱ Counter shaft top gear (27 T)
⑲ 52 mm bearing set ring
⑳ 5205 HS ball bearing
㉑ Transmission main shaft (24 T)
㉒ Main shaft fourth gear (28 T)
㉓ Main shaft second, third gear (22 T, 26 T)
㉔ Main shaft top gear (30 T)
㉕ 20 mm thrust washer
㉖ 22 mm needle bearing
㉗ 8×34×8 oil seal

Fig. 168

7. Install the two bearing set rings and the dowel pins in the upper crankcase. Install the transmission.
8. Reassemble the upper and the lower crankcase in accordance with section 9. C., page 51.
9. Install the clutch in accordance with section 6. C., page 41.
10. Mount the engine in the frame in accordance with 2. B., page 23.

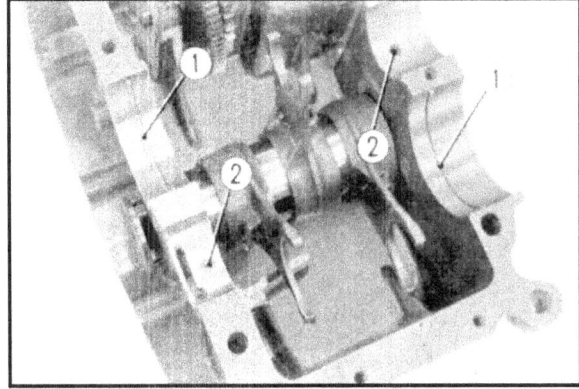

Fig. 169 ① Bearing set rings ② Dowel pins

11. CARBURETOR

A. Disassembly

1. Remove the carburetor unit from the engine in accordance with section 2 A., page 20.

Stay Plate And Carburetor

2. Unhook the throttle return spring from the link lever.
   Note:
   Be careful not to damage the hook end of the spring.
3. Loosen the hex nuts, and remove the stay plate B. Remove the cap nuts.

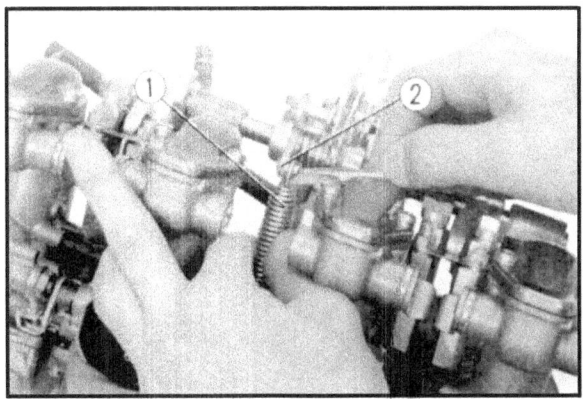

Fig. 170 ① Throttle return spring
② Link lever

Fig. 171 ① Stay nuts ③ Cap nuts
② Stay plate B

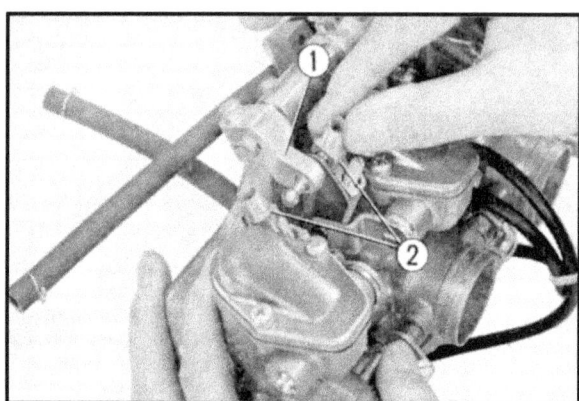

Fig. 172 ① Link arm ② Adjuster holders

4. Remove the adjuster holders from the link arm.
5. Loosen the eight 6 mm flat head screws from the stay plate and remove the carburetor unit.

Throttle Valve And Jet Needle

6. Loosen the two carburetor top mounting screws from each carburetor and remove the tops.

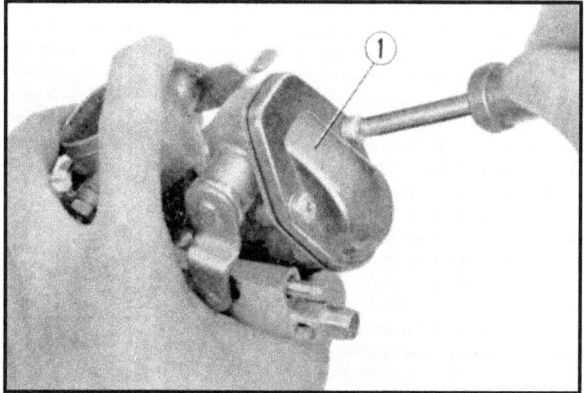

Fig. 173 ① Carburetor top

7. Place the throttle valve in the fully open position and straighten the tabs of the two tongued washers.

Fig. 174 ① Tongued washer

8. Remove the 6 mm bolt from the shaft end and remove the link arm in direction A using a screwdriver.

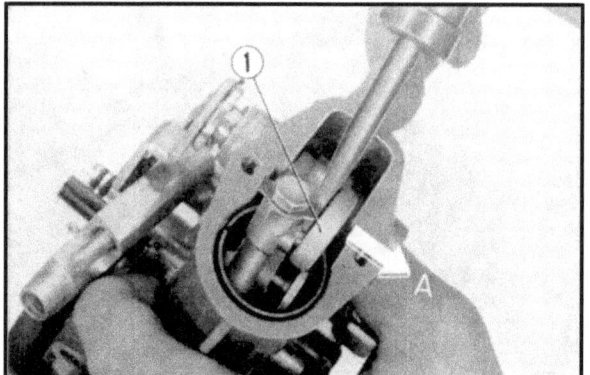

Fig. 175 ① Link arm

9. Loosen the 6 mm bolt on the throttle side about 1/2 turn, insert a screwdriver between the throttle shaft and link arm and pry loose in direction A.

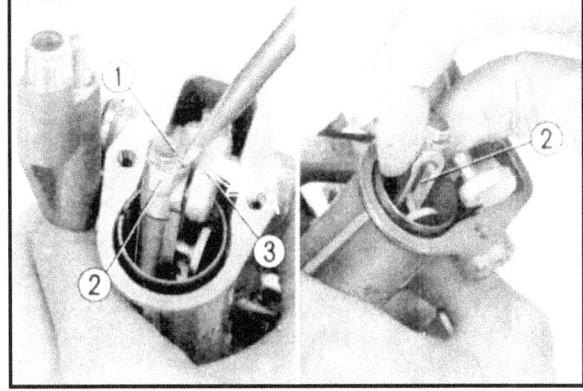

Fig. 176 ① 6 mm bolt ③ Link arm
② Throttle shaft

10. Loosen the two 3 mm screws, rotate the valve plate 90° in either direction and align the tab on the valve plate to the groove in the shaft. Remove the valve plate.
11. Remove the jet needle from the throttle valve.

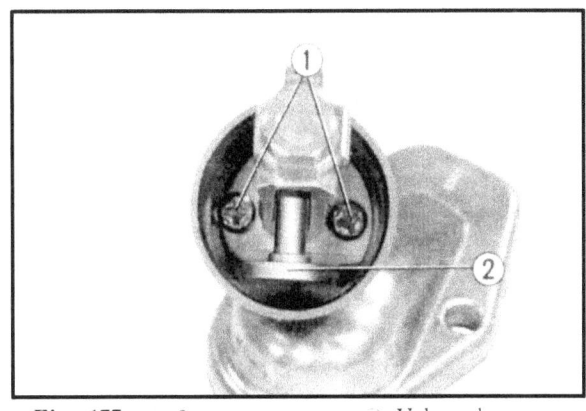

Fig. 177 ① 3 mm screws ② Valve plate

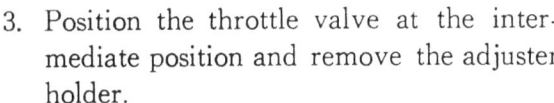

Adjuster Holder

1. Remove the carburetor from the stay plate in accordance with steps 1~5, page 57.
2. Remove the adjusting screw from the adjuster holder.

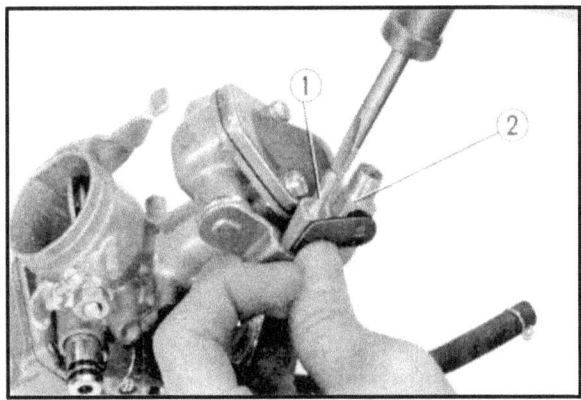

Fig. 178 ① Adjusting screw
② Adjuster holder

3. Position the throttle valve at the intermediate position and remove the adjuster holder.

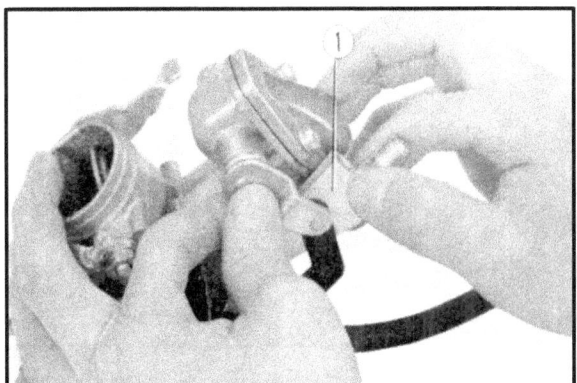

Fig. 179 ① Adjuster holder

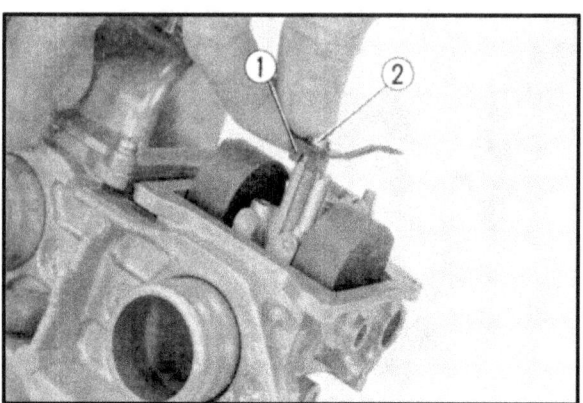

Fig. 180 ① Leaf spring   ② Main jet

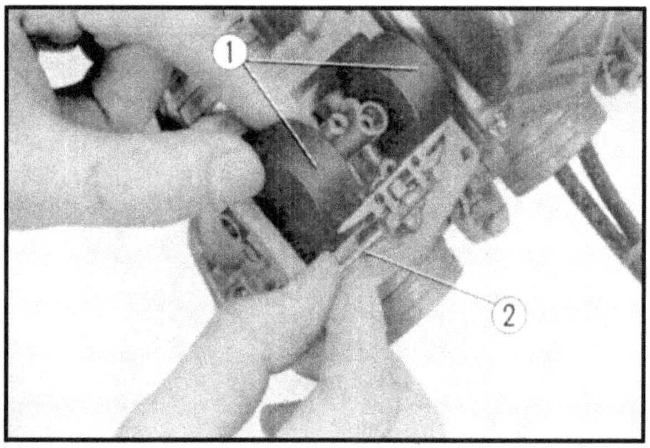

Fig. 181 ① Float   ② Float arm pin

Fig. 182 ① Valve seat   ② Clip plate

Float, Main Jet, And Slow Jet

1. Remove the float chamber body.
2. Remove the leaf spring and the main jet.

3. Pull the float arm pin out and remove the float.

4. Disengage the clip plate and remove the valve seat.

B. Inspection

1. Fuel level adjustment.
   Position the float so that the float arm barely touches the tip of the float valve. Measure the distance from the flange to the top of the float with the float level gauge. The standard value is **22 mm (0.89 in.)**

Fig. 183 ① Floats
② Float level gauge
(Tool No. 07401-0010000)

4. ENGINE

C. Reassembly

Float, Main Jet, And Slow Jet

1. Install the valve seat with the clip plate.
2. Install the float.
3. Place the leaf spring on the main jet and install them on top of the needle jet holder.
4. Install the float chamber body.

Carburetor setting data	
Description	No.
Main jet	≠ 100
Air jet	≠ 150
Slow jet	≠ 40
Throttle valve	≠ 2.5
Air screw opening	1 ± 1/8

Adjuster Holder

1. Insert the coil spring B and spring seat B into the adjuster holder. Position the throttle valve to about 1/2 open and insert approximately 1/4 of the connector shaft into the holder window. Install them while holding the spring seat down with a screwdriver.
2. Mount the carburetor on the stay plate in accordance with sections 7 and 8.

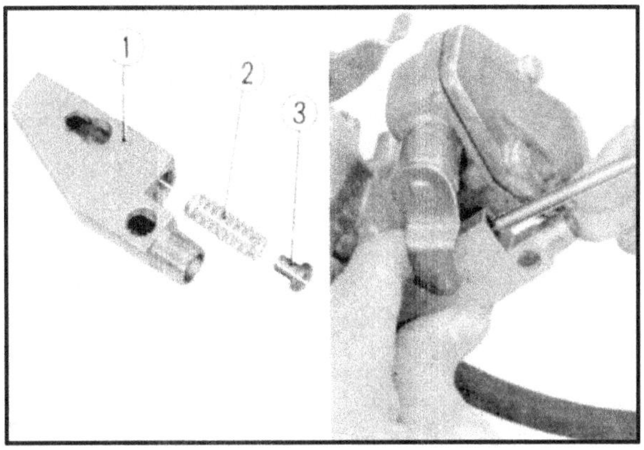

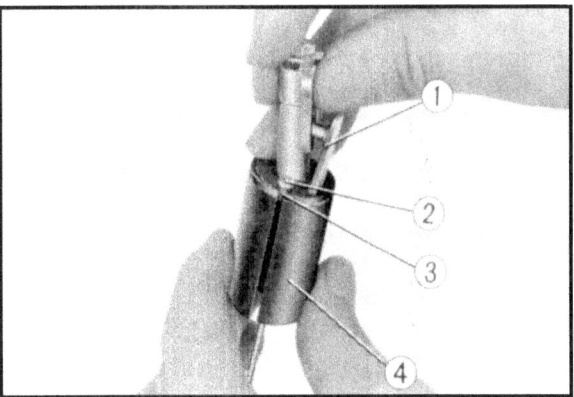

Fig. 184 ① Adjuster holder   ③ Spring seat B
② Coil spring B

Throttle Valve And Jet Needle

1. Install the jet needle on the throttle valve.
2. Place two spring washers and 3 mm screws on the valve plate. Place the valve plate tab to the slot of the throttle valve and push down to the bottom. Rotate the valve plate 90° toward the link arm and install the 3 mm screws.

3. Install the throttle valve in the carburetor body so that the throttle valve cutaway section is facing the choke valve.

Fig. 185 ① Valve plate   ③ Spring washer
② 3 mm screw   ④ Throttle valve

Fig. 186 ① Cutaway section   ② Choke valve

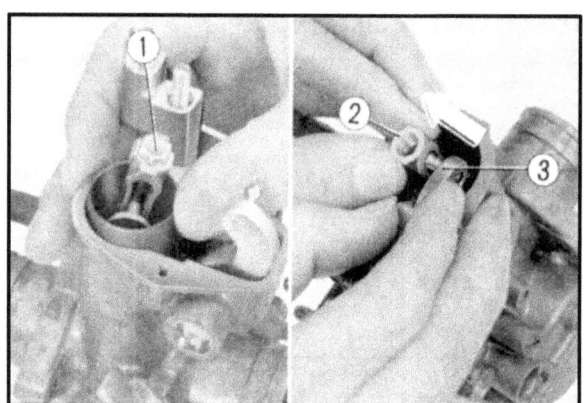

Fig. 187 ① 6 mm bolt   ③ Link arm
② Throttle shaft

4. Loosen the 6 mm bolt from the throttle shaft and push the spherical end of the link arm into the throttle shaft while pulling the throttle shaft up.

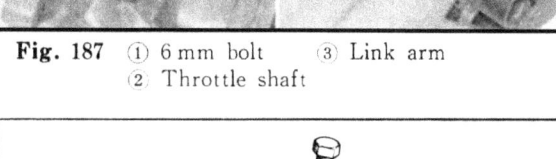

Fig. 188 ① Tongued washer

5. Install the tongued washer with the tongue positioned as shown in Fig. 188. Tighten the 6 mm bolt, and bend the washer tongue up against the bolt head.
6. Install the carburetor top with the two 5 mm screws.

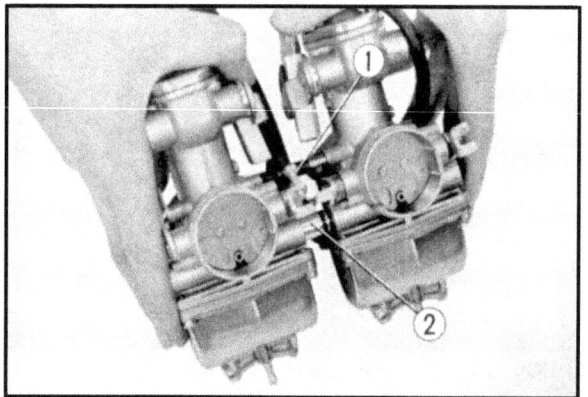

Fig. 189 ① Rubber pipe   ② T type joint

7. Combine the two carburetors with the "T" type joint and the rubber pipe.

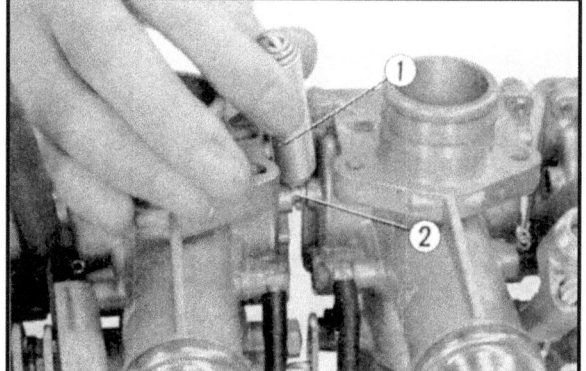

Fig. 190 ① Return spring   ② Spring set plate

8. Mount the spring set plate, and hook up the return spring.
Position the four carburetors, install the set plate, and tighten with the eight 6 mm flat head screws.

4. ENGINE 63

9. Install the dust plate A, and mount the adjuster holder to the link arm.

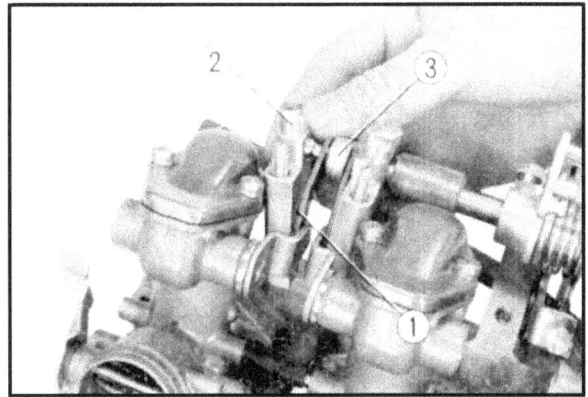

Fig. 191 ① Dust plate A   ③ Link arm
         ② Adjuster holder

10. Insert the coil spring B and tighten it with the cap nut.

Fig. 192 ① Coil spring B   ② Cap nut

11. Install the special washer D, stay plate B, and flat washer on the adjuster screw and tighten the nuts.

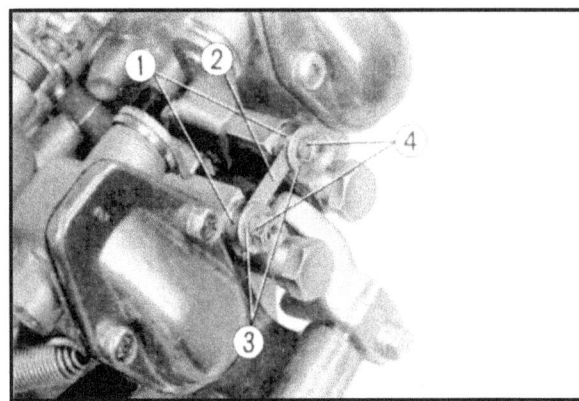

Fig. 193 ① Special washer D   ③ Washers
         ② Stay plate B   ④ Nuts

12. Connect the throttle return spring on the link lever, being careful not to damage the hook.
13. Install and route the two fuel tubes as shown in Fig. 194.
14. Mount the carburetor unit on the engine in the reverse order as described in section 2. A, page 20.

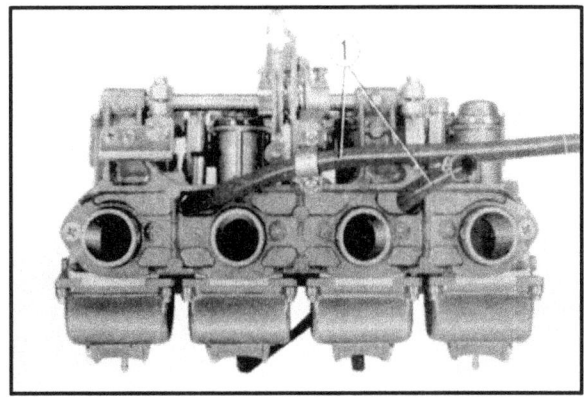

Fig. 194 ① Fuel tubes

MEMO

5. CHASSIS

1. FRONT WHEEL AND FRONT BRAKE

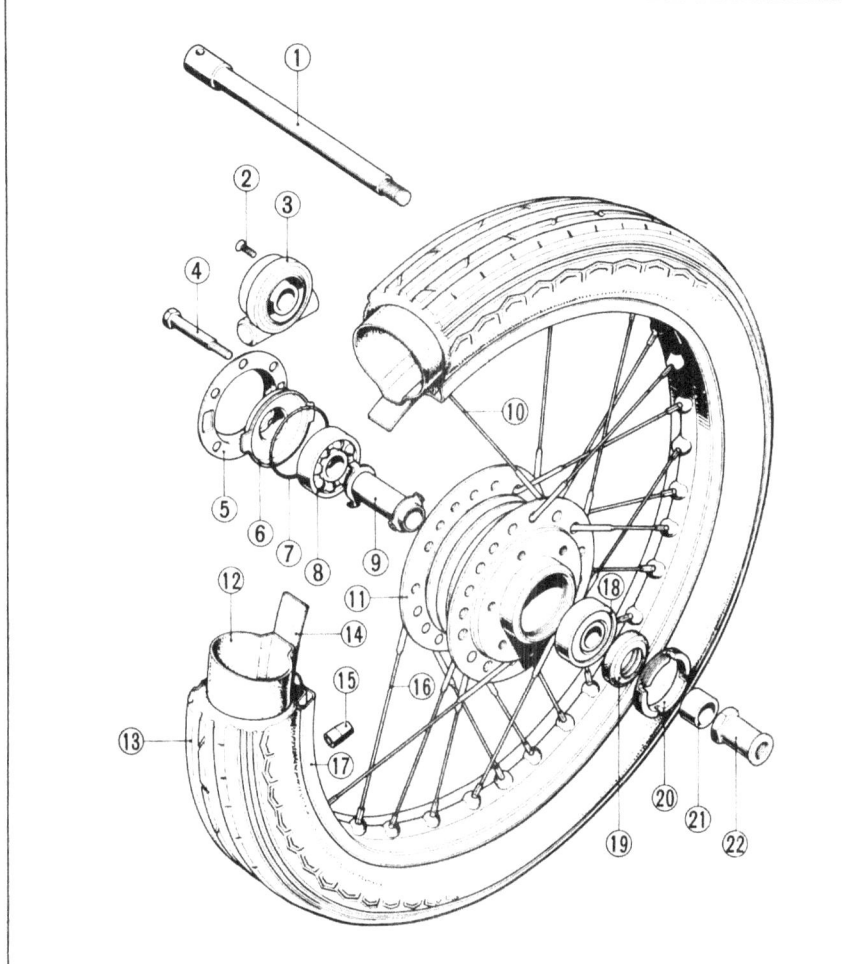

Fig. 195

1. Axle shaft
2. 5×15 mm oval screw
3. Speedometer gear box
4. 8×102 mm bolt
5. Gear box retainer cover
6. Gear box retainer
7. O-ring
8. 6302 R ball bearing
9. Front axle distance collar
10. Front spoke B
11. Front wheel hub
12. Front wheel tube
13. Front wheel tire
14. Front tire flap
15. Wheel balancer
16. Front spoke A
17. Front wheel rim
18. 6302 R ball bearing
19. 22368 dust seal
20. Front wheel bearing retainer
21. Front wheel collar
22. Front wheel axle nut

Front Wheel
A. Disassembly
1. Place a block under the engine to raise the front wheel off the ground.
2. Disconnect the speedometer cable from the speedometer gear box.
3. Loosen the axle holder mounting nuts and remove the front wheel assembly from the front fork.
4. Loosen the front wheel axle nut and remove the front axle.

Fig. 196 ① Speedometer cable

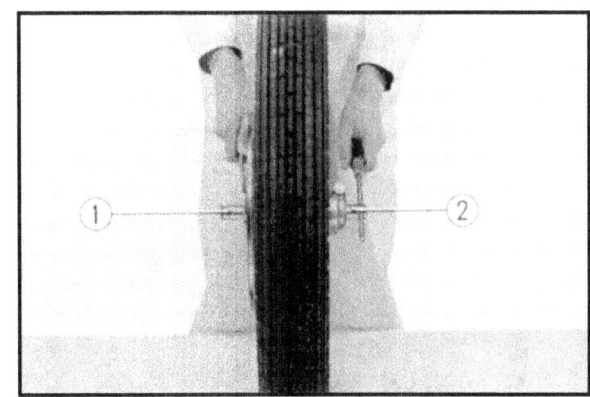

Fig. 197 ① Front axle nut ② Front axle

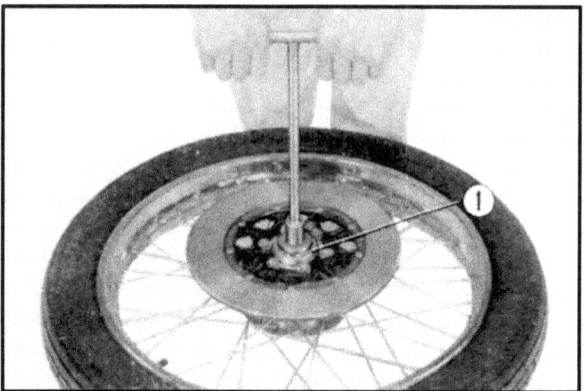

Fig. 198 ① Front wheel bearing retainer

5. Remove the bearing retainer (Tool No. 07910-3230101) from the wheel hub, and the dust seal from the bearing retainer.

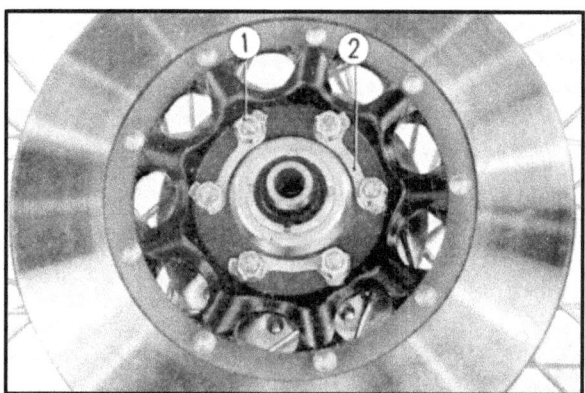

Fig. 199 ① Disc mounting nuts
② Tongued washers

6. To remove the brake disc from the wheel, straighten the tongues on the tongued washers and loosen the disc mounting nuts.
7. Remove the speedometer gear box and retainer cover from the opposite side.
8. Remove the front wheel bearing.

Fig. 200 ① Dial gauge ② Front brake disc

B. Inspection

1. Brake disc inspection.
   Place the disc on a surface plate and measure the trueness using a dial gauge as shown in Fig. 199. Replace the disc if it exceeds the serviceable limit.

Fig. 201 ① Dial gauge

2. Rim wobble and wheel runout check.
   Spin the wheel by hand and check both wobble and runout using a dial gauge as shown in Fig. 201.

5. CHASSIS

3. Wheel bearings check.
   Measure bearing wear in both axial and radial directions.
4. Check for loose or bent spokes.
   Tighten loose spokes and straighten or replace bent spokes.
5. If tire pressure is low, check for leaks around the valve stem and the valve.
6. Check the condition of the tire inside and outside for cuts, bruises, and imbedded nails.
7. Check to be sure that the tire is correctly inflated.
   Tire inflation pressure: 1.3 kg/cm^2
   (25.6 psi)
8. Check if air leaks from the tire valve.

C. Reassembly
Note:
Before installing the front wheel bearings, install the distance collar.

1. Drive the 6302R wheel ball bearing into the hub using a bearing driver.
   Use a driver attachment (Tool No. 07946-9350200) and driver handle (Tool No. 07949-6110000).
2. Install the dust seal in the wheel bearing retainer. Mount the retainer into the wheel hub and install the O-ring into the hub.
3. Install the gear box retainer cover on the gear box retainer so that the cover matches the slot.

4. Mount the brake disc on the wheel with bolts, tongued washers, and nuts. After tightening, bend the tongues up on the washers to lock the nuts.

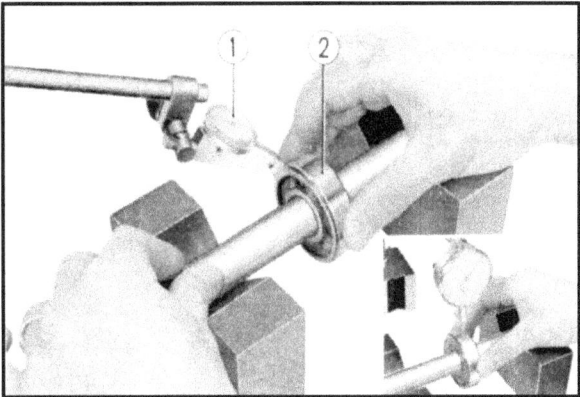
Fig. 202 1 Dial gauge 2 Ball bearing

Fig. 203 1 Bearing driver

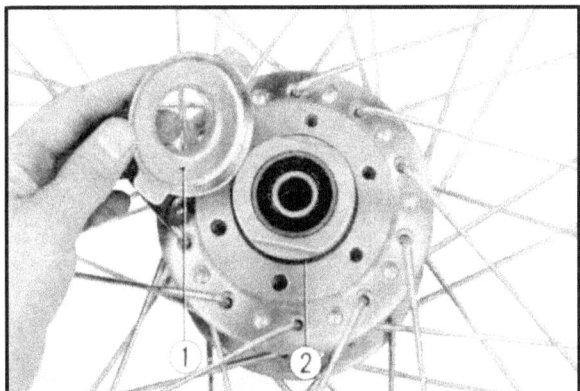
Fig. 204 ① Gear box retainer
         ② O-ring

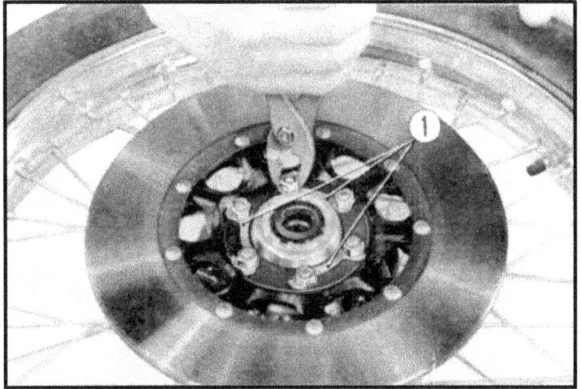
Fig. 205 ① Tongued washers

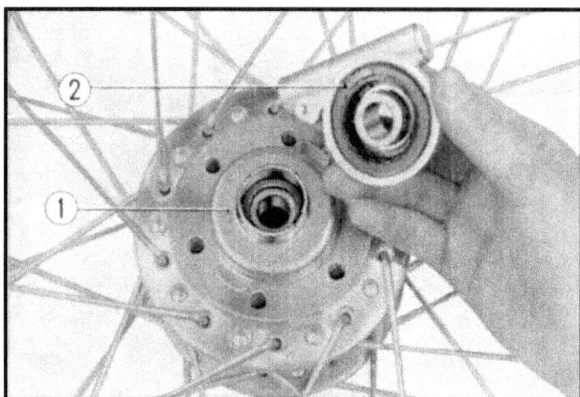

Fig. 206 ① Gear box retainer
② Speedometer gear box

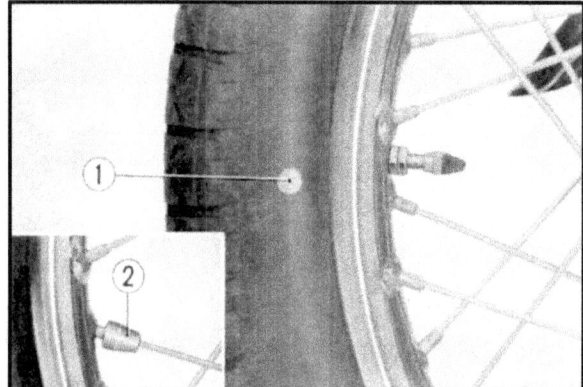

Fig. 207 ① Balance marking ② Balance weight

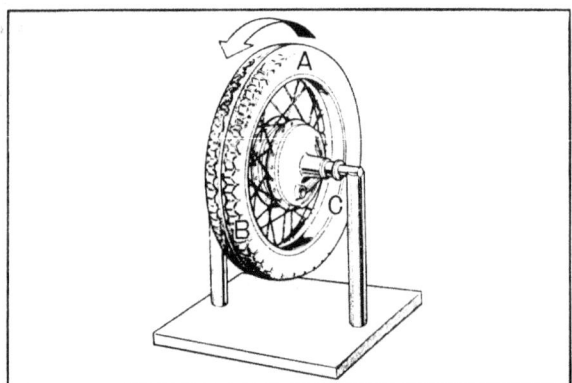

Fig. 208

5. Install the speedometer gear box on the opposite side of the brake disc, and insert the front axle into the hub through the speedometer gear box.
6. Mount the front wheel on the front fork. Install the axle holders and tighten the nuts.

Note:
Make sure that the speedometer gear box is properly mounted.
Tighten the axle holder on the left side first (brake disc side), then the right side. Tighten the front nuts on the axle holder first.

7. Connect the speedometer cable to the gear box.
8. Wheel balance check.
   a. Mark the side of the tire and rotate the wheel lightly several times. Note the position the mark comes to rest.
   b. If the wheel is not statically balanced, the mark on the tire will come to rest at the same position. (Heavier section will be at the bottom).
   c. Attach a balance weight on the spoke at the lighter section (the top).
   d. The wheel is balanced if it does not stop at any definite position after rotating several times.
      The balance weights are available in four different weight sizes (5, 10, 15 and 20 grams).
   e. The front wheel should be balanced with the brake disc installed.

Front disc brake
The disc brake system consists of the brake lever and master cylinder on the right handlebar, the caliper mounted on the left side of the front fork, and the special stainless steel brake disc mounted on the wheel hub.

(Operation)
1. When the brake lever ① is gripped, the cam ② at the base of the lever actuates a piston in the master cylinder.
2. The piston moves the primary cup ③ that blocks the passage to the reservoir and pressurizes the fluid within the master cylinder. This pressure is transmitted to the caliper chamber through the brake hose B ④, the 3 way joint ⑤, and the brake hose A ⑦. The stop light pressure switch ⑥ mounted on the 3 way joint is also actuated.
3. The hydraulic pressure within caliper chamber A applies pressure against the piston ⑨, which forces pad A ⑩ against the brake disc. Since the caliper assembly is mounted on an arm which pivots at the front fork, it is free to swivel, therefore, the reaction from pad A ⑩ is transmitted to pad B, resulting in equalized pressure being applied by the pads to both sides of the brake disc.

5. CHASSIS

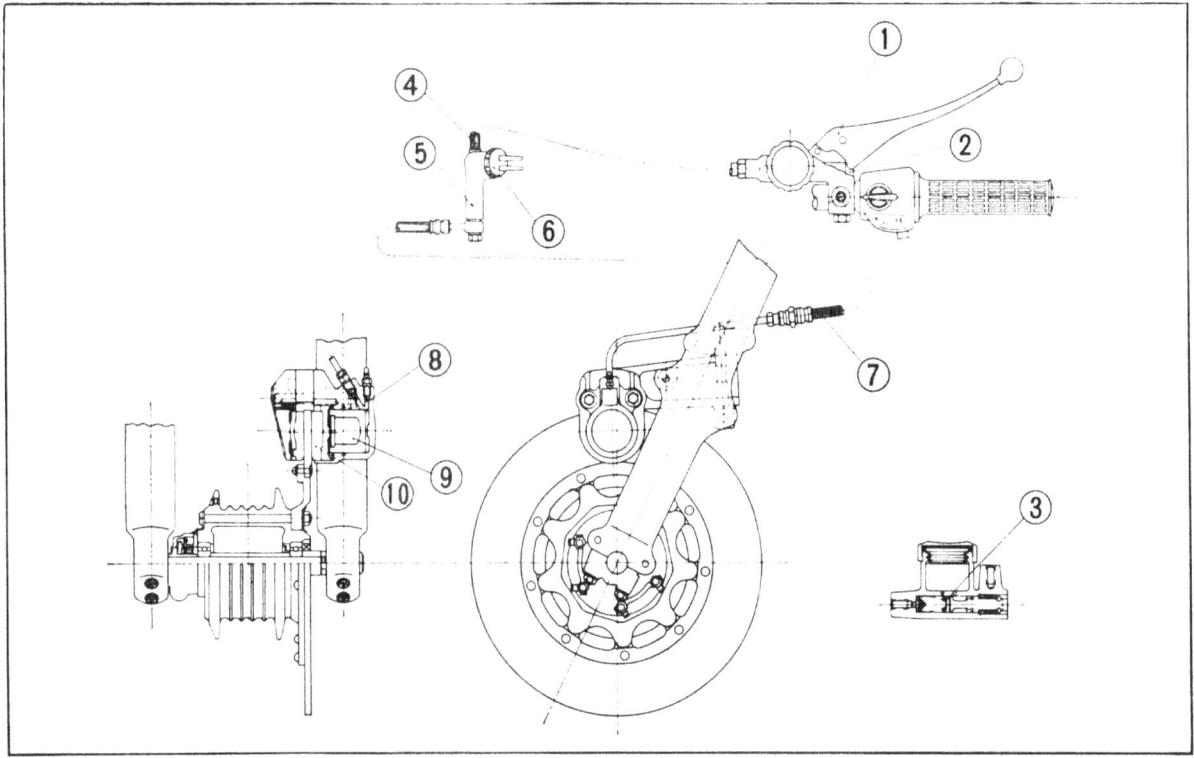

① Front brake lever
② Front brake lever cam
③ Primary cup
④ Front brake hose B
⑤ Three way joint
⑥ Stop switch
⑦ Front brake hose A
⑧ Caliper A
⑨ Piston
⑩ Pad A

Fig. 209

A. Disassembly

1. Remove the front wheel.
2. Loosen the oil joint bolt and disconnect the brake hose.

Fig. 210 ① Oil joint ② Oil joint bolt ③ Brake hose

3. Loosen the three caliper mounting bolts and a caliper adjusting bolt, and remove the caliper assembly.
4. Loosen the two caliper set bolts and separate calipers A and B.

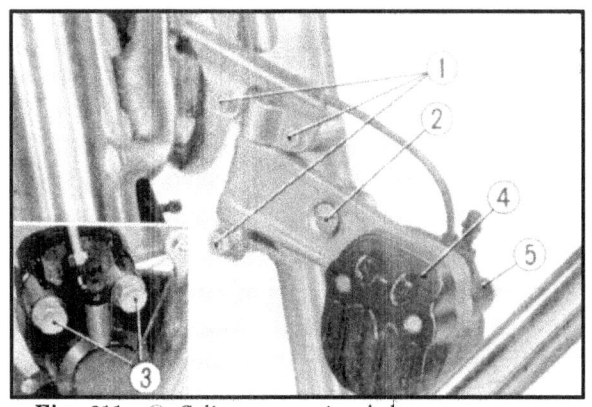

Fig. 211 ① Caliper mounting bolts
② Caliper adjusting bolt
③ Caliper set bolts
④ Caliper B
⑤ Caliper A

5. CHASSIS

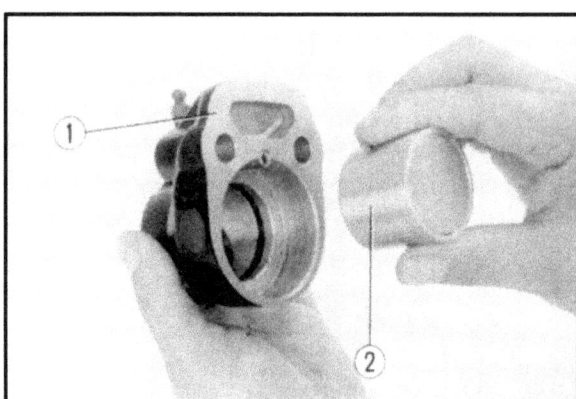

Fig. 212 ① Caliper A ② Piston

5. Remove pad A and the piston from caliper A.
   Use compressed air to remove the piston.
6. Remove pad B from caliper B.

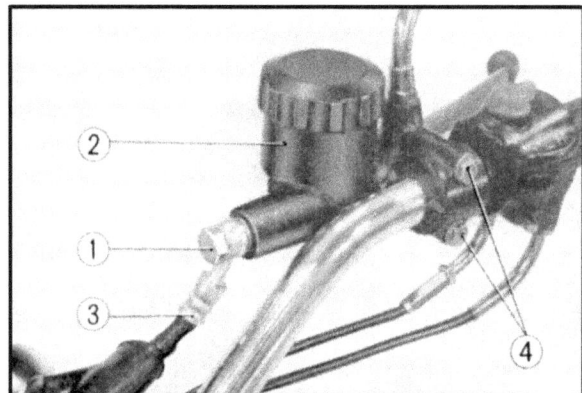

Fig. 213 ① Joint bolt
② Master cylinder unit
③ Brake hose
④ Master cylinder mounting bols

7. Loosen the master cylinder joint bolt and remove the brake hose.
8. Loosen the master cylinder mounting bolts and remove the master cylinder unit from the handlebar.
9. Disassemble the master cylinder.

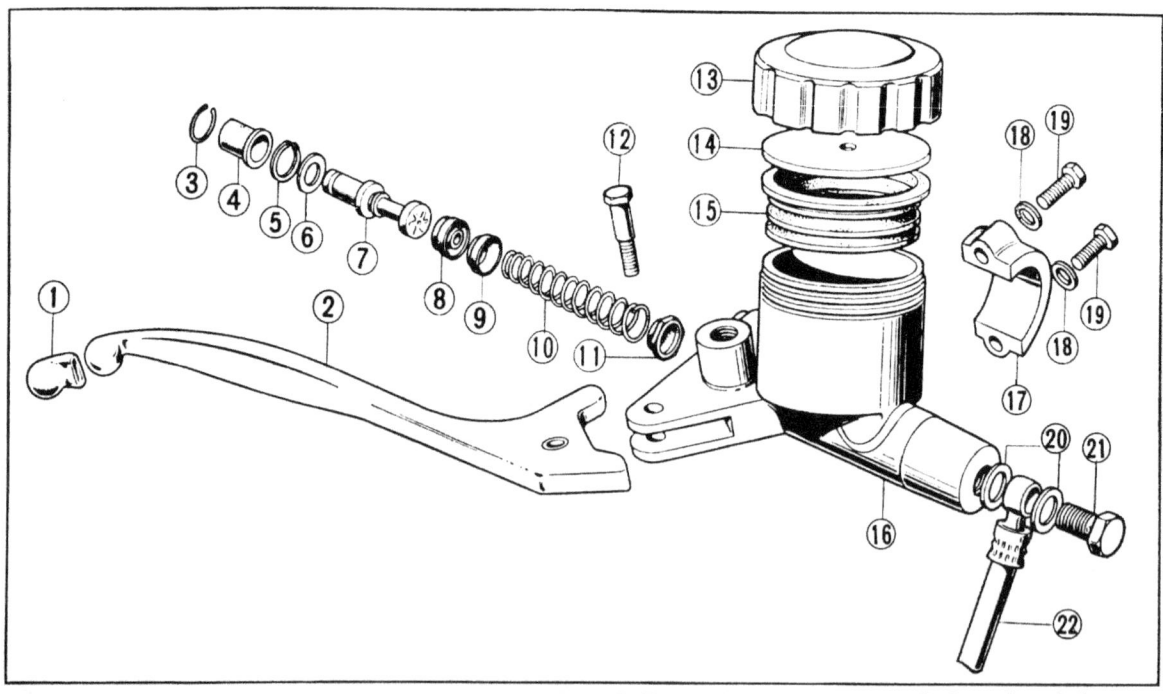

① Brake lever cap
② Brake lever
③ Stopper washer
④ Boot
⑤ 18mm internal snap ring
⑥ 10.5mm washer
⑦ Piston
⑧ Secondary cup
⑨ Primary cup
⑩ Spring
⑪ Check valve
⑫ Handle lever pivot bolt
⑬ Reservoir cap
⑭ Master cylinder plate
⑮ Diaphragm
⑯ Master cylinder body
⑰ Master cylinder holder
⑱ 6mm spring washer
⑲ 6mm hex bolt
⑳ Joint bolt washer
㉑ Joint bolt
㉒ Front brake hose

Fig. 214

5. CHASSIS   71

10. Remove the boot and the snap ring from the master cylinder body with the snap ring plier (Tool No. 07914-3230001) Remove the 10.5 mm washer, piston, secondary cup, spring, and check valve.

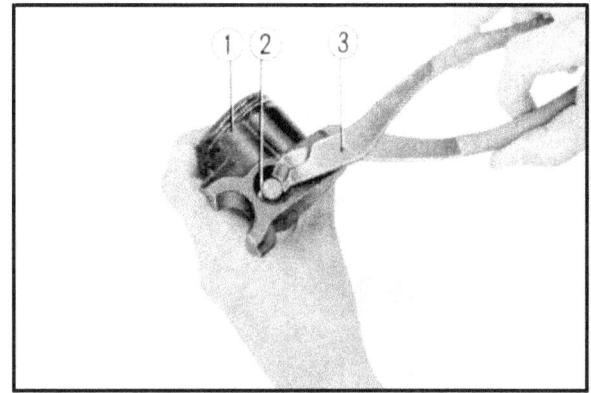

Fig. 215 1) Master cylinder body 3) Special pliers
         2) Snap ring

B. Inspection

1. Checking the disc brake pad wear. Red grooves are provided for both pads A and B as a wear limit indicator. When the pad is worn to this red groove, the pad should be replaced. After replacing the pads, adjust the clearance between the brake disc and pad to **0.15 mm (0.006 in.)** with the caliper adjusting bolt.
   Adjust by turning the caliper adjusting bolt until the pad drags slightly against the brake disc, and from this position back off 1/2 turn and tighten the lock nut.

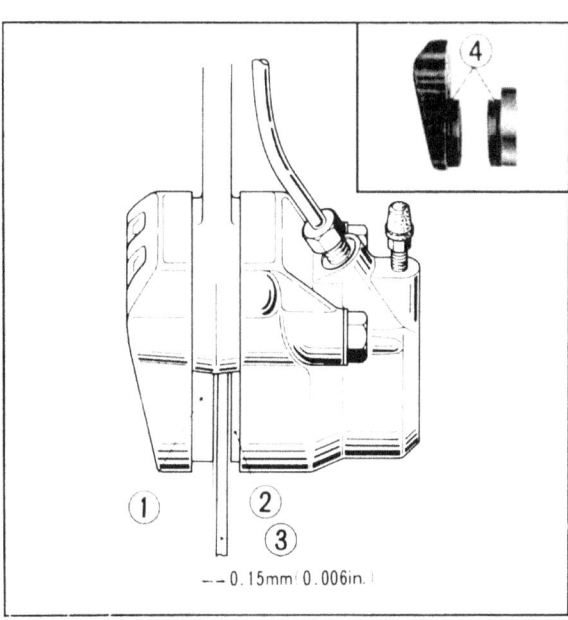

Fig. 216 1) Pad B   3) Brake disc
         2) Pad A   4) Wear limit indicator

2. Checking the caliper cylinder and piston. Measure the inside diameter of the caliper cylinder and the outside diameter of the piston using a cylinder gauge and a micrometer. If the clearance exceeds the serviceable limit. replace the part.

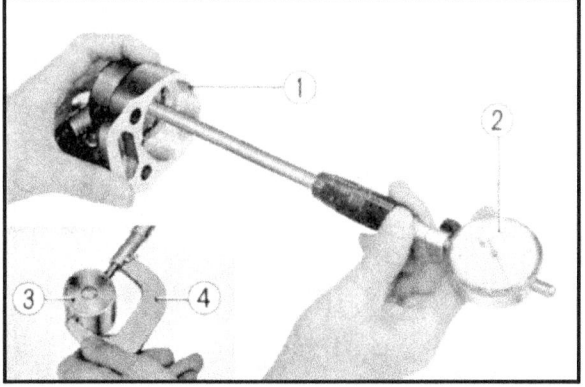

Fig. 217 1) Caliper cylinder 3) Piston
         2) Cylinder gauge   4) Micrometer

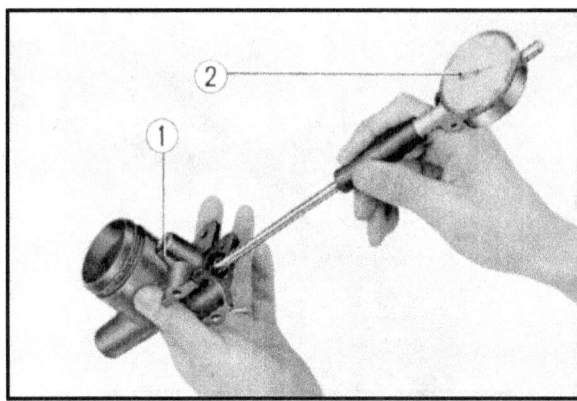

Fig. 218 ① Master cylinder ② Cylinder gauge

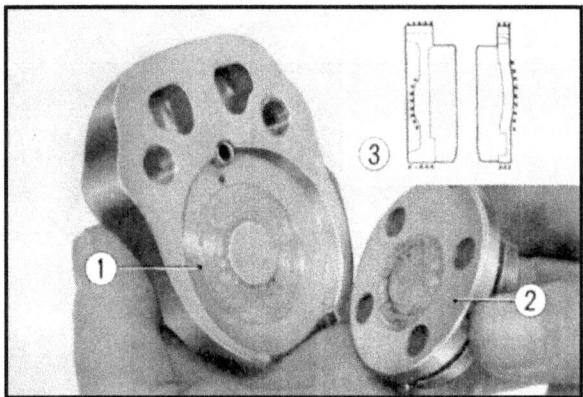

Fig. 218-1 ① Caliper B
② Pad B
③ Apply grease to part marked (X)

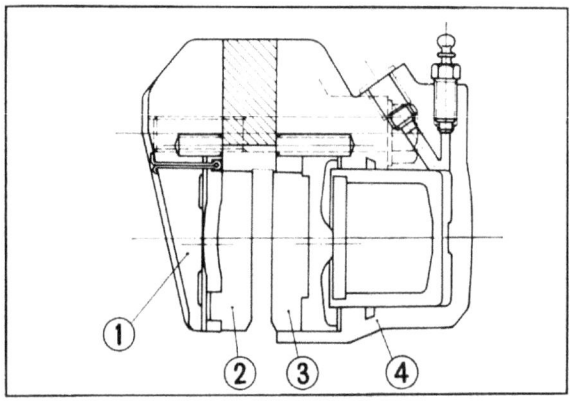

Fig. 219 ① Caliper B　③ Pad A
② Pad B　　④ Caliper A

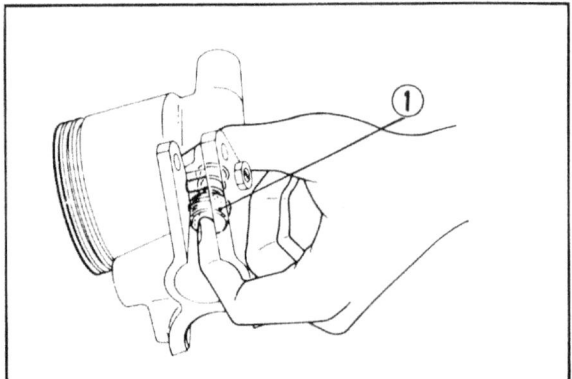

Fig. 220 ① Primary cup

3. Checking the master cylinder and piston. Measure the inside diameter of the cylinder and the outside diameter of the piston using a cylinder gauge and a micrometer. If the clearance exceeds the serviceable limit, replace the part.

C. Reassembly

1. Perform reassembly in the reverse order of disassembly.
2. Assemble pads A and B.

Note:

Apply silicone sealing grease on the pads sliding surfaces of the caliper before assemblying pads A and B. This serves as a dust preventative as well as a water repellent. Do not apply grease on the pad friction surface.

3. Apply a coat of brake fluid to the inside surface of the cylinder.
4. Install the check valve to the return spring and install them both in the cylinder.

CAUTION:

When installing the check valve and return spring in the cylinder, make sure that the valve is facing correctly and that the spring is in the correct position.

5. Apply a thin coat of brake fluid to the outside surface of the primary cup.
   Install the primary cup being careful not to allow dust to attach to it or not to damage it. Make sure that the cup is not inclined or reversed in the cylinder.

Note:

When the primary cup has been disassembled, replace it with a new one.

6. Install the 18 mm internal snap ring.
   Turn the snap ring to check for proper fit.

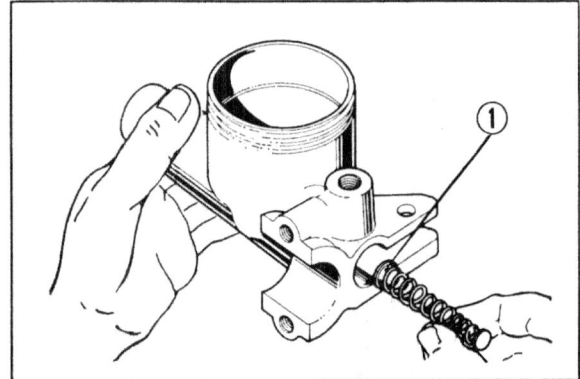

Fig. 221 ① Spring

5. CHASSIS

D. Brake adjustment

When the brake has been disassembled always perform the air bleeding operation of the hydraulic brake and then adjust the brake.

1. Brake lever free play
   Lever free play of **2~5 mm (0.08~0.2 in.)** measured at the end of the lever is normal. If the play is excessive, inspect the brake system and replace any worn or defective part.
2. Brake fluid level
   Fill the reservoir with brake fluid to the level line.

Note:
Brake fluid will damage paint finish, rubber parts, and meter components, therefore, use care in handling and immediately wipe in case of spillage.

- To air bleed the brake system refer page 15.

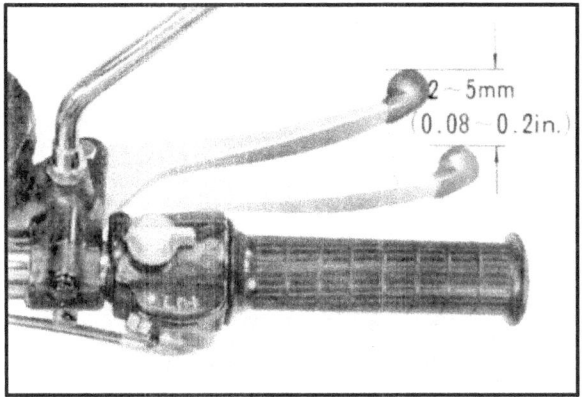

Fig. 222

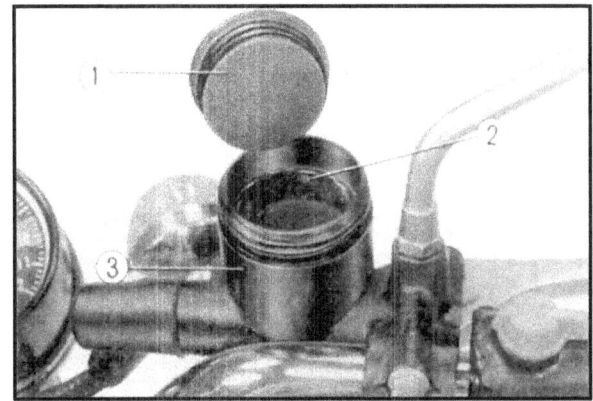

Fig. 223 ① Diaphragm   ③ Master cylinder
         ② Brakefluid

2. REAR WHEEL AND REAR BRAKE

① 6304 U ball bearing
② Distance collar
③ Wheel balancer
④ Tire
⑤ Tube
⑥ Tire flap
⑦ Wheel hub
⑧ Rim
⑨ O-ring
⑩ Wheel damper A
⑪ Wheel damper B
⑫ Final driven flange
⑬ Distance collar B
⑭ 6305 U ball bearing
⑮ Bearing retainer
⑯ 10×48 driven sprocket bolt
⑰ Side collar
⑱ Final driven sprocket
⑲ 34559 oil seal
⑳ O-ring
㉑ Sprocket side plate
㉒ Tongued washer
㉓ 10 mm nut

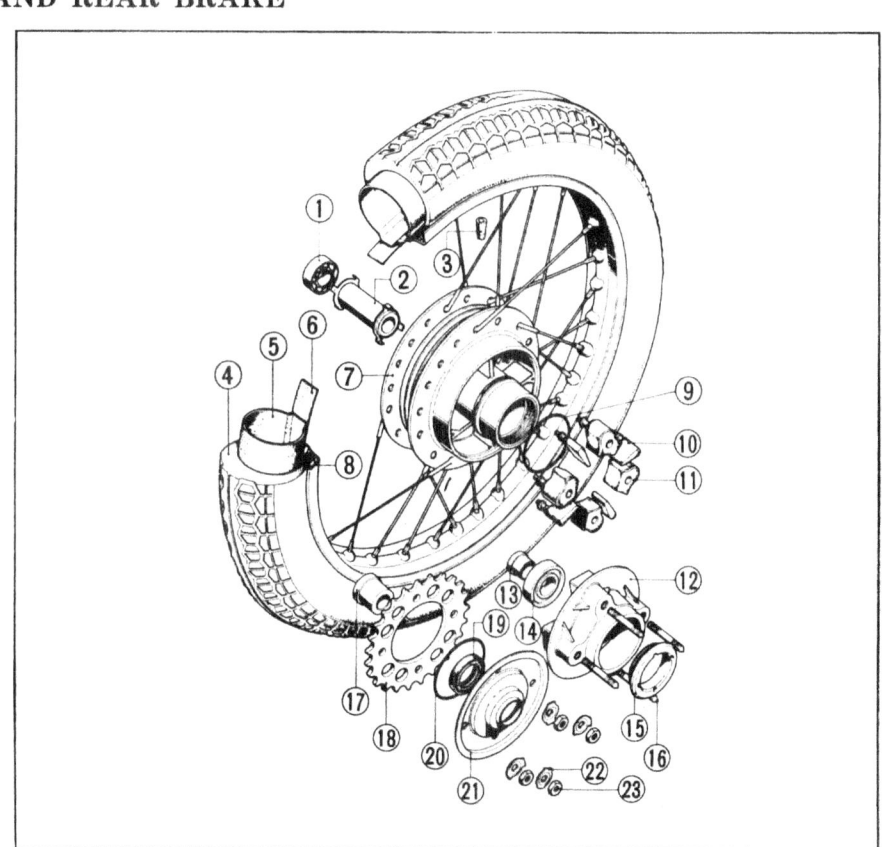

Fig. 224

74   5. CHASSIS

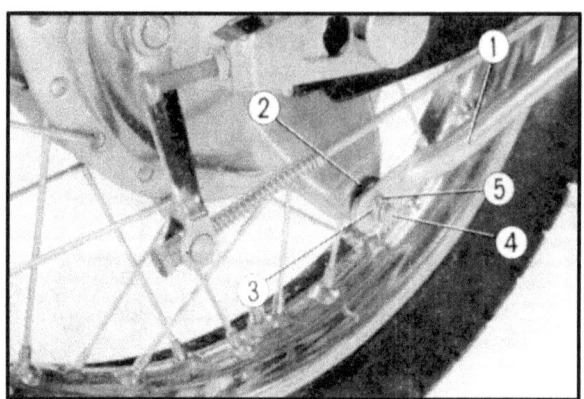

Fig. 225 ① Brake stopper arm
         ② Stopper arm cushion rubber
         ③ 8mm nut
         ④ Panel stopper bolt
         ⑤ Lock pin

A. Disassembly

1. Disconnect the rear brake rod.
2. Remove the rear brake panel stopper bolt to disconnect the brake stopper arm.

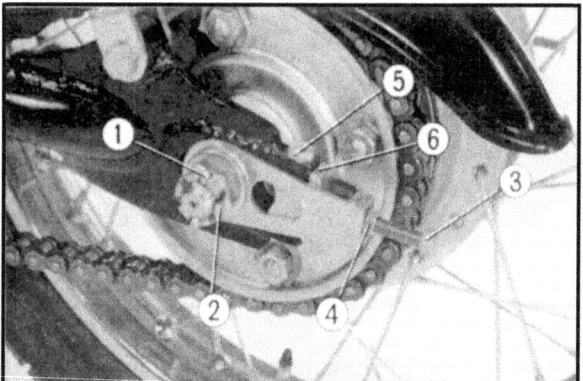

Fig. 226 ① Cotter pin
         ② Axle nut
         ③ Adjusting bolt
         ④ Lock nut
         ⑤ Lock bolt
         ⑥ Chain adjusting stopper

3. Loosen the drive chain adjusting bolt on both sides, remove the cotter pin, and loosen the axle nut.
4. Push the wheel forward, and lift the chain off the driven sprocket. Remove the lock bolts, chain adjusting stoppers and pull the wheel rearward to remove the wheel and axle from the rear wheel.
5. Straighten the tongued washers and loosen the four nuts to remove the driven sprocket.
6. Remove the rear wheel bearing retainer with the bearing retainer remover, and drive the bearing out of the hub.

Note:
The bearing retainer has a left hand thread.

Fig. 227 ① Driven sprocket
         ② Tongued washer
         ③ Lock nut

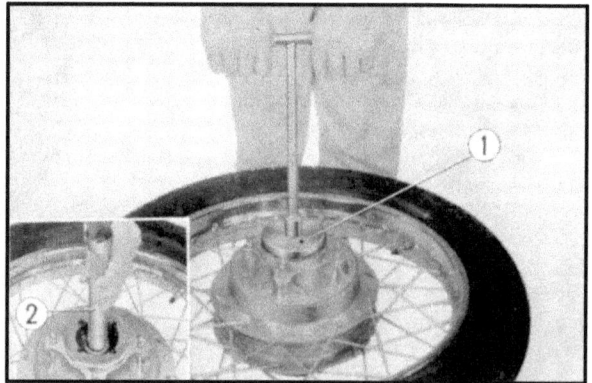

Fig. 228 ① Bearing retainer remover
         ② Bearing driver

7. Remove the two cotter pins and washer from the brake shoe anchor posts.

B. Inspection

1. Check rim runout and wobble.
2. Check rear axle shaft runout.
3. Check brake lining wear.
4. Check brake drum wear.
5. Check ball bearing wear.
6. Check for loose spokes, bending and damage. Tighten, straighten or replace as necessary.
7. Check the tire inside and outside for cuts, bruises, and imbedded nails. Repair or replace as necessary.

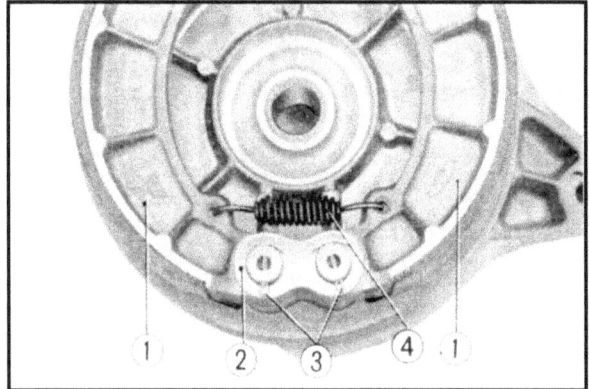

Fig. 229 1) Brake shoes   3) Cotter pins
2) Pin washer   4) Brake shoe spring

Fig. 230 1) Vernier caliper   2) Brake shoe

Fig. 231 1) Vernier caliper

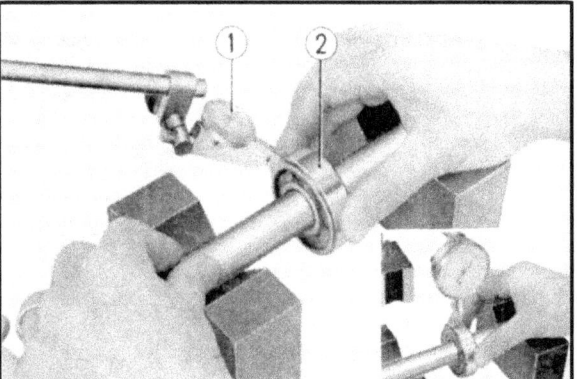

Fig. 232 1) Dial gauge   2) Ball bearing

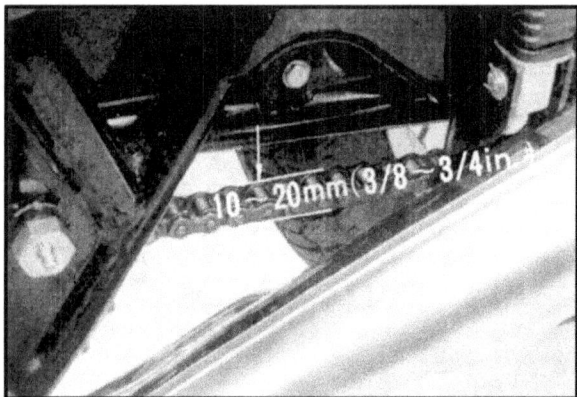

Fig. 233

Fig. 234
① Cotter pin
② Axle nut
③ Adjusting bolt
④ Lock nut
⑤ Lock bolt

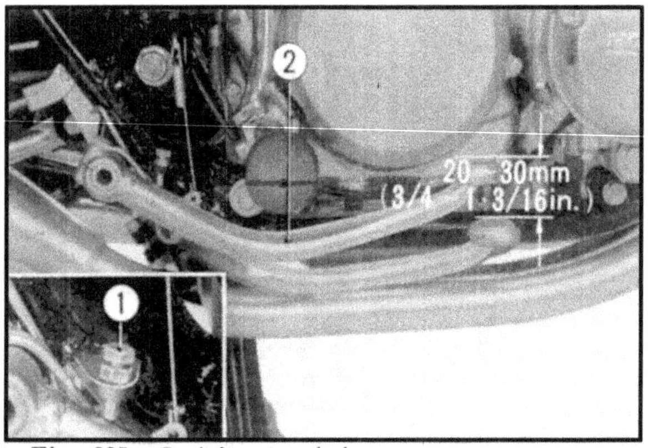

Fig. 235
① Adjusting bolt
② Brake pedal

Fig. 236 ① Adjusting nut

C. Reassembly

1. Perform reassembly in the reverse order of disassembly.
2. Install the brake shoes on the brake panel.

Note:
Do not allow oil, grease, dust or dirt to get inside the brake shoes and wheel hub.
Use thread lock cement when installing the bearing retainer.
Apply grease on the friction surfaces of the flange and wheel hub.

3. Fill the cavity in each ball bearing and inside the wheel hub with grease. Install the bearings using the bearing driver B attachment (Tool No. 07945-3230200), on the CB 550 model. Use a driver attachment (Tool No. 07946-3600000) and driver handle (Tool No. 07949-6110000), being careful not to allow the space collars to incline.
4. Mount the brake panel on the hub and the drive chain on the sprocket. Insert the wheel axle through the assembled wheel hub, and mount the wheel on the rear fork.
5. After completing the reassembly, adjust the drive chain slack.
   a. Normal chain slack is 10~20 mm (3/8~3/4 in) with a slight drag.
   b. Loosen the axle nut and adjust the drive chain with the adjusting bolt, making sure the adjuster marks on both sides are in the same position when completed.
6. Install the rear brake stopper arm, and adjust the height and play of the brake pedal.
   a. Adjust the height of the pedal with the adjusting bolt.
   b. Adjust the free play of the pedal to 20~30 mm ($^3/_4$~1 $^3/_{16}$ in) with the adjusting nut on the end of the brake rod.
7. Check to be sure that the tire is correctly inflated.

5. CHASSIS

3. STEERING

The steel tube handlebar is mounted on the front fork top bridge with the handlebar holders. The top bridge is bolted to the front fork and steering stem. The steering stem is mounted on the frame head pipe.

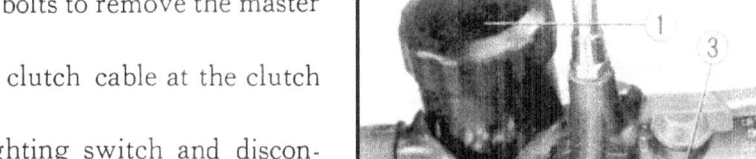

Fig. 237
① Steering handle bar
② Handle bar holder
③ Steering stem nut
④ Steering stem washer
⑤ Fork top bridge
⑥ Steering head top nut
⑦ Steering head top cone race
⑧ Steel ball
⑨ Steering top ball race
⑩ Steering head
⑪ Steering stem
⑫ Steering bottom ball race
⑬ Steel ball
⑭ Steering bottom cone race
⑮ Steering head dust seal

A. Disassembly

1. Loosen the two bolts to remove the master cylinder unit.
2. Disconnect the clutch cable at the clutch lever.
3. Remove the lighting switch and disconnect the throttle cable from the throttle grip pipe.
4. Remove the headlight unit from the headlight case and disconnect the wiring at the harness within the case.
5. Loosen the four bolts, remove the handlebar holders and disconnect the wire harness.

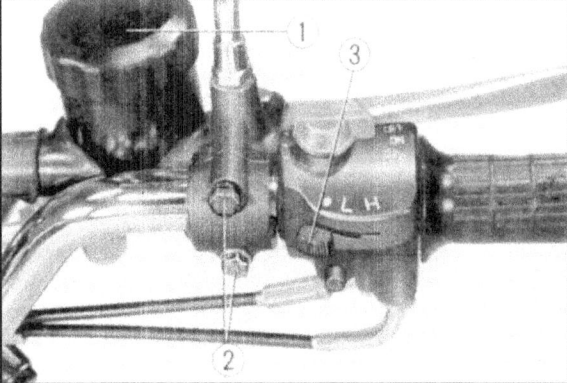

Fig. 238 ① Master cylinder unit ③ Lighting switch
② 6 mm bolts

Fig. 239 ① Upper handle bar holders ② Handle bar

5. CHASSIS

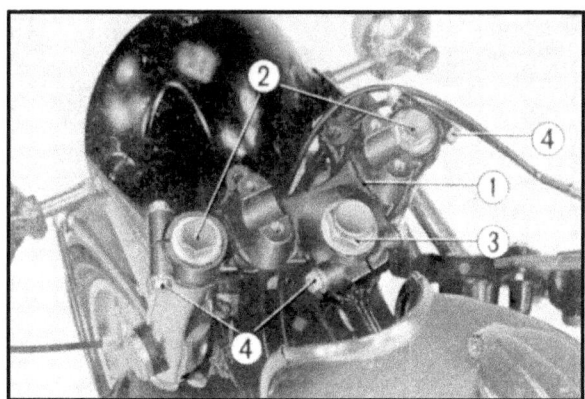

Fig. 240　① Fork top bridge　③ Stem nut
　　　　　② Fork top bolts　④ 8 mm bolts

Fig. 241　① 48 mm pin spanner
　　　　　② Steering stem head nut

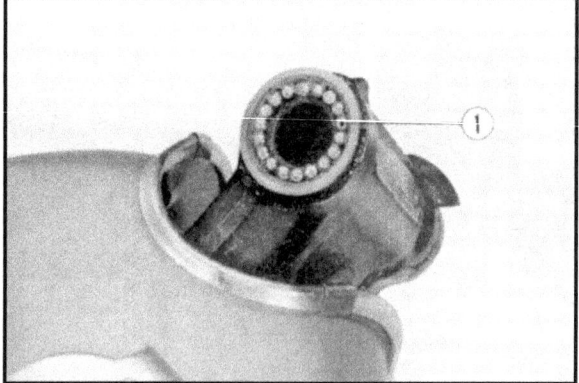

Fig. 242　① Steel balls

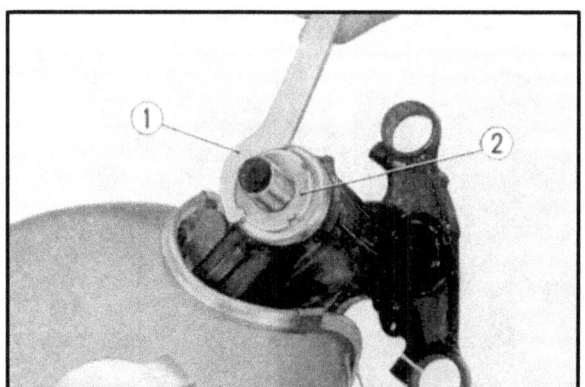

Fig. 243　① 48 mm pin spanner
　　　　　② Steering stem head nut

6. Loosen the two mounting bolts and remove the speedometer and tachometer.
7. Loosen the stem nut, and remove the 8 mm bolts and the fork top bridge.

8. Remove the front fork.
9. Loosen the steering stem head nut with the 48 mm pin spanner (Tool No. 07902-200000).
10. Remove the steering stem from the bottom.

Note:
#8 Steel balls will drop out, therefore, be careful not to lose them.

B. Inspection
1. Check the handlebar for twisting and damage.
2. Check the steering stem for twisting and cracking.
3. Check the steel balls for cracks and wear.
4. Check the cone race wear.
5. Check the stop for deformation or cracks.

C. Reassembly
1. Mix the steel balls in grease and assemble 18 into the upper race and 19 into the lower cone.
2. Install the steering stem into the head pipe being careful not to drop the steel balls.
3. Assemble the top cone race and tighten the steering stem head nut.
   Tighten the steering head top thread fully, then back it off just to the point where the handlebar can be turned with reasonable ease.

Note:
Before assembly, wash the cone and ball races, and steel balls. Mix the balls in new grease.

5. CHASSIS

4. Assemble the front fork.
5. Assemble the front fork top bridge, and mount the speedometer and tachometer.
6. Install the handlebar.

Note:
Align the punch marks on the handlebar to the parting surface of the holder. Tighten the front holder bolts first.

Fig. 244 ① Punch marks

7. Reconnect the electrical wiring.
8. Reconnect the clutch and throttle cables, and the brake hose to the master cylinder unit.

Note:
- Make sure the cables and the electrical wirings are free from binding when the handle is turned fully to both sides.
- Adjust cable freeplay.
  Clutch lever: 10.0~20.0 mm (3/8~3/4 in.)
  at the end of the lever.
  Brake lever: 2~5 mm (5/64~13/64 in.)
  at the end of the lever.

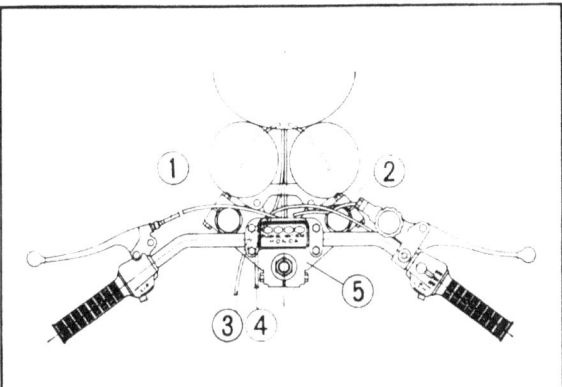

Fig. 245
① Clutch cable　　④ Wire harness
② Front brake hose　⑤ Fork top bridge
③ Throttle cable

4. FRONT SUSPENSION

The front fork unit consists of a lightweight aluminium front fork bottom case with a dual action telescoping shock absorber oil damper. Cushioning travel is 91 mm (3.15 in.) on compression and 31 mm (1.22 in.) on extension strokes.

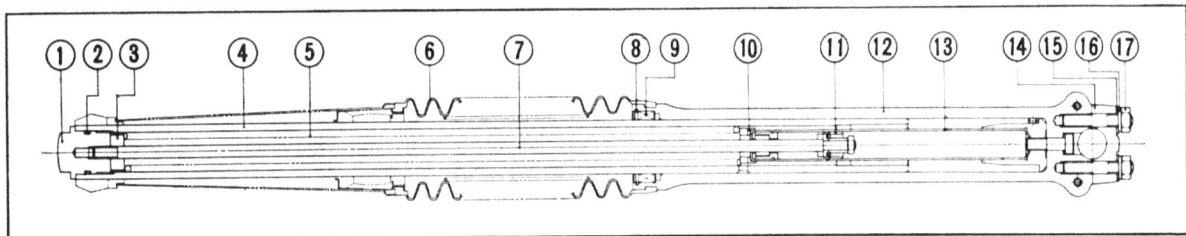

Fig. 246 Front fork unit

① Front fork bolt
② O-ring
③ Lock nut
④ Front fork pipe
⑤ Front suspension spring
⑥ Front fork boot
⑦ Damper rod
⑧ Snap ring
⑨ Oil seal
⑩ Holder
⑪ Collar
⑫ Front fork bottom case
⑬ Damper case
⑭ Axle holder
⑮ Plain washer
⑯ Spring washer
⑰ Nut

80 5. CHASSIS

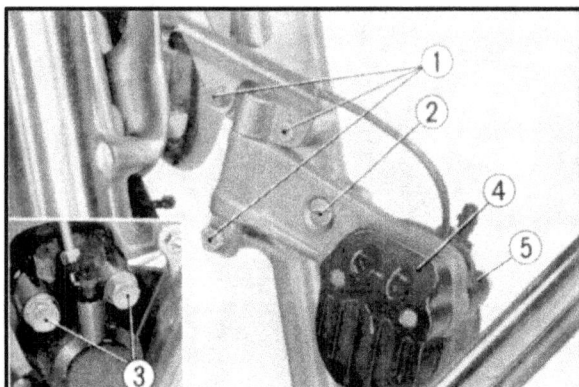

Fig. 247
① Caliper mounting bolts
② Adjusting screw
③ Caliper set bolts
④ Caliper B
⑤ Caliper A

A. Disassembly

1. Loosen the fork bolt, remove the drain plug and drain the damper oil.
2. Remove the front wheel.
3. Loosen the three caliper mounting bolts and an adjusting screw, and remove the caliper from the left front fork.

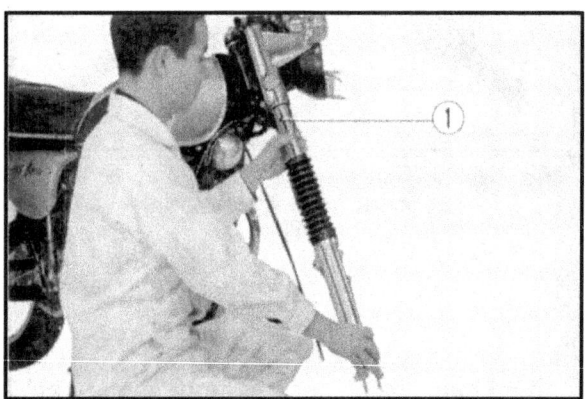

Fig. 248 ① Front fork

4. Loosen the 8×56 mm and the 10×35 mm bolts, and pull the forks off the bottom.

5. Loosen the front fork bolt, from the piston rod lock nut, and remove the front fork spring and cushion spring seat. Separate the front fork pipe and bottom case.

6. Loosen the 8 mm bottom case bolt using a hollow set wrench (Tool No. 07917-3230000) and remove the damper unit from the bottom case. (Fig. 252)

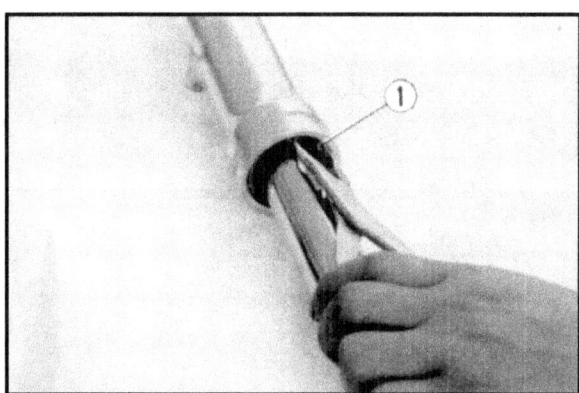

Fig. 249 ① Snap ring

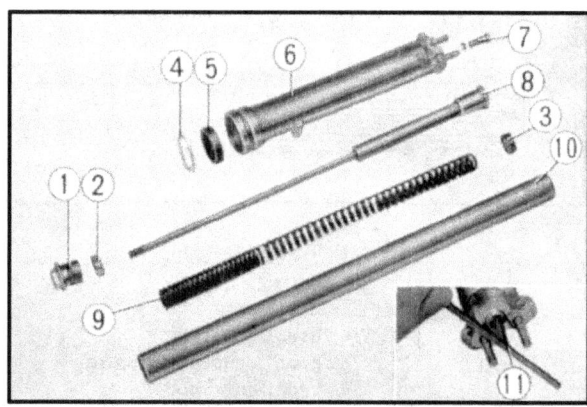

Fig. 250
① Front fork bolt
② Lock nut
③ Cushion spring seat
④ Snap ring
⑤ Oil seal
⑥ Bottom case
⑦ 8 mm bolt
⑧ Damper unit
⑨ Fork spring
⑩ Fork pipe
⑪ Special tool

B. Inspection

1. Check the front suspension spring.
2. Check the fork pipe and bottom case for damage or looseness.
3. Check the oil seal for scratches and damage.
4. Check for excessive clearance between the shock absorber piston and the cylinder.

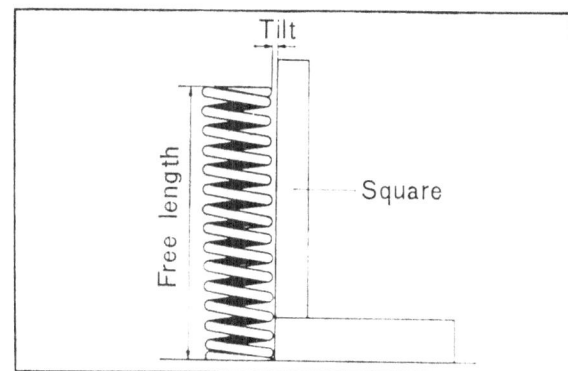

Fig. 251 Measuring the free length

C. Reassembly

1. Reassemble in the reverse order of disassembly. Be careful not to allow dust, or other foreign matters to adhere to the component parts.
2. Install the fork pipe into the bottom case. Apply a coat of thread lock cement to the socket bolt and tighten it using a socket wrench.
3. Apply a coat of Honda ATF (Automatic Transmission Fluid) to both sides of the oil seal and install it using a fork seal driver (Tool No. 07947-3290000).

Note:
- Do not forget to install the snap ring.
- Replace the removed seal with a new one.

4. Apply a coat of thread lock cement to the threaded part of the damper. Making sure that the 8 mm lock nut is completely screwed on the threaded part of the damper, tighten the fork bolt.
5. Remove the front fork bolt and pour a specified amount of Honda ATF into the front fork pipe.
   Capacity: 155~165 cc (5.3~5.6 oz.)
              (at disassembly)
6. Install and tighten the front fork bolt.
7. Route the front forks through the holes in the fork top bridge and tighten them with the 8 mm setting bolts and 10 mm setting bolts.

Note:
Remove any oil from around the front forks.

8. After reassembling, check the front forks for smooth movement. Also check for oil leaks from the oil seals.

Fig. 252 ① Fork pipe

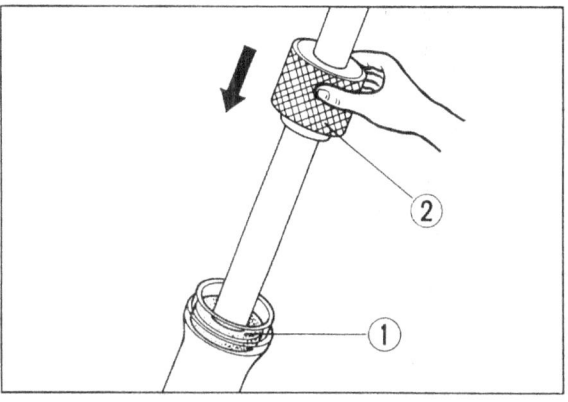

Fig. 252-1 ① Oil seal   ② Fork seal driver

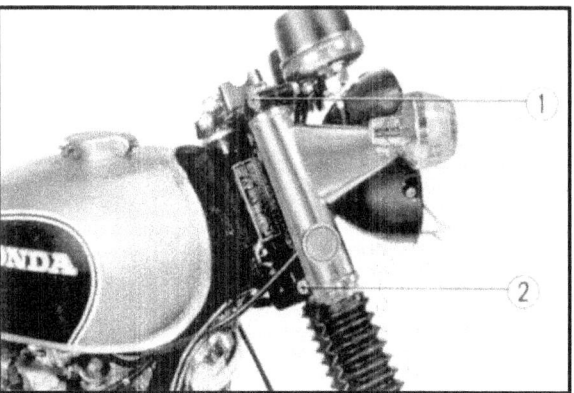

Fig. 253 ① 8 mm setting bolt
          ② 10 mm setting bolt

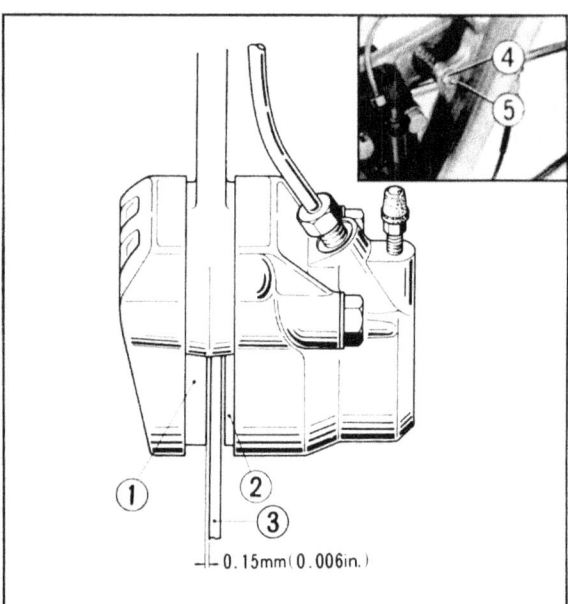

Fig. 254
① Pad B ④ Nut
② Pad A ⑤ Caliper adjusting screw
③ Brake disc

9. Adjust the front brake caliper.
   Adjust the clearance between brake disc and pad B to **0.15 mm (0.006 in.)** with the caliper adjusting screw.

5. REAR SUSPENSION

The rear suspension is equipped with dual action telescoping shock absorbers
The rear fork is a swing arm type of tubular construction that provides greater rigidity.

A. Disassembly

1. Remove the mufflers.
2. Remove the rear wheel.
3. Remove the rear suspension mounting nut and bolt, and then remove the suspension from the frame and rear fork.
4. Compress the rear suspension spring using a special suspension compressor tool (Tool No. 07959-3290000) and disassemble.

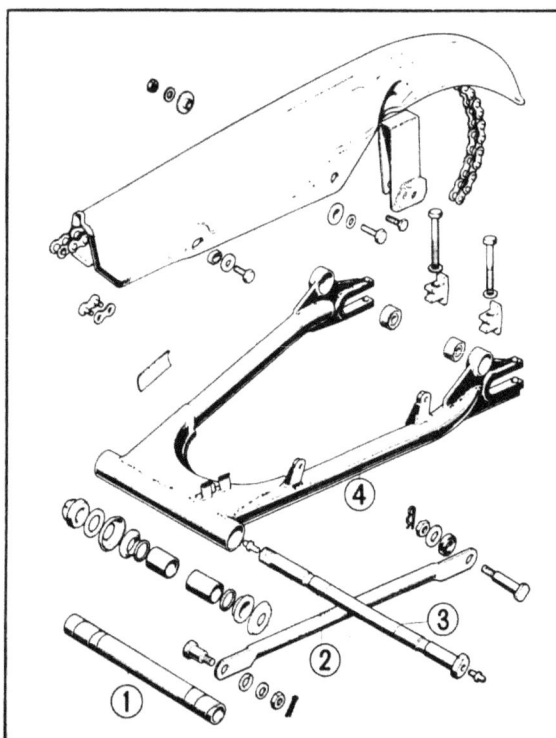

Fig. 255
① Rear fork pivot collar
② Torque link arm
③ Rear fork pivot shaft
④ Rear fork

Fig. 256 ① Rear suspension ② Nut ③ Bolt

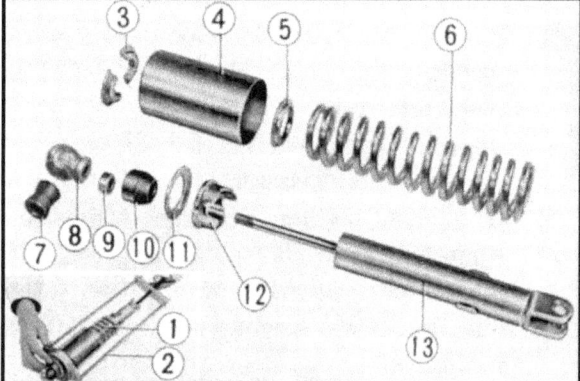

Fig. 257
① Rear suspension assembly
② Suspension compressor tool
③ Spring seat stopper
④ Rear suspension upper cover
⑤ Spring seat
⑥ Rear suspension spring
⑦ Joint rubber   ⑪ Spring seat
⑧ Joint   ⑫ Spring adjuster
⑨ Nut   ⑬ Rear damper
⑩ Rubber

5. CHASSIS

5. Remove the rear fork pivot nut and shaft, and separate the fork from the frame.

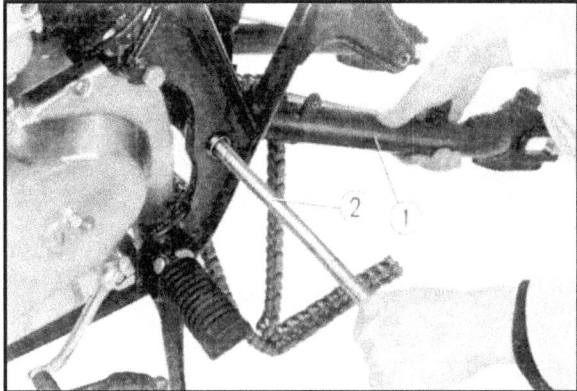

Fig. 258 1 Rear fork   2 Rear fork pivot shaft

B. Inspection

1. Check the rear suspension spring.
2. Check damper for oil leaks.
3. Inspect the damper upper case and rod for dents and bending. Make sure the oil damper operates smoothly in both directions.
4. Inspect the damper case and stopper for damage and dents.
5. Check the clearance between the rear fork pivot bushing and shaft.
6. Check the pivot shaft for bending.
7. Check the rear fork swing arm for bending, twisting, and cracking.

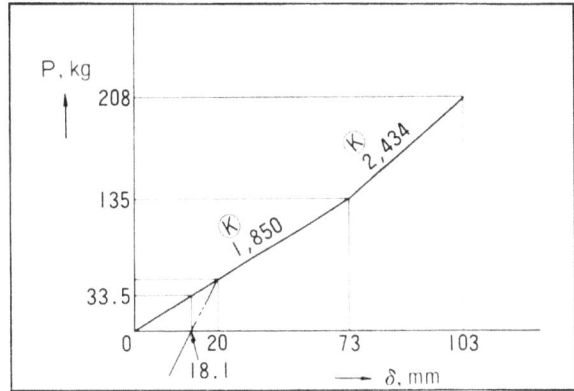

Fig. 259 Rear shock absorber spring characteristic

C. Reassembly

1. Mount the rear brake arm stopper to the rear fork.
2. Apply grease on the fork pivot bushing and install the rear fork on the frame with the pivot shaft.
3. Mount the rear suspension between the frame and fork on both sides and tighten the cap nuts and bolts.
4. Mount the rear wheel.

Note:
When the reassembly is completed, adjust the rear brake and the drive chain tension.

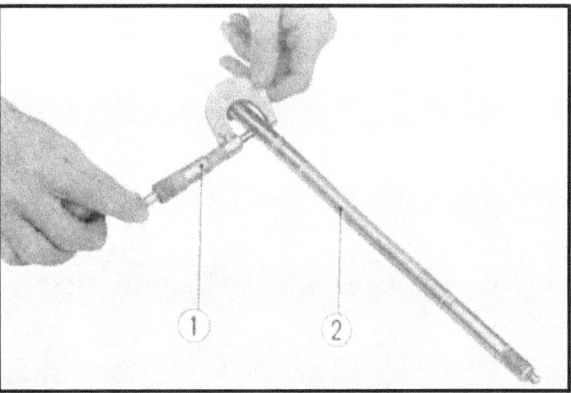

Fig. 260 1 Micrometer   2 Rear fork pivot shaft

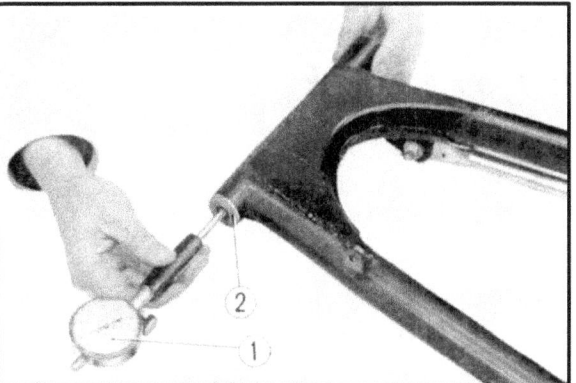

Fig. 261 1 Inside dial gauge
         2 Rear fork bushing

6. FRAME BODY

A. Construction

The double cradle frame is constructed of steel tubes and plates. The head pipe section is of drawn tubing construction which provides high rigidity and strength for good handling at high riding speed.

Fig. 262 ① Fuel tank

B. Disassembly

1. Position the fuel valve lever to 'STOP', disconnect the fuel tube from the fuel valve, and dismount the fuel tank from the frame.
2. Remove the mufflers and dismount the engine.
3. Remove the front wheel and the front fork.
4. Remove the handlebar and the steering stem from the frame.
5. Remove the rear wheel, rear fork, and rear fender.
6. Remove the seat, the tool tray, and the air cleaner element.

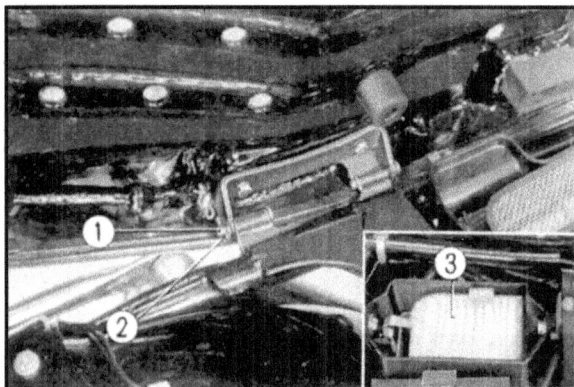

Fig. 263 ① Seat mounting bolt
② Cotter pin
③ Air cleaner

Fig. 264 ① 6 mm bolt ② 6 mm bolt

7. Detach the electrical equipment.
8. To remove the main stand, loosen the two mounting bolts, remove the cotter pin, and extract the main stand pivot pipe.

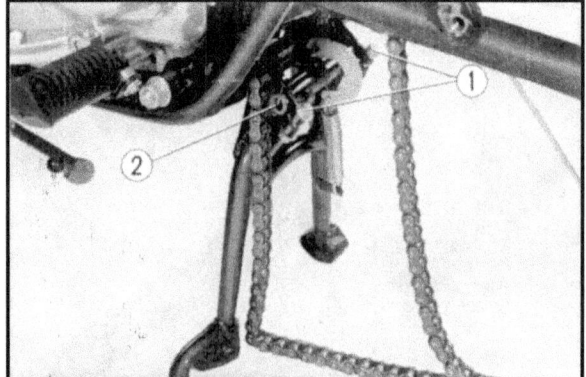

Fig. 265 ① Mounting bolt
② Cotter pin

9. Remove the top and bottom ball races from the steering head pipe.

Note:
Use a **Ball race remover (Tool No. 07953-3330000) to prevent damage when driving out the ball races.**

C. Inspection

1. Check the frame main unit for twisting, deformation, and cracking around the welded areas, and the pipes for bending and cracks.
2. Inspect the top and bottom races for scoring and wear.
3. Check the head pipe for misalignment
4. Check the seat cover for tears.
5. Check the fuel tank for leaks, the fuel tubes for aging or damage, and the fuel valve gasket and strainer cup O-ring for damage.
   Flush the tank interior with clean gasoline.
6. Remove dust from the air cleaner element by blowing compressed air from inside. Check the element for damage.
7. Replace the exhaust pipe gasket if it is damaged.

D. Reassembly

1. Install the main stand on the frame.
2. Install the rear fender and the electrical equipment on the frame.
3. Install the rear fork, rear cushion and the rear wheel.
4. Install the steering stem, front fork and front wheel.
5. Mount the air cleaner case, the battery, the seat, and the fuel tank.

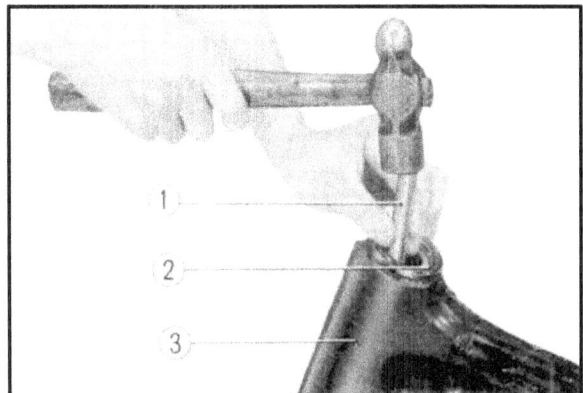

Fig. 265
1) Ball race remover
2) Ball race
3) Head pipe

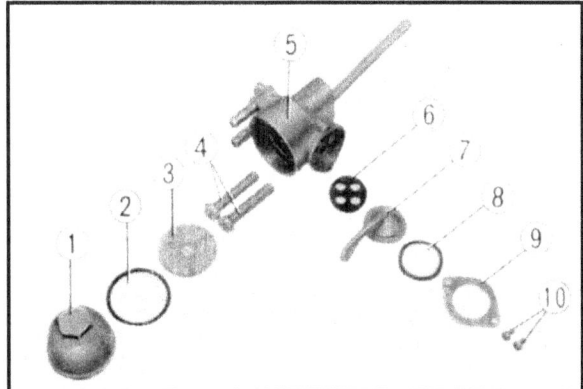

Fig. 267
1) Fuel strainer cup
2) O-ring
3) Fuel strainer screen
4) 6 mm cross screws
5) Fuel valve body
6) Fuel valve gasket
7) Fuel valve lever
8) Valve lever spring
9) Setting plate
10) 6 mm screw

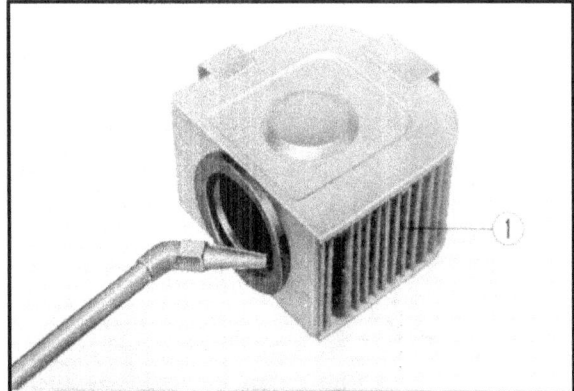

Fig. 268 1) Air cleaner element

MEMO

6. ELECTRICAL

1. GENERAL DESCRIPTION

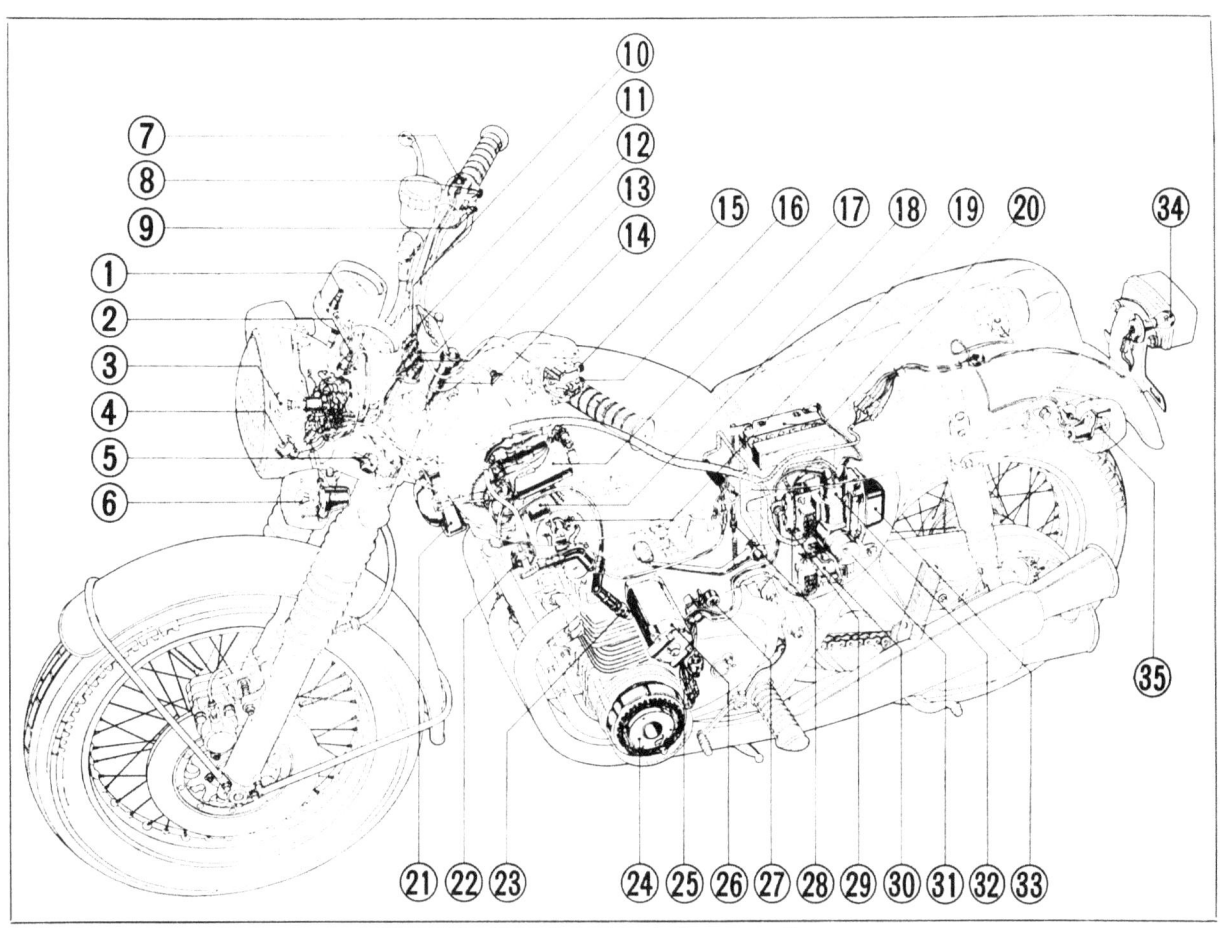

Fig. 269 Complete electrical system diagram

① Tachometer pilot lamp
② Speedometer pilot lamp
③ Head light
④ Position lamp (except USA type)
⑤ Front brake stop switch
⑥ Front winker lamp
⑦ Emergency switch
⑧ Head light switch
⑨ Starter switch
⑩ High beam pilot lamp
⑪ Neutral lamp
⑫ Oil warning lamp
⑬ Winker pilot lamp
⑭ Speed warning lamp (except USA type)
⑮ Winker switch
⑯ Horn button
⑰ Ignition coil
⑱ Speed warning system (except USA type)
⑲ Contact breaker assembly
⑳ Battery
㉑ Horn
㉒ Main switch
㉓ Spark plug
㉔ AC generator
㉕ Oil pressure switch
㉖ Starting motor
㉗ Neutral switch
㉘ Rear brake stop switch
㉙ Fuse holder
㉚ Silicon rectifier
㉛ Winker relay
㉜ Magnetic switch
㉝ Voltage regulator
㉞ Tail/stop lamp
㉟ Rear winker lamp

2. IGNITION SYSTEM

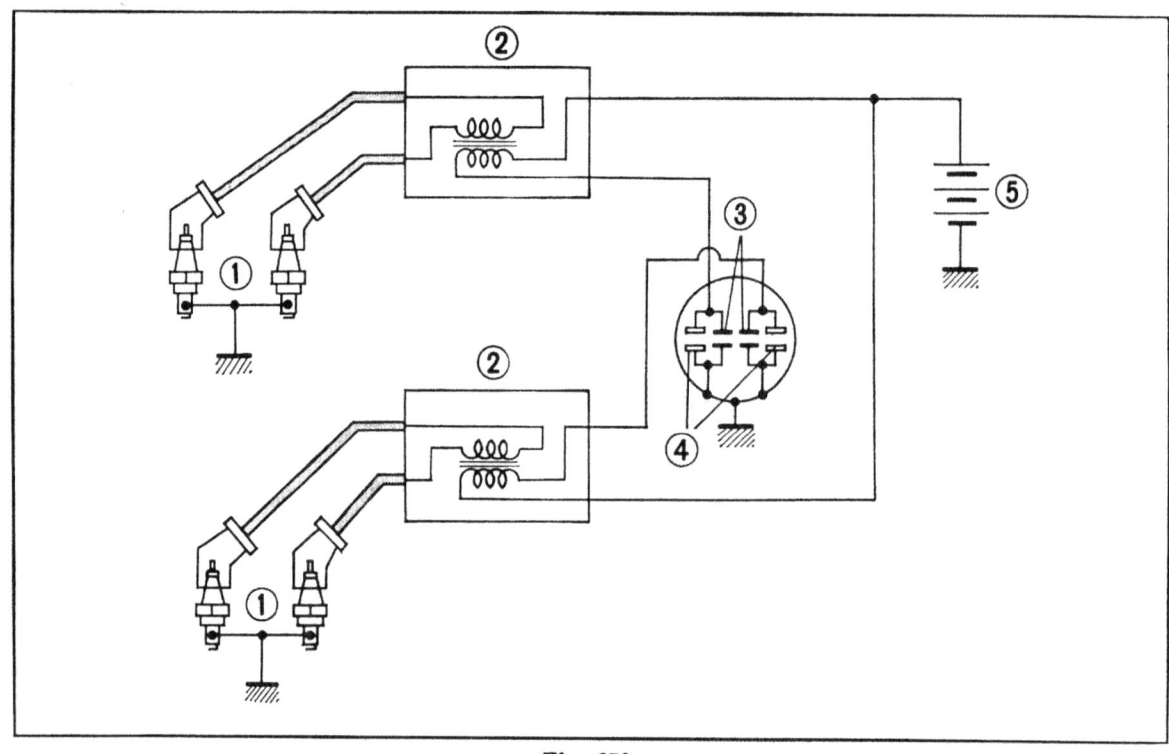

Fig. 270

① Spark plugs ③ Condensers ⑤ Battery
② Ignition coils ④ Contact breaker

The ignition system consists of two ignition coils, two contact breakers, four spark plugs, an ignition switch and a battery.

The current from the battery flows through the primary winding of the ignition coil, and the circuit is completed by grounding through the contact breaker. The contact breaker is contained in the contact breaker housing at the right end of the crankshaft. There are two contact breakers which are 180° out of phase. One of the breakers furnishes high voltage current to spark plugs 1 and 4; the other breaker furnishes current to plugs 2 and 3. The contact breakers ignite the spark plugs in a firing sequence of 1, 2, 4 and 3 which is indicated on the high tension plug cords. Since no distributor is used, the construction is simple and the system is easy to service.

SERVICE DATA

Ignition coil 3 point spark gap opening	7 mm min. (0.27 in.)
Spark plug Type (standard) Plug gap	NGK D-7 ES, DENSO X 22 ES 0.6~0.7 mm (0.023~0.027 in.)
Contact breaker Point gap Spring force	0.3~0.4 mm (0.012~0.016 in.) 680~850 g (1.43~1.87 lbs.)
Condenser Capacity Insulation resistance	0.24 μF ±10% Over 10 MΩ (1,000 megger)
Spark advancer Start of advance (crankshaft speed) Full advance (crankshaft speed) Advance angle	1,150 rpm 2,300~2,500 rpm 25°

Ignition Coil

The ignition coil consists of a primary coil with 420 turns of copper wire wound around an iron core of laminated silicon steel sheets. A secondary coil with 13,000 turns of wire is wound on top of the primary coil. Each secondary coil has two high tension cords to two spark plugs.

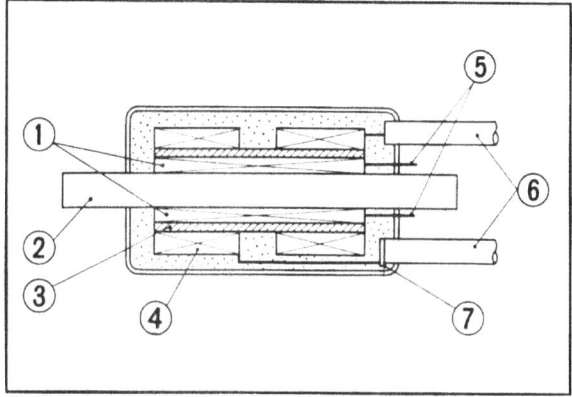

Fig. 271
① Primary coil
② Iron core
③ Bobbin
④ Secondary coil
⑤ Primary terminal
⑥ High tension cord
⑦ High tension terminal

A. Disassembly

1. Open the seat and remove the fuel tank.
2. Disconnect the ignition coil leads. (yellow, blue and black/white)
3. Loosen the two ignition coil mounting bolts, and separate the ignition coil from the frame.

Fig. 272 ① Ignition coil ② Bolts

B. Inspection

1. Ignition coil continuity test
   Primary coils:
   Check for continuity between the primary coil terminals.
   Right coil: yellow and black/white leads
   Left coil: blue and black/white leads
   Secondary coils
   Check for continuity between the terminals of the high tension cords.
   If there is no continuity, the coil is open and must be replaced.

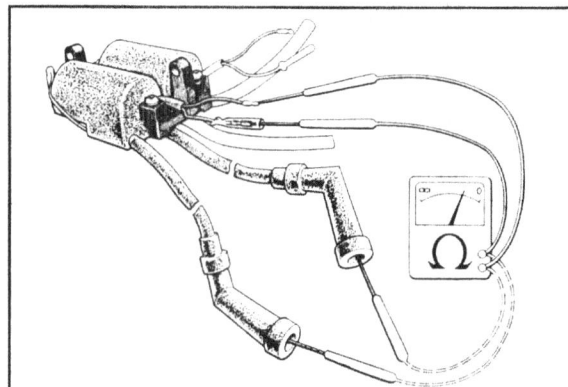

Fig. 273 Ignition coil continuity test

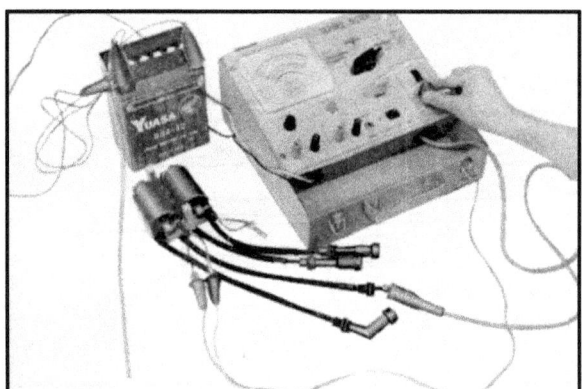

Fig. 274 Ignition coil performance test

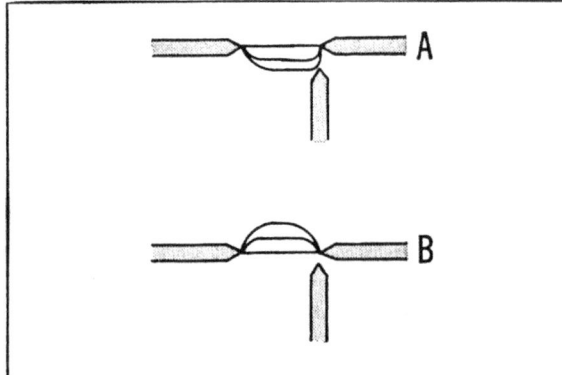

Fig. 275 Spark performance

Ignition coil perfomance test

Coil may test satisfactorily for continuity but it may not perform satisfactorily due to deterioration from long use, therefore, performance should be checked to determine its condition.

Connect the service tester power cord to a 12 V battery and ground the ground cable. Connect the ignition primary test lead to the tester and connect the opposite terminal ends to the primary terminals of the coil. Connect the red test lead to the black terminal of the ignition coil and the white test lead to the yellow cord of the left coil (to the blue cord for the right coil).

Position the selector knob to COIL TEST. Adjust the three point spark tester to the maximum distance spark is maintained.

Measure this distance. The coil is satisfactory if the distance is greater than **7 mm**. **(0.27 in.)**

Note:
Since a dual sparking ignition coil is used, note the spark condition. If the spark appears as B in Fig. 275, the connection to the primary coil is reversed.

6. ELECTRICAL

Spark plug

A. Removal
1. Remove any dirt from around the spark plug by using compressed air.
2. Remove the spark plugs with a plug wrench.

B. Inspection
Inspect the spark plug for worn electrodes, excessive gap, fouled condition and damaged porcelain insulator.
1. Clean dirty spark plug with a plug cleaner or wire brush.
2. Measure the electrode gap with a feeler gauge and, if necessary, adjust to the specified gap.
   Standard gap: **0.6~0.7 mm (0.023~0.027 in.)**
3. Replace the spark plug if the porcelain insulator is damaged, or the gasket if it is damaged or distorted.
   Standard spark plug: **D-7ES (NGK), X22ES (DENSO)**

C. Reinstallation
1. Install the spark plugs in the reverse order of removal.
   Torque: **1.5~2.0 kg-m (11~14 ft-lbs)**

Note:
1. Do not drop the plug gasket.
2. A loose plug will not properly dissipate the heat and may result in engine malfunction.

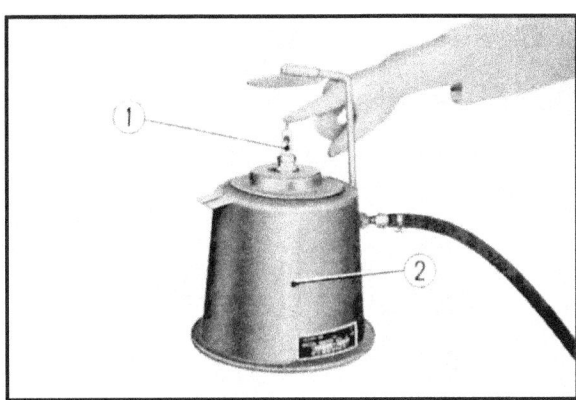

Fig. 276 1) Spark plug   2) Spark plug cleaner

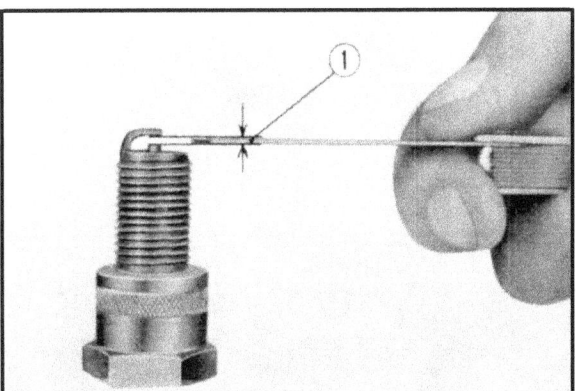

Fig. 277 1) Feeler gauge

Contact Breaker and Condenser

A. Disassembly
1. Remove the point cover.
2. Disconnect the leads (yellow, blue) at the connectors located at the center of the frame.
3. Loosen the 6 mm bolt, remove the special washer, loosen the base plate mounting screws, and then remove the contact breaker assembly.

Fig. 278
① 6 mm bolt
② Special washer
③ Screws
④ Condensers
⑤ Contact breaker plate

B. Inspection
- For adjustment of breaker point and ignition timing, refer to the "Maintenance Operations" section.
- Condenser
  Measure the capacitance of the condenser using the service tester.
  Standard value: **0.22~0.26 μF**

Note:
The points should be open when testing.

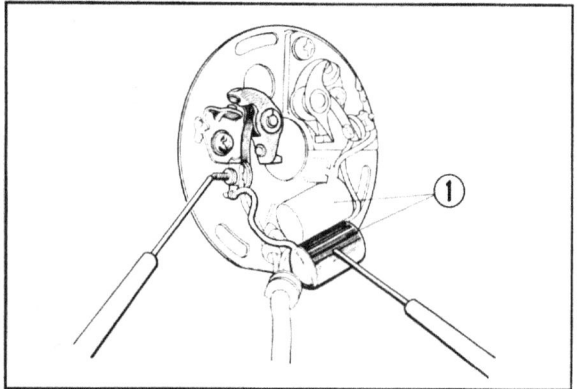

Fig. 279 ① Condenser

Spark Advancer

A. Disassembly
1. Remove the point cover and the contact breaker assembly.
2. Remove the spark advancer from the spark advancer shaft.

B. Inspection
1. Clean dust and foreign matters from friction surfaces, and make sure operation is smooth.
2. Check spring tension and advancer pin wear.
   Standard spring tension:
   680~850 gr. (1.43~1.87 lbs)

Fig. 280 ① Spark advancer

C. Reassembly
1. Install the dowel pin by aligning the hole.
2. Reassemble in the reverse order of removal.

Fig. 281 ① Spark advancer ② Crankshaft

3. CHARGING SYSTEM

The charging system for the CB 500 is made up of the exciter field 3-phase AC generator, rectifier, voltage regulator and the fuse. The generator consists of the field coil, stator coil and the rotor; it does not contain slip rings or brushes.

In order for the stator coil to produce constant voltage, the current from the battery to produce the exciter field is regulated to very close limits by the dual contact regulator. The generator output is rectified by the silicon rectifier before being sent to recharge the battery. The generator performs two functions depending upon the charge condition of the battery. The electrical current from the battery flows through the switch and into the regulator. When the battery voltage is lower than normal (less than 13.5 V at the battery terminal), the current flows through the upper contact to the field coil. The strength of the magnetic field is dependent upon the strength of the battery voltage. When the battery terminal voltage is 12 V, the field coil current is 1.6 A. This produces an output voltage of corresponding strength which is used to charge the battery.

When the battery voltage exceeds approximately 14.5 V, the armature coil pulls the armature away from the upper contacts and closes the lower contacts to insert a 10 Ω resistance into the field coil circuit. The current to the field coil is thus reduced to 0.7 A and, consequently, a lower voltage is produced by the generator, limiting the amount of charge to the battery. This function of inserting or removing the resistance into the generator field coil is performed by the voltage regulator in accordance with the charge condition of the battery.

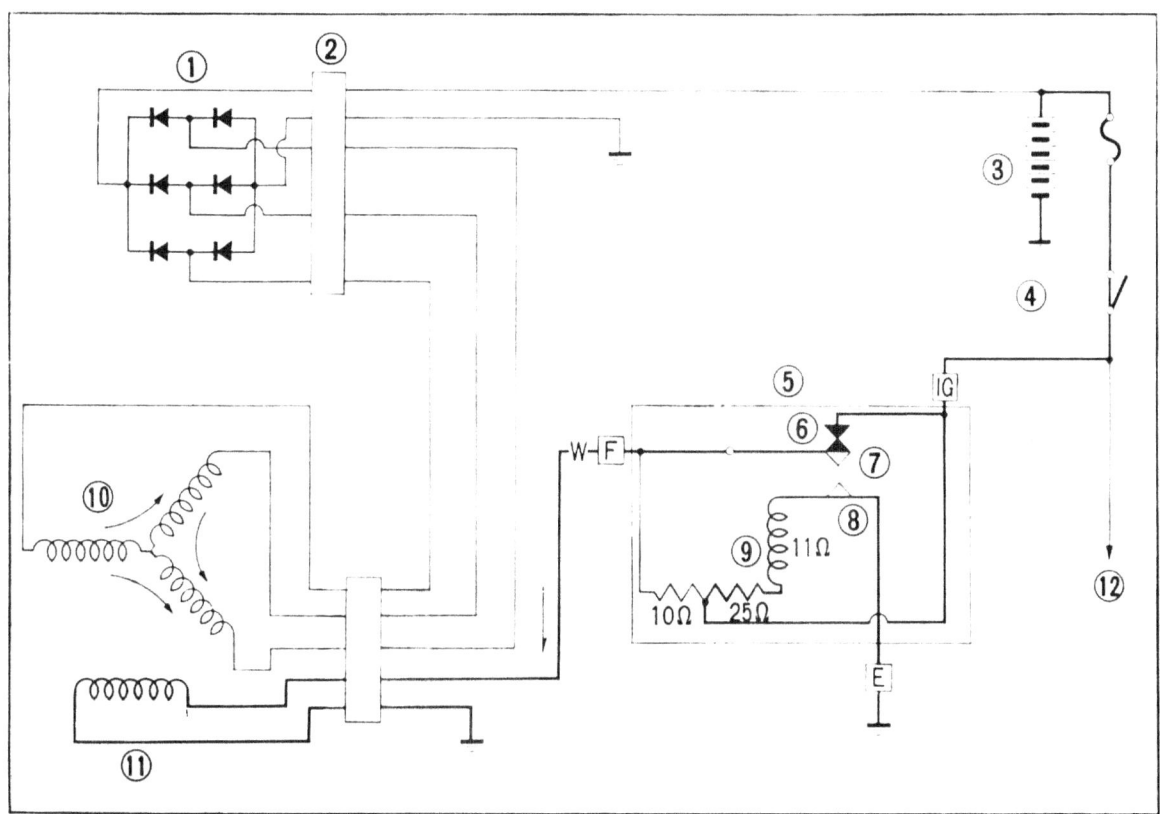

Fig. 282

① Silicon rectifier
② Coupler
③ Battery 12 V, 12 AH
④ Main switch
⑤ Regulator
⑥ Upper contact
⑦ Moving contact
⑧ Lower contact
⑨ Relay coil
⑩ Stator coil
⑪ Field coil
⑫ To load

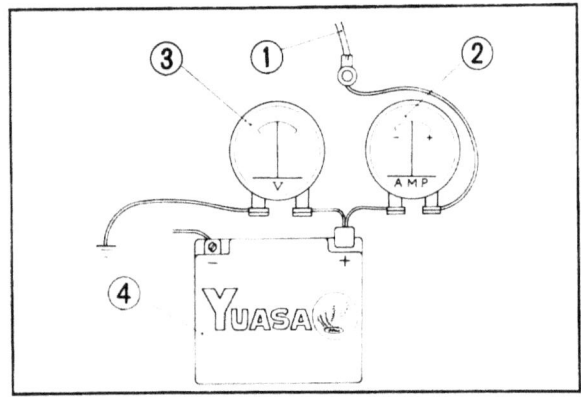

Fig. 283 ① Red/white lead ③ Voltmeter
② Ammeter ④ Battery

Charging Test

1. Perform the test using the ammeter and voltmeter.
2. The battery charge condition is determined by measuring the specific gravity of the battery electrolyte. If the specific gravity is lower than **1.26** (at 20°C/68°F), recharge the battery so that the specific gravity is up to **1.26~1.28** (at 20°C/68°F), and then perform the following test.
3. Disconnect the battery cable from the ⊕ terminal of the battery, and connect it to the ⊕ side of the ammeter.

Next, connect the ⊖ side of the ammeter to the ⊕ terminal of the battery.

Connect the ⊕ side of the voltmeter to the ⊕ end of the battery cable, and ground the ⊖ side of the voltmeter. (Fig. 283)

4. Start the engine, operate it under both the NIGHT RIDING and DAY RIDING conditions and check to see if the measured values conform to those specified in the table below.

If the values are less than those specified, adjust the regulator.

Note:
The charge condition of the battery may cause the charge current to vary slightly.

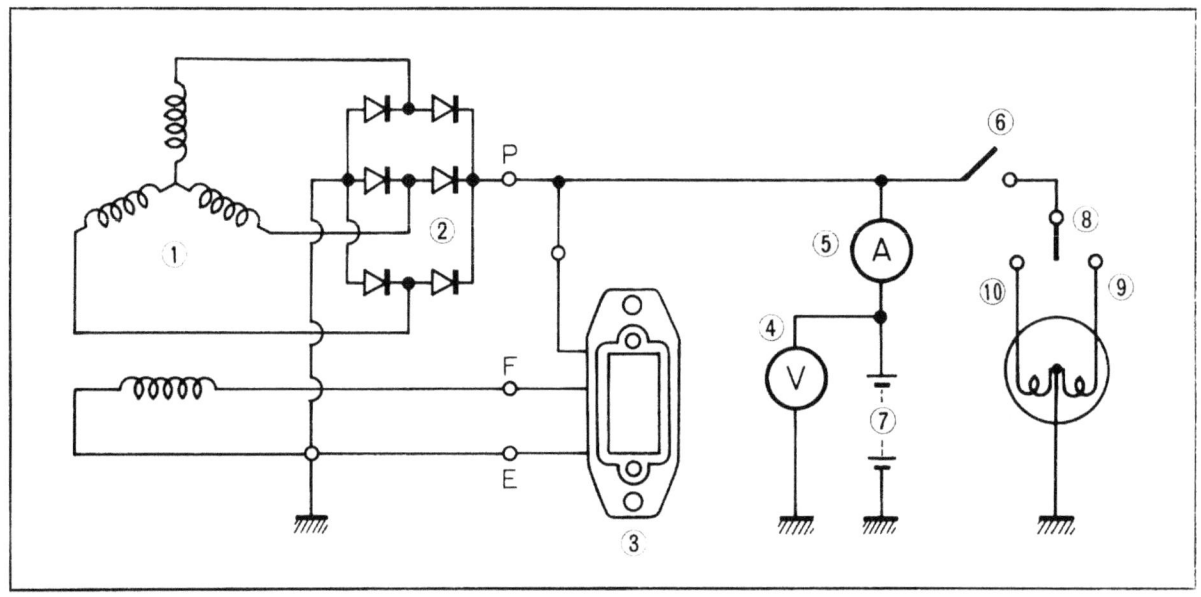

Fig. 284

① A.C. Generator ⑤ Ammeter ⑨ Headlight low beam
② Silicon rectifier ⑥ Main switch ⑩ Headlight high beam
③ Voltage regulator ⑦ Battery
④ Voltmeter ⑧ Headlight switch

Engine RPM Charging current (A)	1,000	2,000	3,000	4,000	5,000	6,000	7,000	8,000
Day riding	6.5	0	2.4	1.3	1.0	1.0	0.8	0.6
Night riding	2-3	1	1	1	1	1	1	1
Battery terminal voltage (v)	12	12.4	13.2	14.5	14.5	14.5	14.5	14.5

6. ELECTRICAL

A.C. Generator

Specifications

Type and manufacture	LD 110-01, Hitachi
Output	150 W
Battery voltage	12 V
Polarity	⊖ ground
Charging speed	1000-9000 rpm
Weight	3 kg (6.6 lbs)

A. Disassembly

1. Remove the generator cover and pull the rotor out using the rotor puller (Special Tool No. 07933-2160000).
2. Loosen the three 6 mm screws from inside the generator cover and remove the stator coil.
3. Loosen the three 6 mm screws from the outside the generator cover and remove the field coil.

B. Inspection

1. Field coil resistance test
   Check resistance between the two field coil leads (White, Green) using the Service Tester OHMS function.
   STANDARD RESISTANCE VALUE:
   4.9Ω ±10%
   NOTE: Test may be performed without removing the field coil.
2. Stator coil resistance test
   a. Check resistance between any two of the three yellow alternator (stator) leads.
   b. Leave either tester lead connected to the yellow wire. Attach another tester lead to the third yellow stator wire.
   STANDARD RESISTANCE VALUE:
   0.35Ω ±10% at a.
   0.35Ω ±10% at b.
NOTE: Test may be performed without removing the stator.

TEST	RESULT	INDICATION
1 (field coil)	No reading or low reading	Defective
2 (stator) a or b	No reading or low reading	Defective

Fig. 285 1) Rotor puller 2) Rotor

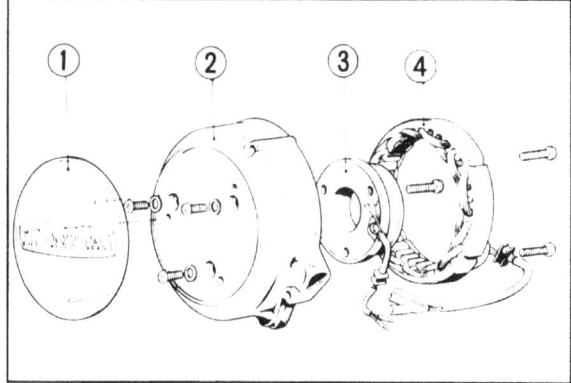

Fig. 286 1) Side cover 3) Field coil
2) Generator cover 4) Stator coil

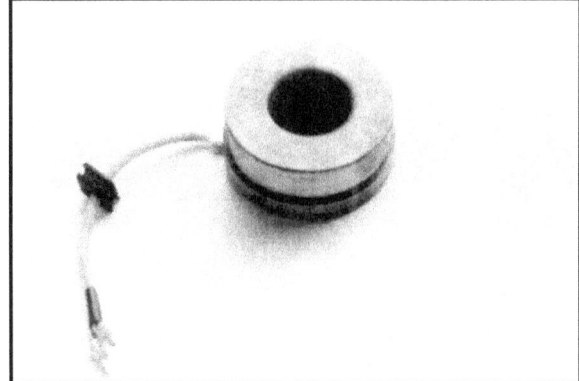

Fig. 287 Field coil

Fig. 288 Stator coil

6. ELECTRICAL

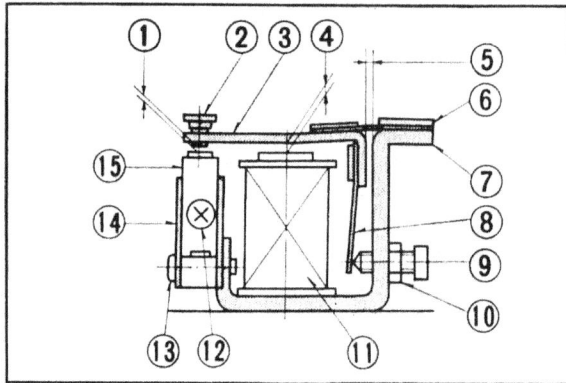

Fig. 289

① Point gap
② Upper contact
③ Armature
④ Core gap
⑤ Yoke gap
⑥ Spring
⑦ Yoke
⑧ Adjusting spring
⑨ Voltage adjusting screw
⑩ Lock nut
⑪ Coil
⑫ Point gap adjusting screw
⑬ Core gap adjusting screw
⑭ Contact set
⑮ Lower contact

Regulator

The regulator is a dual contact type. It maintains a constant voltage by placing the resistance circuit into the field coil circuit when the generating voltage rises to a certain value, and cutting the resistance circuit out when the voltage drops below a set limit.

A. Disassembly

1. Disconnect the leads at the connectors and loosen the two 6 mm regulator mounting bolts.
2. Loosen the two screws and remove the regulator cover.

B. Inspection and Adjustment

Regulating voltage adjustment

1. To adjust for low charge current or low battery voltage, loosen the lock nut on the voltage adjusting screw and turn the adjusting screw clockwise. When the regulator is set too high, turn the adjusting screw counterclockwise.
2. Upon completing the adjustment, recheck regulator performance after installation.

Core gap adjustment
Measure the core gap with a feeler gauge. If it requires adjustment, loosen the core gap adjusting screw and move the point body up or down.
Standard core gap value:

0.6~1.0 mm (0.02~0.40 in.)

Point gap adjustment
Measure the point gap with a feeler gauge. If it requires adjustment, loosen the point gap adjusting screw and move the lower point up or down. Standard point gap value:

0.2 mm (0.008 in.)

Note: If the points are pitted or fouled polish with a ±500~600 emery paper.

Fig. 290 ① Regulator

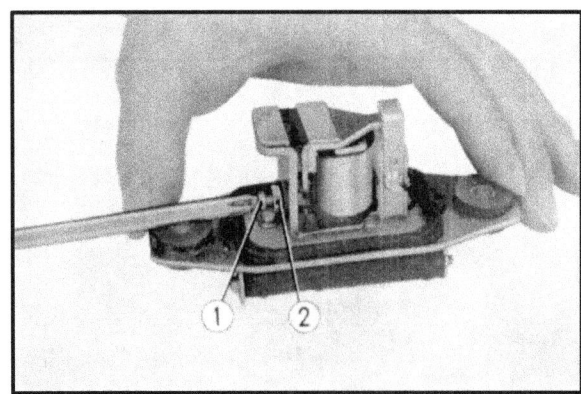

Fig. 291 ① Voltage adjusting screw
② Lock nut

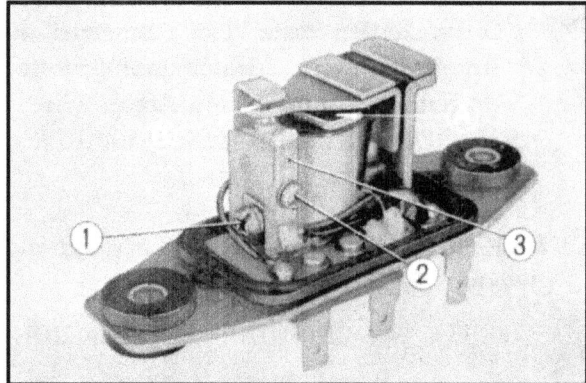

Fig. 292 Ⓐ Core gap
Ⓑ Point gap
① Core gap adjusting screw
② Point gap adjusting screw
③ Lower point

Silicon Rectifier

Inspection

The condition of the silicon rectifier is tested by disconnecting the electrical connections and testing the rectifying function in both the normal and reverse directions. Continuity in the normal direction indicates good condition. Continuity in both directions indicates a defective rectifier.

Note:
1. Do not use a megger for the test as the high voltage will damage the silicon diodes.
2. Observe the polarity of the battery. Connecting the battery terminals in reverse will shorten the battery life as well as cause a large current to flow through the electrical system, causing damage to the silicon rectifier and destroying the wire harness.
3. Do not operate the generator at a high RPM with the "P" terminal red/white cord from the magnetic switch of the silicon rectifier disconnected. The high voltage generated may damage the silicon rectifier.
4. When charging the battery mounted on the motorcycle from an external source with a high charge rate such as a "quick charge", the silicon rectifier wiring should be disconnected at the coupler to prevent damage.

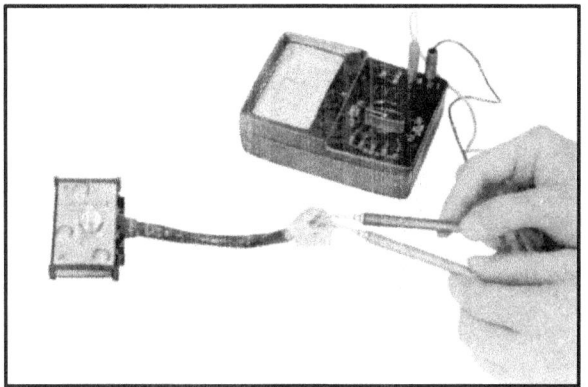

Fig. 293 Silicon rectifier inspection

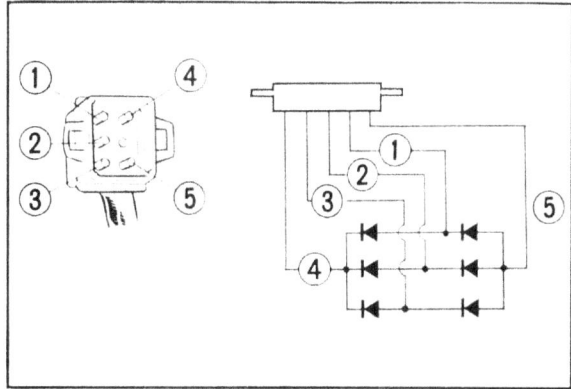

Fig. 294 ①, ②, ③ Yellow
④ Yellow/White
⑤ Green

4. STARTING SYSTEM

The starter is a device which converts the electrical energy of the battery to the mechnical energy to start the engine. The starting circuit consists of a push button switch mounted on the right side of the handlebar which, when the starter button is pressed, energizes the starter magnetic switch and closes the starter circuit contacts. This permits approximately 120 A of current to flow from the battery to the starting motor, which then rotates the engine to perform the starting.

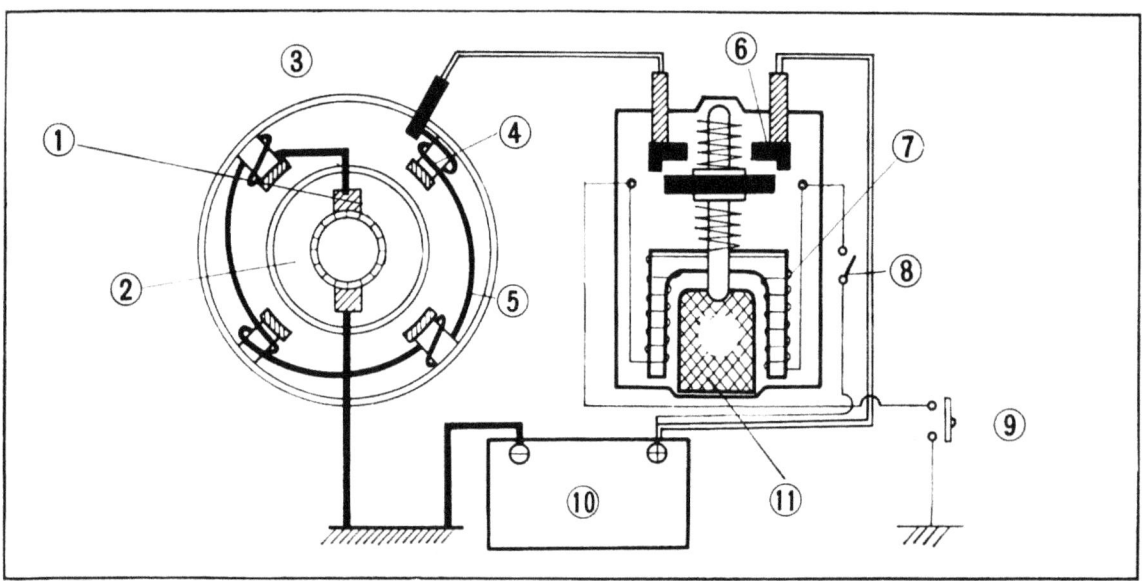

Fig. 295 Starting Circuit

① Brush
② Armature
③ Starting motor
④ Pole
⑤ Field coil
⑥ Starter magnetic switch
⑦ Electromagnet
⑧ Ignition switch
⑨ Starter button
⑩ Battery
⑪ Plunger

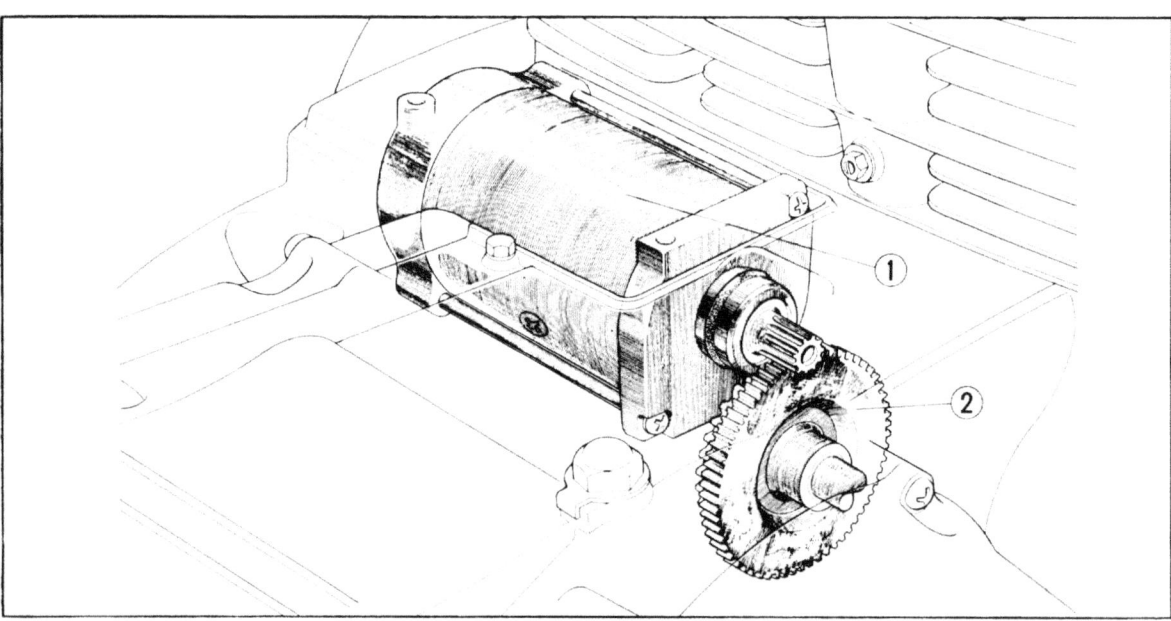

Fig. 296 Starting motor installation
① Starting motor   ② Starter reduction gear

6. ELECTRICAL

Starting Motor

The starting motor is mounted on the crankcase behind the cylinder and drives the crankshaft through the starting clutch.

Specifications
- Rated voltage   12 V
- Rated output   0.6 KW
- Rated operation   Continuous for 30 seconds

	Without load	With load
Voltage	11 V	8.5 V
Amperage	35 A	120 A
Torque	—	0.12 kg-cm (0.86 ft-lbs)
Revolution	11000~20000 rpm	3200 rpm

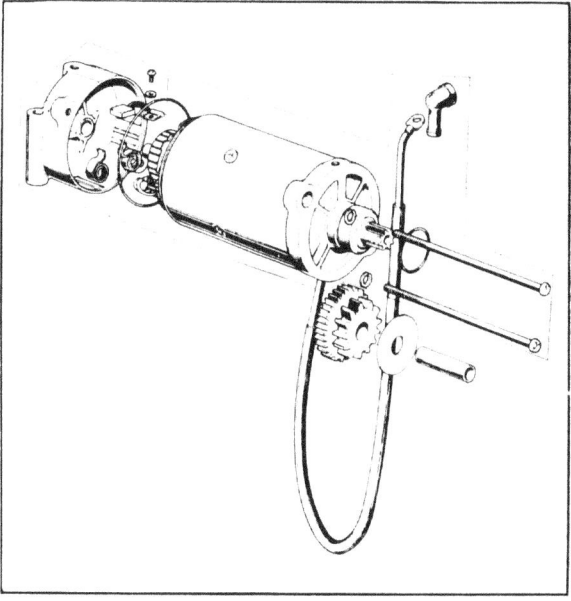

Fig. 297 Starting motor disassembly drawing

A. Disassembly

1. Disconnect the starting motor cable at the magnetic switch.
2. Remove the starting motor cover, left crankcase cover and loosen the two 6 mm starting motor mounting bolts.
3. The starting motor can now be pulled out.
4. Loosen the two 6 mm screws and remove the starting motor side cover.

Fig. 298   1) Magnetic switch
          2) Starting motor cable

Fig. 299   1) Starting motor
          2) 6 mm bolts

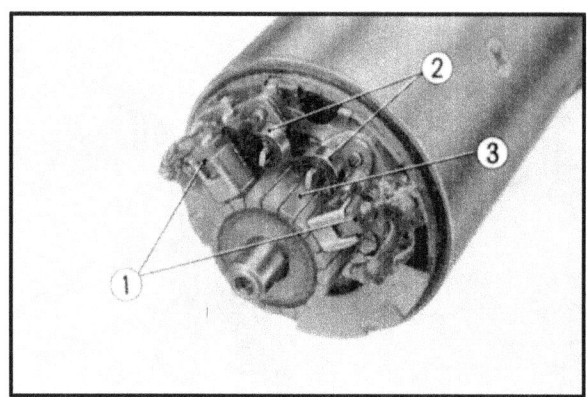

Fig. 300 (1) Carbon brushes
(2) Springs
(3) Commutator

B. **Inspection**
1. Carbon brush inspection
   Worn carbon brush, pitted or rough contact surface and weakened brush spring will cause starting difficulty, therefore, they should be replaced.
2. Commutator cleaning
   Dirty commutator will give poor starting motor performance.
   The commutator surface should be polished with a fine grade emery paper and completely washed before reassembly.

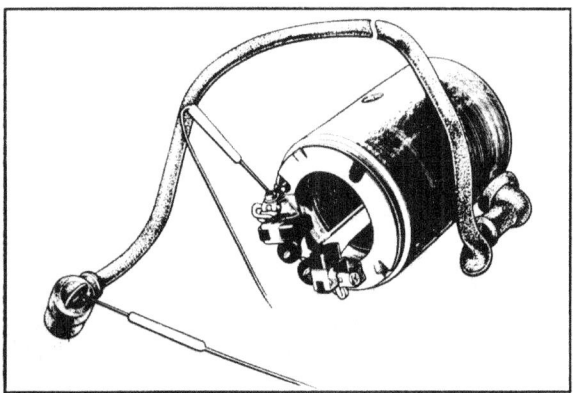

Fig. 301 Stator coil inspection

3. Stator coil inspection
   Check continuity between the brush wired to the stator coil and the starting motor cable. Lack of continuity indicates an open stator coil and should be replaced.

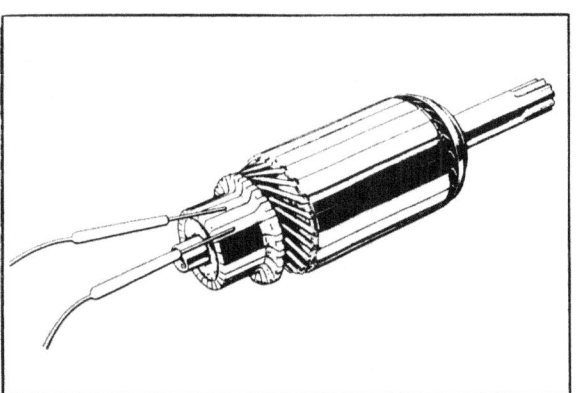

Fig. 302 Armature coil inspection

4. Armature coil inspection
   A grounded armature coil will render the starting motor inoperative.
   Perform a continuity test between the commutator and the core. A continuity condition indicates a grounded stator coil and should be replaced.

6. ELECTRICAL

Starter Magnetic Switch

The starting motor requires a current of approximately 100 A to operate. To minimize resistance, a large cable is used for wiring. A switch with heavy duty contacts is required. Sparking across the contacts will result, as well as resistance depending upon the contact pressure, when the contacts are opened suddenly to shut off the flow of large current. To cope with these conditions, a magnetic switch is used separately which is operated electrically by a small current through a push button starter switch.

Inspection

1. Primary coil continuity test.
   If there is no continuity, the primary coil is open.
   - If a clicking noise is heard when a 12 V battery is connected to the two leads of the coil, the primary coil is satisfactory.
2. After long use, the magnetic switch contacts will become pitted or burnt from the large current which flows across it, and gradually build up resistance which may prevent the current flow.
   Connect 12 V to the primary coil leads of the magnetic switch. If there is no continuity across the switch contacts, the switch is defective.

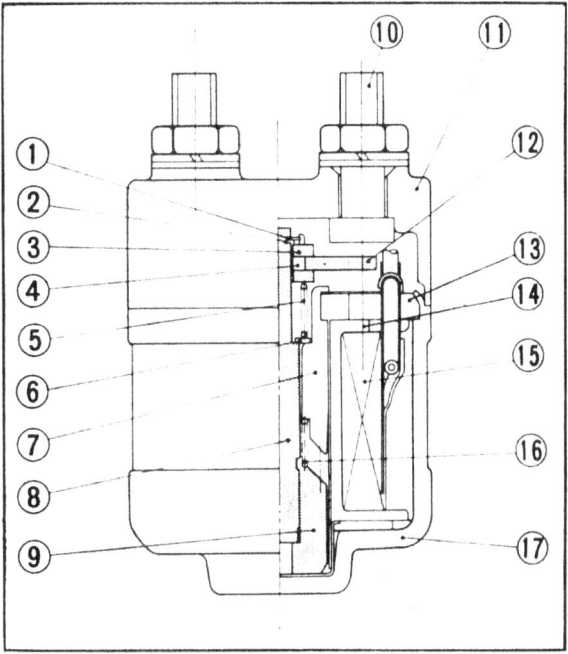

Fig. 303

1. Stopper
2. Stopper holder
3. Washer
4. Roller A
5. Contact spring
6. Flat washer
7. Plunger holder
8. Plunger shaft
9. Plunger
10. Contact bolt
11. Case
12. Contact plate
13. Yoke
14. Coil bobbin
15. Coil complete
16. Return spring
17. Body

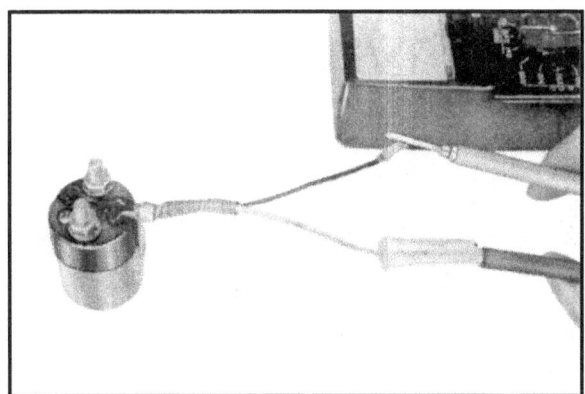

Fig. 304 Primary coil continuity test

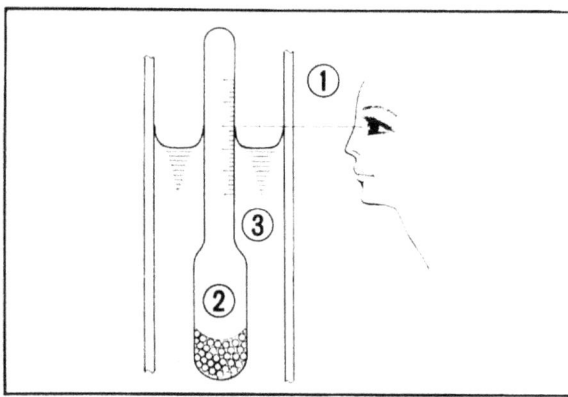

Fig. 305 ① Eye level ③ Electrolyte
② Hydrometer

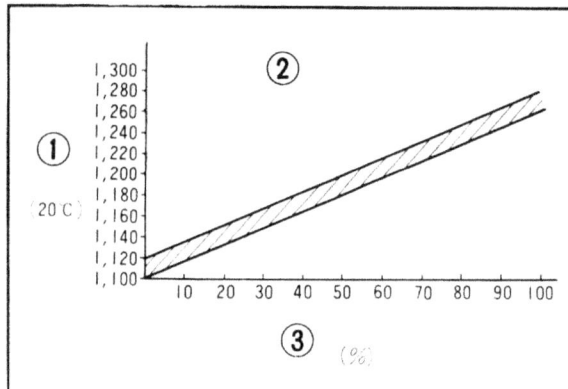

Fig. 306 ① Specific gravity
② Relation between specific gravity
③ Residual charge (%)

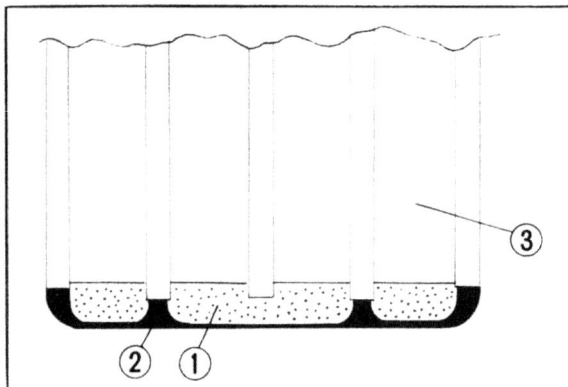

Fig. 307 ① Sediment ③ Plates
② Battery case

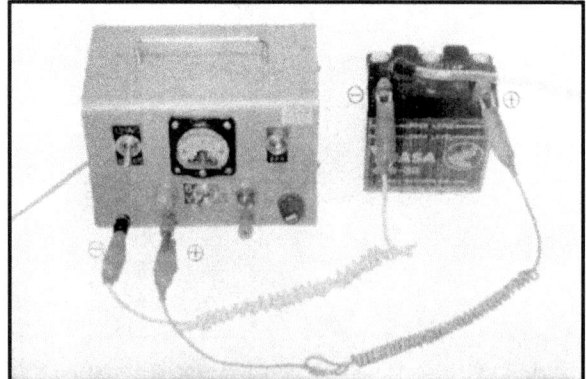

Fig. 308 Charger hook-up

Battery
A. Specification

Type	12N 12A-4A·1
Voltage	12 V
Capacity	12 AH

B. Specific gravity measurement
Battery electrolyte is measured with a bulb type hydrometer. When the specific gravity is below 1.200 (at 20°C), the battery should be recharged.

When making a reading, the hydrometer should be held vertical with the electrolyte liquid level, held at the eye level and the value on the floating scale read at the point where the liquid separates from the stem of the float.

C. Inspection and replenishment
1. Electrolyte in each battery cell should be inspected every three months or 1,500 miles, and distilled water added to bring the level to the upper mark whenever the electrolyte level is below the level mark.
2. Whenever there is rapid lowering of the electrolyte level, the charging system should be inspected.
3. Periodically measure the specific gravity. After adding distilled water, allow the battery to be charged and the electrolyte sufficiently agitated before making the measurement.
4. Primary battery troubles are due to corrosion around the connectors and terminals causing poor contact, separation of the battery paste, and sulfation. A battery which is left in a discharged condition for a long period will have lead sulfate formed on the plates and recharging will not restore it to its original condition. Battery inspection should be performed periodically and thoroughly.

Note:
When sediment has formed at the bottom as shown in Fig. 307, the battery should be replaced.

D. Battery charging
(Caution)
1. Refrain from charging the battery at a fast rate (quick charge) as it shortens battery life. When rapid charging is necessary, limit the charging rate to a maximum of 2.0 A.
2. Hydrogen gas is generated during the charging process, therefore, keep fire away.
3. After battery charging is completed, wash the battery with water to remove spilled electrolyte. Apply grease to the terminals.

5. ELECTRICAL EQUIPMENT

1. Main switch inspection
   With the switch in both the ON and OFF positions, check to see that the continuity conditions in the chart below are satisfied. The switch is defective if there is no continuity where specified, or if there is continuity where not specified.

Color of cords	BAT Red	IG Black	TL_1 Brown/white	TL_2 Brown
Key position OFF				
1	○	○	○	○
2	○			○

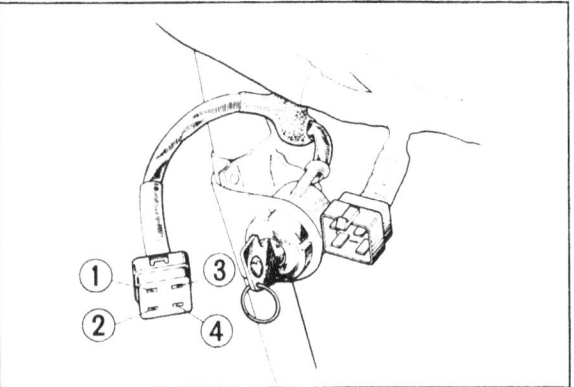

Fig. 309 ① Black   ③ Brown
② Brown/white   ④ Red

2. Front stop switch inspection
   Apply tester lead probes to the terminals of the front stop switch cords (black, green/yellow), operate brake lever and check for continuity.
   - Check the lever free play **2~5 mm (0.08~0.2 in.)**.
   The stop light should come on when the brake lever travels beyond the lever free play.

3. Rear stop switch inspection
   After connecting the stop switch spring, apply the tester lead probes to the switch terminals (green/yellow, black cords) and check for continuity. When the brake pedal is depressed 20 mm (0.8 in.) at the front end of the pedal, the stop light should come on at this point.
   Adjustment.
   If the stop light is late in coming on, turn the adjuster nut clockwise, and if too early, turn counterclockwise.

4. Horn Inspection
   - Check for continuity across the horn lead terminals.
   - An alternate method is to connect the horn to a fully charged 12 V battery and check its operation.

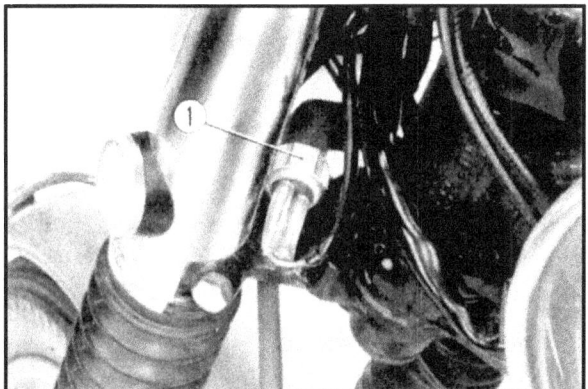

Fig. 310 Front stop switch inspection
① Front stop switch

Fig. 311 ① Rear stop switch adjuster nut

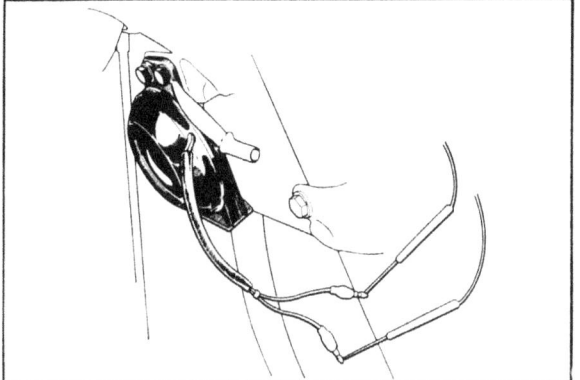

Fig. 312 Horn continuity test

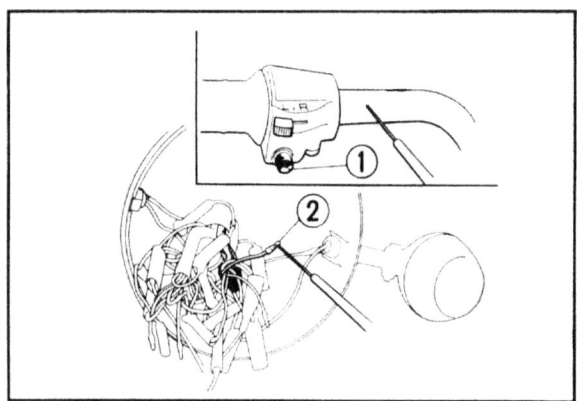

Fig. 313 ① Horn button
② Light green cord

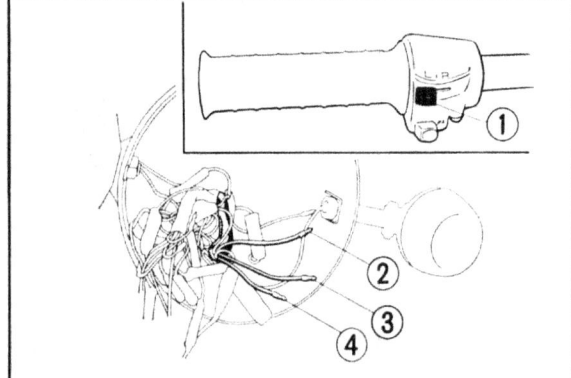

Fig. 314 ① Winker switch
② Light blue cord
③ Gray cord
④ Orange cord

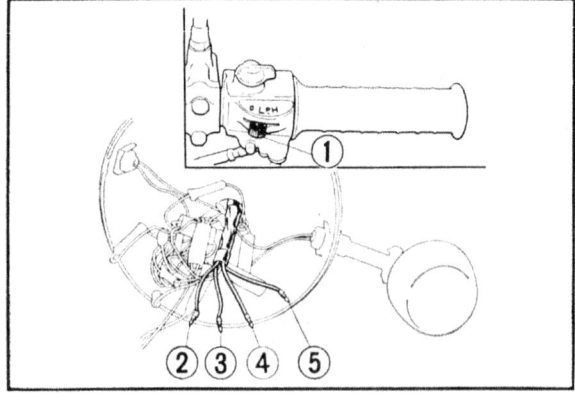

Fig. 315 ① Lighting switch
② Black cord
③ Blue cord
④ Brown/white cord
⑤ White cord

5. Horn button inspection

   With the tester lead probes, contact the light green cord terminal within the headlight case and the handlebar, and then press the horn button to check for continuity. If continuity exists, the horn button is satisfactory.

6. Winker switch inspection.

   Disconnect the winker switch wiring within the headlight case. Check continuity between the gray cord terminal and the orange cord terminal (left winker), and between the gray cord terminal and light blue cord terminal (right winker) of the winker switch. Continuity for the respective tests should exist according to the switch connections shown in the table below.

Knob	Blue cord	Gray cord	Orange cord
R	○———○		
OFF (center)			
L		○———○	

7. Lighting switch inspection.

   Using a tester inspect for broken wires and defective contact between the respective switch cords. Continuity between the different cords should exist in accordance with the switching position table shown below. If continuity exists where not indicated the switch is defective.

Cord color		IG Black	HB Blue	TL Brown/white	LB White
ON	H	○	○	○	
	P	○		○	
	L	○		○	○
OFF					

6. ELECTRICAL

8. Emergency switch and starter switch inspection.

   Inspect for broken wires and defective contact between the respective switch cords. Continuity between the different cords should exist in accordance with the switching position table shown below.

   If continuity exists where not indicated, the switch is defective.

Emergency switch		
Cord color	Black	Black/white
ON	○	○
OFF		

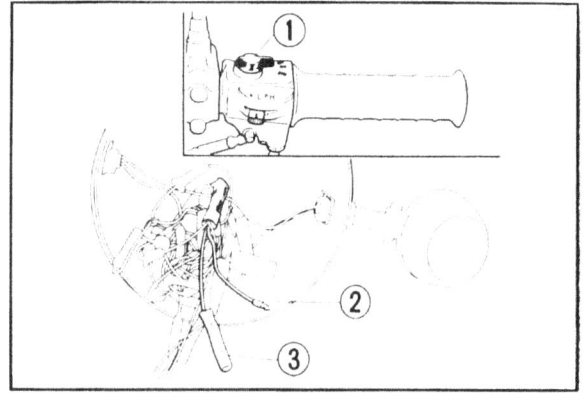

Fig. 316 ① Emergency switch   ③ Black/white
② Black

Starter switch	
Cord color	Yellow/red
ON	○ ○
OFF	

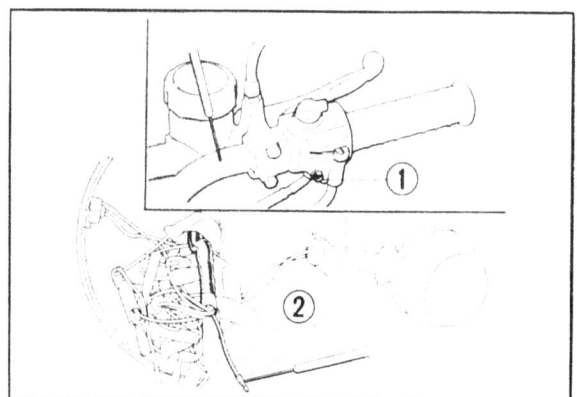

Fig. 317 ① Starter switch
② Yellow/red

9. Oil pressure switch inspection

   Lubricating oil is supplied under pressure of $4 \sim 6\,\text{kg/cm}^2$ ($56.8 \sim 85.3\,\text{lbs/in.}^2$) by the oil pump to various parts of the engine. When the oil pressure drops, the oil supply becomes low. The oil system is designed so that when the oil pressure drops below $0.5\,\text{kg/cm}^2$ ($7\,\text{lbs/in.}^2$), the oil pressure switch operates and the warning lamp comes on.

   Without starting the engine and with the main switch on, check the oil pressure switch for continuity. If there is continuity, the switch is satisfactory. It is normal for the warning lamp to go out when the engine is started.

   If the warning lamp does not go out after starting, and the pressure switch is satisfactory, the oil system should be inspected.

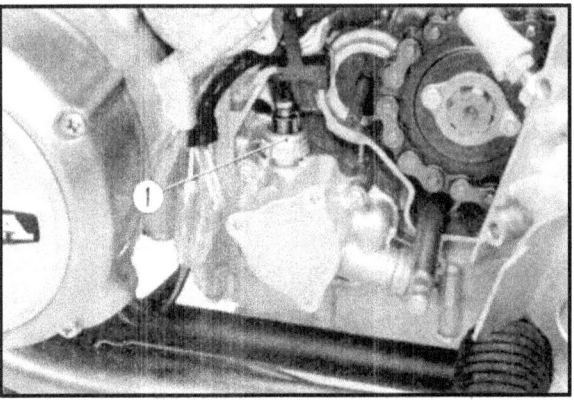

Fig. 318 ① Oil pressure switch

Fig. 319 Neutral switch inspection
① Neutral switch

10. Neutral switch inspection

    The neutral switch is mounted on the left side of the upper crankcase. When the transmission is in neutral, the switch is grounded and the neutral pilot lamp comes on. Place the transmission in neutral, remove the left crankcase cover and check the continuity of the neutral switch. The switch is satisfactory if there is continuity.

7. INSPECTION AND ADJUSTMENT OF CB550

1. Clutch

The clutch must be adjusted so that the engine can be completely disconnected from the transmission when the clutch lever is squeezed, but not to the point where the clutch will slip when accelerating the motorcycle.
The clutch cable should be adjusted to provide **10~20 mm (0.4~0.8 in.)** free play measured at the tip of the clutch lever.
To adjust, proceed as follows:

1. Loosen the clutch adjuster lock nut ① and turn the adjuster ② to align the marks ③ on the actuating arm and the engine side cover.
2. Clutch cable adjustment can be made by means of the adjusters at the upper and lower ends of the clutch cable. Loosen the lock nut ⑤ (⑥ at the lower end) at the clutch lever and turn the cable adjuster bolt ④ (nut ⑦ at the lower end) in either direction. Turning the cable adjuster bolt or nut at the lower end in direction A will increase the free play and turning it in the direction B will decrease the free play. Tighten the lock nut.
3. After adjusting, check to see if the clutch is slipping and if it is properly disengaging.

Start the engine and shift into gear. There should be no excessive grinding from the transmission, and the motorcycle should not creep when the clutch lever is squeezed. Drive the motorcycle to check for clutch slippage.

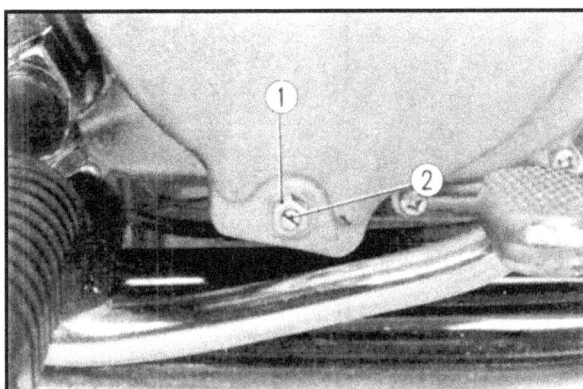

Fig. 320　① Clutch adjuster lock nut
　　　　　② Clutch adjuster

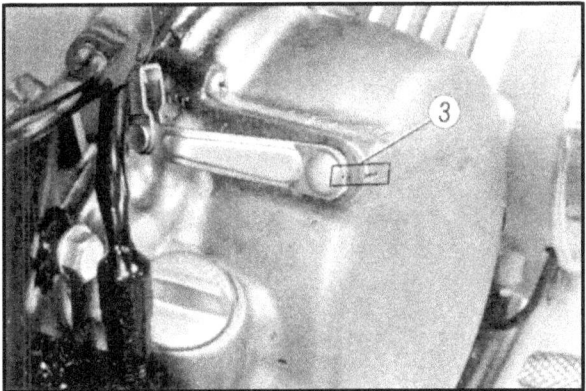

Fig. 321　③ Alignment marks

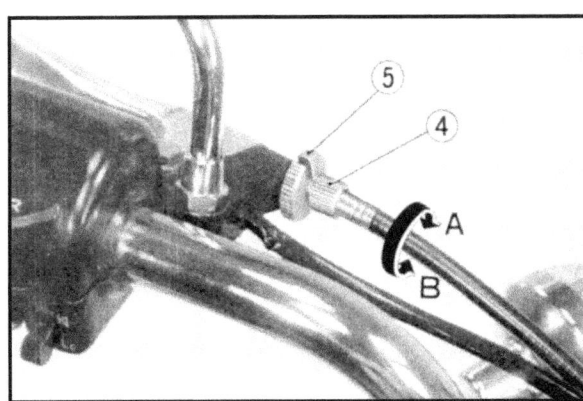

Fig. 322　④ Clutch cable adjuster bolt
　　　　　⑤ Lock nut

Fig. 323　⑥ Lock nut
　　　　　⑦ Clutch cable adjuster nut

8. NEW FEATURES OF THE CB550

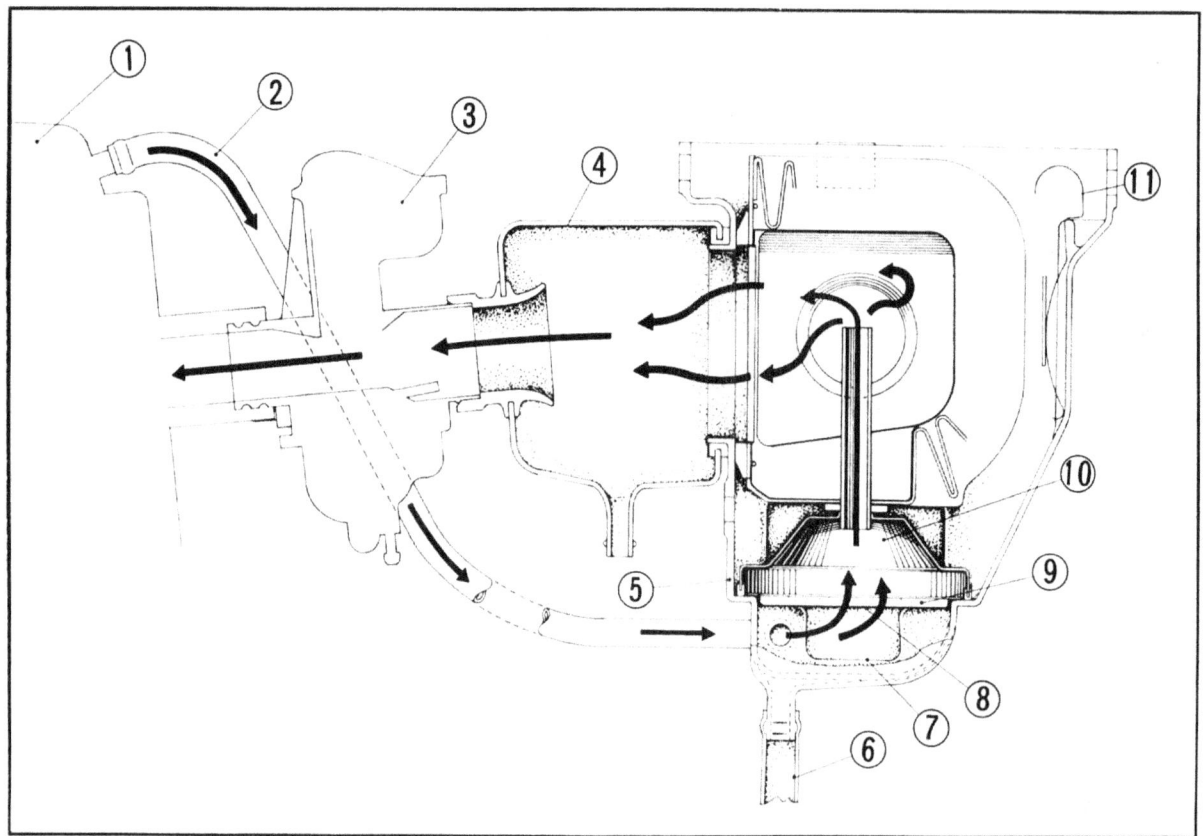

Fig. 323
① Cylinder head
② Breather tube
③ Carburetor
④ Air cleaner chamber
⑤ Element seal case
⑥ Drain tube
⑦ Seal plate
⑧ Punching metal
⑨ Element B
⑩ Element cover
⑪ Air cleaner element spring

1. BLOW-BY GAS SCAVENGING DEVICE

The blow-by gas scavenging device was added to minimize pollution. The description given here refers to Fig. 323 above.

The blow-by gas within the cylinder head is conducted into the element seal case through the breather tube. Gas is then conducted into the element B through the openings on both sides in the seal plate and punching metal, where oil is separated from the gas at each section. The gas enters the air cleaner element on the upper part of the seal case through the pipe within the element cover and is filtered again. The gas so filtered is drawn into the carburetor chamber and returns to the combustion chamber for burning through the carburetor. Now the gas is again burnt in the combustion chamber to minimize pollution by the exhaust gases.

Fig. 324

Fig. 325

• Blow-by gas

The exhaust gases contain carbon monoxide, hydrocarbon, hydrogen sulfide, nitrogen dioxide, selenium oxide, etc. which are poisonous ingredients contributing to pollution.

The exhaust gases consist of not only the remainder of burned mixture and combustion products, but also a compression leakage past the cylinder wall or from the crankcase. The latter is known as "blow-by gas", and accounts for 20 to 40% of the total hydrocarbon amount to be emitted in the air. Since blow-by gases have not been completely burned, they must be burned again by means of the blow-by gas scavenging device to minimize the amount of the gas to be emitted into the air.

2. STARTING MOTOR SAFETY UNIT

• Description

The starting motor safety unit operates in the way that the starting motor functions only when the transmition is in neutral or while the clutch lever is being squeezed in any gear position, assuring rider safety and preventing engine and transmission damage.

• Circuits and operations

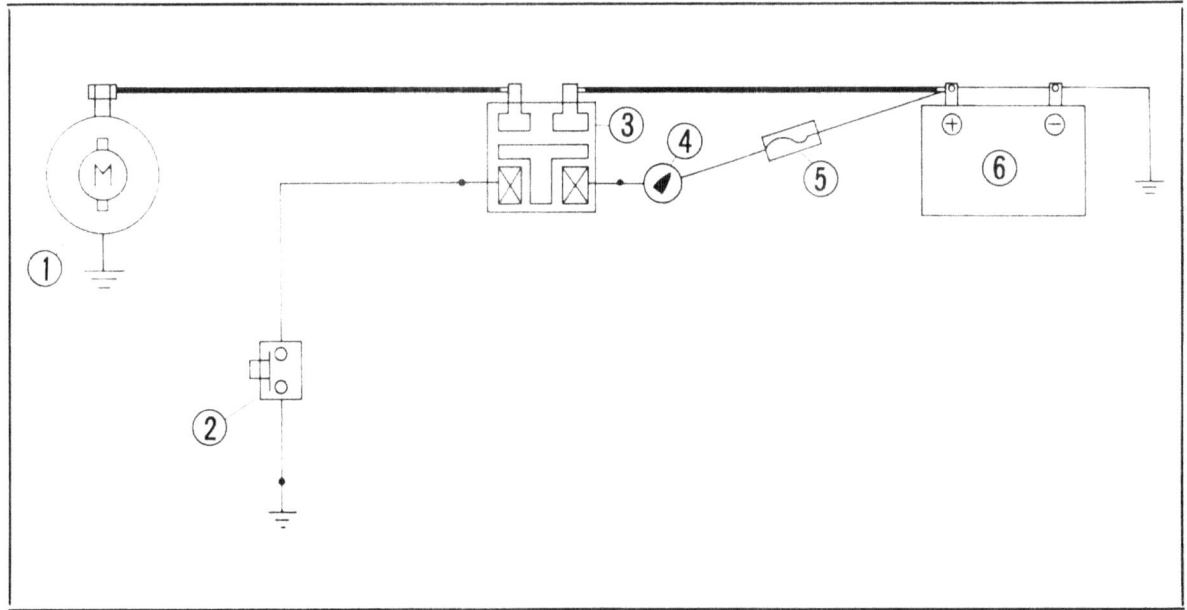

Fig. 326 Circuit of models without safety unit
① Starting motor   ④ Main switch
② Starter button switch   ⑤ Fuse
③ Starter magnetic switch   ⑥ Battery

When the engine switch is turned on, electricity is usually applied to the starter magnetic switch coil. If the starter button switch is then turned on, the starter magnetic switch will operate to cause the starting motor to turn. In other words, the motorcycle begines to move when the main switch and starter button switch are turned on with the transmission in gear.

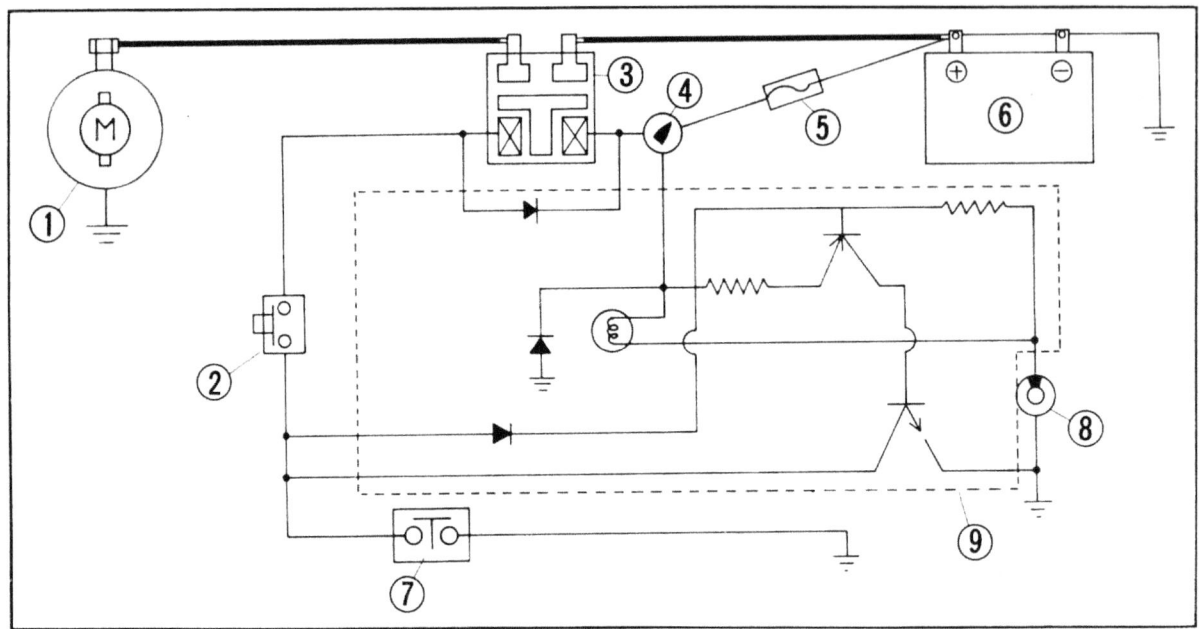

Fig. 327 Circuit of model (CB 550) with safety unit
① Starting motor
② Starter button Switch
③ Starter magnetic switch
④ Main switch
⑤ Fuse
⑥ Battery
⑦ Clutch lever switch
⑧ Neutral switch
⑨ Safety unit

The ground side of the starter button switch is connected to the body through the clutch lever switch and neutral switch. When the clutch lever switch or the neutral switch is turned on, the starter magnetic switch will operate, causing the starting motor to turn.
(1) Clutch lever switch
   The clutch lever switch is designed to be turned on when the clutch lever is squeezed to cause the clutch to be disengaged only. (This switch has the same construction and function as those of the front stop switch.)

3. FRONT SUSPENSION

The front fork used on the CB 550 is a free valve type which is used in a telescopic type shock absorber.
The damping force can be adjusted by changing its stroke to meet different road conditions, and it will always provide a comfortable ride even under severe driving conditions. The CB 500 is incorporated with a rod type shock absorber which is also used in a Telescopic type.

8. NEW FEATURES OF THE CB550

Operation

- When the wheel meets holes or bumps in the road, it moves up and down. This up-and-down movement of the wheel is transmitted to the bottom leg.

  Since the bottom leg is integrated with a pipe, the pipe also moves up and down. With either action, two springs on the pipe flux and rebound, absorbing the road shocks.

  In this case, oil in the chamber Ⓑ pushes the free valve up and flows into the space Ⓐ freely.

  At the same time, oil in the chamber Ⓑ also flows through orifices in the lower end of the spring under the seat into the space Ⓒ by the amount the pipe moves up.

- Extension

  As the wheel passes the bump or hole, it moves down. To eliminate excessive up-and-down motion of the spring and wheel, there will be a restraint on the spring and wheel action.

  In operation, as the wheel moves down, the free valve is closed, introducing high pressure in the space Ⓐ. This high pressure then forces the oil out and into the space Ⓒ through the orifices in the spring under the seat.

  Since the oil encounters a restraint as it passes through the orifices, excessive wheel and spring movement, as well as spring oscillation, are prevented.

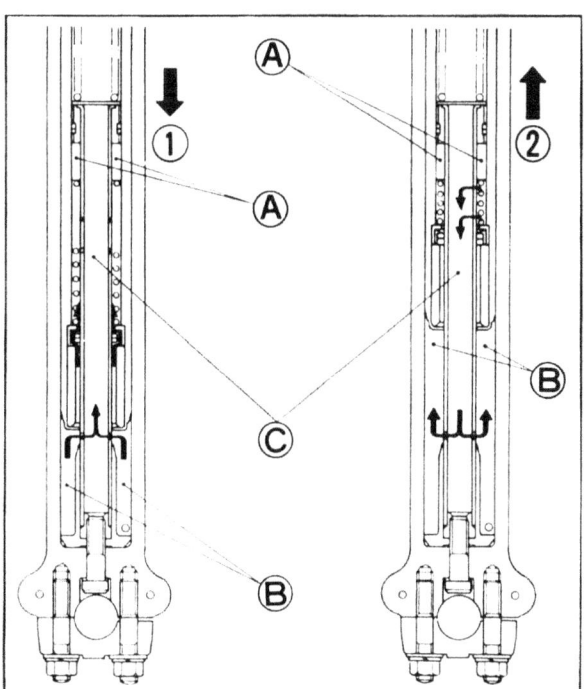

Fig. 328 ① Compression ② Extension

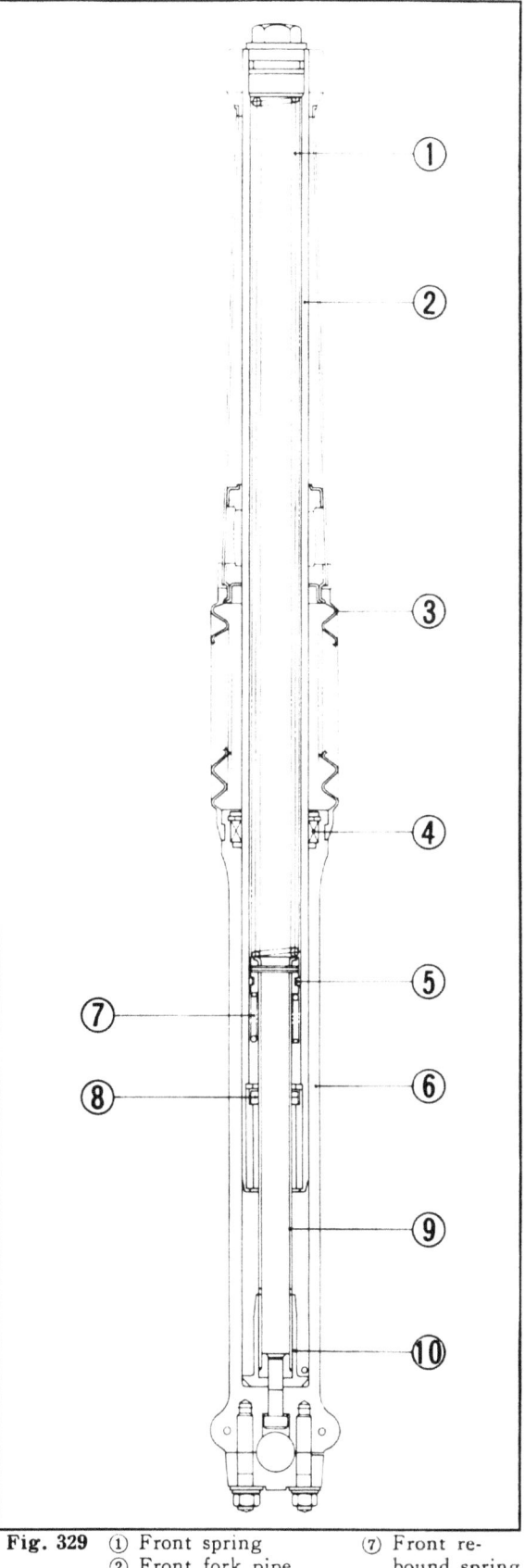

Fig. 329
① Front spring
② Front fork pipe
③ Front fork dust seal
④ Oil seal
⑤ Piston ring
⑥ Front fork bottom leg
⑦ Front rebound spring
⑧ Free valve
⑨ Bottom pipe
⑩ Oil lock piece

4. BRAKE LINING WEAR INDICATOR

Discription

The brake lining wear indicator is provided to check the brake lining wear condition visually from outside. As shown in the figure below, the indicator plate is attached to the brake cam. As the brake lining wears, the brake cam moves excessively. Such cam movement is checked by the arrow on the periphery of the indicator. The brake panel cam boss is also provided with the "wear limit" mark to make it possible to check the service limit (replacement time) of the lining easily with the brake panel installed.

Descriptive illustration

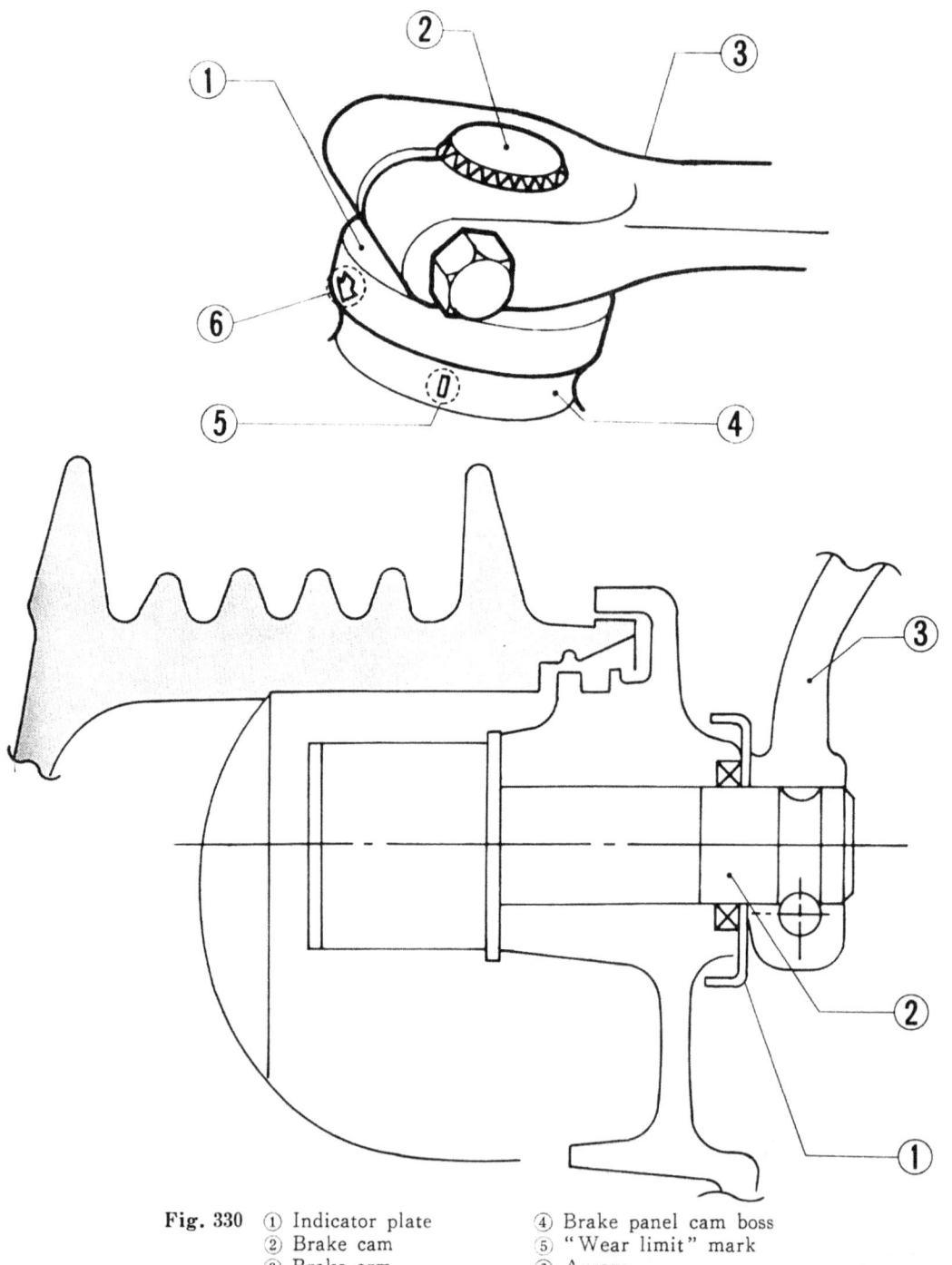

Fig. 330 ① Indicator plate   ④ Brake panel cam boss
② Brake cam   ⑤ "Wear limit" mark
③ Brake arm   ⑥ Arrow

9. COMPARISON OF CB550 TO CB500

(Engine)

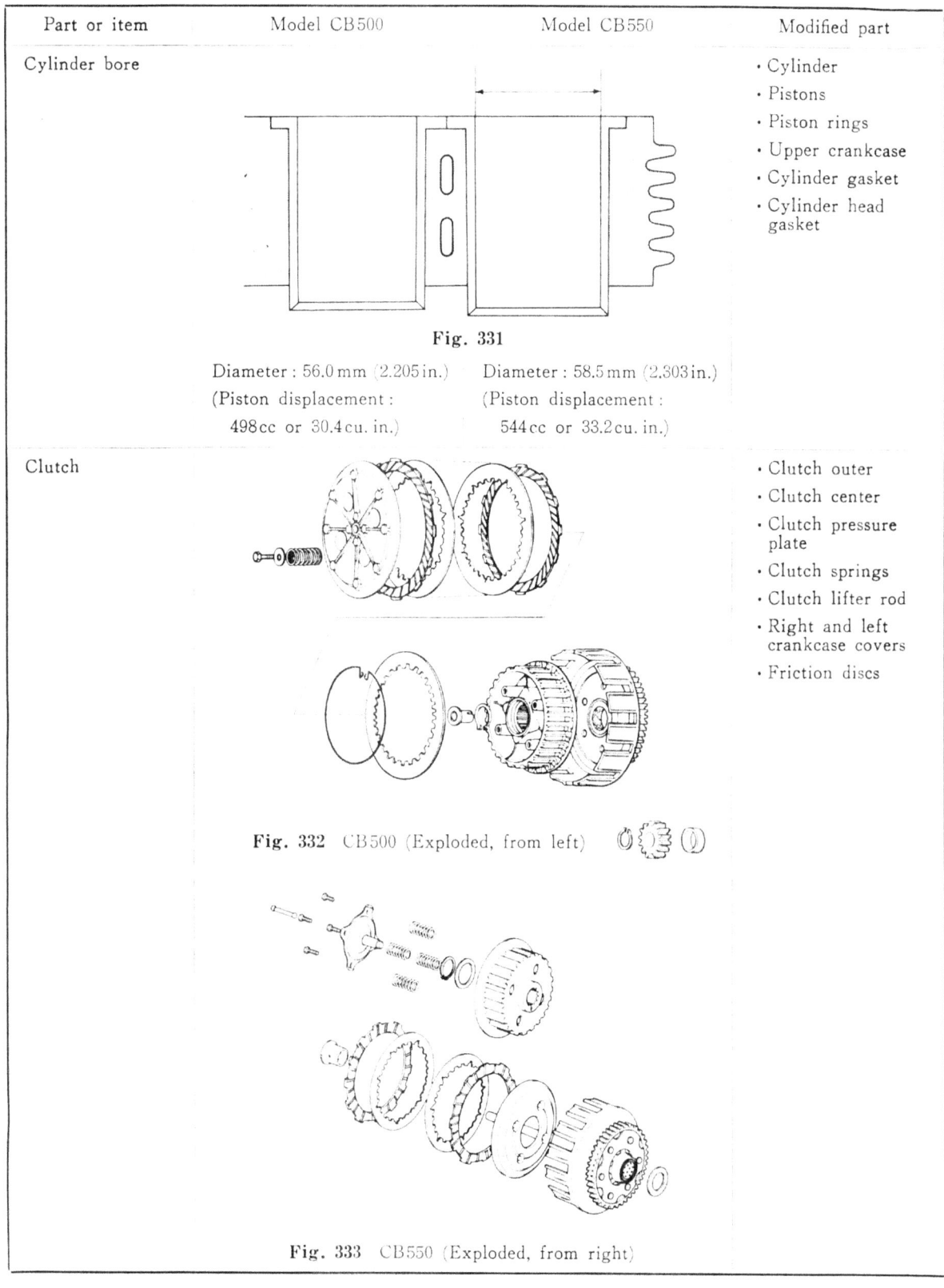

Part or item	Model CB500	Model CB550	Modified part
Cylinder bore	Diameter: 56.0 mm (2.205 in.) (Piston displacement: 498cc or 30.4 cu. in.)	Diameter: 58.5 mm (2.303 in.) (Piston displacement: 544cc or 33.2 cu. in.)	· Cylinder · Pistons · Piston rings · Upper crankcase · Cylinder gasket · Cylinder head gasket
Clutch	Fig. 332 CB500 (Exploded, from left)	Fig. 333 CB550 (Exploded, from right)	· Clutch outer · Clutch center · Clutch pressure plate · Clutch springs · Clutch lifter rod · Right and left crankcase covers · Friction discs

Fig. 331

Clutch operation

Model CB 500	Model CB 550
Refer to Fig. 334 on page 115. The clutch connects and disconnects the engine from the transmission. As shown in Fig. 334, the clutch plates ④ ("drive plates"), which are capable of sliding axially on the clutch center ⑤, are "sandwiched" between the friction discs ③ ("driven discs") engaged in the clutch outer ②. In normal engaged condition of the clutch, the pressure plate ⑦, upon which the clutch springs ⑥ force is acting, presses the stacks of the discs and plates against the clutch outer. Under this condition, the engine power is transmitted through the primary drive gear ①, clutch outer, friction discs, plates and clutch center to the transmission main shaft. As the clutch lever is squeezed to disengage the clutch, the clutch lifter ⑪, connected to the clutch cable, is rotated and forced out. This clutch ball force is transmitted through the #10 steel ball ⑩, clutch lifter rod ⑨ and clutch lifter joints piece ⑧ to the clutch pressure plate to compress the clutch springs producing clearance between the friction discs and plates. Now the face pressure on the friction surfaces of the power transmitting parts is reduced to zero, resulting in clutch disengagement.	Refer to Fig. 335 on page 115. As shown in the figure, the clutch plates ⑨, which are capable of sliding axially on the clutch center ⑥, are sandwiched between the friction discs ⑧ engaged in the clutch outer ⑦. In normal engaged condition of the clutch, the pressure plate ⑩, upon which the clutch springs ⑤ force is acting, presses the stacks of the discs and plates against the clutch outer. Under this condition, the engine power is transmitted through the primary drive gear, clutch outer, friction discs, plates and clutch center to the transmission mainshaft. As the clutch lever is squeezed to disengage the clutch, the clutch arm connected to the clutch cable operates and the clutch lifter cam ① rotates to cause the clutch adjusting lever ② to be forced against the clutch lifter rod ③. This force is transmitted through the clutch lifter plate ④ to the clutch center, producing clearance between the friction discs and plates. Now the face pressure on the friction surfaces of the power transmitting parts is reduced to zero, resulting in clutch disengagement.

Construction of CB500 clutch system

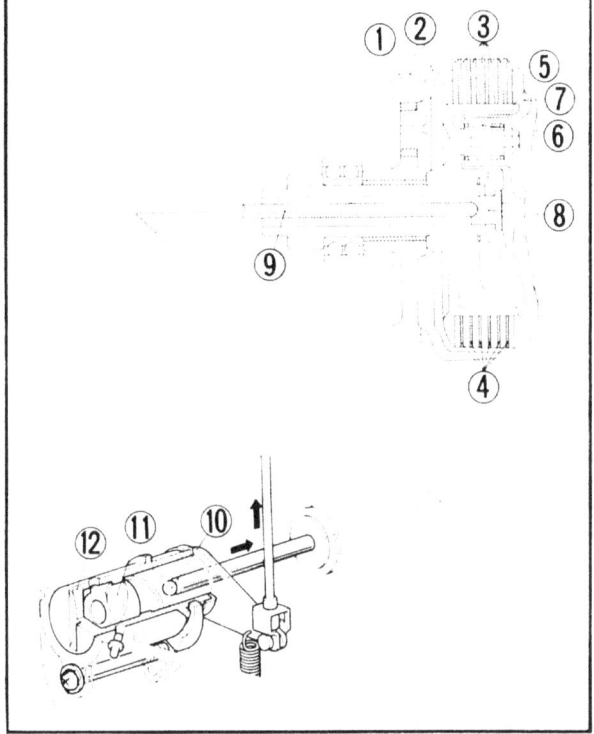

Fig. 334

Construction of CB550 clutch system

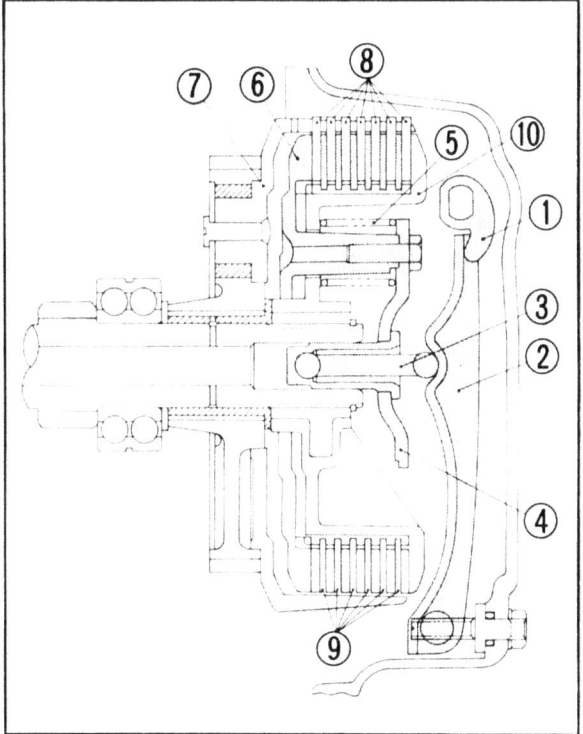

Fig. 335

9. COMPARISON OF CB550 TO CB500

Part or item	Model CB500	Model CB550	Modified part
Countershaft lubrication	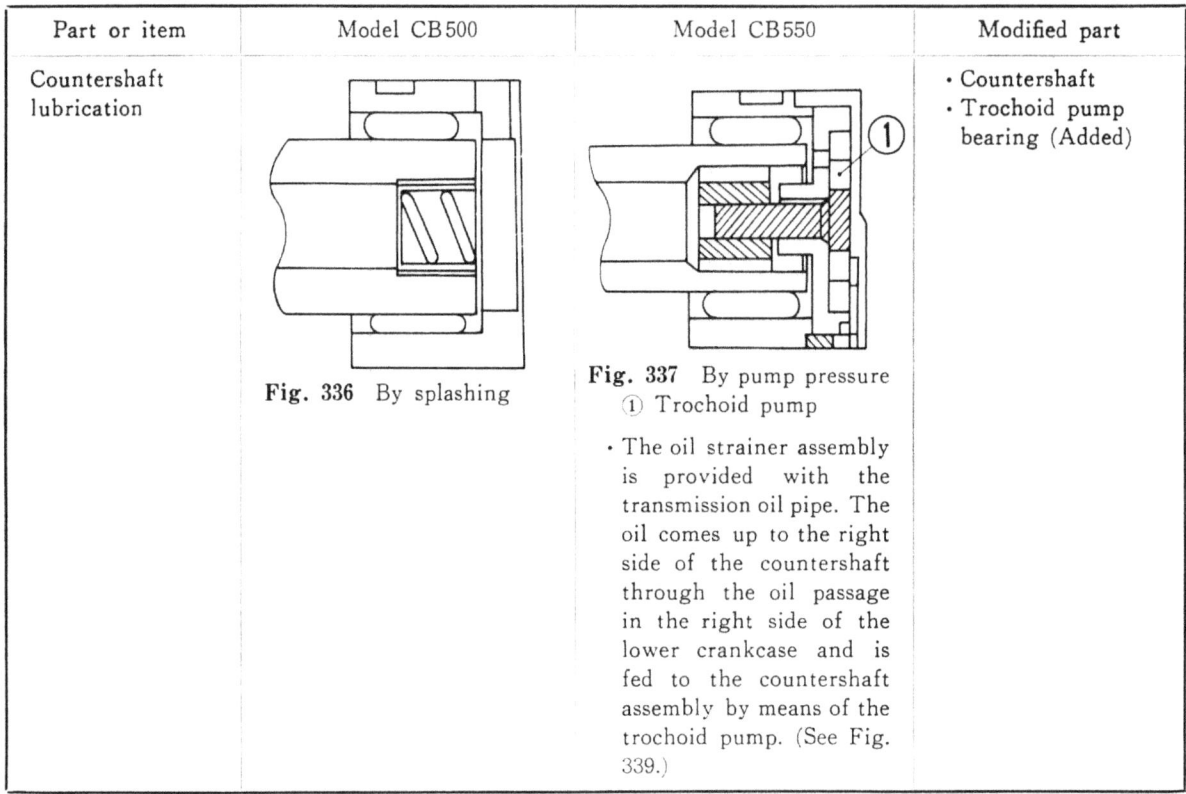 Fig. 336 By splashing	Fig. 337 By pump pressure ① Trochoid pump • The oil strainer assembly is provided with the transmission oil pipe. The oil comes up to the right side of the countershaft through the oil passage in the right side of the lower crankcase and is fed to the countershaft assembly by means of the trochoid pump. (See Fig. 339.)	• Countershaft • Trochoid pump bearing (Added)

Fig. 338 ① Trochoid pump
② Countershaft assembly

9. COMPARISON OF CB550 TO CB500

117

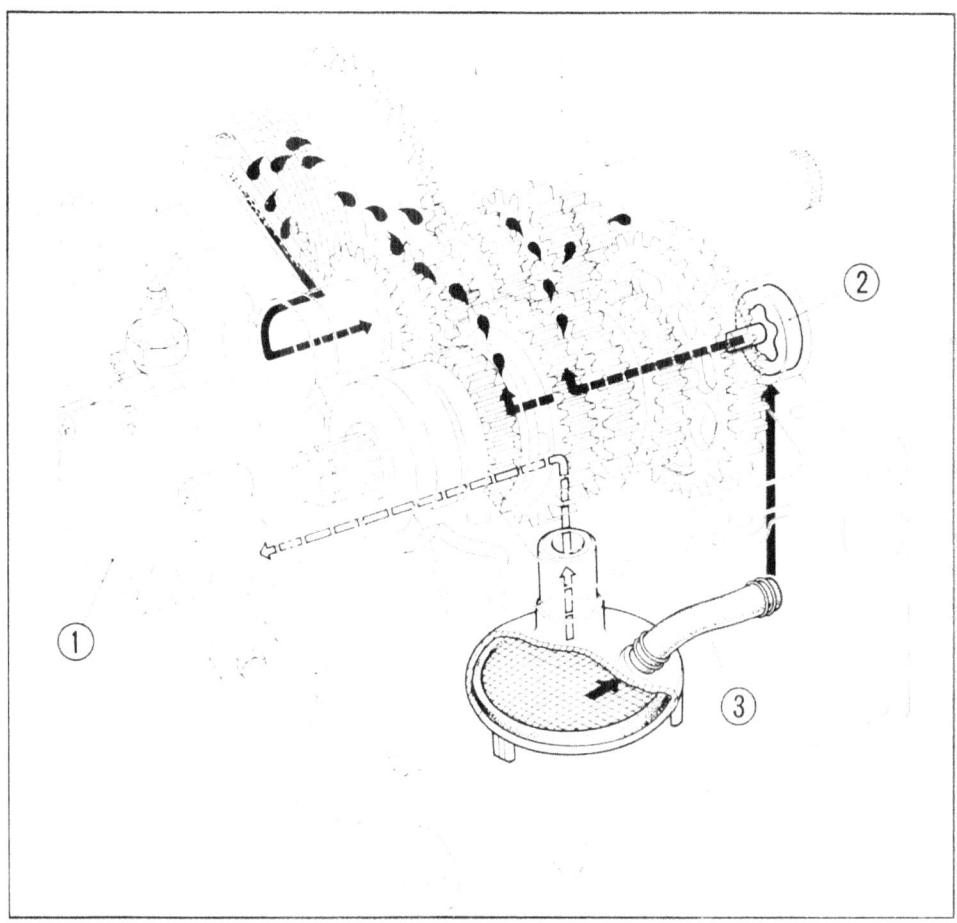

Fig. 339　① Oil pump
　　　　　② Trochoid pump
　　　　　③ Transmission oil pipe

➡　Oil to countershaft
▫▫▫▷　Oil to cylinder head and crankshaft through oil pump

118   9. COMPARISON OF CB550 TO CB500

Unit: mm

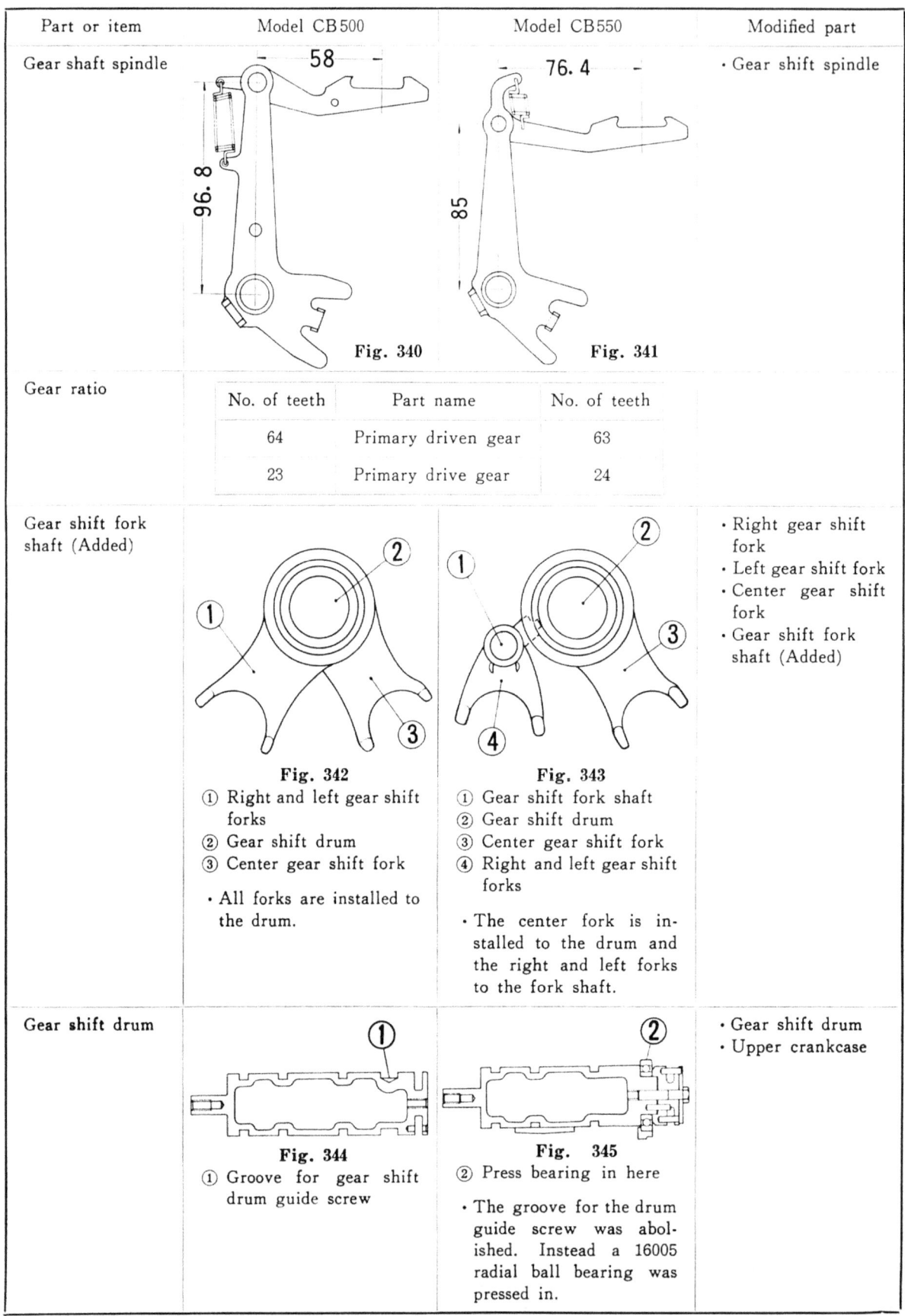

Part or item	Model CB500	Model CB550	Modified part
Gear shaft spindle	58 / 96.8 Fig. 340	76.4 / 85 Fig. 341	• Gear shift spindle
Gear ratio	No. of teeth: 64 / 23	Part name: Primary driven gear / Primary drive gear — No. of teeth: 63 / 24	
Gear shift fork shaft (Added)	Fig. 342 ① Right and left gear shift forks ② Gear shift drum ③ Center gear shift fork • All forks are installed to the drum.	Fig. 343 ① Gear shift fork shaft ② Gear shift drum ③ Center gear shift fork ④ Right and left gear shift forks • The center fork is installed to the drum and the right and left forks to the fork shaft.	• Right gear shift fork • Left gear shift fork • Center gear shift fork • Gear shift fork shaft (Added)
Gear shift drum	Fig. 344 ① Groove for gear shift drum guide screw	Fig. 345 ② Press bearing in here • The groove for the drum guide screw was abolished. Instead a 16005 radial ball bearing was pressed in.	• Gear shift drum • Upper crankcase

9. COMPARISON OF CB550 TO CB500

(Frame)

Part or item	Model CB500	Model CB550	Modified part
Air cleaner	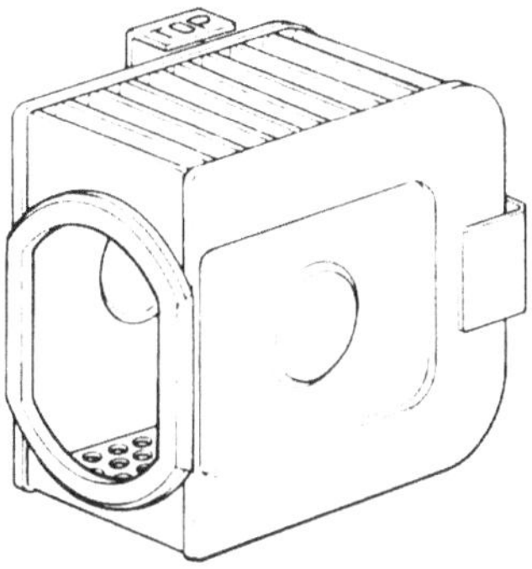 Fig. 346 Air cleaner element seal case	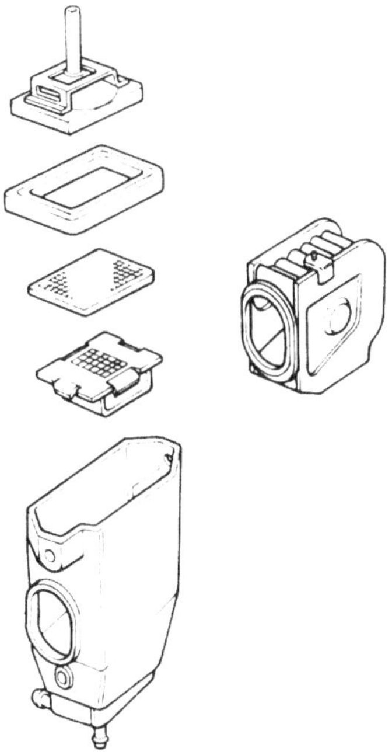 Fig. 347 · In connection with employment of the blow-by gas scavenging device, the air cleaner shape was changed.	· Air cleaner chamber · Element cover · Element cover seal · Element (wet type) · Plate seal · Air cleaner element (dry type)
Final driven sprocket	Number of teeth: 34	Number of teeth: 37	
Turn signal/ horn switch	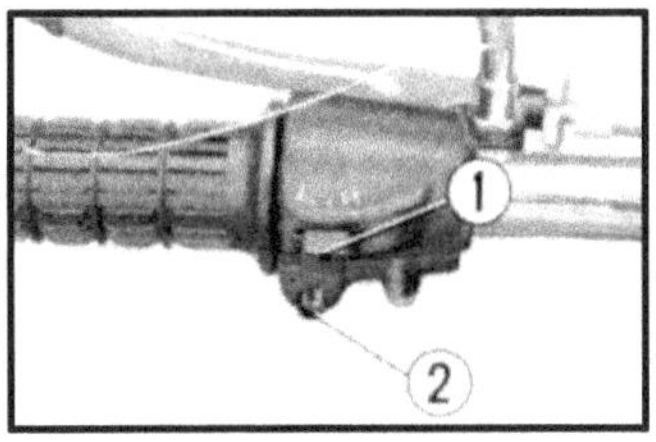 Fig. 348 ① Turn signal switch ② Horn switch	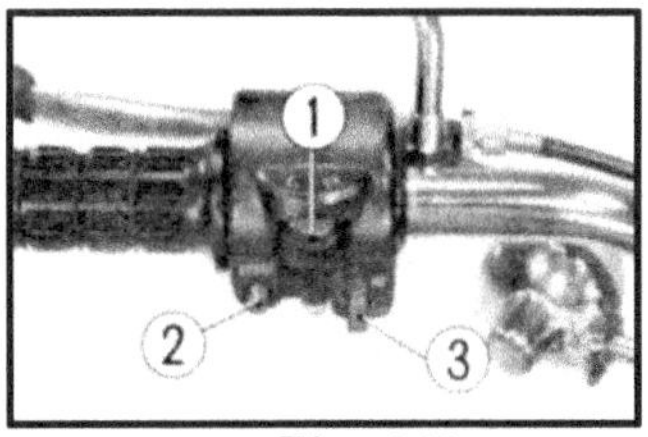 Fig. 349 ① Turn signal switch ② Horn switch ③ Dimmer switch	· The turn signal/ horn switch was changed to the turn signal/horn/ dimmer switch (common with that of CB750).
Starter/ headlight/ ignition switch	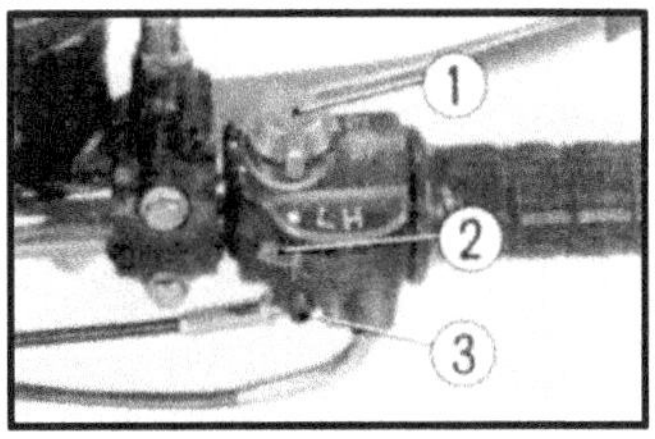 Fig. 350 ① Ignition switch ② Headlight switch ③ Starter switch	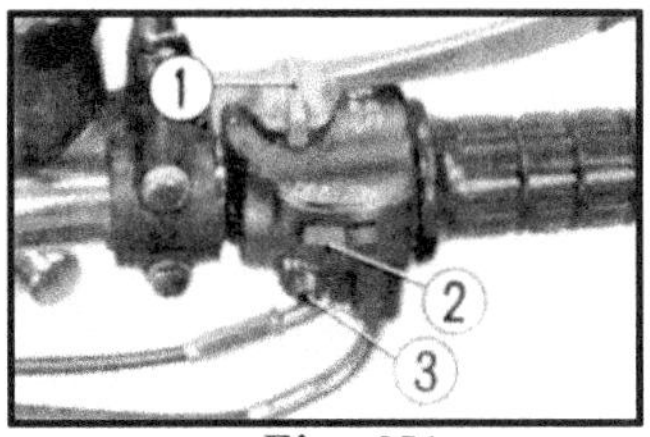 Fig. 351 ① Ignition switch ② Headlight switch ③ Starter switch	· The starter/head-light/ignition switch shape was changed.

MEMO

10. ENGINE

1. CLUTCH

A. Disassembly

1. Drain the engine oil. (See page 20 of the CB500 Shop Manual issued separately).
2. Remove the kick starter pedal.
3. Remove the ten 6mm screws and the right crankcase cover.

Fig. 352 1 Right crankcase cover

4. Remove the clutch lifter rod.
5. Remove the four clutch pressure plate mounting bolts.
6. Remove the clutch lifter plate.

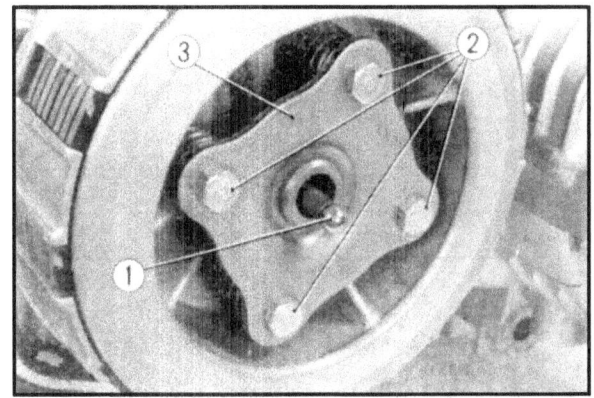

7. Remove the 25mm snap ring and shim and remove the clutch assembly from the mainshaft.
8. Remove the clutch outer and inner at the same time.

(Refer to page 40, Fig. 110)

Fig. 353 ① Clutch lifter rod
2 Mounting bolts
3 Lifter plate

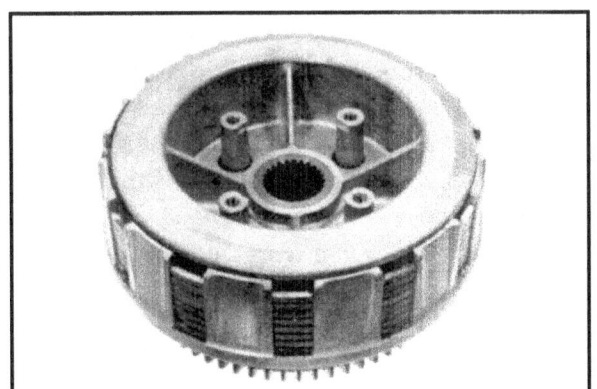

Fig. 354 ① Clutch assembly

Fig. 355 1 25mm snap ring
2 Shim
3 Main shaft

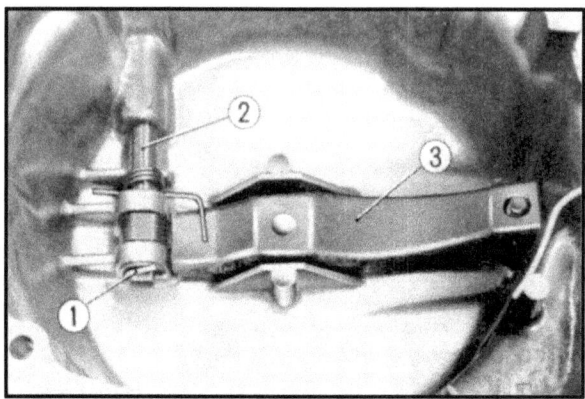

Fig. 356 ① Cotter pin ③ Clutch adjusting lever
② Clutch lever

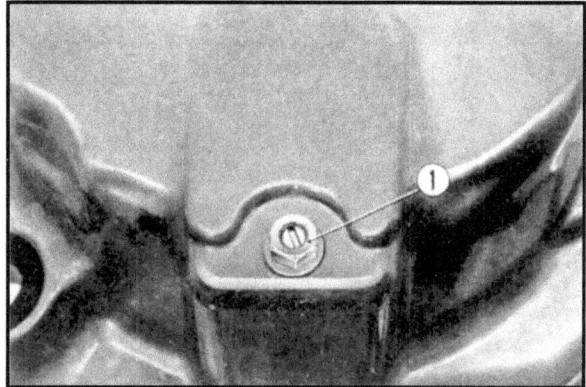

Fig. 357 ① 6 mm nut

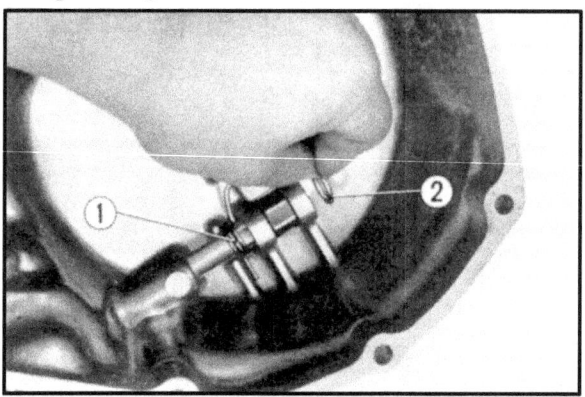

Fig. 358 ① Clutch lever spring ② 10 mm washer

Fig. 359 ① Clutch center
② Friction discs and plates
③ Clutch outer
④ 25 mm collar

9. Remove the cotter pin from inside the right crankcase cover and pull the clutch lever out.

10. Remove the 6 mm nut and the clutch adjusting lever.

B. Inspection

See page 41 of the CB500 Shop Manual issued separately.
Measurement of friction disc thickness.
Using a vernier caliper, measure the thickness of each friction disc. Replace a disc whose thickness is below the service limit.

Unit: mm (in.)

Assembly standard	Service limit
2.7 (0.1063)	2.4 (0.0945)

C. Assembly

1. Install and tighten the 6 mm nut attaching the clutch adjusting lever.
2. As shown in Fig. 358, install the clutch lever spring and 10 mm washer on the clutch lever. Insert the cotter pin and spread its ends.
3. Install the 25 mm collar in the clutch outer.
4. Install the seven friction discs and six plates alternatively to the clutch center and to the clutch outer. Install to the mainshaft.

5. Attach a dial gauge to the end face of the clutch assembly to check for excessive looseness. If it exceeds 0.1 mm (0.0039 in.), install a washer or washers behind the snap ring. The washers are available in three thicknesses: 0.1 mm (0.0039 in.), 0.3 mm (0.0118 in.) and 0.5 mm (0.0197 in.).
6. Install the four clutch springs. Install the lifter plate and tighten the four 6 mm bolts in a criss-cross pattern.
7. Insert the lifter rod.
8. Install the right crankcase cover and kick starter pedal.

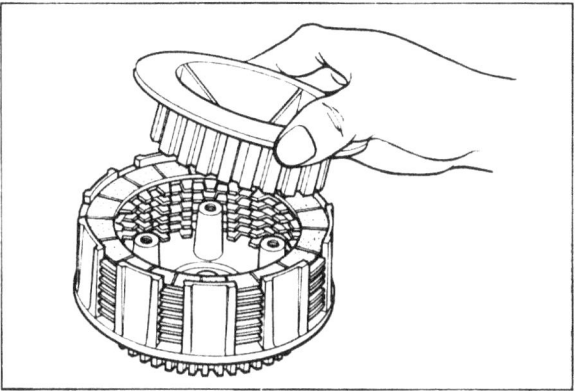

Fig. 360

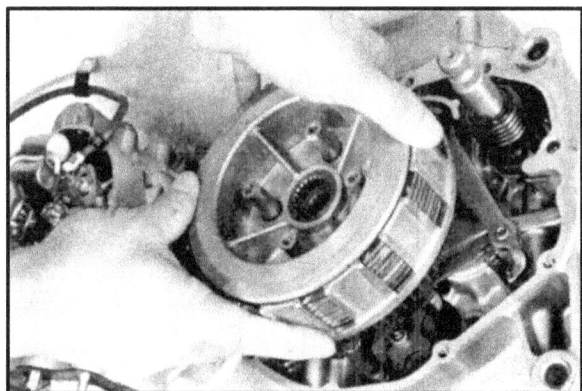

Fig. 361

2. GEARSHIFT MECHANISM

A. Disassembly

1. Remove the clutch. (See page 121.)
2. Remove the gear change pedal.
3. While holding the gearshift arm down as shown in Fig. 262, pull the gearshift spindle out.

Fig. 262 ① Gearshift arm

Fig. 363 ① Shift drum neutral stop bolt
② Shift drum stop bolt
③ Shift drum stop   ④ Neutral stop

4. Remove the shift drum stop bolt, the neutral stop bolt, the shift drum stop and the neutral stop.

5. Remove the 6 mm bolt and the bearing set plate on the primary shaft side.
6. Remove the two 6 mm bolts and the bearing set plate on the gearshift drum side.

Fig. 364 ① Bearing set plate on primary shaft side
② Bearing set plate on shift drum side

7. Remove the 6 mm bolt, the drum stop cam plate and the drum gearshift center.

Fig. 365 ① 6 mm bolt   ③ Drum gearshift center
② Stop cam plate

10. ENGINE

8. Separate the crankcase into the upper and lower parts and remove the transmission gears. (See page 43 of the CB500 Shop Manual issued separately.)
9. Remove the neutral stop switch from the gearshift drum.

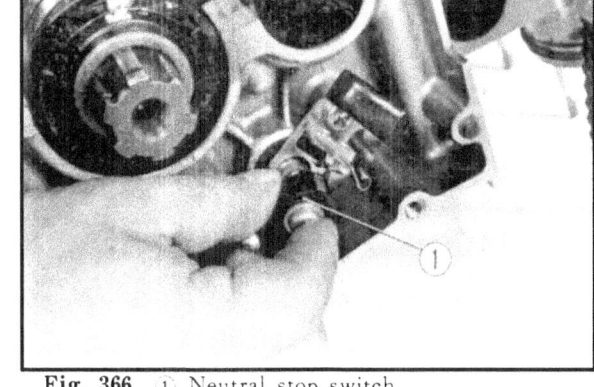

Fig. 366 ① Neutral stop switch

10. Remove the guide pin clip and guide pin and pull the gearshift drum from the upper crankcase.

B. Inspection

See page 44 of the CB500 Shop Manual issued separately.

Fig. 367 ① Guide pin clip   ② Guide pin

C. Assembly

1. Position the center gearshift fork on the drum as shown in Fig. 368.
2. Insert the guide pin into the center gearshift fork and secure with the guide pin clip.

NOTE:
Install the guide pin clip with it facing correctly. (See Fig. 367.)

Fig. 368 ① Center gearshift fork   ② Drum

3. Put the right and left gearshift forks in the upper crankcase and insert the gearshift fork shaft as shown in Fig. 369.

Fig. 369 ① Right gearshift fork
② Left gearshift fork
③ Gearshift fork shaft

Fig. 370

4. Make sure that the gearshift forks are installed correctly and securely.
5. Instal the neutral stop switch to the gearshift drum by fitting the lug into the groove in the drum and secure with the 6 mm screw.

Fig. 371

6. Install the transmission gears in the upper crankcase and put the upper and lower crankcases together. Install the primary shaft and tighten the crankcases securely.
7. Install the bearing set plate on the drum side and secure with the two 6 mm bolts.

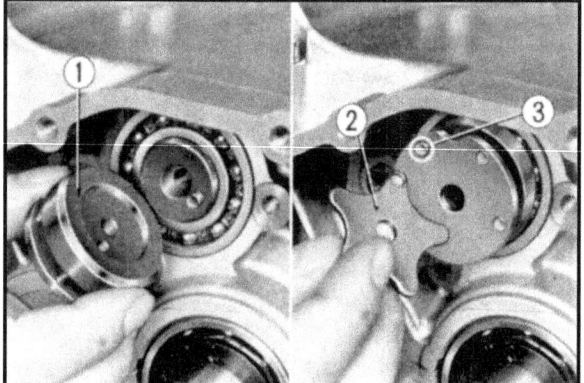

Fig. 372
1. Drum gearshift center
2. Drum stop cam plate
3. Lug

8. Install the drum gearshift center.
NOTE:
Properly fit the lug of the drum into the hole in the drum gearshift center.
9. Install the drum stop cam plate.
NOTE:
Properly fit the gearshift drum pin into the hole in the drum stop cam plate.

Fig. 373 1. Bearing set plate on primary shaft side

10. Instal the bearing set plate on the drum side.
11. As shown in Fig. 373, install the gearshift drum stop spring to the drum stop and the neutral stop and tighten the drum stop bolt, and neutral stop bolt securely. Also tighten the bearing set plate on the primary shaft side as shown in Fig. 373.

10. ENGINE

12. Rotate the gearshift drum and check each component for smooth movement.
13. Install the gearshift arm and check to see if it moves smoothly and equally in both directions.
14. Install the clutch. (See page 121.)

Fig. 374

11. TROUBLE SHOOTING

ENGINE

Trouble	Probable Causes	Remedies
Engine does not start	1. Excessive piston ring or cylinder wear	Replace
	2. Seized valve in valve guide	Replace
	3. Seized piston	Replace
	4. Faulty valve timing	Adjust
	5. Low or lack of compression pressure · Pressure leak	Lap the valve to obtain good valve seating or replace
	5. Blown out cylinder head gasket	Replace
	6. Warped gasketing surface of the cylinder and cylinder head	Repair or replace
Poor engine idling	**Valve Mechanism**	
	1. Incorrect tappet clearance	Adjust to standard value
	2. Low or lack of compression pressure	Repair
	3. Excessive valve guide clearance	Replace valve and guide
Loss of power	1. Valve sticking open	Replace
	2. Incorrect seating of valve	Lap valve
	3. Weak or broken valve spring	Replace
	4. Faulty valve timing	Check valve timing and adjust if necessary
	5. Blown out cylinder head gasket	Replace
	6. Excessive cylinder and piston wear	Replace
	7. Worn, weak or broken piston ring	Replace
	8. Loose spark plug	Retighten
Overheating	1. Heavy carbon deposit on combustion chamber and piston head	Remove carbon
	2. Lean fuel mixture	Adjust the carburetor
	3. Retarded ignition timing	Adjust ignition timing
	4. Low oil level, poor quality	Add good grade oil
	5. Extended operation in low gear	
Backfire	1. Incorrect seating of intake valve	Check the valve seating
	2. Faulty valve timing	Adjust
	3. Incorrect ignition timing	Adjust
	4. Excessive spark plug gap	Adjust the gap to 0.024~0.028 in (0.6~0.7 mm)
	5. Improper fuel	Replace
White exhaust smoke	1. Excessive cylinder and piston wear	Replace the piston
	2. Overfilled engine oil	Adjust the oil level
	3. Excessively high oil pressure	Check the breather
	4. Poor quality oil	Replace with good quality oil
Black exhaust smoke	Rich fuel mixture	Adjust the carburetor

11. TROUBLE SHOOTING

Trouble	Probable Causes	Remedies
Difficult gear shifting	1. Improper clutch disengagement	Adjust the clutch
	2. Damaged gear or foreign object lodged in the gear	Replace the defective parts
	3. Gear shift fork inoperative	Repair or replace
	4. Incorrect operation of the gear shift drum stopper and change pedal	Repair or replace
	5. Mainshaft and countershaft out of alignment	Repair or replace
	6. High oil viscosity	Change the oil
Excessive high gear noise	1. Excessive gear backlash	Repair or replace
	2. Worn main and countershaft bearing	Repair or replace
Gear slip out	1. Worn fingers on gear shift fork	Replace
	2. Worn gear dog hole	Replace
	3. Worn spline	Replace
Clutch slippage	1. No clutch lever play	Adjust the clutch lever
	2. Weak or no uniform clutch pressure plate spring	Replace the weak spring
	3. Worn or glazed friction disc	Replace
Poor clutch engagement	1. Excessive clutch lever play	Adjust clutch lever play
	2. Warped friction disc	Replace
	3. Warped pressure plate	Replace
	4. Bent main shaft	Replace
Pedal does not return	1. Faulty return spring	Replace
	2. Unhook return spring	Hook return spring
Kick starter gear does not rotate	1. Excessive kick starter pawl wear	Replace
Engine does not start	**Carburetor**	
	1. Choke fully open	Close choke
	2. Carburetor air screw improperly set	Adjust air screw
	3. Air leaking into the cylinder head	Retighten carburetor connecting tube
	4. Clogged carburetor slow jet	Check, clean and retighten
	5. Clogged fuel valve or piping	Disassemble and clean
	6. Clogged vent hole in the fuel tank cap	Disassemble and clean
	7. No fuel in the tank	Fill tank with gasoline
Poor engine idling	**Carburetor**	
	1. Clogged or loose carburetor slow jet	Check, clean and retighten
	2. Improper float level	Adjust
	3. Incorrect air screw adjustment	Adjust
	4. Carburetor linkage malfunction	Adjust
	5. Air leaks	Tighten all air passage connections
Improper running of engine	**Carburetor**	
	1. Jet size too small	Replace with larger size jet
	2. Improper float level	Adjust
	3. Clogged carburetor main jet	Clean and retighten
	4. Carburetor linkage malfunction	Adjust
	5. Air leaks	Tighten all air passage connections

CHASSIS

Trouble	Probable Causes	Remedies
Heavy steering	1. Steering stem excessively tightened	Loosen the steering stem nut
	2. Damaged steering stem steel balls	Replace
	3. Bent steering	Replace
	4. Low front tire pressure	Add air to the specified pressure of 1.8 kg/cm² (25.6 psi)
Front and rear wheel wobble	1. Loose steering stem mounting bolt	Retorque
	2. Worn front and rear wheel bearings	Replace bearing
	3. Front or rear wheel runout or distorted	Repair or replace
	4. Loose spoke	Retorque
	5. Defective tire	Replace
Soft suspension	1. Loss of spring tension	Replace
	2. Excessive load	
Hard suspension	1. Ineffective front fork damper	Repair
	2. Ineffective rear damper	Replace
Suspension noise	1. Front case or rear damper rubbing	Inspect cushion spring and case
	2. Interference between cushion case and spring	Repair or replace
	3. Faulty fork stopper rubber	Replace
	4. Insufficient front fork oil	Add damper oil
Defective brake	1. Front brake fluid	
	· Insufficient brake fluid	Add brake fluid
	· Air in the brake system	Bleed brake system
	· Worn brake pad	Replace pad
	· Worn piston	Replace piston
	· Worn or distorted front brake disc	Replace disc
	· Brake lever out of adjustment	Readjust
	2. Rear brake	
	· Worn brake lining	Replace
	· Worn brake shoe or poor contacts	Replace
	· Worn brake cam	Replace
	· Wet brake from water or oil	Clean
	· Worn brake shaft	Replace
	· Brake pedal out of adjustment	Readjust

11. TROUBLE SHOOTING

ELECTRICAL

Troubles	Probable causes	Remedies
Engine does not start	1. Battery	
	· Discharged	Recharge or replace
	· Poor battery terminals contact	Repair
	2. Main switch	
	· Open or shorted circuit, disconnected connections	Repair
	· Poor contact between main switch wire and wire harness	Repair
	3. Ignition coil	
	· Improperly insulated high tension coil	Replace
	· Open or shorted circuit in ignition coil	Replace
	4. Contact breaker	
	· Open circuit in the primary coil	Repair
	· Dirty ground point with oil or dust	Clean
	· Point gap out of adjustment	Readjust
	· Improperly charged condenser	Replace
Starting motor does not operate	1. Defective battery	Charge or replace
	2. Poor magnetic switch contact	Repair or replace
	3. Poor starting motor carbon brush contact	Repair or replace
Horn inoperative, poor sound or too weak sound	1. Horn	
	· Cracked diaphragm	Replace
	2. Horn button	
	· Poor grounding	Repair
	3. Wiring	
	· Poor contact	Repair
	4. Adjusting screw	
	· Out of adjustment	Readjust
Tail light and head light inoperative	1. Fuse	
	· Blown fuse or burnt bulb filament	Replace
	2. Bulb	
	· Burnt bulb filament	Readjust
	3. Switch	
	· Poor lighting switch contact	Readjust
	4. Wiring	
Stop light inoperative	1. Bulb	
	· Burnt or broken bulb filament	Replace
	2. Front and tail stop light switch	
	· Malfunction of switch	Readjust
	3. Wiring	
	· Poor contact of leads	Readjust
Winker lamp blinks too fast or too slow	1. Bulb	
	· Blinks unusually fast: improperly connected relay	Replace
	2. Wiring	
	· Blinks too fast: bulb with unsuitable wattage	Replace
	· Blinks too slow: burnt or broken bulb	Replace
	3. Defective relay	Replace

11. TROUBLE SHOOTING

Trouble	Probable causes	Remedies
Winker lamp inoperative	1. Winker lamp switch	
	• Poor winker relay contact	Replace
	• Open circuit in winker relay coil	Replace
	2. Bulb	
	• Bulb wattage is smaller than rated wattage	Replace
	3. Relay	
	• Poor winker relay contact	Replace
	• Improperly connected leads	Replace
No charging	1. Broken wire or shorted, loose connection	Repair or replace
	2. Faulty coil due to short or grounding	Replace
	3. Faulty or shorted silicon diode	Replace
	4. Broken or shorted lead wire at regulator	Repair or replace
	5. Regulator voltage at no load is too low	Readjust
Insufficient charging	1. Wiring	
	• Broken wire, intermittent shorting or loose connection	Repair, retighten
	2. Generator	
	• Shorting across layer in the field coil (resistance indicated in continuity test)	Replace
	• Shorting across layer in stator coil	Replace
	• Open circuit in one of the stator coil	Replace
	• Faulty or shorted silicon diode	Replace
	3. Regulator	
	• Voltage below specified value at no load	Readjust
	• Dirty or pitted points	Polish or replace
	• Coil or resistor internally shorted	Replace
	4. Battery	
	• Low electrolyte level	Add distilled water
	• Defective battery plates	Replace
Excessive charging	1. Wiring	
	P terminal circuit and F terminal circuit shorted resulting in split wound generator	Repair
	2. Battery	
	Internal short	Replace
	3. Regulator	
	• Excessive voltage at no load voltage	Repair
	• Improper grounding	Provide proper ground
	• Broken coil lead wire	Repair, replace
Unstable charging voltage	1. Wiring	
	• Bare wire shorting intermittently under vibration or broken wire making partial contact	Repair or replace
	2. Generator	
	• Layer short (intermittent shorting)	Repair or replace
	3. Generator	
	• Intermittent open circuit in the coil	Repair or replace
	• Improperly adjusted voltage	Readjust
	• Defective key switch	Replace
	• Dirty points	Clean

11. TROUBLE SHOOTING

Trouble	Probable causes	Remedies
Self discharge Battery discharges in addition to that caused by the connected load.	1. Dirty contact areas and case. 2. Contaminated electrolyte or electrolyte excessively concentrated.	1. Always keep the exterior clean. 2. Handle the replenishing electrolyte with care.
C. Large discharge rate Specific gravity gradually lowers and around 1.100 (S. G.), the winker and horn no longer function.	1. The fuse and the wiring are satisfactory, but loads such as winker and horn do not function. In this condition the motorcycle will operate but with long use, both $\oplus$ and $\ominus$ plates will react with sulfuric acid and form lead sulfide deposits, (sulfation) making it impossible to recharge.	1. When the specific gravity falls below 1,200 (20°C : 68°F), the battery should be recharged immediately. 2. When the battery frequently becomes discharged while operating at normal speed, check the generator for proper output. 3. If the battery discharges under normal charge output, it is an indication of overloading. Remove some of the excess load.
High charging rate The electrolyte level drops rapidly but the charge is always maintained at 100% and the condition appears satisfactory. (Specific gravity over 1.260)	1. The deposit will heavily accumulate at the bottom and will cause internal shorting and battery damage.	1. Check to assure proper charging rate
Specific gravity drop Electrolyte evaporates	1. Shorted. 2. Insufficient charging. 3. Distilled water overfilled. 4. Contaminated electrolyte.	1. Check specific gravity measurement. 2. If the addition of distilled water causes a drop in specific gravity, add sulfuric acid and adjust to proper value.
Sulfation The electrode plates are covered with a white layer or spots.	1. Charging rate is too small or too large. 2. The specific gravity or the mixture of the electrolyte is improper. 3. Battery left in a discharge condition for a long period. (left with the switch turned on) 4. Exposed to excessive vibration due to improper insulation. 5. Motorcycle stored during the cold season with the battery connected.	1. When motorcycle is in storage, the battery should be recharged once a month even though the motorcycle is not used. 2. Check the electrolyte periodically and always maintain the proper level. 3. In a lightly discharged condition, perform recharging and discharging several times by starting the engine.
Spark plug electrode coated with carbon deposit	1. Too rich a fuel mixture. 2. Excessive idle speed. 3. Poor quality gasoline. 4. Clogged air cleaner. 5. Use of cold spark plug.	Adjust carburetor. Adjust idle speed. Use good quality gasoline Service the air cleaner. Use proper heat range plug.
Spark plug electrode fouled with oil	1. Worn piston ring. 2. Worn piston and cylinder. 3. Excessive clearance between valve guide and valve stem.	Replace piston ring. Replace piston or cylinder. Replace valve guide or valve.
Spark plug electrode overheated or burnt	1. Use of hot spark plug. 2. Engine overheating. 3. Improper ignition timing 4. Loose spark plug or damaged spark plug hole thread. 5. Too lean a fuel mixture.	Use proper heat range plug. Readjust ignition timing. Retighten plug or replace cylinder head. Adjust carburetor.
Damage	Spark plug overtorqued.	Replace with a new spark plug.

12. MAINTENANCE SCHEDULE

This maintenance schedule is based upon average riding conditions. Machines subjected to severe use, or ridden in unusually dusty areas, require more frequent servicing.	INITIAL SERVICE PERIOD	REGULAR SERVICE PERIOD Perform at every indicated month or mileage interval, whichever occurs first.				
	500 miles 800 km	1 month 500 miles 800 km	3 months 1,500 miles 2,500 km	6 months 3,000 miles 5,000 km	12 months 6,000 miles 10,000 km	
ENGINE OIL—Change	●		○			
OIL FILTER ELEMENT—Replace	●			○		
OIL FILTER SCREEN—Clean					○	
SPARK PLUGS —Clean and adjust gap or replace if necessary.				○		
*CONTACT POINTS AND IGNITION TIMING —Clean, check, and adjust or replace if necessary.	●			○		
*VALVE TAPPET CLEARANCE —Check, and adjust if necessary.	●			○		
*CAM CHAIN TENSION—Adjust	●			○		
PAPER AIR FILTER ELEMENT AND POLYURETHAN FOAM ELEMENT—Clean	(Service more frequently if operated in dusty areas)			○		
PAPER AIR FILTER ELEMENT—Replace					○	
*CARBURETORS—Check, and adjust if necessary.	●			○		
THROTTLE OPERATION —Inspect cables. Check, and adjust free play.	●			○		
FUEL FILTER SCREEN—Clean				○		
FUEL LINES—Check				○		
*CLUTCH—Check operation, and adjust if necessary.	●			○		
DRIVE CHAIN —Check, lubricate, and adjust if necessary.	**●	○				
BRAKE FLUID LEVEL —Check, and add fluid if necessary.	●			○		
*BRAKE SHOES/PADS —Inspect, and replace if worn.				○		
BRAKE CONTROL LINKAGE —Check linkage, and adjust free play if necessary.	●			○		
*WHEEL RIMS AND SPOKES—Check. Tighten spokes and true wheels, if necessary.	●			○		
TIRES—Inspect and check air pressure.	●	○				
FRONT FORK OIL—Drain and refill.	***●				○	
FRONT AND REAR SUSPENSION —Check operation.	●			○		
REAR FORK BUSHING —Grease, check for excessive looseness.				○		
*STEERING HEAD BEARING—Adjust					○	
BATTERY—Check electrolyte level, and add water if necessary.	●		○			
LIGHTING EQUIPMENT —Check and adjust if necessary.	●	○				
ALL NUTS, BOLTS, AND OTHER FASTENERS —Check security and tighten if necessary.	●	○				

Items marked * should be serviced by an authorized Honda dealer, unless the owner has proper tools and is mechanically proficient. Other maintenance items are simple to perform and may be serviced by the owner.

** INITIAL SERVICE PERIOD   200 MILES
*** INITIAL SERVICE PERIOD 1,500 MILES

13. TECHNICAL DATA

A. Specifications of CB 500 (CB 500 K1, K2)

	Item	Metric	English
DIMENSION	Overall Length	2,105 mm (2,120 mm)	83.0 in. (83.5 in.)
	Overall Width	825 mm	32.5 in.
	Overall Height	1,115 mm	44.0 in.
	Wheel Base	1,405 mm	55.5 in.
	Seat Height	805 mm	31.7 in.
	Foot Peg Height	315 mm	12.4 in.
	Ground Clearance	165 mm	6.5 in.
	Dry Weight	183 kg	403.5 lb.
FRAME	Type	Double cradle tubular steel	
	F. Suspension, Travel	Telescopic fork, travel 121 mm,	4.8 in.
	R. Suspension, Travel	Swing arm, travel 78.5 mm,	3.1 in.
	F. Tire Size, Type	3.15-19 (4 PR) / (3.25-19) (4 PR) Rib tire, tire air pressure 1.8 kg/cm² / 2.0 kg/cm²	25.6 psi / 28.5 psi
	R. Tire Size, Type	3.50-18 (4 PR) Block tire, tire air pressure 2.0 kg/cm²	28.5 psi
	F. Brake, Lining Area	Disc brake, lining area 288.8 cm²×2	32.36 in²×2
	R. Brake, Lining Area	Internal expanding shoe, lining area 169.6 cm²×2	26.28 in²×2
	Fuel Capacity	14.0 lit.	3.7 U.S. gal. 3.1 Imp. gal.
	Fuel Reserve Capacity	4.0 lit.	1.6 U.S. gal. 0.9 Imp. gal.
	Caster Angle	64°	
	Trail Length	105 mm	4.1 in.
	Front Fork Oil Capacity	160 cc	5.4 ozs
ENGINE	Type	Air-cooled, 4-stroke, O.H.C. engine	
	Cylinder Arrangement	4-cylinder in-line	
	Bore and Stroke	56.0×50.6 mm	2.205×1.992 in.
	Displacement	498 cc	30.38 cu. in.
	Compression Ratio	9.0	
	Carburetor, Venturi Dia.	Four, piston valve, 22 mm dia.	
	Valve Train	Chain drive overhead camshaft	
	Maximum Horsepower	50 BHP (SAE)/9,000 rpm (44 BHP (SAE)/9,000 rpm)	
	Maximum Torque	4.2 kg-m/7,500 rpm	30.4 lb-ft/7,500 rpm
	Oil Capacity	3.0 lit.	3.2 U.S. qt. 2.6 Imp. qt
	Lubrication System	Forced pressure and wet sump	

13. TECHNICAL DATA CB 500

	Item	Metric	English
ENGINE	Air Filter	Paper element	
	Valve Tappet Clearance	IN: 0.05, EX: 0.08 mm	IN: 0.002, EX: 0.003 in.
	Engine weight	69 kg	152 lb.
	Air Screw Opening	1 ± 1/8 turns	
	Idle Speed	1,000 rpm	
DRIVE TRAIN	Clutch	Wet, multi-plate	
	Transmission	5-speed, constant mesh	
	Primary Reduction	2.000	
	Gear Ratio I	2.353	
	" II	1.636	
	" III	1.269	
	" IV	1.036	
	" V	0.900	
	Final Reduction	2.000, drive sprocket 17, driven sprocket 34 T	
	Gear Shift Pattern	Left foot return type	
ELECTRICAL	Ignition	Battery and ignition coil	
	Starting System	Electrical motor and kick pedal	
	Alternator	Three phase A.C. 12 V-0.2 KW/5,000 rpm	
	Battery Capacity	12 V-12 AH	
	Spark Plug	NGK D-7 ES, DENSO X-22 ES	
	Headlight	Low/high, 12 V-40 W/50 W	
	Tail/stoplight	Tail/Stop, 12 V-32 W/3 CP (12 V-4 CP/32 CP)	
	Turn Signal light	Front/Rear 12 V-25 W/25 W (12 V-32 CP/32 CP)	
	Speedometer Light	12 V- 3 W (12 V-2 CP)	
	Tachometer Light	12 V- 3 W (12 V-2 CP)	
	Neutral Indicator Light	12 V- 3 W (12 V-2 CP)	
	Turn Signal Indicator Light	12 V- 3 W (12 V-2 CP)	
	High Beam Indicator Light	12 V- 3 W (12 V-2 CP)	

13. TECHNICAL DATA

A. Specifications of CB 550

	Item	Metric	English
DIMENSION	Overall Length	2,120 mm	83.5 in.
	Overall Width	825 mm	32.5 in.
	Overall Height	1,115 mm	43.9 in.
	Wheel Base	1,405 mm	55.3 in.
	Seat Height	805 mm	31.7 in.
	Foot Peg Height	315 mm	12.4 in.
	Ground Clearance	160 mm	6.3 in.
	Dry Weight	192 kg	423 lb.
FRAME	Type	Double cradle frame	
	F. Suspension, Travel	Telescopic fork, travel 121 mm	4.8 in.
	R. Suspension, Travel	Swing arm, travel 77.3 mm	3.0 in.
	F. Tire Size, Type	3.25-19 (4 PR) Rib tire, tire air pressure 2.0 kg/cm^2	28 psi
	R. Tire Size, Type	3.75-18 (4 PR) Block tire, tire air pressure 2.4 kg/cm^2	34 psi
	F. Brake, Lining Area	Disk brake, lining area 288.8 cm$^2 \times 2$	32.36 in$^2 \times 2$
	R. Brake, Lining Area	Internal expanding shoe, lining area 169.6 cm$^2 \times 2$	26.28 in$^2 \times 2$
	Fuel Capacity	14.0 lit.	3.7 U.S. gal. 3.1 Imp. gal.
	Fuel Reserve Capacity	4.0 lit.	1.1 U.S. gal. 0.9 Imp. gal.
	Caster Angle	64°	
	Trail Length	105 mm	4.1 in.
	Front Fork Oil Capacity	185-191 cc	6.3-6.5 ozs
ENGINE	Type	Air-cooled, 4-stroke, O.H.C. engine	
	Cylinder Arrangement	4-cylinder in-line	
	Bore and Stroke	58.5 × 50.6 mm	2.303 × 1.992 in.
	Displacement	544 cc	33.19 cu. in.
	Compression Ratio	9.0	
	Carburetor, Venturi Dia.	Four, piston valve, 22 mm dia.	
	Valve Train	Chain drive overhead camshaft	
	Maximum Horsepower	50 BHP (SAE)/8,500 rpm	
	Maximum Torque	4.2 kg-m/7,500 rpm	30.4 lb-ft/7,500 rpm
	Oil Capacity	3.0 lit.	3.2 U.S. qt., 2.6 Imp. qt
	Lubrication System	Forced pressure and wet sump	

13. TECHNICAL DATA CB 550

	Item	Metric	English
ENGINE	Air Filter	Paper element	
	Valve Tappet Clearance	IN: 0.05, EX: 0.08 mm	IN: 0.002, EX: 0.003 in.
	Engine weight	72 kg	159 lb.
	Air Screw Opening	$1\ 1/2 \pm 3/8$ turns	
	Idle Speed	1,000 rpm	
DRIVE TRAIN	Clutch	Wet, multi-plate	
	Transmission	5-speed, constant mesh	
	Primary Reduction	3.063	
	Gear Ratio I	2.353	
	″ II	1.636	
	″ III	1.269	
	″ IV	1.036	
	″ V	0.900	
	Final Reduction	2.176, drive sprocket 17, driven sproket 37 T	
	Gear Shift Pattern	Left foot return type	
ELECTRICAL	Ignition	Battery and ignition coil	
	Starting System	Electrical motor and kick pedal	
	Alternator	Three phase A.C. 12 V-0.11 KW/2,000 rpm	
	Battery Capacity	12 V-12 AH	
	Spark Plug	NGK D-7 ES, DENSO X-22 ES	
	Headlight	Low/high,	12 V-40 W/50 W
	Tail/stoplight	Tail/Stop	12 V-32 W/3 CP
	Turn Signal light	Front/Rear	12 V-32 W/32 W
	Speedometer Light	12 V-3 W	
	Tachometer Light	12 V-3 W	
	Neutral Indicator Light	12 V-3 W	
	Turn Signal Indicator Light	12 V-3 W	
	High Beam Indicator Light	12 V-3 W	

13. TECHNICAL DATA CB 500

B. Service Data (CB 500)

ENGINE

mm (in.)

Item	Standard value	Serviceable limit
Intake cam height	34.93~34.97 (1.3742~1.3768)	34.85 (1.3720)
Exhaust cam height	34.53~34.57 (1.3595~13.610)	34.45 (1.3563)
Runout	—	0.1 (0.004)

Item	Standard value	Serviceable limit
Cylinder bore	56~56.01 (2.204~2.205)	56.1 (2.208)

Item	Standard value	Serviceable limit
Piston dia.	55.99~55.97 (2.204~2.203)	55.85 (2.198)
Piston pinhole	—	15.08 (0.593)

Item	Standard value	Serviceable limit
Piston ring end gap	0.15~0.35 (0.005~0.013)	0.7 (0.027)

Piston ring Side clearance	Standard value	Serviceable limit
Top ring	0.040~0.075 (0.0015~0.0029)	0.18 (0.007)
Second ring	0.025~0.06 (0.0009~0.0023)	0.15 (0.005)
Oil ring	0.020~0.055 (0.0007~0.0021)	0.15 (0.005)

Item	Standard value	Serviceable limit
Ring groove clearance	15.002~15.008 (0.59063~0.59087)	Replace if over 15.080 (0.5937)

	Standard value	Serviceable limit
Valve stem clearance	Intake 0.010~0.035 (0.00039~0.00137)	0.080 (0.0031)
	Exhaust 0.030~0.050 (0.0011~0.0019)	0.10 (0.0039)
Valve stem diameter	Intake 5.450~5.465 (0.2145~0.2150)	
	Exhaust 5.430~5.445 (0.2137~0.2142)	
Valve face runout	—	0.05 (0.009)

mm (in.)

Item	Standard value	Serviceable limit
Cylinder head flatness	—	0.3 (0.011)

Item	Standard value	Serviceable limit
Valve spring free length	Outer 40.4 (1.59)	39 (1.53)
	Inner 35.7 (1.40)	34.5 (1.35)
Loading (reference)	Outer 27.9 mm/45.6~50.6 kg (1.0 in/ 100.54~111.57 lbs-ft) Inner 23.2 mm/19.1~21.1 kg (0.9 in/ 421.15~464.35 lbs-ft)	
Clutch plate warp	—	0.3 (0.011)

Oil pump	Standard value	Serviceable limit
Inner and outer rotor clearance	—	0.35 (0.013)
Outer rotor and body clearance	—	0.35 (0.013)

Item	Standard value	Serviceable limit
Friction disc thickness	3.3 (0.13)	3.0 (0.11)

	Standard value	Serviceable limit
Clutch spring free length	31.9 (1.25)	30.5 (1.20)
Spring strength	31.4~33 kg at 23 mm (227.84~238.6 at 0.90 in)	

Item	Standard value	Serviceable limit
Gear shift drum O.D.	39.975~39.95 (1.5738~1.5728)	39.9 (1.5709)
Shift fork I.D.	40.00~40.025 (1.5748~1.5757)	40.075 (1.5797)

Gear shift fork	Standard value	Serviceable limit
Center	5.93~6.00 (0.233~0.236)	5.60 (0.220)
Right & left	4.93~5.0 (0.194~0.197)	4.60 (0.181)

Item	Standard value	Serviceable limit
Crankshaft journal clearance	0.020~0.046 (0.00079~0.00181)	0.080 (0.0031)
Runout	—	0.05 (0.0019)
Journal and taper	—	0.05 (0.0019)

13. TECHNICAL DATA

Item	Standard value	Serviceable limit
Connecting rod large end clearance	0.02~0.046 (0.00079~0.00181)	0.08 (0.0031)

mm (in.)

Item	Standard value	Serviceable limit
Connecting rod side clearance	0.12~0.27 (0.0047~0.0106)	0.35 (0.0138)

Item	Standard value	Serviceable limit
Connecting rod small end clearance	15.016~15.034 (0.5911~0.5918)	15.07 (0.5930)

Item	Standard value	Serviceable limit
1st, 2nd, 3rd gears backlash	0.044~0.133 (0.0017~0.0051)	0.2 (0.0078)
4th and 5th gears backlash	0.046~0.140 (0.0018~0.0055)	0.2 (0.0078)

CHASSIS

Wheel	Standard value	Serviceable limit
Rim wobble	0.5 (0.020)	2.0 (0.08)
Wheel runout	0.5 (0.020)	2.0 (0.08)

Wheel bearing	Standard value	Serviceable limit
Front wheel bearing axial direction, TIR	0.07 (0.028)	0.1 (0.004)
Front wheel bearing radial direction, TIR	0.003 (0.00012)	0.05 (0.002)

Front brake	Standard value	Serviceable limit
Caliper cylinder inside dia.	38.18~38.20 (1.5031~1.5039)	38.215 (1.504)
Caliper piston outside dia.	38.115~38.48 (1.5006~1.5149)	38.105 (1.500)

Front brake	Standard value	Serviceable limit
Master cylinder	14.0~14.043 (0.5511~0.5528)	14.055 (0.533)
Piston	13.957~13.984 (0.5494~0.5505)	13.940 (0.549)

Wheel	Standard value	Serviceable limit
Rim runout, TIR (vertical and side)	0.5 (0.02)	2.0 (0.08)

Item	Standard value	Serviceable limit
Disc trueness	—	0.3 (0.011)
Caliper and piston clearance	—	0.11 (0.004)
Master cylinder and piston clearance	—	0.11 (0.004)

mm (in.)

Rear axle shaft	Standard value	Serviceable limit
Bent, TIR	0.01 (0.0004)	0.2 (0.009)

Brake lining	Standard value	Serviceable limit
Thickness	5.0 (0.200)	2.0 (0.080)

Brake Drum	Standard value	Serviceable limit
Inside dia.	179.8~180.0 (7.079~7.087)	181.0 (7.125)

Item	Standard value	Serviceable limit
Axial, TIR	0.07 (0.0028)	0.1 (0.004)
Radial, TIR	0.003 (0.00011)	0.05 (0.002)

	Standard value	Serviceable limit
Front suspension spring I.D.	42 (1.65)	
Free length	451.7 (17.78)	425 (16.73)
Tilt	5 (0.02)	8 (0.03)

Item	Standard value	Serviceable limit
Rear suspension free length	210.4 (8.283)	205 (8.070)

Item	Standard value	Serviceable limit
Clearance	0.1~0.3 (0.004~0.012)	0.5 (0.02)
Rear fork bushing inside dia.	21.448~21.5 (0.844~0.846)	21.8 (0.858)
Center collar outside dia.	21.427~21.46 (0.843~0.844)	21.4 (0.842)

ELECTRICAL

Item	Standard value	Serviceable limit
Carbon brush length	12~31 mm (0.47~0.51 in)	5.5 mm (0.22 in)
Brush spring tension	0.5~0.5 kg (1.1~1.3 lbs)	0.4 kg (0.8 lbs)

13. TECHNICAL DATA

B. Service Data (CB 550)

ENGINE

mm (in.)

Item	Standard value	Serviceable limit
Intake cam height	34.93~34.97 (1.3742~1.3768)	34.85 1.3720
Exhaust cam height	34.53~34.57 (1.3595~13.610)	34.45 (1.3563)
Runout	—	0.1 (0.004)

Item	Standard value	Serviceable limit
Cylinder bore	58.50~58.51 (2.303~2.304)	58.6 (2.307)

Item	Standard value	Serviceable limit
Piston dia.	54.47~58.49 (2.301~2.30)	58.35 (2.302)
Piston pinhole	—	15.08 (0.593)

Item		Standard value	Serviceable limit
Piston ring end gap	Top	0.15~0.35 (0.005~0.013)	0.7 (0.027)
	2nd		
	oil	0.3~0.9 (0.01~0.035)	1.1 (0.043)

Piston ring Side clearance	Standard value	Serviceable limit
Top ring	0.040~0.075 (0.0015~0.0029)	0.18 (0.007)
Second ring	0.025~0.06 (0.0009~0.0023)	0.15 (0.005)
Oil ring	—	—

Item	Standard value	Serviceable limit
Ring groove clearance	15.002~15.008 (0.59063~0.59087)	Replace if over 15.080 (0.6937)

	Standard value	Serviceable limit
Valve stem clarance	Intake 0.020~0.045 (0.00079~0.00177)	0.080 (0.0031)
	Exhaust 0.030~0.050 (0.0011~0.0019)	0.10 (0.0039)
Valve stem diameter	Intake 5.450~5.465 (0.2145~0.2150)	
	Exhaust 5.430~5.445 (0.2137~0.2142)	
Valve face runout	—	0.05 (0.009)

mm (in.)

Item	Standard value	Serviceable limit
Cylinder head flatness	—	0.3 (0.011)

Item	Standard value	Serviceable limit
Valve spring free length	Outer 40.4 (1.59)	39 (1.53)
	Inner 35.7 (1.40)	34.5 (1.35)
Loading (reference)	Outer 27.9 mm 45.6~50.6 kg/ (1.0 in/ 100.54~111.57 lbs-ft)	
	Inner 23.2 mm/19.1~21.1 kg (0.9 in/ 421.15~464.35 lbs-ft)	
Clutch plate warp	—	0.3 (0.011)

Oil pump	Standard value	Serviceable limit
Inner and outer rotor clearance	—	3.35 (0.013)
Outer rotor and body clearance	—	0.35 (0.013)

Item	Standard value	Serviceable limit
Friction disc thickness	2.6 (0.12)	2.3 (0.09)

	Standard value	Serviceable limit
Cutch spring free length	36.8 (1.45)	35.4 (1.39)
Spring strength	22.1~33.2 at 23 mm (227.84~238.6 at 0.90 in)	

Item	Standard value	Serviceable limit
Gear shift drum O.D.	39.975~59.95 (1.5738~1.5728)	39.9 (1.5709)
Shift fork I.D.	40.00~40.025 (1.5748~1.5757)	40.075 (1.5797)

Gear shift fork	Standard value	Serviceable limit
Center	5.93~6.00 (0.233~0.236)	5.60 (0.220)
Right & left	4.93~5.0 (0.194~0.197)	4.60 (0.181)

Item	Standard value	Serviceable limit
Crankshaft journal clearance	0.020~0.046 (0.00079~0.00181)	0.080 (0.0031)
Runout	—	0.05 (0.0019)
Journal and taper	—	0.05 (0.0019)

13. TECHNICAL DATA

Item	Standard value	Serviceable limit
Connecting rod large end clearance	0.02~0.046 (0.00079~0.00181)	0.08 (0.0031)

mm (in.)

Item	Standard value	Serviceable limit
Connecting rod side clearance	0.12~0.27 (0.0047~0.0106)	0.35 (0.0138)

Item	Standard value	Serviceable limit
Connecting rod small end clearance	15.016~15.034 (0.5911~0.5918)	15.07 (0.5930)

Item	Standard value	Serviceable limit
1st, 2nd, 3rd gears backlash	0.044~0.133 (0.0017~0.0051)	0.2 (0.0078)
4th and 5th gears backlash	0.046~0.140 (0.0018~0.0055)	0.2 (0.0078)

CHASSIS

Wheel	Standard value	Serviceable limit
Rim wobble	0.5 (0.020)	2.0 (0.08)
Wheel runout	0.5 (0.020)	2.0 (0.08)

Wheel bearing	Standard value	Serviceable limit
Front wheel bearing axial direction, TIR	0.07 (0.028)	0.1 (0.004)
Front wheel bearing radial direction, TIR	0.003 (0.00012)	0.05 (0.002)

Front brake	Standard value	Serviceable limit
Caliper cylinder inside dia.	38.18~38.20 (1.5031~1.5039)	38.215 (1.504)
Caliper piston outside dia.	38.115~38.48 (1.5006~1.5149)	38.105 (1.500)

Front brake	Standard value	Serviceable limit
Master cylinder	14.0~14.043 (0.5511~0.5528)	14.055 (0.533)
Piston	13.957~13.984 (0.5494~0.5505)	13.940 (0.549)

Wheel	Standard value	Serviceable limit
Rim runout, TIR (vertical and side)	0.5 (0.02)	2.0 (0.08)

Item	Standard value	Serviceable limit
Disc trueness	—	0.3 (0.011)
Caliper and piston clearance	—	0.11 (0.004)
Master cylinder and piston clearance	—	0.11 (0.004)

mm (in.)

Rear axle shaft	Standard value	Serviceable limit
Bent, TIR	0.01 (0.0004)	0.2 (0.009)

Brake lining	Standard value	Serviceable limit
Thickness	5.0 (0.200)	2.0 (0.080)

Brake Drum	Standard value	Serviceable limit
Inside dia.	179.8~180.0 (7.079~7.087)	181.0 (7.125)

Item	Standard value	Serviceable limit
Axial, TIR	0.07 (0.0028)	0.1 (0.004)
Radial, TIR	0.003 (0.00011)	0.05 (0.002)

	Standard value	Serviceable limit
Front suspension spring I.D.	42 (1.65)	
Free length	451.7 (17.78)	425 (16.73)
Tilt	5 (0.02)	8 (0.03)

Item	Standard value	Serviceable limit
Rear suspension free length	210.4 (8.283)	205 (8.070)

Item	Standard value	Serviceable limit
Clearance	0.1~0.3 (0.004~0.012)	0.5 (0.02)
Rear fork bushing inside dia.	21.448~21.5 (0.844~0.846)	21.8 (0.858)
Center collar outside dia.	21.427~21.46 (0.843~0.844)	21.4 (0.842)

ELECTRICAL

Item	Standard value	Serviceable limit
Carbon brush length	12~31 mm (0.47~0.51 in)	5.5 mm (0.22 in)
Brush spring tension	0.5~0.5 kg (1.1~1.3 lbs)	0.4 kg (0.8 lbs)

14. WIRING DIAGRAM

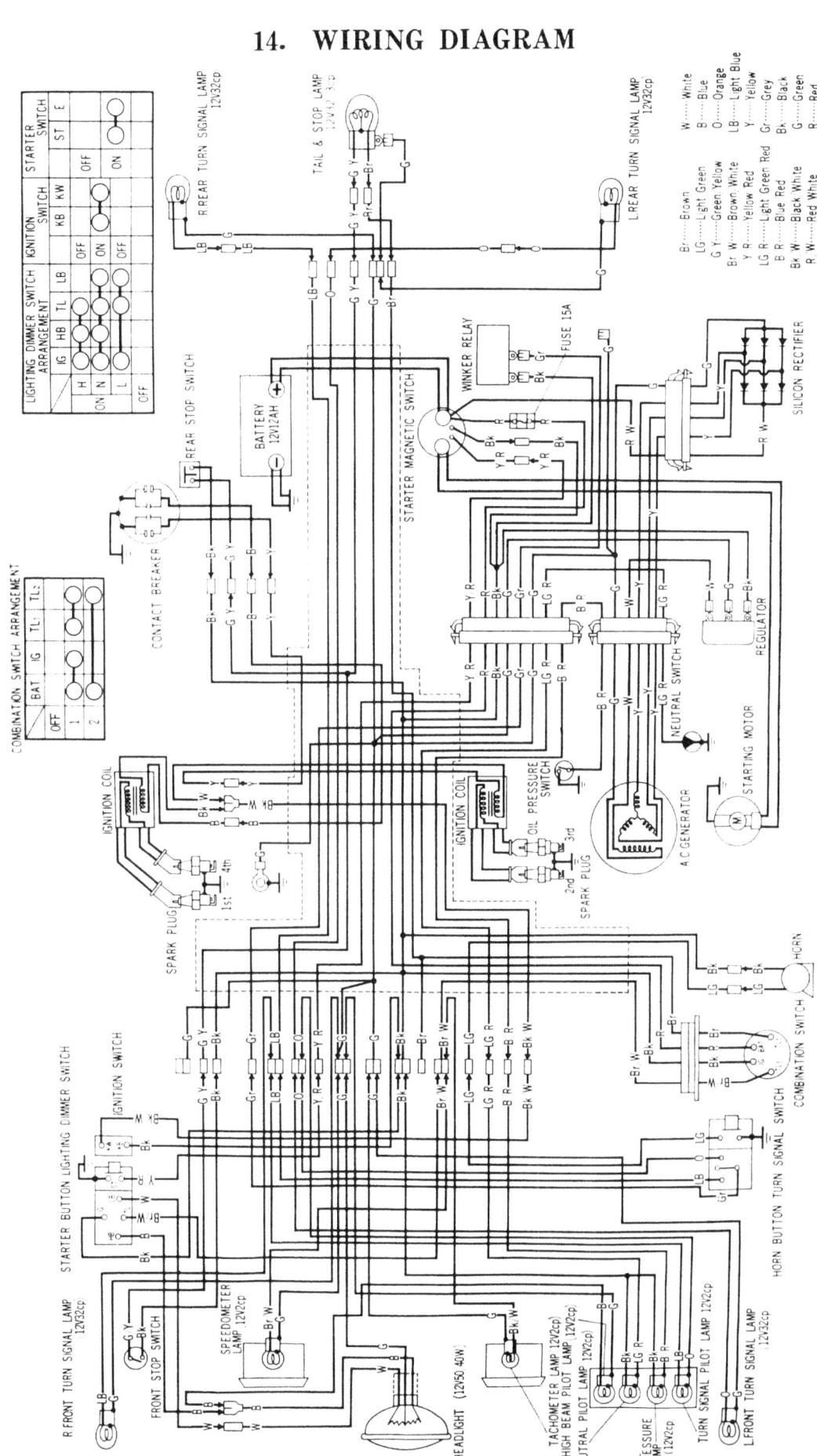

14. WIRING DIAGRAM

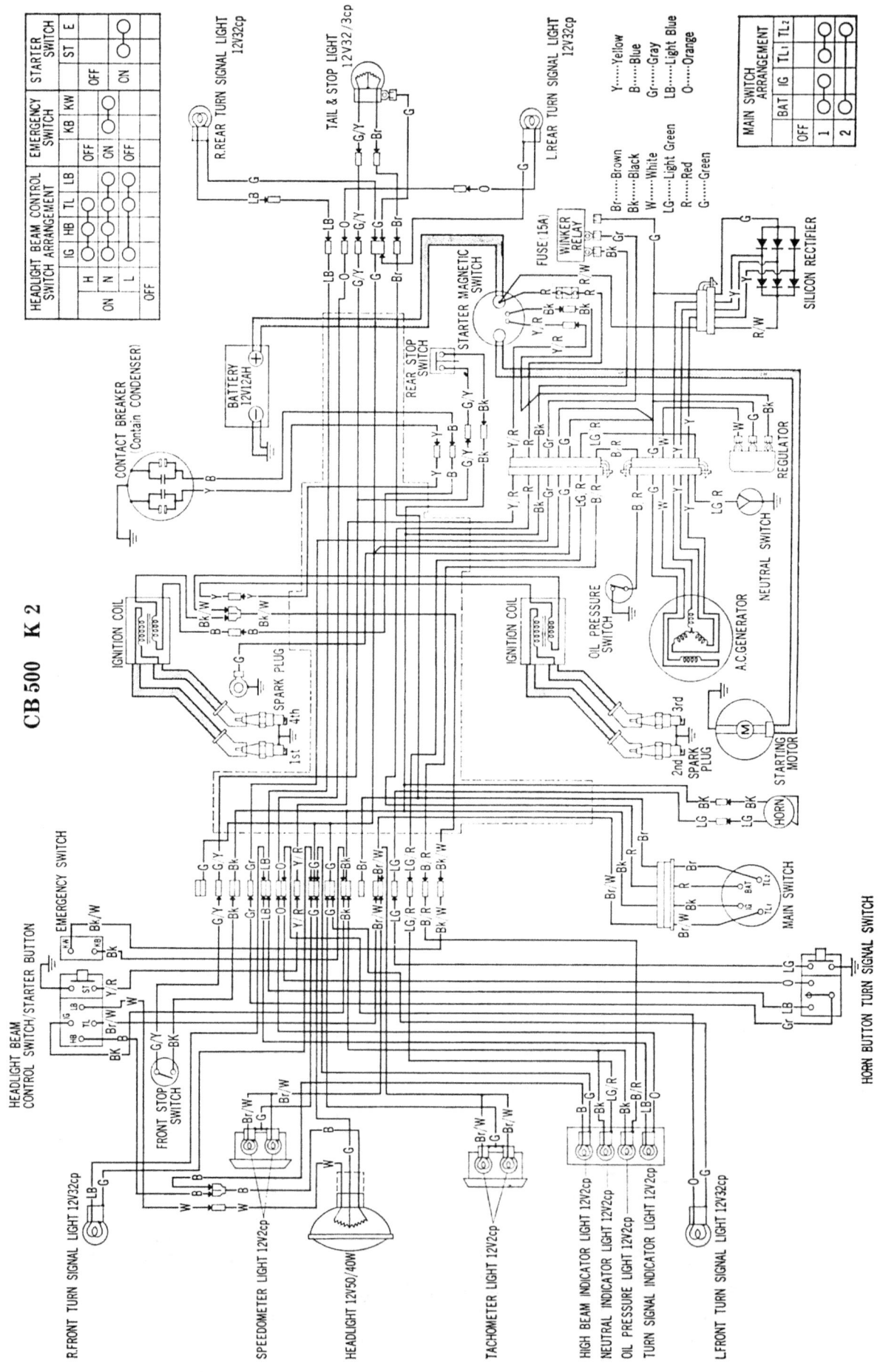

14. WIRING DIAGRAM

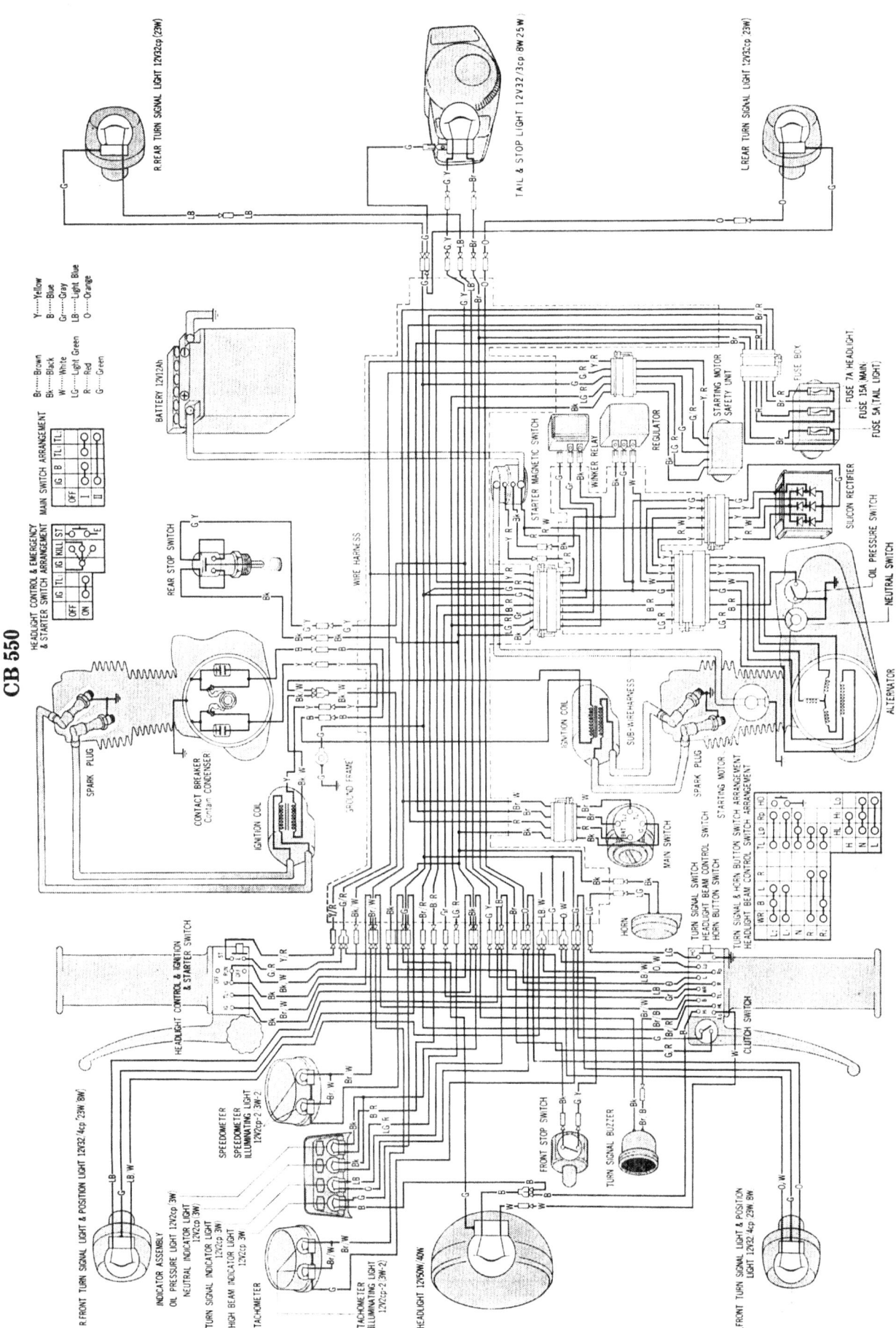

14. WIRING DIAGRAM

Wiring diagram of CB 550

Refer to the following illustrations for the location of wires, cables, and leads.

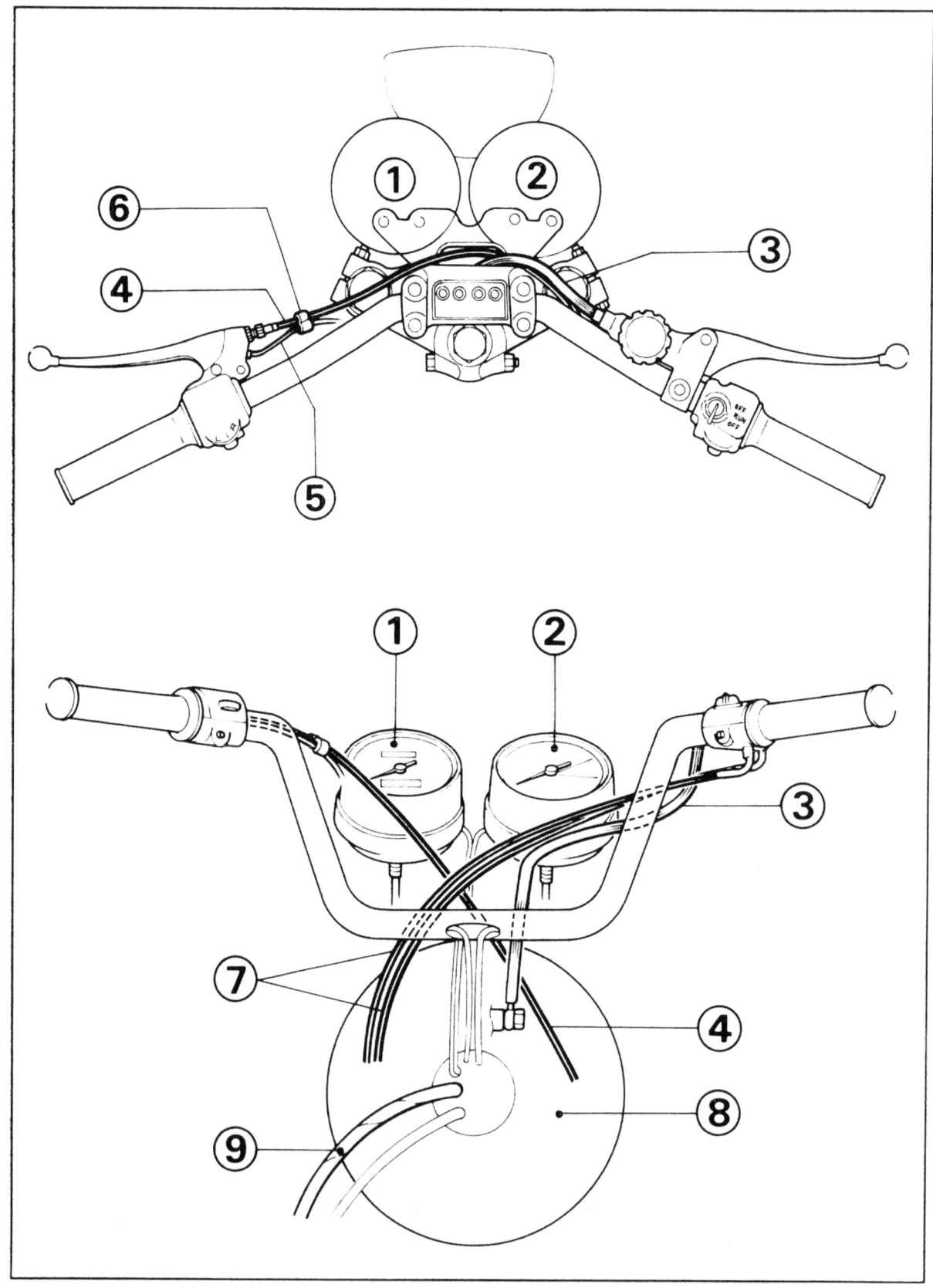

① Speedometer
② Tachometer
③ Front brake hose
④ Clutch cable
⑤ Clutch switch wire
⑥ Clip
⑦ Throttle cables
⑧ Headlight case
⑨ Wire harness

14. WIRING DIAGRAM

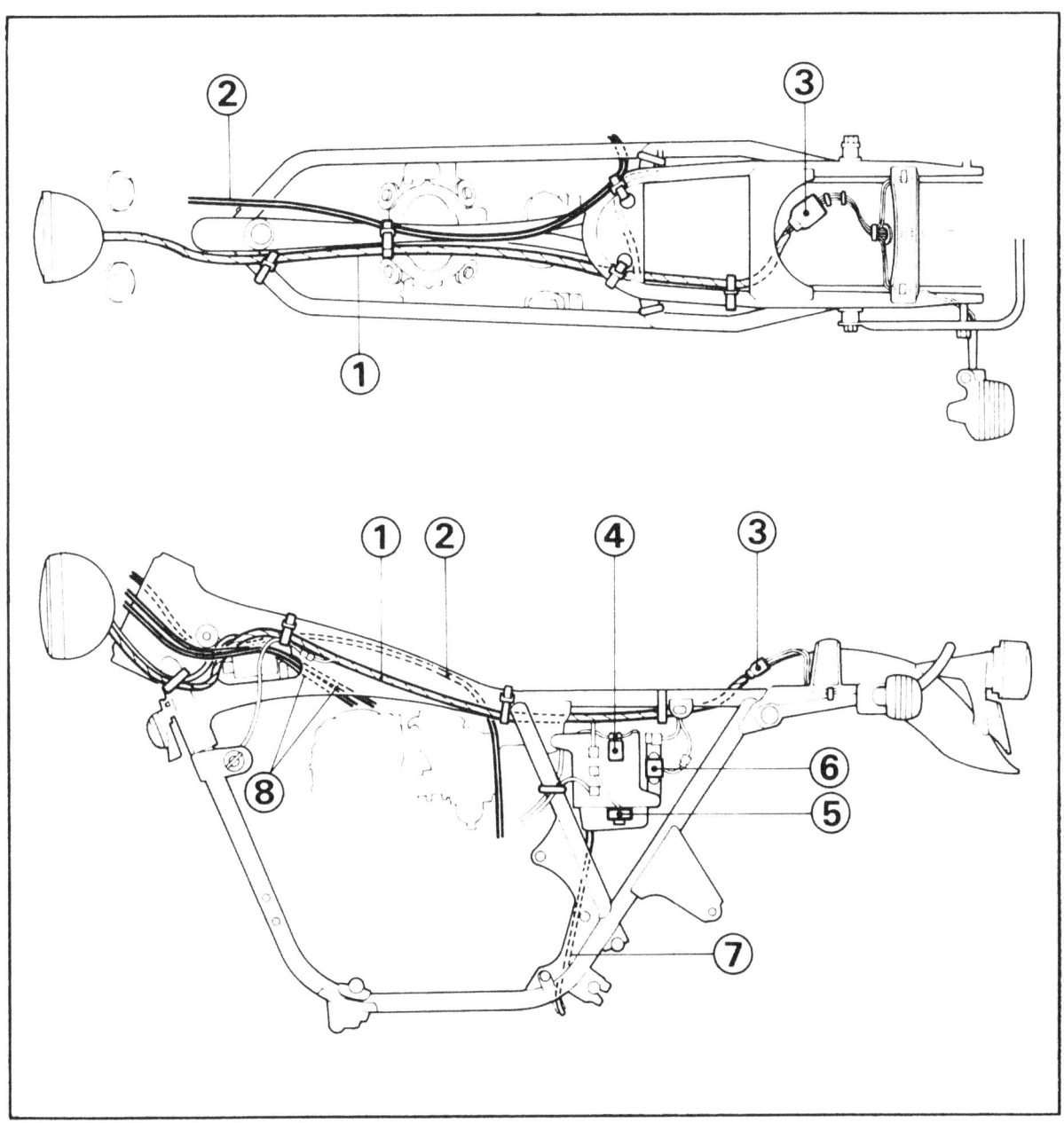

1. Wire harness
2. Clutch cable
3. Terminal cover
4. Starter magnetic switch
5. Siricon rectifier
6. fuse box
7. Air cleaner tube
8. Throttle cables

MEMO

15. SUPPLEMENT TO CB550 K1

1. FUEL VALVE

The fuel valve is new for the revised model. The indication marks and the fuel valve positions were changed.

Inspection and cleaning

1. Place the fuel lever in the "OFF" position; disconnect the fuel tubes. Take the fuel tank out.
2. Drain the fuel tank thoroughly.
3. Loosen the fuel valve fixing nut and remove the fuel valve and fuel filter from the fuel tank.
4. Check the gasket for damage. Replace with a new one, if it is damaged.
5. Wash the fuel filter in solvent and dry with compressed air. Replace the filter with a new one if it is clogged.
6. Install the fuel filter to the fuel valve with the fixing nut. Install the gasket into the groove of the fixing nut.
7. Install the fuel valve to the fuel tank with the fixing nut.
8. Install the fuel tank in place on the frame. Connect the tubes and secure with the clips.
9. Fill the tank with fuel. With the fuel valve lever in the "ON" position, check for leaks past the tube joints or connections.

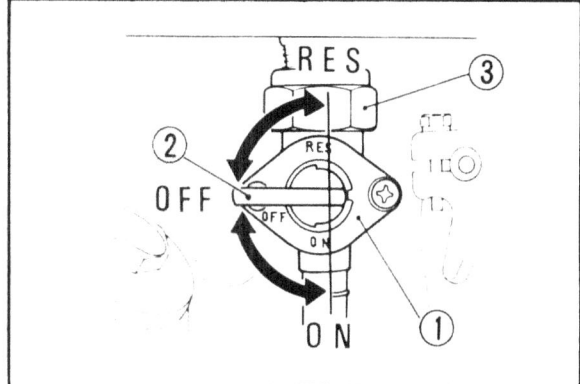

Fig. K1-1
1) Fuel valve
2) Lever
3) Fuel valve fixing nut

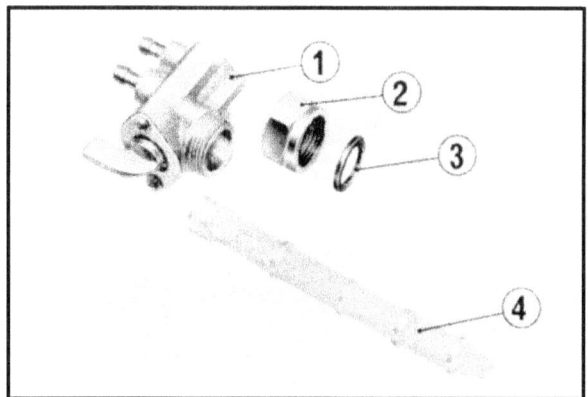

Fig. K1-2
1) Fuel valve
2) Fixing nut
3) Gasket
4) Fuel filter

15. SUPPLEMENT TO CB550 K1

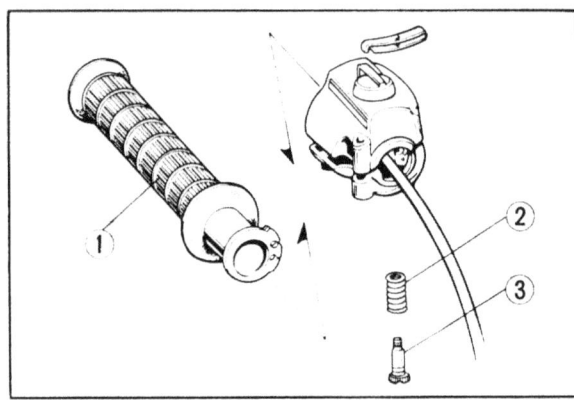

Fig. K1-3 ① Throttle grip ② Spring adjuster ③ Adjusting bolt

2. THROTTLE GRIP

The throttle grip adjuster, Fig. K1-3, was discontinued.

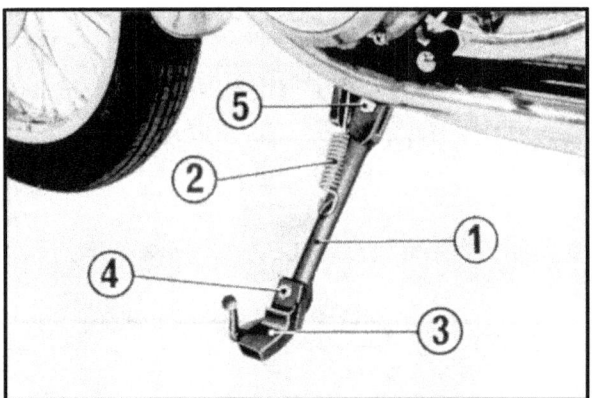

Fig. K1-4 ① Side stand bar ④ 6 mm bolt
② Spring ⑤ Side stand pivot
③ Rubber pad bolt

3. SIDE STAND

The side stand was changed to a new type with a shock absorbing rubber pad. The side stand must be inspected periodically to determine that it is in good condition.

Inspection

1. Check the entire stand assembly (side stand bar, bracket and rubber pad) for installation, deformation or excessive damage.
2. Check the spring for damage or other defects.
3. Check the side stand for proper return operation:
   a. With the side stand applied, raise the stand off the ground by using the main stand.
   b. Attach a spring scale to the lower end of the stand and measure the force with which the stand is returned to its original position.
   c. The stand condition is correct if the measurement falls within 2~3 kg (4.4~6.6 lbs.).
      If the stand requires force exceeding the above limit, this may be due to neglected lubrication, overtightened side stand pivot bolt, worn stand bar or bracket, or excessive tension. Replace if necessary.
4. Check the rubber pad for deterioration or wear. When the rubber pad wear is so excessive it is worn to the wear line, replace it with a new one.

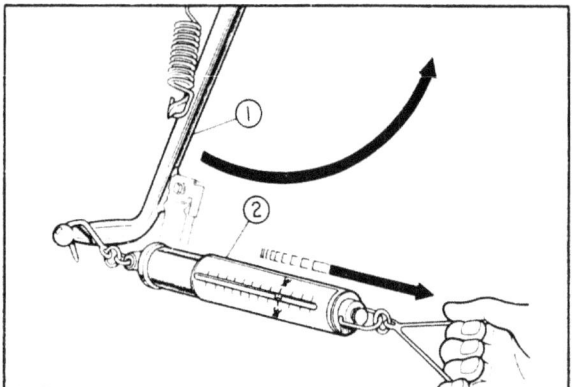

Fig. K1-5 ① Side stand bar ② Spring scale

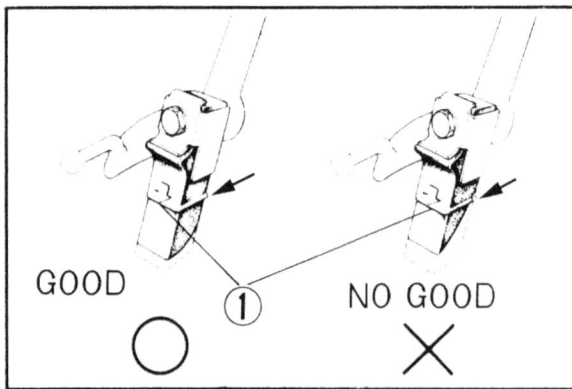

Fig. K1-6 ① Wear line

Rubber pad replacement

1. Remove the 6 mm bolt. Separate the rubber pad from the bracket at the side stand.
2. After the collar is installed, place a new rubber pad in the bracket with the arrow mark out.
   Note:
   Use a rubber pad having the mark "OVER 260 lbs ONLY".
3. Secure the rubber pad with the 6 mm bolt.

Fig. K1-7 1 Rubber pad
2 Collar

4. TURN SIGNAL LIGHT

The front and rear turn signal lights were changed to new, larger types. See Figs. K1-8 and K1-9.

Fig. K1-8 1 Front turn signal light

Fig. K1-9 1 Rear turn signal light

5. MAINTENANCE SCHEDULE

Some additions occurred in the MAINTENANCE SCHEDULE. They are shown below:

This maintenance schedule is based upon average riding conditions. Machines subjected to severe use, or ridden in unusually dusty areas, require more frequent servicing.	INITIAL SERVICE PERIOD	REGULAR SERVICE PERIOD Perform at every indicated month or mileage interval, whichever occures first.			
		1 month	3 months	6 months	12 months
	500 miles 800 km	500 miles 800 km	1,500 miles 2,500 km	3,000 miles 5,000 km	6,000 miles 10,000 km
*SIDE STAND—Check installation, operation, deformation, damage and wear.					○

Items marked * should be serviced by an authorized Honda dealer, unless the owner has proper tools and is mechanically proficient. Other maintenance items are simple to perform and may be serviced by the owner

6. WIRING DIAGRAM CB550K1

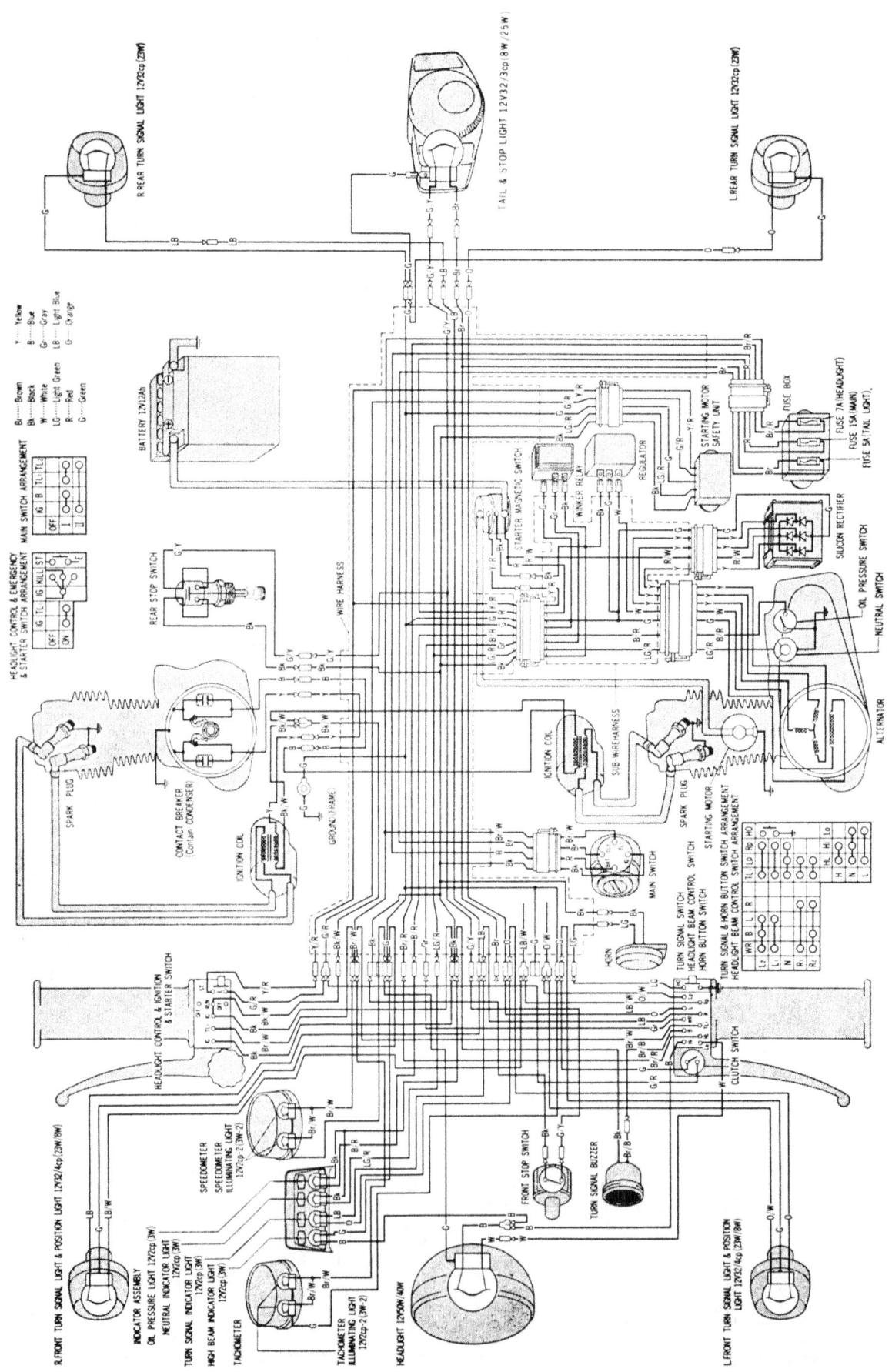

16. SUPPLEMENT TO CB 550 F

ENGINE

GEAR SHIFT MECHANISM

A. Disasembly

1. Remove the clutch assembly. (See page 121.)
2. Remove the gear change pedal.
3. Remove the shift drum stop bolt, the neutral stop bolt, shift drum stop and neutral stop.

Fig. 1-1 1) Shift drum stop bolt
2) Neutral stop bolt

4. Lower the gear shift arm as shown in Fig. 1-2 and remove the gear shift spindle.

B. Inspection

1. Check the shift drum stop and neutral stop for bending or damage.
2. Check the shift drum stop and neutral stop rollers for wear.

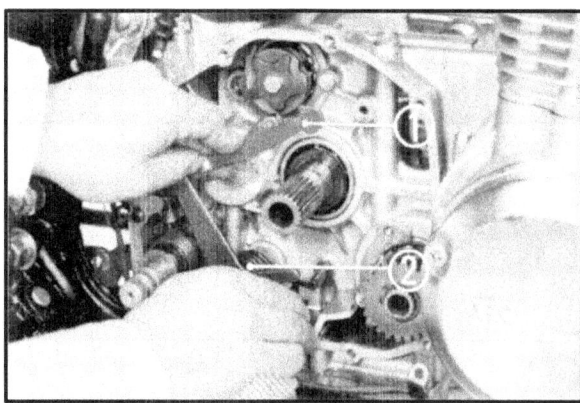

Fig. 1-2 1) Gear shift arm
2) Gear shift spindle

16. SUPPLEMENT TO CB550F

Fig. 1-3
① Shift drum stop
② Shift drum stop springs
③ Shift drum neutral stop

Fig. 1-4
① Bearing set plate on shift drum side
② Shift drum neutral stop
③ Shift drum stop
④ Bearing set plate on primary shaft side
⑤ Gear shift spindle

C. Reassembly

To reassemble the gear shift mechanism, reverse the disassembly procedure. Note the following items:

1. As shown in Fig. 1-3, attach one of the shift drum stop springs to the shift drum stop and shift drum neutral stop, then attach the other shift drum stop spring to the arm and body of the shift drum stop. Secure the shift drum stop and shift drum neutral stop using the neutral stop bolt and shift drum stop bolt and collar.
2. Turn the gear shift drum and check if each part moves smoothly.
3. Install the gear shift arm and check that it moves smoothly in either direction.
4. Install the clutch assembly. (See page 122.)

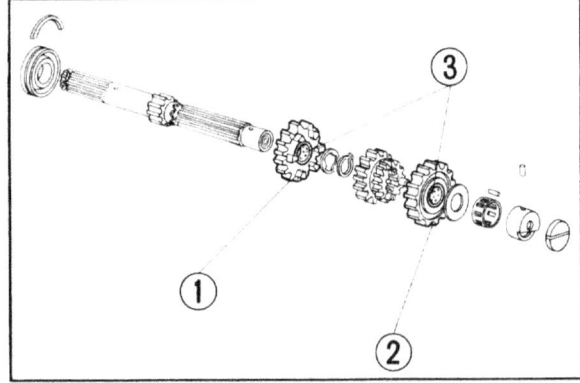

Fig. 1-5
① Main shaft fourth gear
② Main shaft top gear
③ Bushings

Bushings

A bushing is pressed in the main shaft fourth gear and top gear. (The CB550 model gears do not contain bushings.)

FRAME

FRONT SUSPENSION

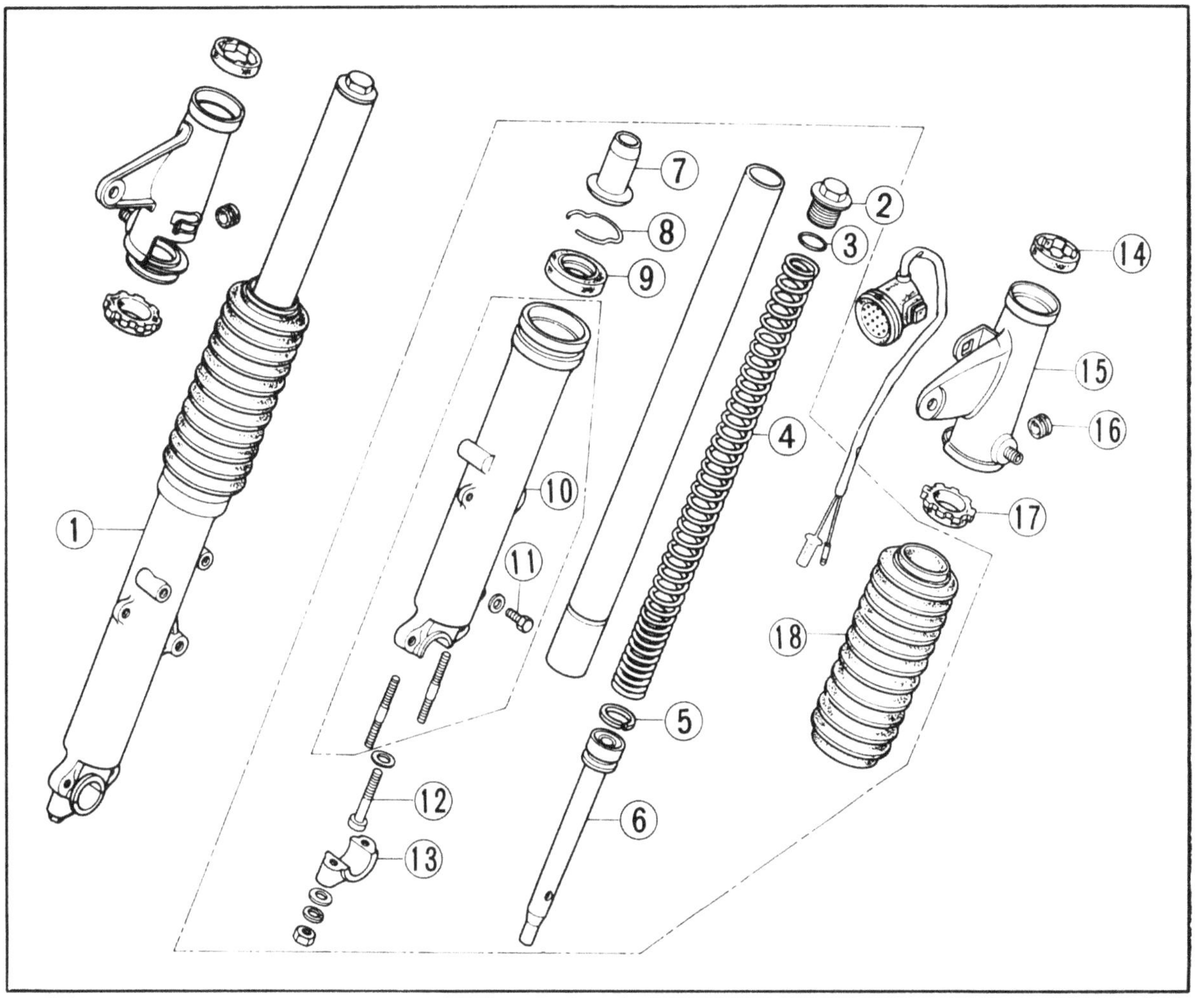

Fig. 2-1
1. Right front fork
2. Front fork bolt
3. 23 × 2.8 mm O-ring
4. Front shock absorber spring
5. Piston ring
6. Bottom pipe
7. Oil lock piece
8. Oil seal stop ring
9. 35 × 48 × 11 mm oil seal
10. Bottom case
11. 6 × 10 mm bolt
12. Oil lock bolt
13. Axle holder
14. Fork cover shock absorber A
15. Left front cover
16. Wire cord grommet
17. Fork cover shock absorber B
18. Front fork boot

A. Disassembly

1. Loosen the front fork bolt, but do not remove it.
2. Remove the front wheel referring to page 65.
3. Remove the caliper assembly from the left front fork.
4. Remove the front fender, the front fork pipe retaining bolts, and pull the front fork out and down.
5. Remove the front fork bolt and drain the front shock absorber oil.

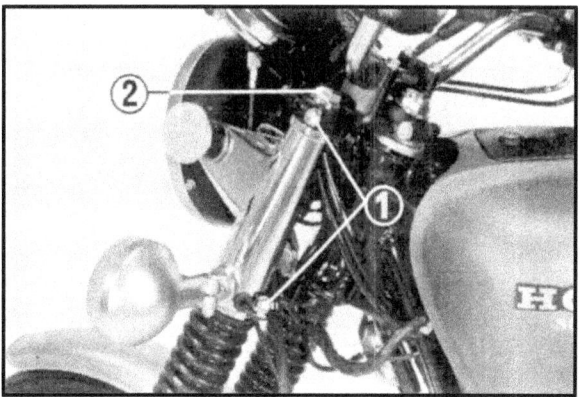

Fig. 2-2
1. Front fork retaining bolt
2. Front fork bolt

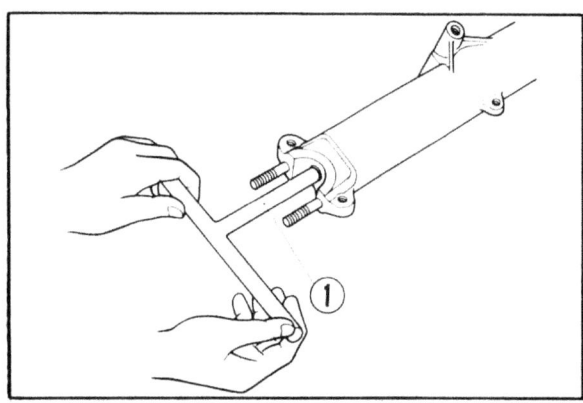

Fig. 2-3 ① Allen head wrench

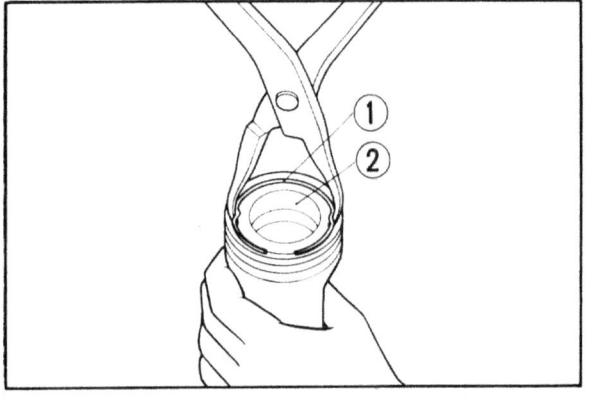

Fig. 2-4 ① Oil seal stop ring ② Oil seal

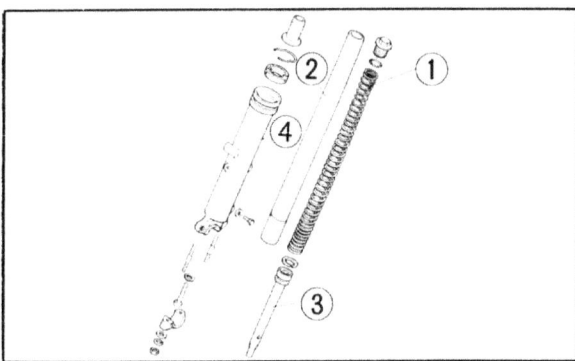

Fig. 2-5 ① Front shock absorber spring
② Front fork pipe
③ Bottom pipe
④ Bottom case

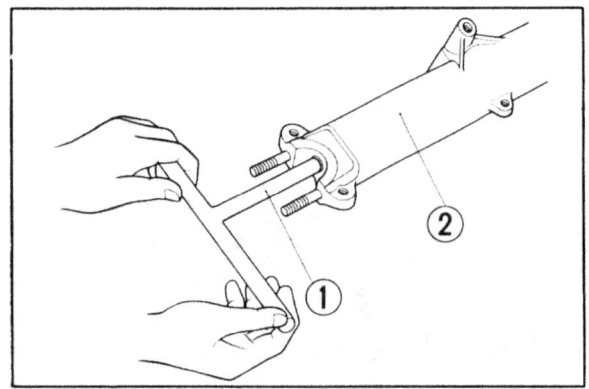

Fig. 2-6 ① Allen head wrench ② Bottom case

6. With the front fork bottom case held in a vise, remove the socket bolt using an Allen head wrench (Tool No. 07917-3230000) and separate the fork pipe from the fork bottom case.
7. Remove the front shock absorber spring and bottom pipe.
8. Remove the oil lock piece from the bottom case.
9. Remove the front fork oil seal stop ring and the oil seal.

B. Inspection

1. Measure the front shock absorber spring free length. Check the spring for tension.
2. Check the front fork piston ring wear.
3. Check the front fork pipe to bottom case clearance.
4. Check the oil seal for scores, scratches or breakage.
5. Check the front fork pipe sliding surface for scores or scratches.

C. Reassembly

To reassemble the front suspension, reverse the disassembly procedure. Note the following items:

1. Install the fork pipe into the bottom case. Apply a coat of thread lock cement to the socket bolt and tighten it using an Allen head wrench.

16. SUPPLEMENT TO CB550F

2. Apply a coat of ATF (automatic transmisson fluid) to the inner and outer circumferences of the oil seal, then install it using a fork seal driver (Tool No. 07947-3290000).

NOTES:
1. **Install the oil seal stop ring properly.**
2. **Use a new oil seal.**
3. Fill the fork pipe with ATF to the specified amount.

   Capacity: 165~170cc (5.6~5.8ozs)

   To fill dry fork assembly

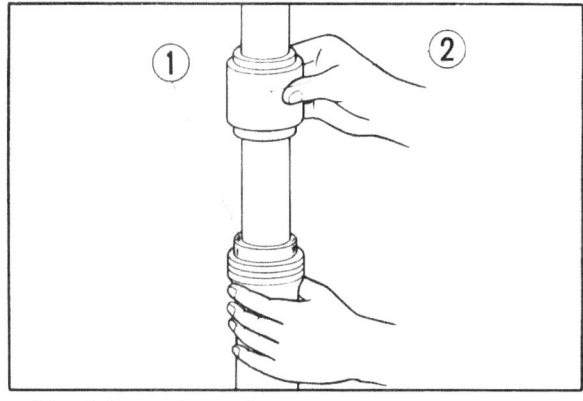

Fig. 2-7 1. Oil seal
         2. Fork seal driver

4. Install the right and left front forks so that their heights are equal. The chamfered edge on the fork pipe should align with the upper surface of the fork top bridge as shown.

NOTE:
Wipe oil, if any, off the fork pipes.

5. After installing the front fork, check:
   - Smooth movement of the fork.
   - Oil leakage from the oil seal.

Fig. 2-8 1. Chamfered edge on front fork pipe

Front shock absorber oil change

1. Remove the front fork bolt and drain bolt. With the front brake applied and the handlebar held, move the front five or six times to drain the oil.
2. Install the drain bolt and fill the fork pipe with new ATF from the upper side to the specified amount.

Fig. 2-9 1. Front fork drain bolt

16. SUPPLEMENT TO CB550F

Fig. 2-10
(1) Air cleaner case
(2) Retaining clip
(3) Air cleaner element

AIR CLEANER

1. Raise the seat, loosen the wing nuts, and remove the air cleaner cover.
2. Remove the retaining clip, and the air cleaner element.

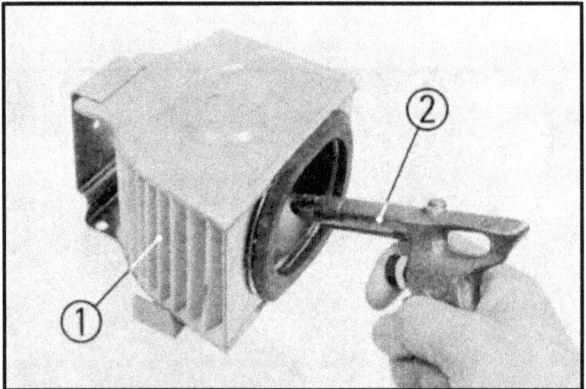

Fig. 2-11 (1) Air cleaner element (2) Air gun

3. Clean the element by tapping it lightly If the element is still dirty, apply air from inside of the element with an air nozzle.

Fig. 2-12 (1) Breather element cover

4. Remove the element cover, and the breather element.

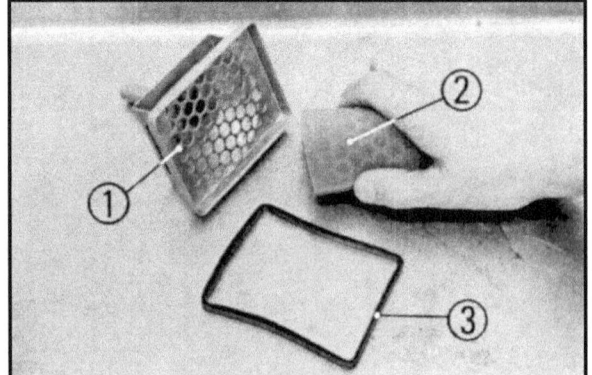

Fig. 2-13 (1) Breather element cover
(2) Breather element
(3) Element cover seal

5. Immerse the breather element in soapsuds and lightly squeeze it. Then immerse the element in new ATF, squeeze it lightly, and install.

WARNING:
Gasoline or low flash point solvents are highly flammable and must not be used to clean the breather elements.

6. Squeeze the end of the drain tube as shown in Fig. 2-14 and drain any oil or water that remains in the tube.
7. Install the air cleaner in the reverse order of the removal procedure.

NOTE:
Check the drain tube for clogging and routing.

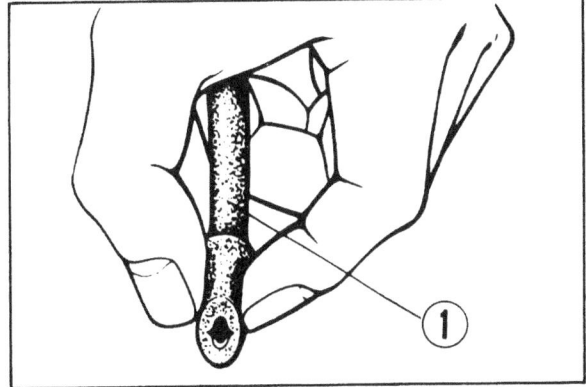

Fig. 2-14 1 Drain tube

EXHAUST MUFFLER

A. Disassembly

1. Remove the 10 mm bolt, and the exhaust muffler.

Fig. 2-15 1 10 mm bolt

2. Remove the eight joint nuts, loosen the exhust pipe joints and joint collars, and remove the exhaust pipes.

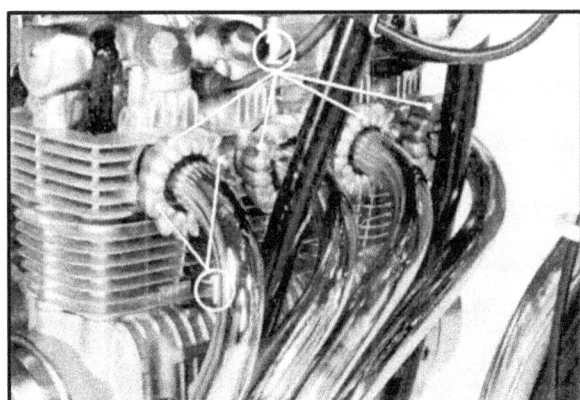

Fig. 2-16 1 Joint nuts
        2 Exhaust pipe joints

16. SUPPLEMENT TO CB550F

3. Remove the protector bands A and B, and the protector. Remove the muffler stay and the muffler band bolt. Separate the four exhaust pipes and sealing gasket from the muffler.

B. Inspection

1. Check for exhaust pipe gaskets damage.
2. Check for muffler sealing gasket damage.

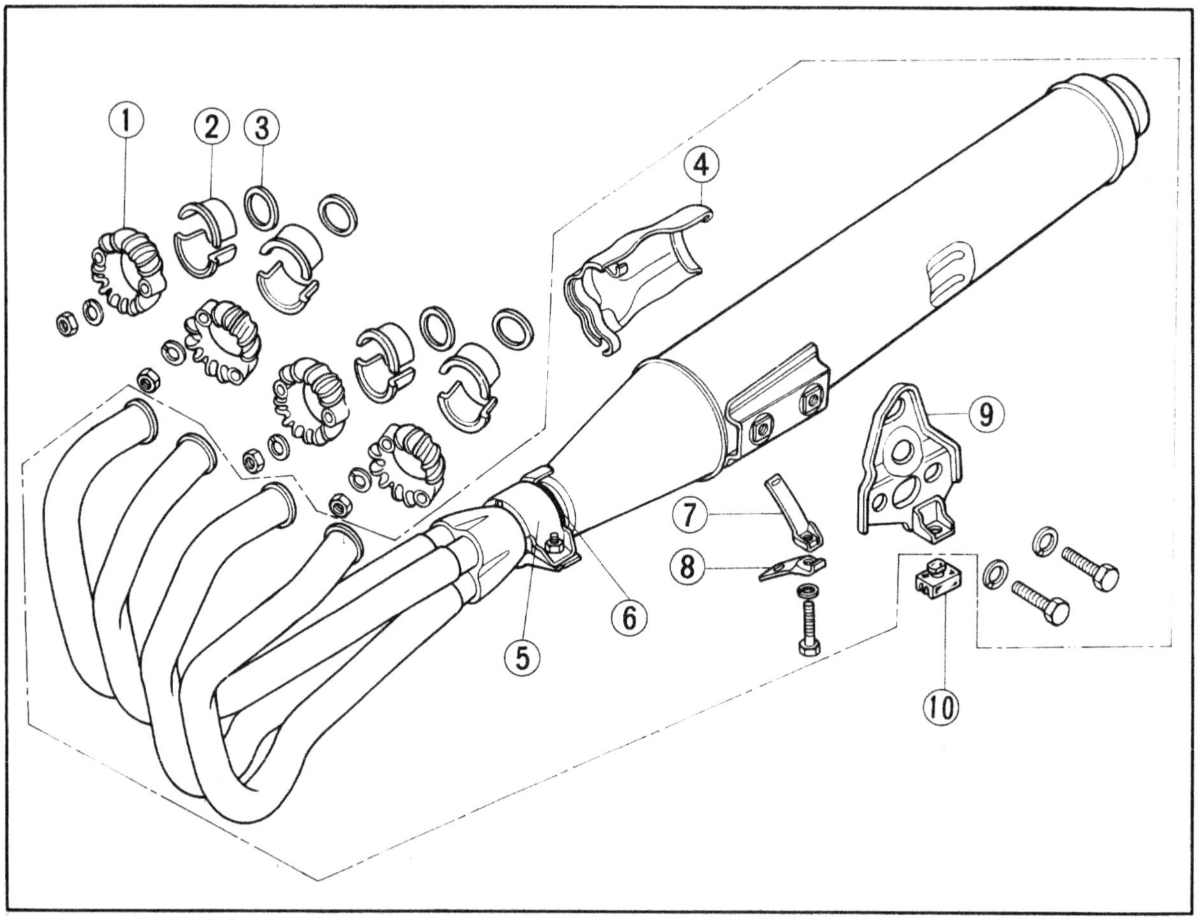

Fig. 2-17
① Exhaust pipe joint
② Exhaust pipe joint collar
③ Exhaust pipe gaskets
④ Exhaust pipe protector
⑤ Muffler band
⑥ Muffler sealing gasket
⑦ Protector band B
⑧ Protector band A
⑨ Muffler stay
⑩ Stand stop rubber A

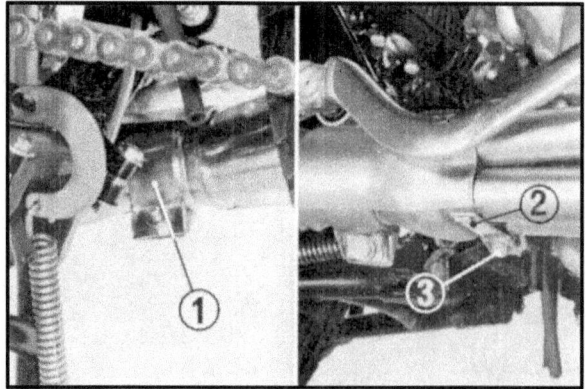

Fig. 2-18
① Muffler band
② Protector band A
③ Muffler band bolt

C. Reassembly

1. Install the sealing gasket and connect the exhaust pipes to the muffler.
2. Install the muffler band, attach the protector bands A and B to the exhaust pipe protector, and tighten the screws securely.
3. Install the exhaust muffler.

ELECTRICAL SYSTEM INSPECTION

1. Clutch switch

Attach the service tester probes to the green and green/red leads of the clutch switch contained in the headlight case and operate the clutch lever to check for continuity. There should be continuity only when the clutch is disengaged.

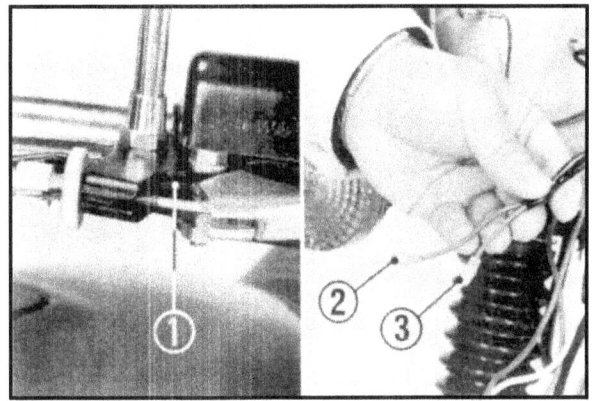

Fig. 2-19　1 Clutch switch　3 Green/red lead
　　　　　2 Green lead

2. Starting Switch

Remove the fuel tank and the connector cover by loosening the 6mm screw. Take the starting switch terminal out of the connector.

Fig. 2-20　1 Connector cover　3 Connector
　　　　　2 6mm screw

Check the switch for continuity between the circuits (○—○) shown in the table below. If there is continuity, the switch is in good condition.

Terminal	ST1	ST2	HL
Wire color	Black	Yellow/red	Black/red
FREE	○———————○		
PUSH	○———○		

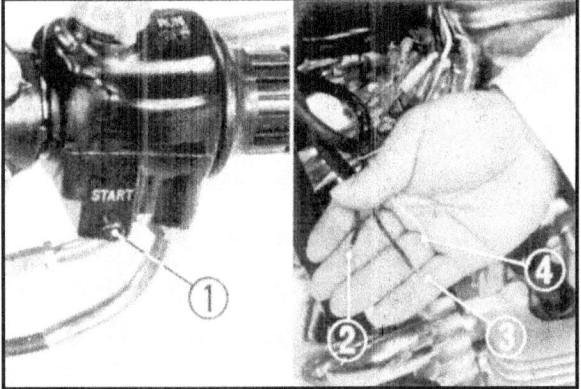

Fig. 2-21　1 Starting switch　3 Black/red lead
　　　　　2 Black lead　　　 4 Yellow/red lead

3. Silicon diode

Using a service tester, check the diode for continuity in the normal and reverse directions. If there is continuity in the normal direction only, the diode is in good condition. If there is continuity or no continuity in both directions, the diode is defective.

CAUTION:
Do not use a megger for this test. High voltage applied to the diode may damage it.

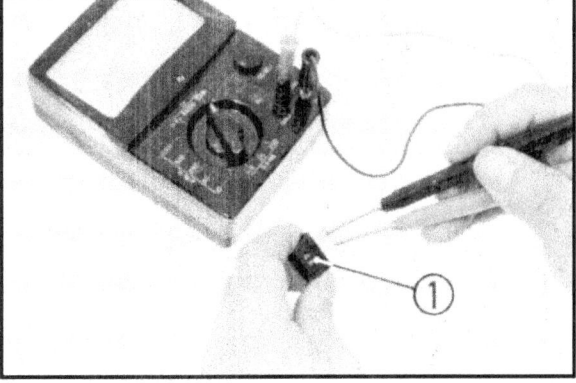

Fig. 2-22　1 Silicon diode

16. SUPPLEMENT TO CB550F

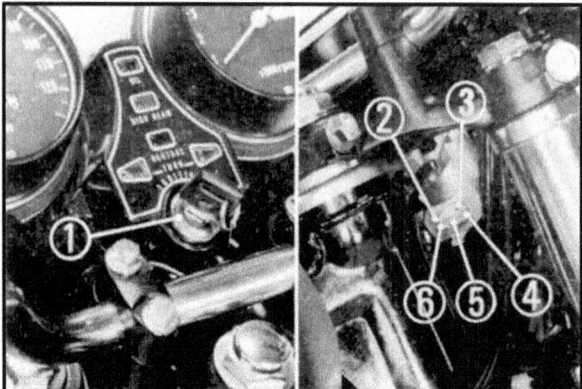

Fig. 2-23 ① Main switch ④ Brown
② Brown ⑤ Red
③ Brown/white ⑥ Black

4. Main switch

Place the switch key in OFF, ON or PARK position and check the switch for continuity between the circuits (○—○) shown in the table below. If there is no continuity or if there is continuity between circuits other than those shown in the table, the switch is defective.

Terminal	BAT	IG	TL1	TL2	PA
Wire color	Red	Black	Brown	Brown/White	Brown
Lock					
OFF					
RUN	○—○	○	○	○	⚬
PA	○—	—⚬			○

5. Dimmer switch and turn signal control switch

Remove the fuel tank, and the connector cover. Take the leads out as shown in the table below. Check each switch for continuity between the circuits (○—○) shown in the table. If there is continuity, the switch is in good condition. If there is no continuity, the switch is defective.

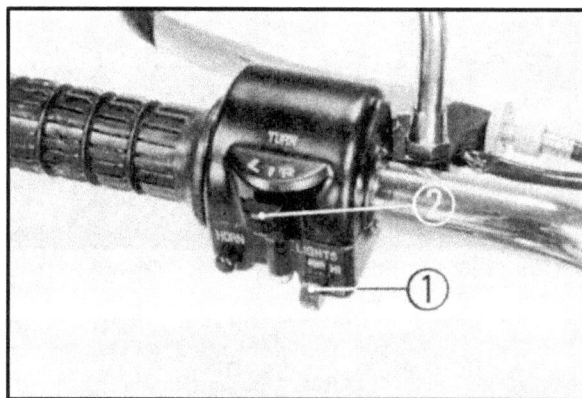

Fig. 2-24 ① Dimmer switch
② Turn signal control switch

Terminal	W	B	L	R
Wire color	Green	Blue/Brown	Orange	Light Blue
L₂	○—○—○			
L₁	○—○			
N				
R₁	○—○			
R₂	○—○—○			

Terminal	TL₁	PL	PR	HO
Wire color	Brown/white	Orange/white	Light blue/white	Light green
L₂	○—○		○	
L₁	○	○		
N	○	○		
R₁	○—○			
R₂	○—○			

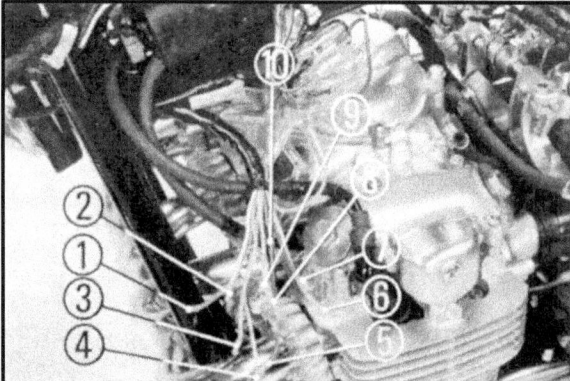

Fig. 2-25 ① Brown/blue ⑦ Light blue
② White ⑧ Orange
③ Blue ⑨ Brown/white
④ Black/yellow ⑩ Green
⑤ Light blue/white ⑪ Light green
⑥ Orange/white

Terminal	HL	Hi	Lo
Wire color	Black/yellow	Blue	white
Hi	○—○		
(N)	○	○	
Lo	○—○		

6. Horn switch

Remove the fuel tank and remove the connector cover. Then take out the light green lead as shown in Fig. 2-26. Attach one probe of a radio tester to the body and the other probe to the gray lead. There should be continuity when the horn button is pushed.

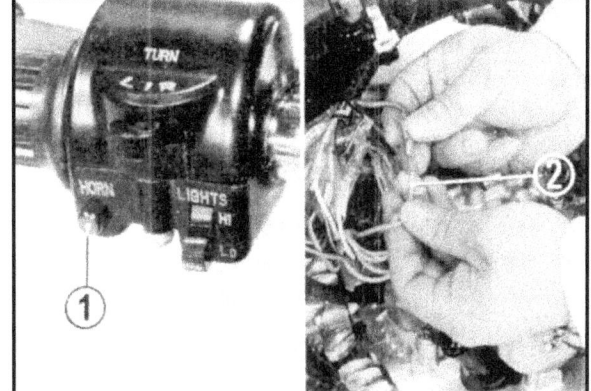

Fig. 2-26 ① Horn switch
② Light green lead

7. Engine stop switch

Remove the fuel tank and the connector cover. Check the switch for continuity between the circuits (○–○) shown in the table below. If there is no continuity, the switch is defective.

Terminal	IG	RUN
Wire color	Black	Black/white
OFF		
RUN	○———	———○
OFF		

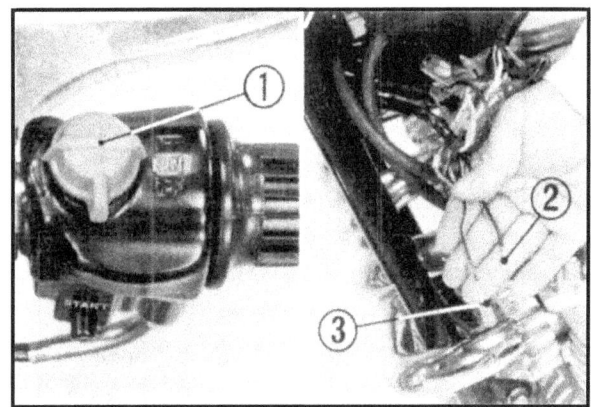

Fig. 2-27 ① Engine stop switch
② Black
③ Black/white

COMBINATION LIGHT

A. Disassembly

1. Remove the three 4 mm screws and the combination light cover.

Fig. 2-28 ① 4 mm tapping screws

2. Remove each bulb.
   To remove a bulb, turn it counterclockwise while pushing it in.

Fig. 2-29 ① Bulb (12V, 3.4W)

3. Remove the combination light case.
   To remove the case, remove the 8 mm nut securing the speedometer and tachometer stay. Straighten the stay and remove the 5 mm screws as shown.

B. Reassembly

To reassemble the combination light, reverse the disassembly procedure.

Fig. 2-30 ① 8 mm nut

Fig. 2-31 ① 5 mm screws
② Combination light case

16. SUPPLEMENT TO CB550F

REAR WHEEL

The CB550F differs from the CB550 in that the rear ends of the rear fork are constructed to prevent the rear wheel from coming off.

A. Disassembly

See page 74 of CB500~550, steps 1-4. Push the wheel forward, and lift the chain off the driven sprocket. Remove the back bolts and the chain adjusting stoppers. Pull the wheel backward and the axle to the left to remove the wheel.

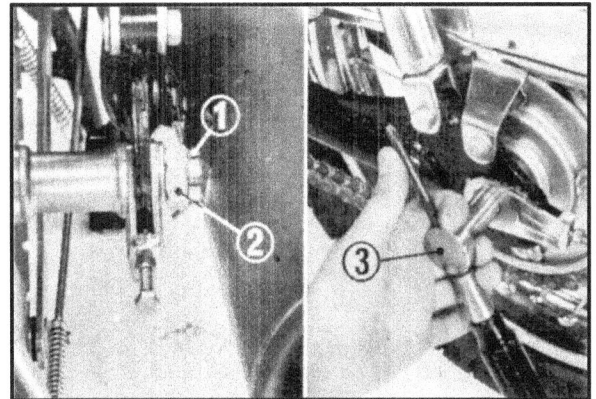

Fig. 2-32
① Cotter pin
② Axle nut
③ Rear wheel axle shaft

Carburetor setting table

CB500	Item	CB550F-A
022A	Setting no.	069A
#100	Main jet	#98
2.515φ—2°30′—4 grooves	Jet needle	2.495φ—3°00′—2 grooves
1-1/2±3/8 taper 12°	Air screw	1-1/2±1/2 taper 18°
0.9φ×2	Air bleed 1	0.7φ×2
0.9φ×2	Air bleed 2	0.7φ×2
0.9φ×2	Air bleed 3	0.7φ×2
0.9φ×2	Air bleed 4	0.7φ×2
0.9φ×2	Air bleed 5	0.7φ×2

16. SUPPLEMENT TO CB550F

	Item	Metric	English
ENGINE	Air Filter	Paper element	
	Valve Tappet Clearance	IN: 0.05, EX: 0.08 mm	IN: 0.002, EX: 0.003 in.
	Engine weight	72 kg	159 lb.
	Air Screw Opening	1-3/4 ± 1/2 turns	
	Idle Speed	1,000 rpm	
DRIVE TRAIN	Clutch	Wet, multi-plate	
	Transmission	5-speed, constant mesh	
	Primary Reduction	3.062	
	Gear Ratio I	2.353	
	″ II	1.636	
	″ III	1.269	
	″ IV	1.036	
	″ V	0.900	
	Final Reduction	2.176, drive sprocket 17, driven sproket 37T	
	Gear Shift Pattern	Left foot return type	
ELECTRICAL	Ignition	Battery and ignition coil	
	Starting System	Electrical motor and kick pedal	
	Alternator	Three phase A.C. 12V-0.11kW/2,000 rpm	
	Battery Capacity	12V-12AH	
	Spark Plug	NGK D-7ES. DENSO X-22ES	
	Headlight	Low/high,	12V-50W/50W
	Tail/stoplight	Tail/Stop	12V- 8W/27W
	Turn Signal light	Front/Rear	12V-23W/23W
	Speedometer Light	12V-3.4W	
	Tachometer Light	12V-3.4W	
	Neutral Indicator Light	12V-3.4W	
	Turn Signal Indicator Light	12V-3.4W	
	High Beam Indicator Light	12V-3.4W	

16. SUPPLEMENT TO CB550F

WIRING DIAGRAM

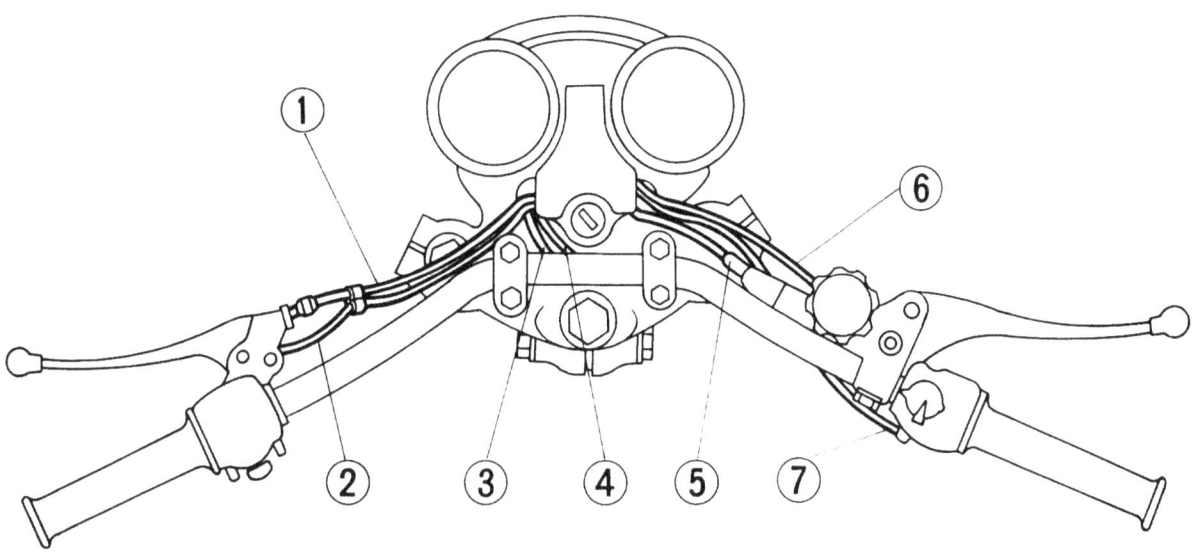

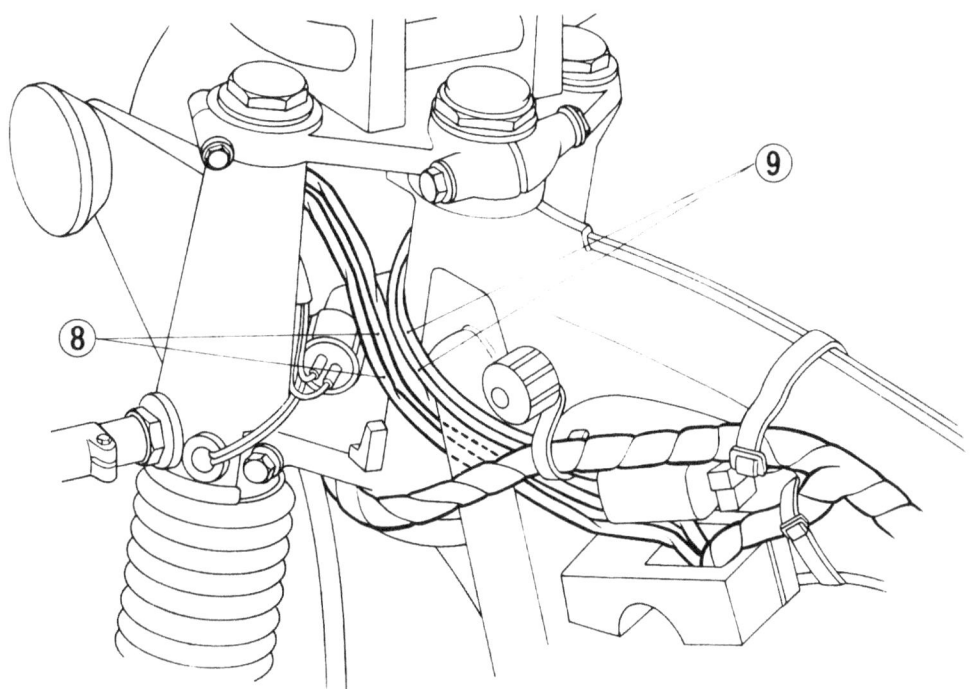

① Clutch cable
② Clutch lever switch cable
③ Handle switch (L) cord
④ Handle switch (R) cord
⑤ Front brake hose
⑥ Throttle cable
⑦ Throttle cable
⑧ Handle (R) (L) switch cord
⑨ Throttle cable (R) (L)

16. SUPPLEMENT TO CB550F

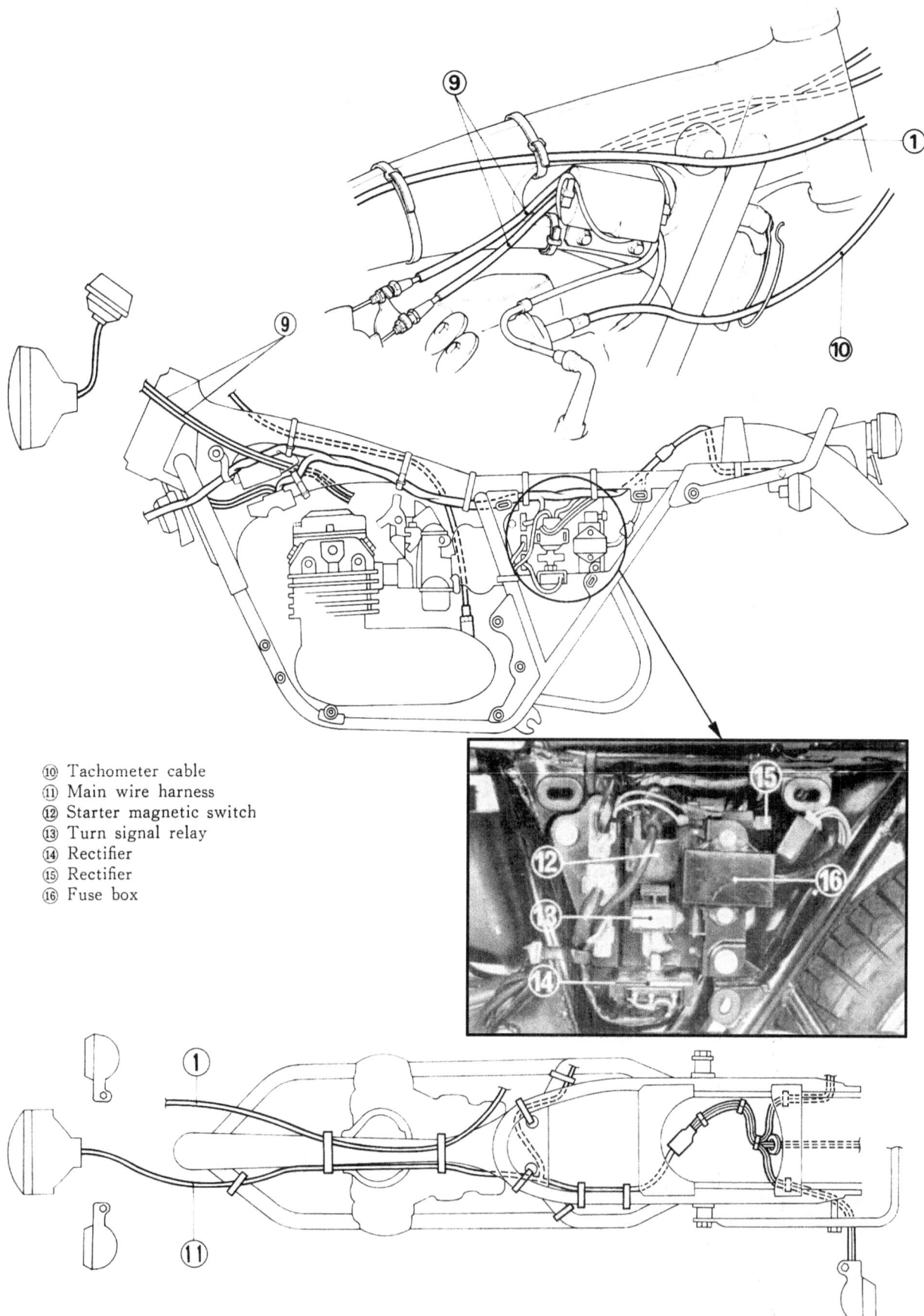

⑩ Tachometer cable
⑪ Main wire harness
⑫ Starter magnetic switch
⑬ Turn signal relay
⑭ Rectifier
⑮ Rectifier
⑯ Fuse box

16. SUPPLEMENT TO CB550F

WIRING DIAGRAM CB 550 F-A

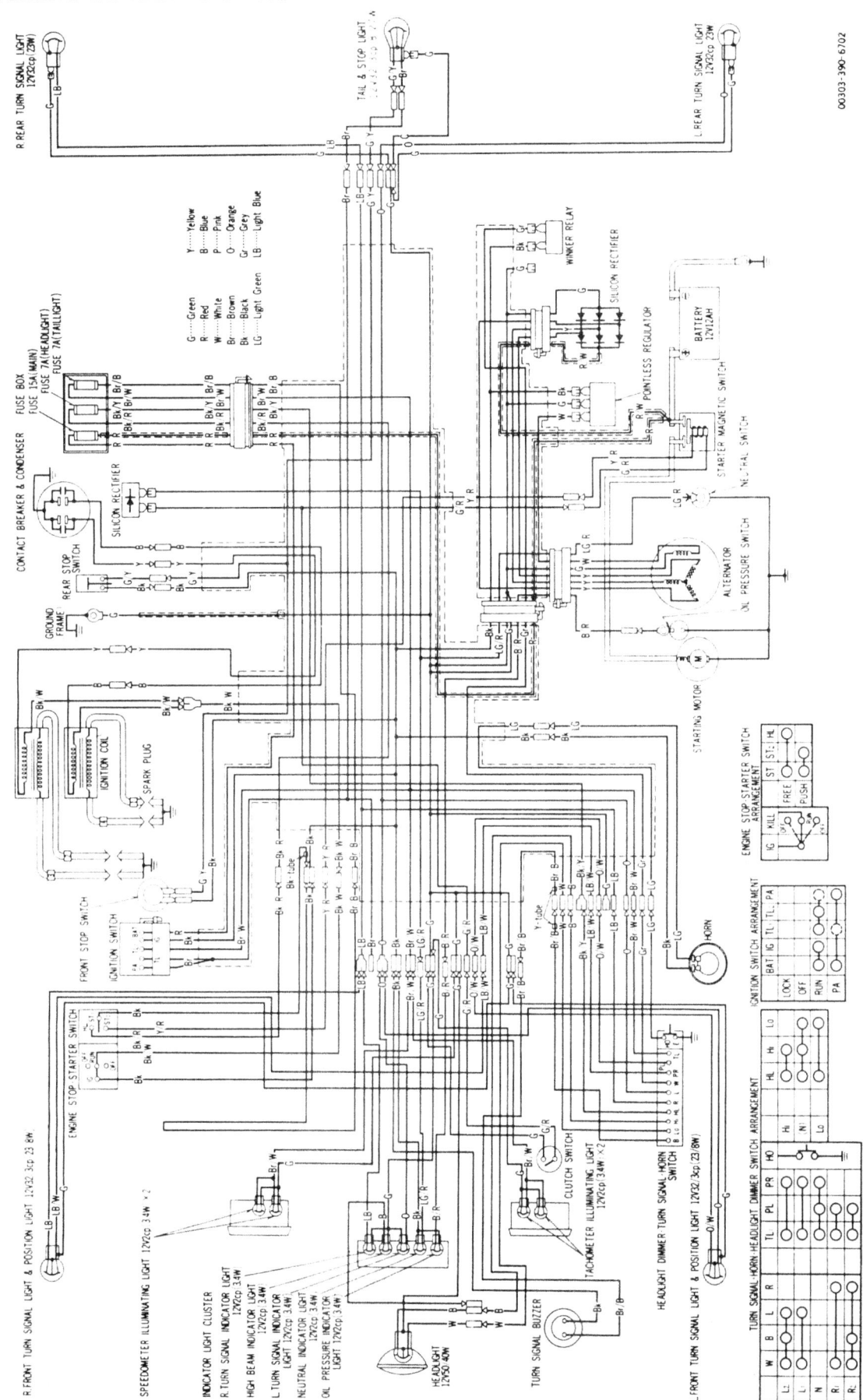

17. SUPPLEMENT TO CB 550 K2 ('76)

Engine No. CB550E—1067334 and subsequent
Frame No. CB550E—1230001 and subsequent

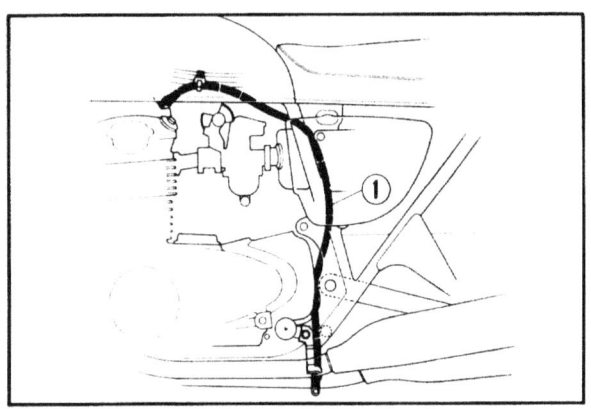

Fig. K2-1 ① Breather tube

1. BREATHER TUBE

The breather tube has been rerouted as shown in Fig. K2-1.

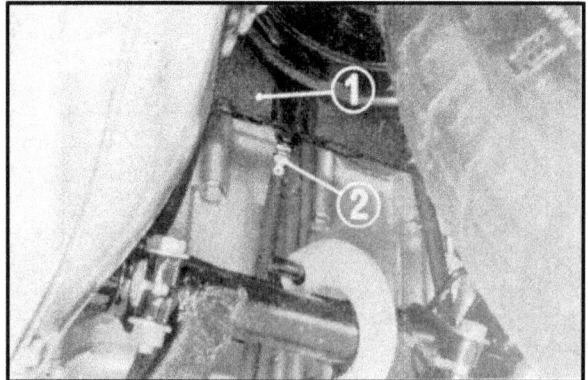

Fig. K2-2 ① Front brake disc
② UBS nut

2. FRONT WHEEL

The front brake will no longer use the tanged washer and nut arrangement for the attachment of the brake disc to the wheel hub. The disc is now tightened with UBS nuts.
Tightening torque: 270–330 kg-cm
(20-24 lbs-ft)

3. FORK TOP BRIDGE

Flange bolts used for tightening the fork top bridge will be changed from 8 mm to 7 mm.
Tightening torque: 180–250 kg-cm
(13-18 lbs-ft)

4. REAR FORK

The rear fork pivot pipe now has a grease nipple at its center. The grease nipples formerly located at both ends of the rear fork pivot bolt were discontinued.

Fig. K2-3 ① Rear fork
② Grease nipple

17. SUPPLEMENT TO CB550 K2 ('76)

4. SPECIFICATIONS (CB550 '76)

Item	
DIMENSION	
Overall Length	2,120 mm (83.5 in.)
Overall Width	825 mm (32.5 in.)
Overall Height	1,115 mm (44.0 in.)
Wheel Base	1,405 mm (55.5 in.)
Seat Height	805 mm (31.7 in.)
Foot Peg Height	315 mm (12.4 in.)
Ground Clearance	150 mm (6.3 in.)
Dry Weight	192 kg (423 lb.)
FRAME	
Type	Double cradle frame
F. Suspension, Travel	Telescopic fork, travel 121 mm (4.8 in.)
R. Suspension, Travel	Swing arm, travel 77.3 mm (3.0 in.)
F. Tire Size, Type	3.25-19-4PR Rib, tire air pressure 1.75/2.0 kg/cm² (25/28 psi)
R. Tire Size, Type	3.75-18-4PR Block, tire air pressure 2.0 /2.5 kg/cm² (28/36 psi)
F. Brake	Disc brake
R. Brake	Internal expanding shoe
Fuel Capacity	14.0 lit. (3.7 U.S.gal. 3.1 Imp.gal.)
Fuel Reserve Capacity	5.0 lit. (1.3 U.S.gal. 1.1 Imp.gal.)
Caster Angle	64°
Trail Length	105 mm (4.1 in.)
ENGINE	
Type	Air-cooled 4-stroke O.H.C. engine
Cylinder Arrangement	4 cylinder in line
Bore and Stroke	58.5 × 50.6 mm (2.303 × 1.992 in.
Displacement	544 cc (33.19 cu in.)
Compression Ratio	9 : 1
Carburetor, Venturi Dia.	Four Piston valve type, venturi dia. 22 mm (0.866 in.)
Valve Train	Chan driven over head camshaft
Oil Capacity	3.0 lit. (3.2 U.S. qt 2.6 Imp. qt)
Lubrication System	Forced pressure and wet sump
Fuel Required	Low-lead gasoline with 91 octane number or higher
Air Filter	Paper filter
Valve Tappet Clearance	IN : 0.05, EX : 0.08 mm (IN : 0.002, EX : 0.003 in.)
Air Screw Opening	1 1/2
Idle Speed	1000 rpm
DRIVE TRAIN	
Clutch	Wet multi-plate
Transmission	5-Speed constant mesh
Primary Reduction	3.063
Gear Ratio I	2.353
II	1.636
III	1.269
IV	1.036
V	0.900
Final Reduction	2.176, drive sprocket 17 T, driven sprocket 37 T
Gear Shift Pattern	Left foot operated return system
ELECTRICAL	
Ignition	Battery and ignition coil
Starting System	Starting motor and kick starter
Alternator	A.C. Generator 0.13 kw/2,000 rpm
Battery Capacity	12 V–12 AH
Spark plug	NGK D7ES or ND X22ES

17. SUPPLEMENT TO CB550 K2 ('76)

5. WIRING DIAGRAM (CB550 '76)

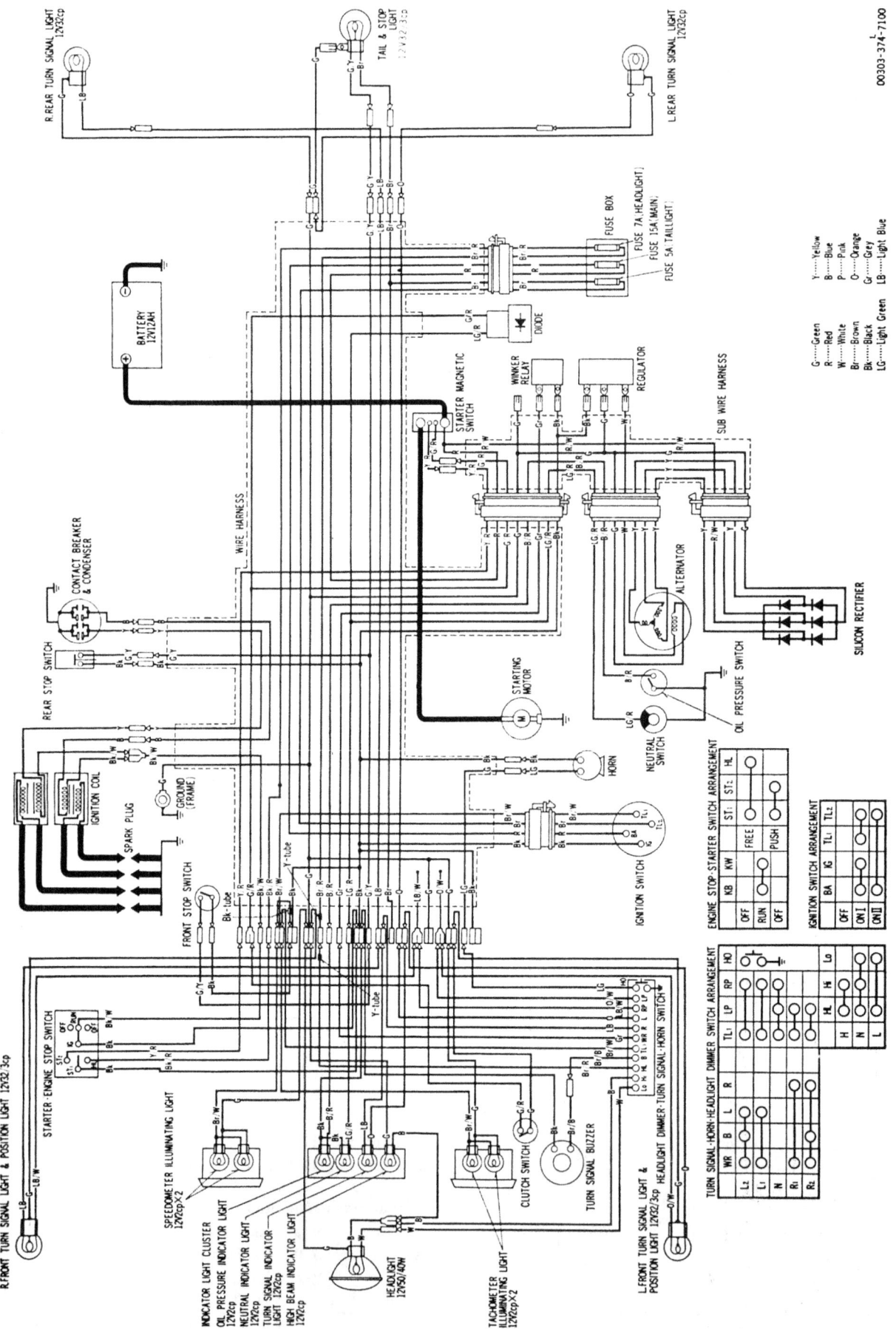

18. INDEX
(Up to and including page 163)

— A —

Adjust ignition timing 11
—— valve tappet clearnce...... 7
—— cam chain 13
—— carburetor 8
Alternator generator 93
Air cleaner 16, 119

— B —

Battery 102
Bleeding brake system 15, 73
Brakes 65
Brake caliper adjustment 14
Brake lever travel 73
Brake pedal travel 15
Brake lining wear monitor ...112
Body electrical 87
Body 84
Bore and stroke....................113
Blow-by gas 108
Bulb 164

— C —

Cam chain tensioner 13, 46
Carburetor 57
Camshaft 24
—— holder 24
Charging system 93
Change oil and oil filter 13
Clutch 40, 107, 114, 115
Compression ratio 18
—— test 18
—— pressure 18
Condenser 92
Connecting rod 51
Contact breaker 92
Crankshaft 48
Cylinder 24
—— arrangement 24
—— bore 27
Cylinder head 24

— D —

Displacement 113
Drive chain 17

— E —

Engine installation 20

Engine removal 20

— F —

Final drive 56
Final reduction 136
Front brake 65
Front suspension 79, 110
Front wheel and tire............65
Fuel tank capacity 137
Fuel strainer....................85
Fuel tank 84

— G —

Gear ratio 136
Gear shift drum 43
Gear shift drum stopper 43
Generator 95

— H —

Horn 104

— I —

Idling speed 9
Ignition timing 11
Ignition system 89
Ignition coil 89

— K —

Kick starter pedal 53

— L —

Lubrication system 36

— M —

Main ignition switch 162
Maintenance operation 7

— N —

Neutral switch 106

— O —

Oil filter 14, 39
—— element 14
Oil pump 39
Oil pressure switch 105
Oil warning lamp 87
Oil screen 37
Oil drain plug 20

— P —

Piston 24
Piston pin 26
Piston ring 28
Primary chain 48
Primary shaft 54

— R —

Rear brake 15, 73
Rear suspension 82
Rear fork 82
Rear wheel 73
Regulator 96
Relief valve 37
Rocker arm 35
—— shaft 35

— S —

Service air cleaner 16
—— battery 16, 102
—— spark plug 13, 91
Special tools 3
Silicone rectifier 97
Spark advancer 92
Spark plug 13, 91
Specifications 137
Starting clutch................48
Starter magnetic switch 101
Starting motor................99
Starting motor safety unit ...109
—— cable 99
Steering 77
Stop switch..................103

— T —

Technical data 135
Throttle valve 61
Trouble shooting 128
Transmission..................53

— V —

Valve 33
Vacuum gauge.................. 8
Valve timing 31

— W —

Winker switch 104
Wiring diagram..............143

MEMO

19. SUPPLEMENT TO CB500K3/CB550K3 ('77)

Engine No. CB550E—2000001 and subsequent

Frame No. CB550K—2000001 and subsequent

Engine No. CB500E—2200001 and subsequent

Frame No. CB500—1000001 and subsequent

1. CARBURETOR

A. Removal and installation

1. Turn the fuel valve lever to the "OFF" position and disconnect the fuel tube at the fuel valve and remove the over flow tube.
2. Open the seat and remove the fuel tank.
3. Remove the air cleaner case.
4. Remove the choke and throttle cables from the cable holders and disconnect them from each shaft lever.

Fig. K3-1　① Choke cable
　　　　　　② Throttle cables
　　　　　　③ Cable holders

5. Loosen the carburetor insulator bands and the air cleaner connecting bands. Take the carburetor assembly out.
6. To install the carburetor assembly, reverse the removal procedure.

Fig. K3-2　① Carburetor insulator band
　　　　　　② Air cleaner connecting band

19. SUPPLEMENT TO CB 500 K3/CB 550 K3 ('77)

Fig. K3-3 ① Bolt   ② Rear stay

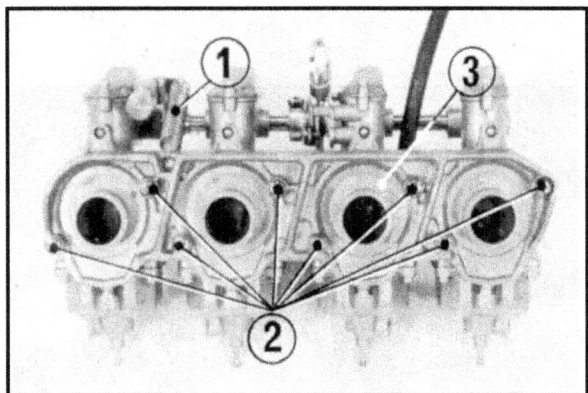

Fig. K3-4 ① Throttle return spring
② Screw   ③ Stay plate

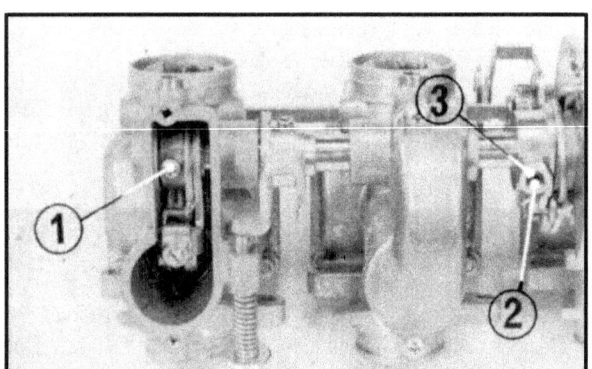

Fig. K3-5 ① Link arm fixing screw
② Set screw   ③ Lock nut

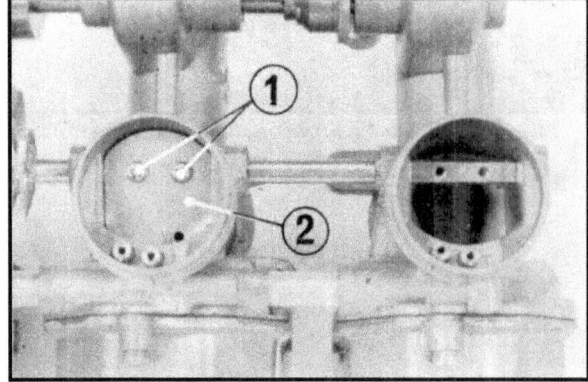

Fig. K3-6 ① Screw   ② Choke valve

B. Disassembly

Carburetor, throttle valve and jet needle:

1. Remove the carburetor assembly from the engine.
2. Remove the rear stays from the carburetor assembly by removing the four bolts.

3. Unhook the throttle return spring from the stopper arm. Remove the stay plate by removing the eight screws.
   Unhook the choke relief spring at the choke lever.

4. Remove the carburetor top by removing the two screws. Loosen the link arm fixing screw.
   Loosen the lock nut and remove the throttle lever set screw.

5. Remove the choke valve from the choke shaft by removing the two screws.
6. Separate the carburetors.

19. SUPPLEMENT TO CB 500 K3/CB 550 K3 ('77)

7. Remove the link arm assembly from the carburetor.
8. Remove the two screws and remove the throttle valve and jet needle from the link arm.

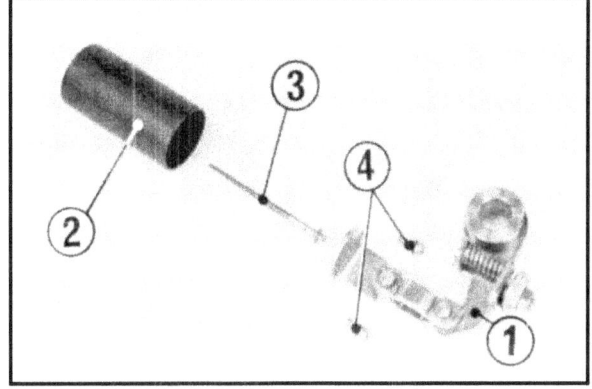

Fig. K3-7 1 Link arm 3 Jet needle
2 Throttle valve 4 Screw

Float, main jet and slow jet:
1. Remove the carburetor assembly from the engine.
2. Remove the three screws and the float chamber body from the carburetor.
3. Remove the float and float valve by pulling the float arm pin out.
4. Remove the main jet and slow jet.

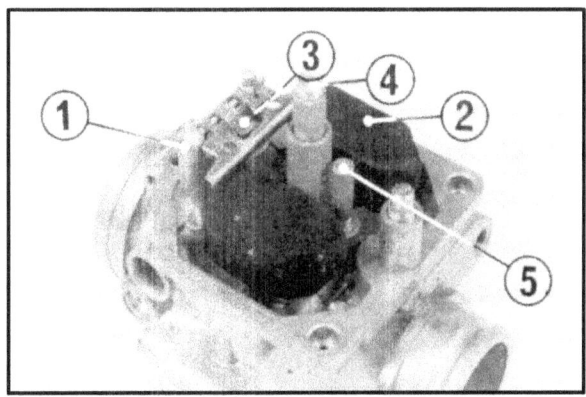

Fig. K3-8 1) Float arm pin 4) Main jet
2) Float 5) Slow jet
3) Float valve

C. Assembly

To assemble the carburetors reverse the disassembly procedure. Observe the following notes:

1. Install the throttle valve to the link arm so that the throttle valve cutaway faces the choke valve when it is installed in the carburetor body.

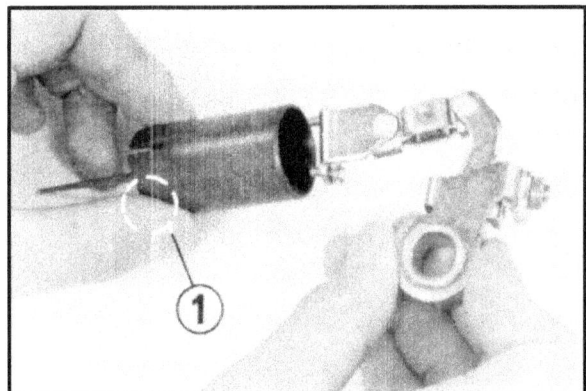

Fig. K3-9 1) Throttle valve cutaway

2. The link arm which is not equipped with the adjusting screw should be installed in the No. 2 carburetor.

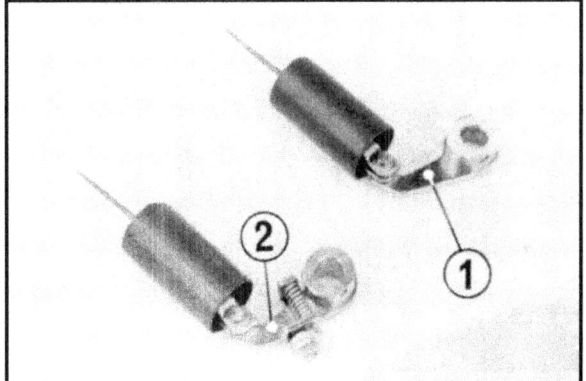

Fig. K3-10 1) Link arm for No. 2 carburetor
2) Link arm for No. 1, 3 and 4 carburetor

Fig. K3-11

3. Install the choke shaft levers and springs as shown in Fig. K3-11.

4. Install the choke valve to the choke shaft by using the lock washer and hex head screws. Bend the lock tabs to lock the screws.

NOTE:
The choke valve securing screws are peened when assembling the carburetor at the factory. Discard the used screws.

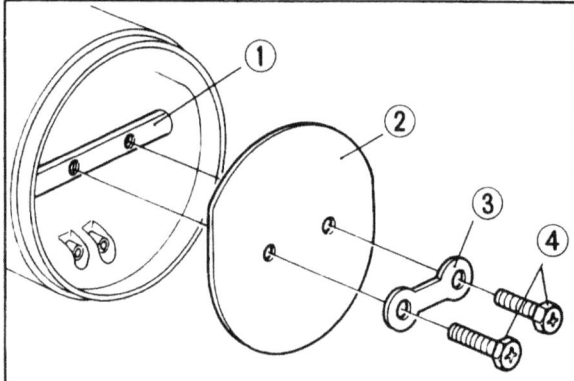

Fig. K3-12
① Choke shaft
② Choke valve
③ Lock washer
④ Hex head screw

D. Carburetor setting table

Item	CB550K3	CB500K3
Main jet	#90	#90
Air jet	#130	#120
Slow jet	#38	#42
Slow air jet	#150	#150
Jet needle setting	3rd. groove E2349F	2nd groove E2350F
Float height	14.5 mm (0.57 in.)	14.5 mm (0.57 in.)

E. Adjustment

Idle speed:

Make the adjustment with the engine warmed up.

1. Adjust the idle stop screw to allow the engine to run at the idle speed of 1050 rpm.
2. Turn the pilot screws either in or out to obtain the highest idle speed. Usually the correct setting will be found to be $1^1/_2$ turns open from a fully closed position.
3. If idle speed changes after adjusting the pilot screw, readjust the idle stop screw.

Fig. K3-13
① Idle stop screw
② Pilot screw

19. SUPPLEMENT TO CB 500 K3/CB 550 K3 ('77)

Synchronizing carburetors:
1. Remove the fuel tank. Position the fuel tank higher than the carburetors and reconnect with a longer fuel tube.
2. Connect the vacuum gauge set to the carburetors.
3. Run the engine at the specified idle speed and read the vacuum. The vacuum gauge readings should be the same on all four gauges.
4. To adjust, proceed as follows:
   a. Remove the carburetor tops from the No. 1, 3 and 4 carburetors.
   b. Loosen the lock nut and turn the adjusting screw until the vacuum reading is the same as the No. 2 carburetor reading.

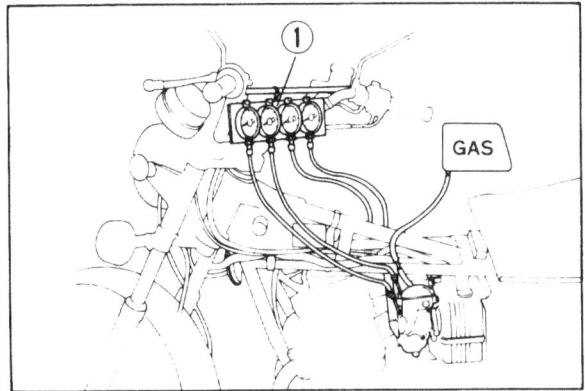

Fig. K3-14 (1) Vacuum gage set

Fig. K3-15 (1) Lock nut
(2) Adjusting screw

Fast idle:
1. Remove the fuel tank.
2. Pull the choke knob out fully and turn the adjusting screw until it touches the stopper.
3. Push the choke knob in and turn the adjusting screw in 2½ turns.
   Fast choke idle speed: 3000–4000 rpm

Fig. K3-16 (1) Adjusting screw

2. SWITCH HOUSING

When installing the right or left switch housing, align the mating edges of the housing with the punch mark on the handlebar and tighten the two screws securely.
The aligning mark on the brake lever bracket holder should also be lined up with the punch mark.

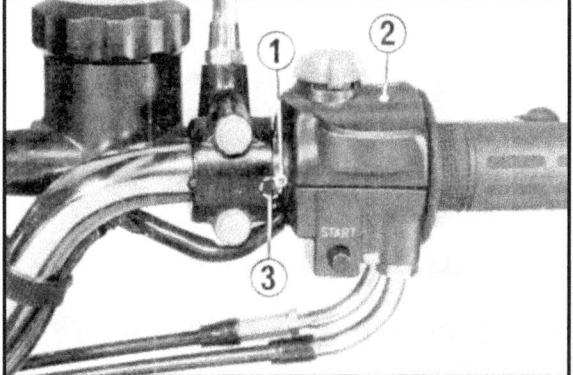

Fig. K3-17 (1) Punch mark
(2) Switch housing
(3) Aligning mark on holder

19. SUPPLEMENT TO CB 500 K3/CB 550 K3 ('77)

3. SERVICE DATA

		Standard value	Service limit
Front shock absorber spring free length		443.5 mm (17.46 in.)	409.5 mm (16.12 in.)
Rear shock absorber spring free length		210.4 mm (8.28 in.)	205 mm (8.07 in.)
Front brake	Caliper cylinder I.D.	38.18–38.23 mm (1.503–1.505 in.)	38.245 mm (1.506 in.)
	Caliper piston O.D.	38.115–38.148 mm (1.501–1.502 in.)	38.105 mm (1.500 in.)

4. SPECIFICATIONS (CB 500 K3/CB 550 K3 '77)

Item \ Type	U.S.A. (Canada)	General and Australia	Europe ⟨CB 500⟩	France
DIMENSION				
Overall Length	2,150 mm (84.7 in.)		2,160 mm	2,155 mm
Overall Width	825 mm (32.5 in.)		750 mm	
Overall Height	1,115 mm (44.0 in.)		1,100 mm	
Wheel Base	1,405 mm (55.5 in.)			
Seat Height	800 mm (31.5 in.)		825 mm (32.5 in.)	
Ground Clearance	160 mm (6.3 in.)			
Dry Weight	193.5 kg (426 lb.)		196 kg	
FRAME				
Type	Double cradle frame			
F. Suspension, Travel	Telescopic fork, travel 121 mm (4.8 in.)			
R. Suspension, Travel	Swing arm, travel 90.0 mm (3.5 in.)			
F. Tire Size, Type	3.25S19-4PR Rib, tire air pressure 1.75/2.0 kg/cm² (25/28 psi)			
R. Tire Size, Type	3.75S18-4PR Block, tire air pressure 2.0 /2.5 kg/cm² (28/36 psi)			
F. Brake	Disc brake			
R. Brake	Internal expanding shoe			
Fuel Capacity	16.0 lit. (4.2 U.S.gal. 3.5 Imp.gal.)			
Fuel Reserve Capacity	4.0 lit. (1.0 U.S.gal. 0.9 Imp.gal.)			
Caster Angle	64°			
Trail Length	104 mm (4.1 in.)			
ENGINE				
Type	Air-cooled 4-stroke O.H.C. engine			
Cylinder Arrangement	4 cylinder in line			
Bore and Stroke	58.5 × 50.6 mm (2.303 × 1.992 in.) ⟨56.0 × 50.6 mm⟩			
Displacement	544 cc (33.19 cu-in.) ⟨498 cc⟩			
Compression Ratio	9 : 1			
Carburetor, Venturi Dia.	Four Piston valve type, venturi dia. 22 mm (0.866 in.)			
Valve Train	Chain driven overhead camshaft			
Oil Capacity	3.2 lit. (3.4 U.S. qt 2.8 Imp. qt)			
Lubrication System	Forced pressure and wet sump			
Fuel Required	Low-lead gasoline with 91 octane number or higher			
Air Filter	Paper filter			
Intake Valve: Opens / Closes	5° BTDC / 35° ABDC			
Exhaust Valve: Opens / Closes	35° BBDC / 5° ATDC			
Valve Tappet Clearance	IN: 0.05 mm, EX: 0.08 mm (IN: 0.002 in, EX: 0.003 in.)			
Pilot Screw Opening	1 1/2 ± 1/2			
Idle Speed	1050 rpm			

19. SUPPLEMENT TO CB 500 K3/CB 550 K3 ('77)

Item	
DRIVE TRAIN	
Clutch	Wet multi-plate
Transmission	5-Speed constant mesh
Primary Reduction	3.063
Gear Ratio I	2.353
II	1.636
III	1.269
IV	1.036
V	0.900
Final Reduction	2.176, drive sprocket 17T, driven sprocket 37T
Gear Shift Pattern	Left foot operated return system
ELECTRICAL	
Ignition	Battery and ignition coil
Ignition Advance:	
"F" mark	5° BTDC
Max. advance	28°–31° BTDC
PPM from "F" to max. advance	1,200–2,500 rpm
Dwell Angle	190 ± 5°
Starting System	Starting motor and kick starter
Alternator	A.C. Generator 0.13 kw/2,000 rpm
Battery	12V-12AH
Spark plug	NGK D7ES or ND X22ES (NGK DR7ES or ND X22ESR-V) NGK DR7ES or ND X22ESR-U
Condenser Capacity	0.02–0.24 μF

19. SUPPLEMENT TO CB 500 K3/CB 550 K3 ('77)

5. WIRING DIAGRAM CB550K3 '77 (U.S.A. Type and Canada Type)

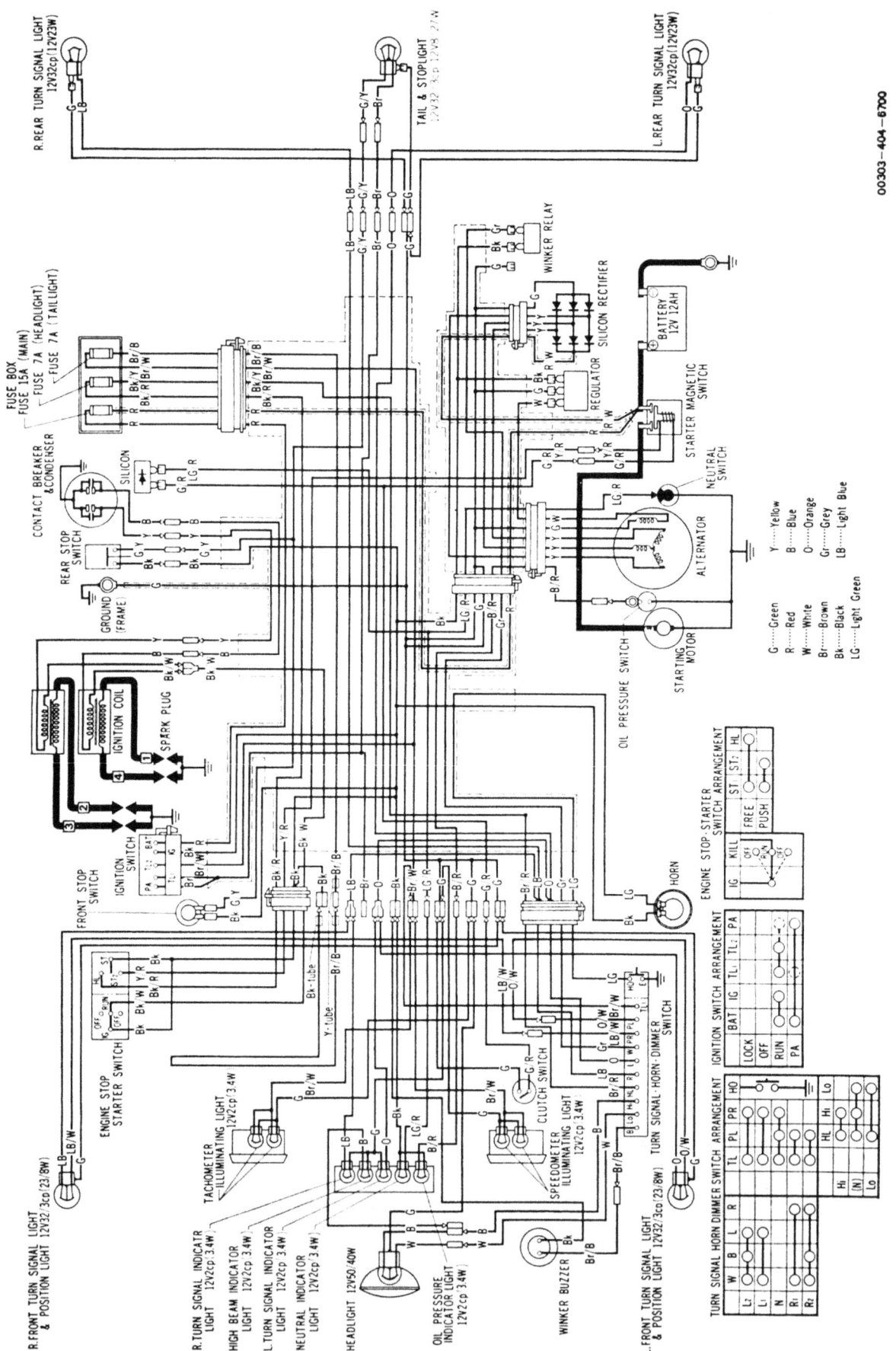

19. SUPPLEMENT TO CB 500 K3/CB 550 K3 ('77)

CB500K3/CB550K3 '77 (Europe Type)

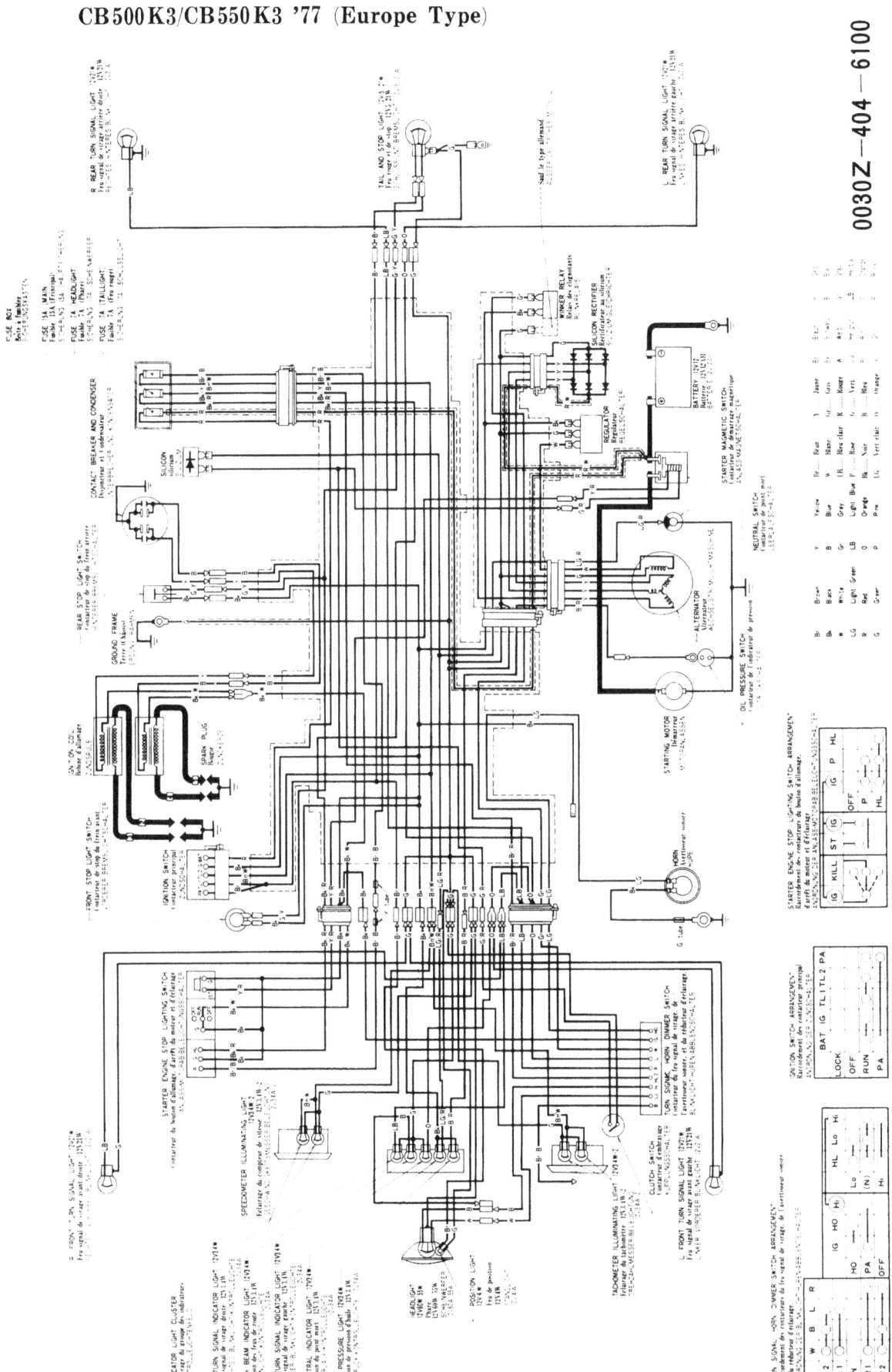

19. SUPPLEMENT TO CB 500 K3/CB 550 K3 ('77)

CB550K3 '77 (General Type and Australia Type)

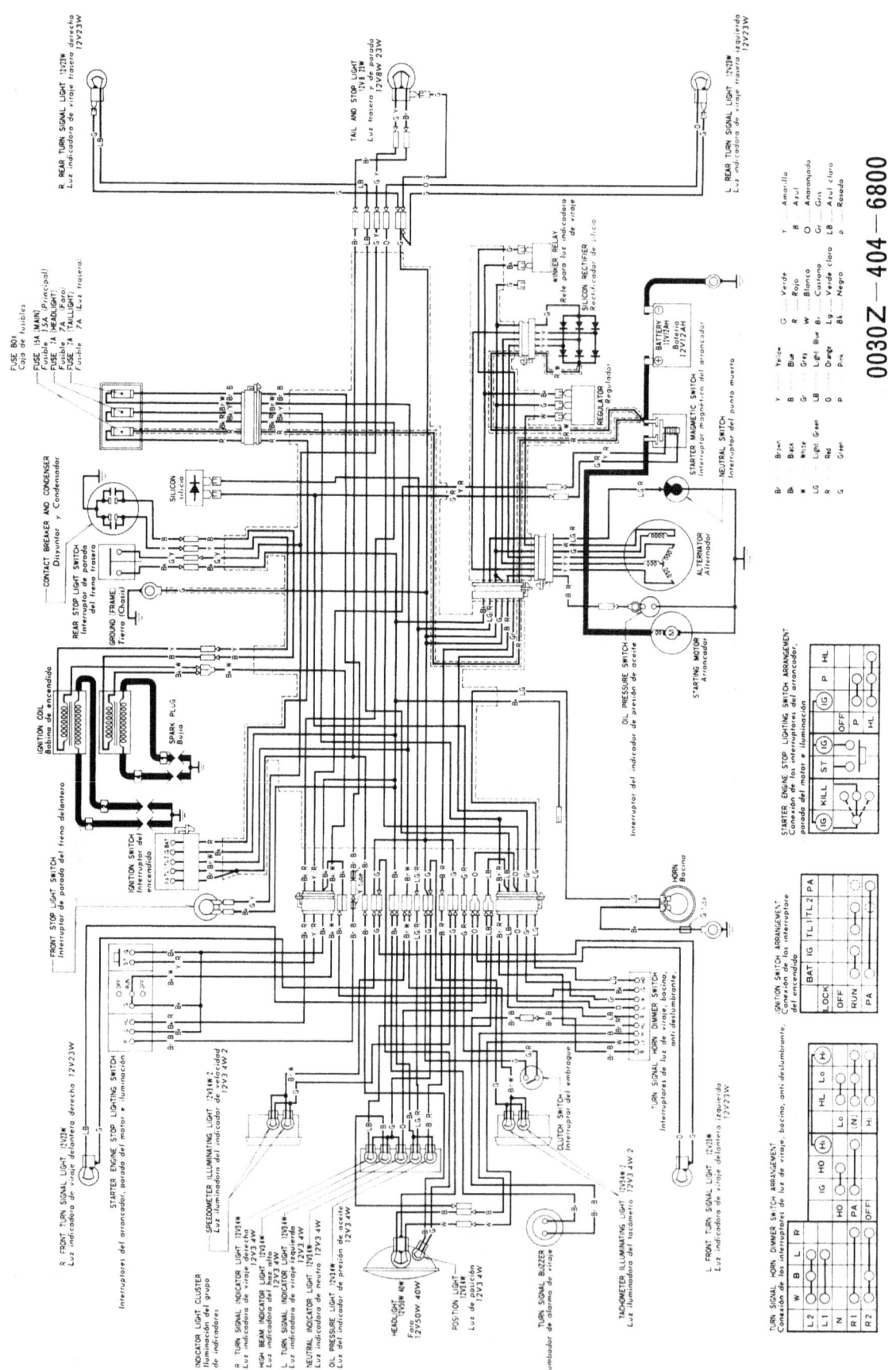

20. SUPPLEMENT TO CB550F2 ('77)

Engine No. CB550E—1135380 and subsequent
Frame No. CB550F—2100001 and subsequent

1. CLUTCH

The clutch plate B ⑤ differs in construction from the five other cluch plates B ③.
Install the clutch plate B ⑤ at the fourth position as counted from the clutch center ①.

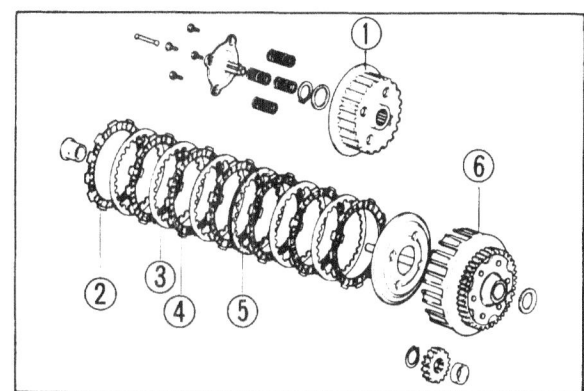

Fig. F2-1
① Clutch center
② Clutch friction disk B
③ Clutch plate B
④ Clutch friction disk
⑤ Clutch plate B comp.
⑥ Clutch outer comp.

2. FUEL VALVE

The valve positions are indicated by the arrow on the lever.
Inspection and cleaning:
1. Place the fuel lever in the "OFF" position and disconnect the fuel lines. Remove the fuel tank.
2. Drain the fuel tank thoroughly.
3. Loosen the fuel valve fixing nut and remove the fuel valve and fuel filter from the fuel tank.
4. Check the gasket to see that it is not damaged.
5. Wash the fuel filter in solvent and dry with compressed air. No damage can be tolerated here. Replace the filter with a new one if it is clogged and not cleanable.
6. Install the fuel filter to the fuel valve with the fixing nut. Do not forget to install the gasket into the groove of the fixing nut.
7. Install the fuel valve to the fuel tank with the fixing nut.
8. Install the fuel tank on the frame and connect the fuel lines and secure with the clip.
9. Fill the tank with fuel. With the fuel valve lever in the "ON" position, check for any leakage past the tube joints or connections.

Fig. F2-2 ① Arrow

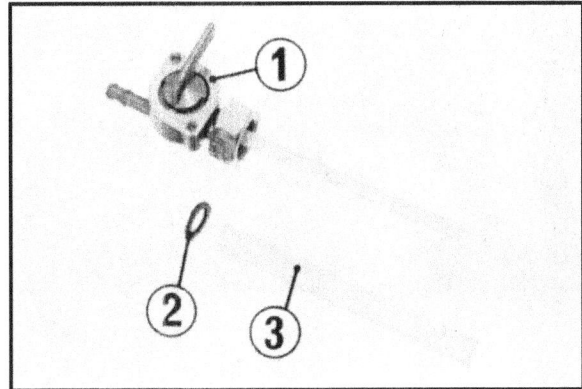

Fig. F2-3
① Fuel valve
② Gasket
③ Fuel filter screen

20. SUPPLEMENT TO CB 550 F2 ('77)

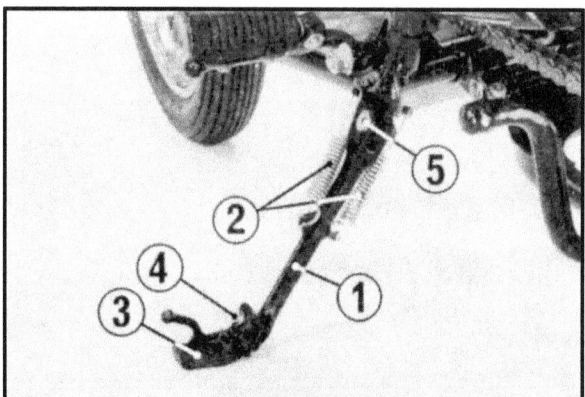

Fig. F2-4
① Side stand bar ④ 6 mm bolt
② Spring ⑤ Side stand pivot bolt
③ Rubber pad

3. SIDE STAND (German Type)

Two springs are installed on the side stand.

4. ELECTRICAL SYSTEM INSPECTION (Except U.S.A. and Canadian Type)

1. Clutch switch
See Page 161.

2. Starting switch
Remove the fuel tank and the connector cover by loosening the 6 mm screw. Take the starting switch terminal out of the connector. Check the switch for continuity between the sircuits (○—○) shown in the table below. If there is continuity, the switch is in good condition.

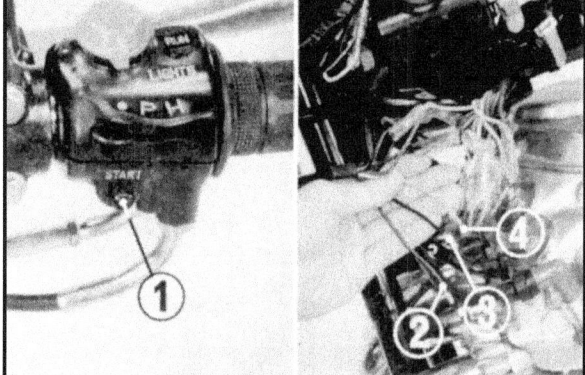

Fig. F2-5
① Starting switch
② Black/red lead
③ Black lead
④ Yellow/red lead

Terminal	ST1	ST2	HL
Wire color	Black	Yellow/red	Black/red
FREE	○——	——	——○
PUSH	○——	——○	

3. Main switch
Place the switch key in OFF, ON or PARK position and check the switch for continuity between the circuits (○—○) shown in the table below. If there is no continuity or if there is continuity between circuits other than those shown in the table, the switch is defective.

Fig. F2-6
① Main switch ④ Brown lead
② Brown lead ⑤ Red lead
③ Brown/white lead ⑥ Black lead

Terminal	BAT	IG	TL1	TL2	PA
Wire color	Red	Black	Brown	Brown/White	Brown
OFF					
ON	○—	—○	○—	—○	○
PA	○—	—	—○		○

20. SUPPLEMENT TO CB 550 F2 ('77)

4. Dimmer switch and turn signal control switch

Remove the fuel tank, and the connector cover. Then take out the leads shown in the table below. Check each switch for continuity between the circuits (O—O) shown in the table. If there is continuity, the switch is in good condition. If there is no continuity, the switch is defective.

Terminal	W	B	L	R
Wire color	Green	Brown/Blue	Orange	Light Blue
L₂	O	O	O	
L₁	O		O	
N				
R₁	O			O
R₂	O	O		O

Terminal	HL	Lo	Hi
Wire color	Black/Yellow	White	Blue
L	O	O	
H	O		O

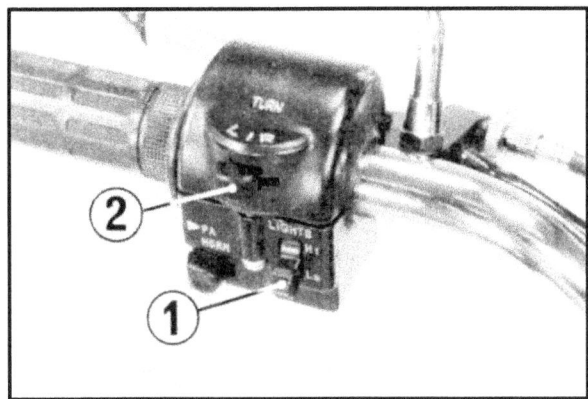

Fig. F2-7 ① Turn signal control switch
② Dimmer switch

Fig. F2-8 ① Brown lead ⑥ Light blue lead
② Brown/blue lead ⑦ Orange lead
③ Black/yellow lead ⑧ Green lead
④ White lead ⑨ Light green lead
⑤ Blue lead

5. Horn switch and passing switch

Remove the fuel tank, and the connector cover. Then take out the light green lead as shown. Attach one probe of a radio tester to the body or the black lead and the other probe to the light green lead.

There should be continuity when the horn button is pushed.

To test the passing switch, follow the same instructions as for the horn switch.

Terminal	IG	HO	Hi
Wire color	Black	Light green	Blue
HORN(push)	O	O	
PA(push)	O		O

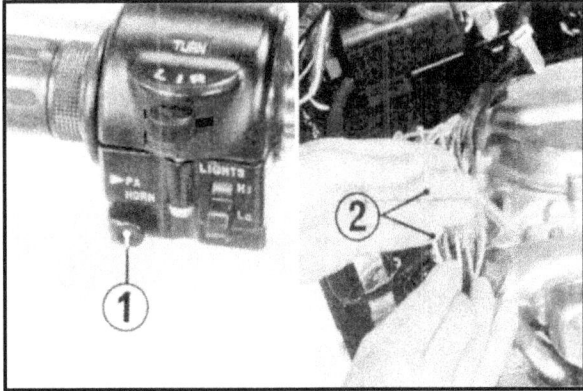

Fig. F2-9 ① Horn and passing switch
② Light green lead

20. SUPPLEMENT TO CB 550 F2 ('77)

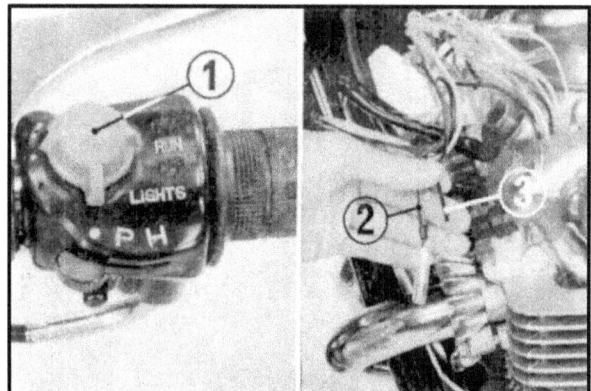

Fig. F2-10
① Engine stop switch
② Black/white lead
③ Black lead

6. Engine stop swich

Remove the fuel tank and the connector cover. Check the switch for continuity between the circuits (○—○) shown in the table below. If there is no continuity, the switch is defective.

Terminal	IG	RUN
Wire color	Black	Black/white
OFF		
RUN	○—	—○
OFF		

7. Lighting switch

Remove the Fuel tank and the connector cover. Check the switch for continuity between the circuits (○—○) shown in the table below. If there is no continuity, the switch is defective.

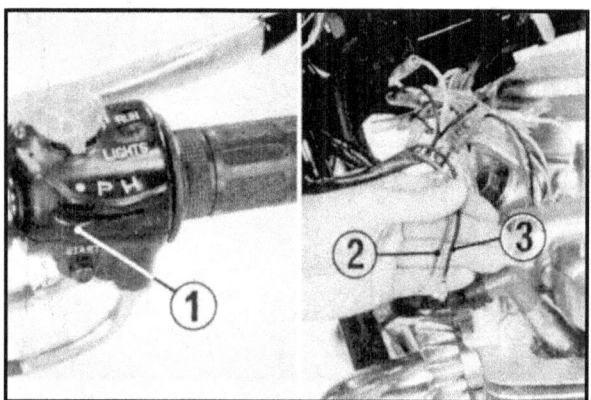

Fig. F2-11
① Lighting switch
② Brown/blue lead
③ Black/red lead

Terminal	IG	P	HL
Wire color	Black	Brown/blue	Black/red
●			
P	○—	—○	
H	○—	—○—	—○

5. BRAKE INSPECTION

Replenishing Brake Fluid

Remove the reservoir cap, washer and diaphram, and whenever the level is lower than the level mark engraved inside the reservoir (Up to the line shown for semi-transparent reservoir), fill the reservoir with DOT 3 BRAKE FLUID (or SAE J 1703) up to the level mark. Reinstall the diaphram and washer, and tighten the reservoir cap securely.

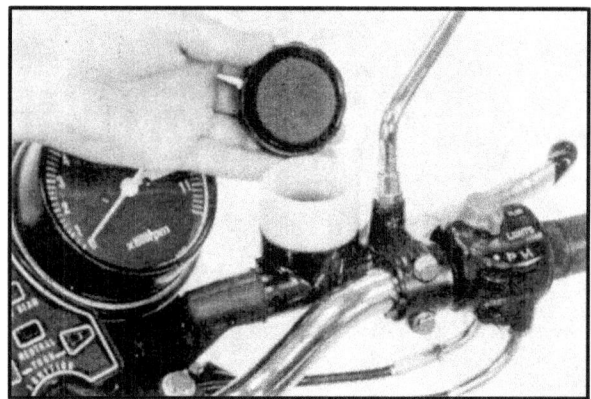

Fig. F2-12

NOTE:
- Do not mix different brands of brake fluid as chemical action will take place and may cause brake trouble.
- Do not use any other fluid in the brake system.
- Remove any brake fluid which may become spilled on the painted surface, rubber parts, and meter as it will produce chemical action and cause damage to these parts.

20. SUPPLEMENT TO CB 550 F2 ('77)

3. SPECIFICATIONS (CB 550 F 2 '77)

Item / Type	U.S.A. (Canada)	Australia	General	France	U.K.	Europe	Germany
DIMENSION							
Overall Length mm (in.)	2,115 (83.3)		2,105 (82.8)	2,110 (83.1)		2,115 (84.8)	
Overall Width mm (in.)			835 (32.9)				
Overall Height mm (in.)	1,100 (43.3)		1,111 (43.7)				
Wheel Base mm (in.)			1,405 (55.3)				
Seat Height mm (in.)	805 (31.7)		800 (31.5)				
Ground Clearance mm (in.)			160 (6.3)				
Dry Weight		191 kg (421 lb.)			192 kg (423 lb.)		
FRAME							
Type	Double cradle frame						
F. Suspension, Travel	Telescopic fork, Travel 121 mm (4.8 in.)						
R. Suspension, Travel	Swing Arm, Travel 90 mm (3.5 in.)						
F. Tire Size, Type	3.25S19-4PR Rib, tire air pressure 2.0 kg/cm² (28 psi)						
R. Tire Size, Type	3.75S18-4PR Block, tire air pressure 2.5 kg/cm² (36 psi)						
F. Brake	Disc brake						
R. Brake	Internal expanding shoe						
Fuel Capacity	16.0 lit. (4.2 U.S. gal. 3.5 Imp. gal.)						
Caster Angle	26°						
Trail Length	105 mm (4.1 in.)						
ENGINE							
Type	Air cooled 4-stroke O.H.C. engine						
Cylinder Arrangement	4 cylinder in line						
Bore and Stroke	58.5 × 50.6 mm (2.303 × 1.992 in.)						
Displacement	544 cc						
Compression Ratio	9.0 : 1						
Carburetor, Venturi Dia.	4 Piston valve Type, Venturi dia. 22 mm (0.866 in.)						
Valve Train	Chain driven over head camshaft						
Oil Capacity	3.2 lit. (3.4 U.S. qt. 2.8 Imp. qt)						
Lubrication System	Forced pressure and wet sump						
Fuel Required	Low-lead gasoline with 91 octane number or higher						
Air Filtration	Paper filter						
Valve Tappet Clearance	IN.: 0.05 mm (0.002 in.) EX.: 0.08 mm (0.003 in.)						
Air Screw Opening	1 1/2						
Idle Speed	1,000 r.p.m.						
DRIVE TRAIN							
Clutch	Wet multi plate						
Transmission	5-Speed constant mesh.						
Primary Reduction	3.062						
Gear Ratio I	2.353						
″ II	1.636						
″ III	1.269						
″ IV	1.036						
″ V	0.900						
Final Reduction	2.176 drive sprocket 17T, driven sprocket 37T						
Gear Shift Pattern	Left foot operated return system						
ELECTRICAL							
Ignition	Battery and Ignition coil						
Starting System	Electric motor and kick pedal						
Alternator	A.C. Generator 0.13 kW/2,000 r.p.m.						
Battery Capacity	12 V-12 AH						
Spark plug	NGK D7ES or ND X22ES (NGK DR7ES or ND X22ESR-U)						

20. SUPPLEMENT TO CB 550 F2 ('77)

4. WIRING DIAGRAM CB 550 F 2 '77
(U.S.A. Type and Canada Type)

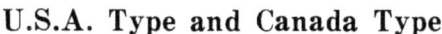

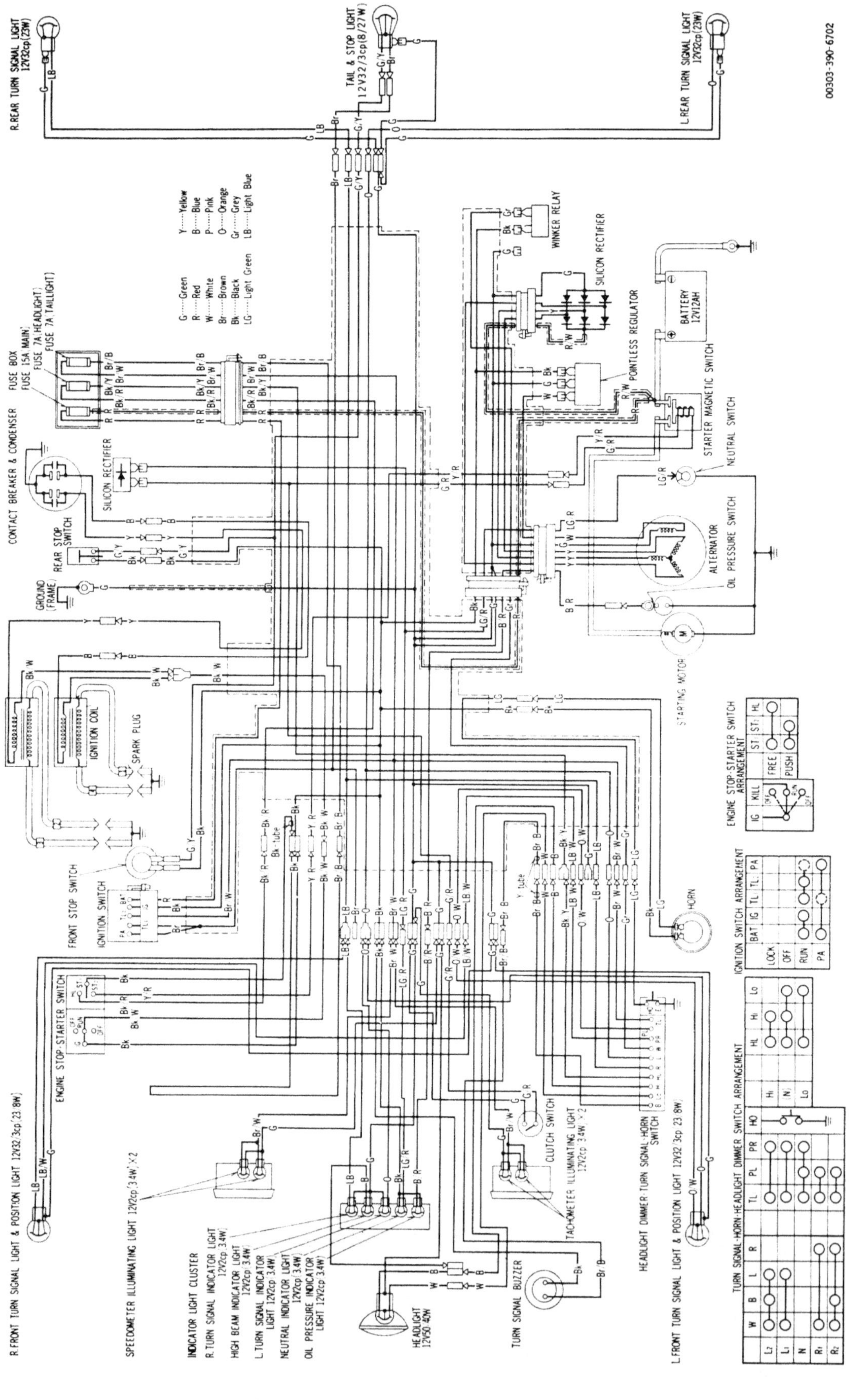

20. SUPPLEMENT TO CB550 F2 ('77)

(GENERAL TYPE)

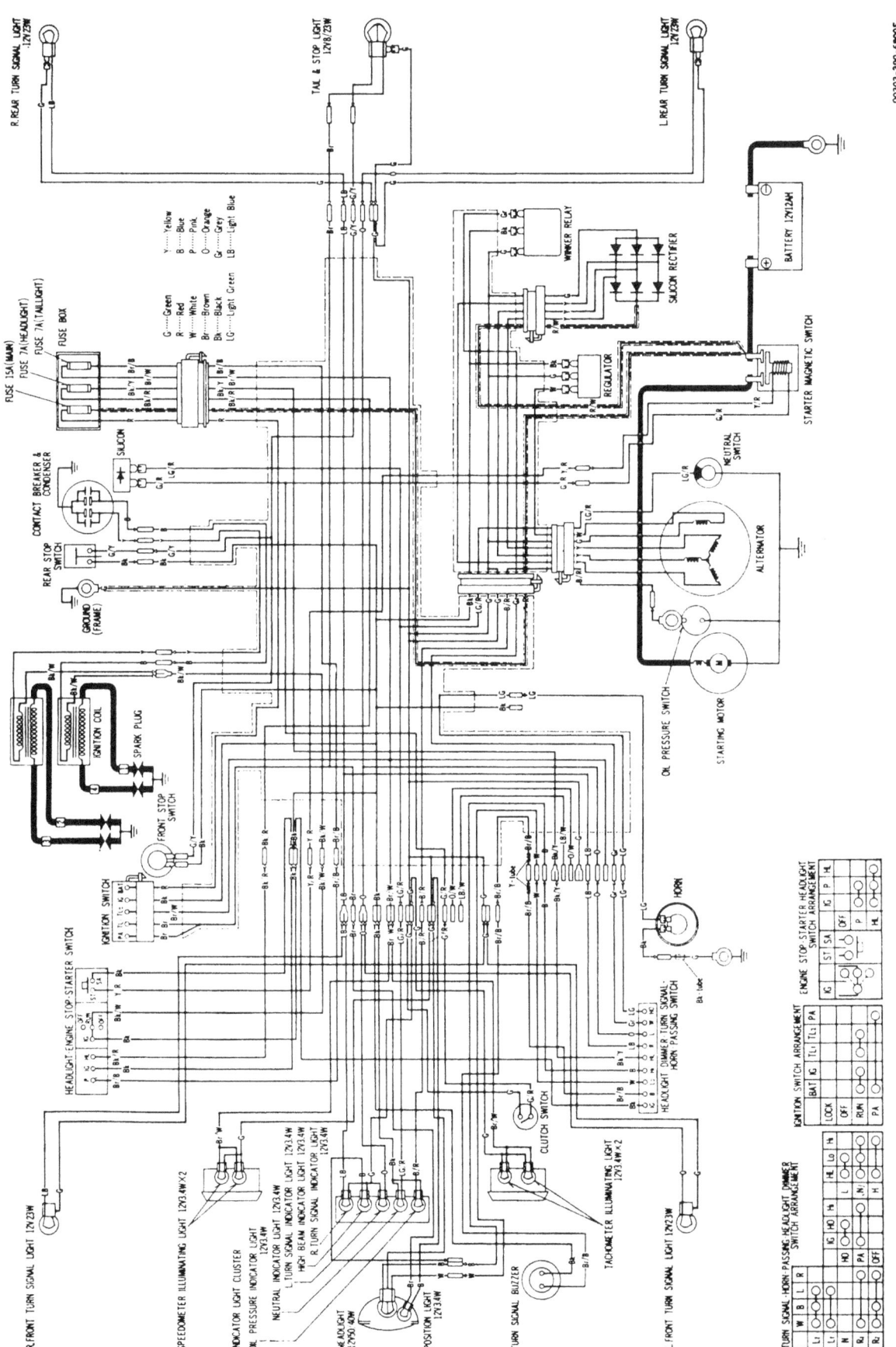

20. SUPPLEMENT TO CB 550 F2 ('77)

(U.K. EUROPEAN TYPE)

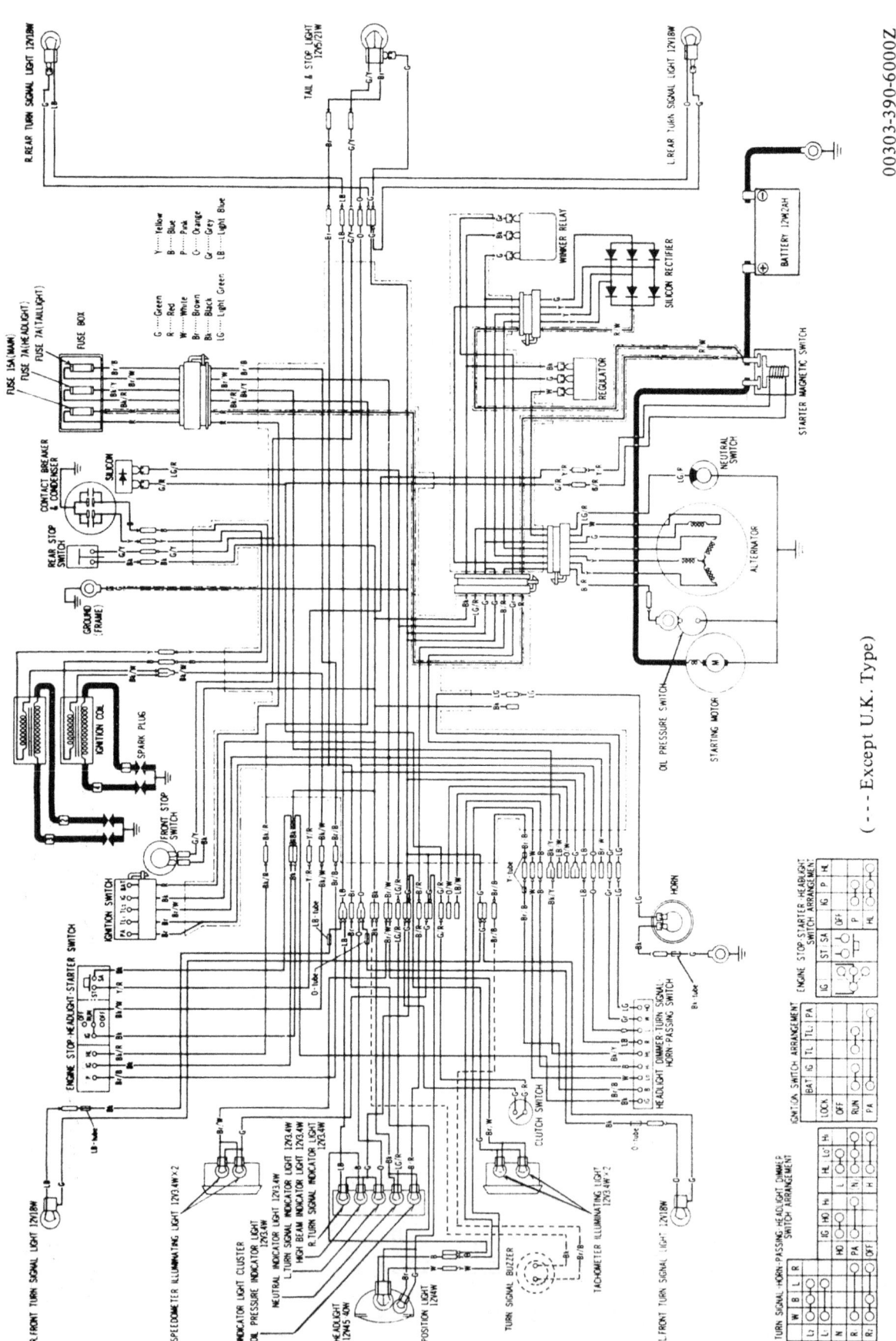

20. SUPPLEMENT TO CB 550 F2 ('77)

(FRENCH TYPE)

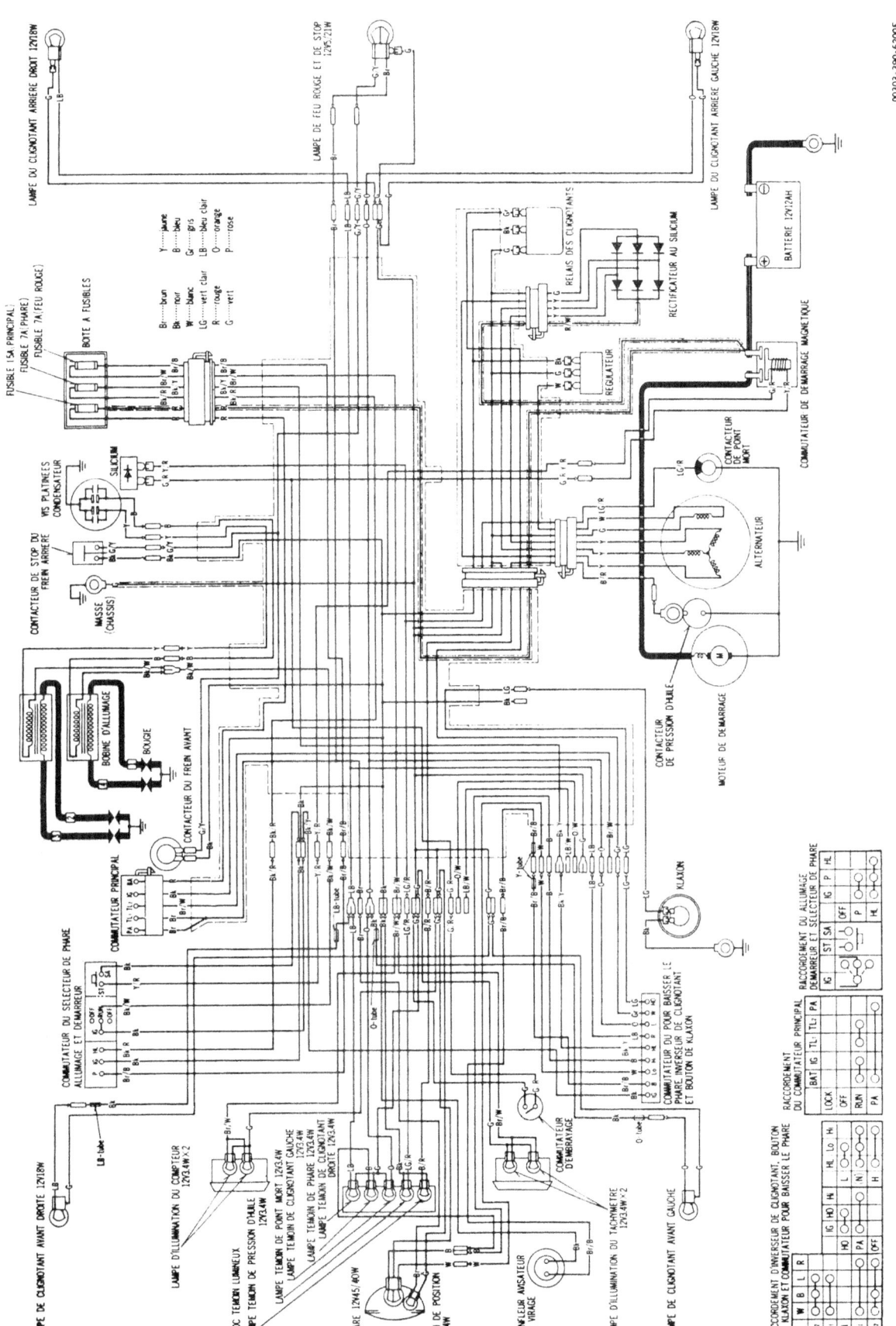

20. SUPPLEMENT TO CB 550 F2 ('77)

(GERMANY TYPE)

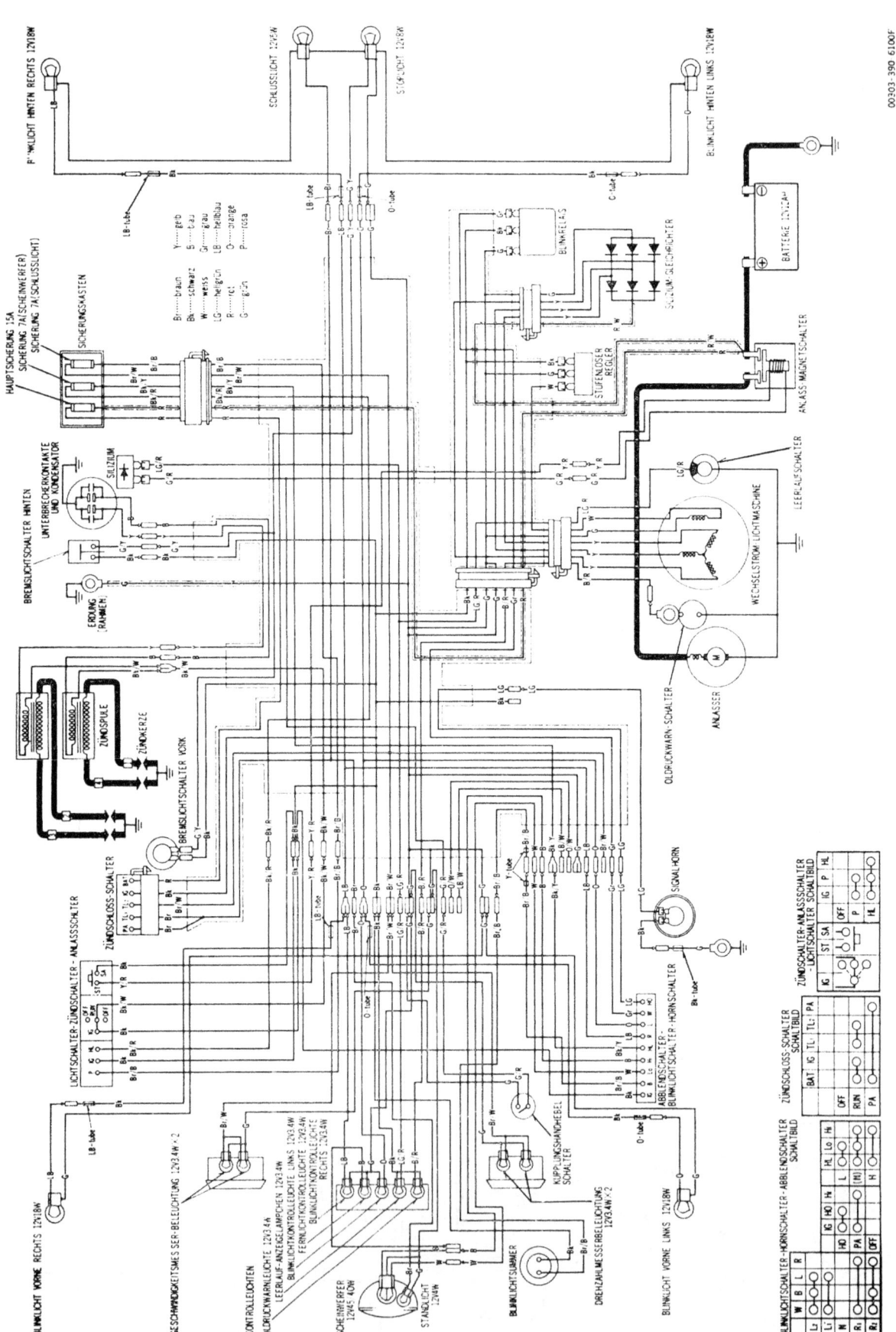

VELOCEPRESS MANUALS – MOTORCYCLE BY MAKE

AJS 1932-1948 SINGLES & TWINS 250cc THRU 1000cc (BOOK OF)
AJS 1945-1960 SINGLES 350cc & 500cc MODELS 16 & 18 (BOOK OF)
AJS 1955-1965 SINGLES 350cc & 500cc (BOOK OF)
AJS 1957-1966 FACTORY WSM - ALL SINGLES & TWINS
ARIEL UP TO 1932 (BOOK OF)
ARIEL 1932-1939 PREWAR MODELS (BOOK OF)
ARIEL 1933-1951 (WORKSHOP MANUAL)
ARIEL 1939-1960 4 STROKE SINGLES (BOOK OF)
ARIEL 1958-1964 LEADER & ARROW (BOOK OF)
BMW R26 R27 (1956-1967) FACTORY WORKSHOP MANUAL
BMW R50 R50S R60 R69S (1955-1969) FACTORY WORKSHOP MANUAL
BRIDGESTONE 90 SERIES FACTORY WSM & PARTS CATALOGUE
BRIDGESTONE 175 SERIES FACTORY WSM & PARTS CATALOGUE
BRIDGESTONE 350 SERIES FACTORY WSM & PARTS CATALOGUES
BSA SERVICE SHEETS MASTER CATALOGUE ALL MODELS 1945-1967
BSA BANTAM D1 TO D7 1948-1966 FACTORY SERVICE SHEETS MANUAL
BSA BANTAM ALL MODELS FROM 1948 ONWARDS (BOOK OF)
BSA DANDY FACTORY WORKSHOP MANUAL (COMPILATION)
BSA SINGLES & V-TWINS UP TO 1927 (BOOK OF)
BSA SINGLES & V-TWINS UP TO 1930 (BOOK OF)
BSA SINGLES & V-TWINS UP TO 1935 (BOOK OF)
BSA SINGLES & V-TWINS 1936-1939 (BOOK OF)
BSA C10, C11 & C12 1945-1958 FACTORY SERVICE SHEETS MANUAL
BSA OHV & SV SINGLES 250-600cc 1945-1959 (BOOK OF)
BSA C15 & B40 1958-1967 FACTORY SERVICE SHEETS MANUAL
BSA OHV & SV SINGLES 250cc (ONLY) 1954-1970 (BOOK OF)
BSA B31, B32, B33 & B34 1945-60 FACTORY SERVICE SHEETS MANUAL
BSA OHV SINGLES 350 & 500cc 1955-1967 (BOOK OF)
BSA M20, M21 & M33 1945-1963 FACTORY SERVICE SHEETS MANUAL
BSA TWINS A7 & A10 1948-1962 FACTORY SERVICE SHEETS MANUAL
BSA TWINS A7 & A10 1948-1962 (BOOK OF)
BSA TWINS A50 & A65 1962-1965 FACTORY WORKSHOP MANUAL
BSA TWINS A50 & A65 1962-1969 (SECOND BOOK OF)
DOUGLAS 1929-1939 PREWAR ALL MODELS (BOOK OF)
DOUGLAS 1948-1957 POSTWAR ALL MODELS FACTORY SHOP MANUAL
DUCATI 160cc, 250cc & 350cc OHC MODELS FACTORY SHOP MANUAL
HONDA 50cc ALL MODELS UP TO 1970 INC MONKEY & TRAIL (BOOK OF)
HONDA 90cc ALL MODELS UP TO 1966 (BOOK OF)
HONDA 50-65-70-90cc OHC SINGLES 1959-1983 FACTORY WSM
HONDA 100-125cc SINGLES CB/CD/CL/SL/TL 1970-1984 FACTORY WSM
HONDA 125-150cc TWINS C/CS/CB/CA FACTORY WORKSHOP MANUAL
HONDA 125-160-175-200cc TWINS 1965-1978 WORKSHOP MANUAL
HONDA 250-305cc TWINS C/CS/CB 1959-1967 FACTORY WSM
HOHDA 250-350cc TWINS CB/CL/SL 1968-1973 FACTORY WSM
HONDA 450cc CB/CL 1965-1974 K0 TO K7 WORKSHOP MANUAL
HONDA 500cc & 550cc 4 CYL 1971-1978 FACTORY WORKSHOP MANUAL
HONDA 750cc SHOC 4 CYL 1969-1978 K0~K8 WORKSHOP MANUAL
HONDA C100 SUPER CUB FACTORY WORKSHOP MANUAL
HONDA C110 SPORT CUB 1962-1969 FACTORY WORKSHOP MANUAL
HONDA TWINS & SINGLES 50cc THRU 305cc 1960-1966 (BOOK OF)
HONDA TWINS ALL MODELS 125cc THRU 450cc UP TO 1968 (BOOK OF)
INDIAN PONYBIKE, BOY RACER & PAPOOSE ILL PARTS LIST & SALES LIT
J.A.P. ENGINES 1927-1952 & MOTORCYCLES 1934-1972 (BOOK OF)
MATCHLESS 1931-1939 ALL MODELS 250cc THRU 990cc (BOOK OF)
MATCHLESS 1945-1956 350 & 500cc SINGLES (BOOK OF)
MATCHLESS 1955-1965 350 & 500cc SINGLES (BOOK OF)
MATCHLESS 1957-1966 FACTORY WSM - ALL SINGLES & TWINS
NEW IMPERIAL ALL SV & OHV FROM 1935 ONWARDS (BOOK OF)
NORTON 1932-1939 PREWAR MODELS (BOOK OF)
NORTON 1932-1947 (BOOK OF)
NORTON 1938-1956 (BOOK OF)
NORTON 1955-1963 MODELS 19, 50 & ES2 (BOOK OF)
NORTON 1955-1965 DOMINATOR TWINS (BOOK OF)
NORTON 1960-1970 TWIN CYLINDER FACTORY WORKSHOP MANUAL
NORTON 1970-1975 COMMANDO 850 & 750cc FACTORY WSM
NORTON 1975-1978 MK 3 COMMANDO 850 cc FACTORY WSM
PANTHER 1932-1958 LIGHTWEIGHT MODELS 250 & 350cc (BOOK OF)
PANTHER 1938-1966 HEAVYWEIGHT MODELS 600 & 650cc (BOOK OF)
RALEIGH MOTORCYCLES 1919-1933 (BOOK OF)
ROYAL ENFIELD 1934-1946 SINGLES & V TWINS (BOOK OF)
ROYAL ENFIELD 1937-1953 SINGLES & V TWINS (BOOK OF)
ROYAL ENFIELD 1946-1962 SINGLES (BOOK OF)
ROYAL ENFIELD 1958-1966 250cc & 350cc SINGLES (SECOND BOOK OF)
ROYAL ENFIELD 1962-1970 INTERCEPTOR WSM'S & PARTS (Compilation)
RUDGE 1933-1939 (BOOK OF)
SUNBEAM 1928-1939 (BOOK OF)
SUNBEAM 1946-1957 S7 & S8 (BOOK OF)
SUZUKI 50cc & 80cc UP TO 1966 (BOOK OF)
SUZUKI T10 1963-1967 FACTORY WORKSHOP MANUAL
SUZUKI T20 & T200 1965-1969 FACTORY WORKSHOP MANUAL
SUZUKI TWINS 1962 ONWARDS 125-500cc WORKSHOP MANUAL
TRIUMPH 1935-1949 SINGLES & TWINS (BOOK OF)
TRIUMPH 1937-1951 (WORKSHOP MANUAL)
TRIUMPH 1945-1955 FACTORY WORKSHOP MANUAL
TRIUMPH 1945-1959 TWINS (BOOK OF)
TRIUMPH 1956-1969 TWINS (BOOK OF)
TRIUMPH 1963-1970 UNIT CONSTRUCTION 650cc FACTORY WSM
TRIUMPH 1963-1974 UNIT CONSTRUCTION 350-500cc FACTORY WSM
TRIUMPH 1968-1974 TRIDENT T150 & T150V FACTORY WSM
VELOCETTE 1925-1970 ALL SINGLES & TWINS (BOOK OF)
VELOCETTE 1933-1952 MOV-MAC-MSS RIGID FRAME FACTORY WSM
VELOCETTE 1954-1971 MSS-VENOM-THRUXTON-VIPER FACTORY WSM
VILLIERS ENGINE UP TO 1959 INC. 3 WHEELERS (BOOK OF)
VILLIERS ENGINE UP TO 1969 (BOOK OF)
VINCENT 1935-1955 (WORKSHOP MANUAL)
YAMAHA 1961-1967 YA5 & YA6 (WORKSHOP MANUAL & ILL PARTS LIST)
YAMAHA 1971-1972 JT1& JT2 (WORKSHOP MANUAL & ILL PARTS LIST)

www.VelocePress.com

VELOCEPRESS TECHNICAL BOOKS – MOTORCYCLE

1930'S BRITISH MOTORCYCLE CARBS & ELEC COMPONENTS (BOOK OF)
1930'S BRITISH MOTORCYCLE ENGINES (OVERHAUL & MAINTENANCE)
1930'S BRITISH MOTORCYCLE GEARBOXES & CLUTCHES (BOOK OF)
CATALOG OF BRITISH MOTORCYCLES (1951 MODELS)
LUCAS ELECTRONICS BRITISH M/CYCLES REPAIR & PARTS (1950-1977)
MOTORCYCLE ENGINEERING (P.E. Irving)
MOTORCYCLE ROAD TESTS 1949-1953 (Motor Cycle Magazine UK)
SPEED AND HOW TO OBTAIN IT (Motor Cycle Magazine UK)
TUNING FOR SPEED (P.E. Irving)
WIPAC (COMBO) MANUAL NUMBER 3 + M/CYCLE & SCOOTER MANUAL

VELOCEPRESS MANUALS – SCOOTERS BY MAKE

BSA SUNBEAM SCOOTER WORKSHOP MANUAL 1959-1965
BSA SUNBEAM SCOOTER 1959-1965 (BOOK OF)
LAMBRETTA 1947-1957 ALL 125 & 150cc MODELS (BOOK OF)
LAMBRETTA 1957-1970 LI & TV MODELS (SECOND BOOK OF)
NSU PRIMA 1956-1964 ALL MODELS (BOOK OF)
TRIUMPH TIGRESS SCOOTER WORKSHOP MANUAL 1959-1965
TRIUMPH TIGRESS SCOOTER (BOOK OF)
VESPA 1951-1961 (BOOK OF)
VESPA 1955-1963 125 & 150cc & GS MODELS (SECOND BOOK OF)
VESPA 1955-1968 GS & SS (BOOK OF)
VESPA 1963-1972 90, 125 & 150cc (THIRD BOOK OF)

VELOCEPRESS MANUALS – MOPEDS & MOTORIZED BICYCLES

CYCLEMOTOR (BOOK OF)
NSU QUICKLY 1953-1963 ALL MODELS (BOOK OF)
PUCH MAXI N & S MAINTENANCE & REPAIR (3 MANUAL COMPILATION)
RALEIGH MOPEDS 1960-1969 (BOOK OF)

VELOCEPRESS MANUALS - THREE WHEELER'S

BOND MINICAR THREE WHEELER 1948-1967 (BOOK OF)
BMW ISETTA FACTORY WORKSHOP MANUAL
BSA THREE WHEELER (BOOK OF)
RELIANT REGAL THREE WHEELER 1952-1973 (BOOK OF)
VINTAGE MORGAN THREE WHEELER (BOOK OF)

VELOCEPRESS MANUALS – AUTOMOBILE BY MAKE

ALFA ROMEO GIULIA WORKSHOP MANUAL 1300 TO 2000cc 1962-1975
ALFA ROMEO GIULIA TECH MANUAL CARBURETED CARS FROM 1962
ALFA ROMEO GIULIA TECH MANUAL FUEL INJECTED CARS FROM 1969
ALFA ROMEO GIULIETTA & GIULIA 750 & 101 SERIES 1955-1965 WSM
AUSTIN-HEALEY SPRITE & MG MIDGET WORKSHOP MANUAL 1958-1971
BMW 600 LIMOUSINE FACTORY WORKSHOP MANUAL
BMW 600 LIMOUSINE OWNERS HAND BOOK & SERVICE MANUAL
BMW 2000 & 2002 1966-1976 WORKSHOP MANUAL
CORVAIR 1960-1969 WORKSHOP MANUAL
CORVETTE V8 1955-1962 WORKSHOP MANUAL
FERRARI HANDBOOK ROAD & RACE CARS (SERVICE/SPECS) 1948-1958
FERRARI 250/GT SERVICE & MAINTENANCE MANUAL 1956-1965
FIAT 500 FACTORY WORKSHOP MANUAL 1957-1973
FIAT 600, 600D & MULTIPLA FACTORY WORKSHOP MANUAL 1955-1969
JAGUAR E-TYPE 3.8 & 4.2 SERIES 1 & 2 WORKSHOP MANUAL
JAGUAR MK 7, 8, 9 & XK120, 140, 150 WORKSHOP MANUAL 1948-1961
METROPOLITAN FACTORY WORKSHOP MANUAL
MGA & MGB OWNERS HANDBOOK & WORKSHOP MANUAL
MG MIDGET TC, TD, TF & TF1500 WORKSHOP MANUAL
PORSCHE 356 1948-1965 WORKSHOP MANUAL
PORSCHE 911 2.0, 2.2, 2.4 LITRE 1964-1973 WORKSHOP MANUAL
PORSCHE 911 2.7, 3.0, 3.2 LITRE 1973-1989 WORKSHOP MANUAL
PORSCHE 912 WORKSHOP MANUAL
PORSCHE 914/4 & 914/6 1.7, 1.8, 2.0 LITRE 1970-1976 WSM
TRIUMPH TR2, TR3, TR4 1953-1965 WORKSHOP MANUAL
VOLKSWAGEN TRANSPORTER, TRUCKS & WAGONS 1950-1979 WSM
VOLVO 1944-1968 ALL MODELS WORKSHOP MANUAL

VELOCEPRESS TECHNICAL BOOKS - AUTOMOBILE

HOW TO BUILD A FIBERGLASS CAR
HOW TO BUILD A RACING CAR
HOW TO RESTORE THE MODEL 'A' FORD
MASERATI OWNER'S HANDBOOK
PERFORMANCE TUNING THE SUNBEAM TIGER
SOUPING THE VOLKSWAGEN
SOLEX CARBURETORS (EMPHASIS ON UK & EU AUTOMOBILES)
SU CARBURETORS (EMPHASIS ON UK AUTOMOBILES)
WEBER CARBURETORS (EMPHASIS ON ALFA & FIAT)

VELOCEPRESS BOOKS & GUIDES - AUTOMOBILE

COMPLETE CATALOG OF JAPANESE MOTOR VEHICLES
FERRARI 308 SERIES BUYER'S AND OWNER'S GUIDE
FERRARI BROCHURES AND SALES LITERATURE 1968-1989
FERRARI SERIAL NUMBERS PART I - ODD NUMBERS TO 21399
FERRARI SERIAL NUMBERS PART II - EVEN NUMBERS TO 1050
HENRY'S FABULOUS MODEL "A" FORD
MASERATI BROCHURES AND SALES LITERATURE

VELOCEPRESS BOOKS – RACING

CARRERA PANAMERICANA - MEXICAN ROAD RACE (BOOK OF)
DIALED IN - THE JAN OPPERMAN STORY
VEDA ORR'S NEW REVISED HOT ROD PICTORIAL

Please check our website:

www.VelocePress.com

for a complete
up-to-date list of
available titles

www.ingramcontent.com/pod-product-compliance
Lightning Source LLC
Chambersburg PA
CBHW060251240426
43673CB00047B/1908